Kitzur Halachos

קיצור הלכות:
ספירת העומר ובין המצרים

Sefiras Haomer & The THREE WEEKS

THE HALACHOS OF SEFIRAS HAOMER & THE THREE WEEKS
-BASED ON THE-

MISHNAH BERURAH

-RAV ZEV HOFSTEDTER-

והוא מקיף כל ההלכות המצויות המבוארים בשו״ע הלכות ספירת העומר ובין המצרים ומיוסד על דברי המשנה ברורה, ביאור הלכה ושער הציון. בנוסף עליו מדברי גדולי פוסקים אחרונים במקומות שלא נמצא מפורש בדברי המ״ב או בדברים שנתחדשו. נכתב ונערך בדרך קצרה ובאופן מעשי שיהא תועלת להבין כל דין בנקל.

מאת זאב בן הרב הגאון דוד מרדכי שליט״א הופשטטר

– מהדורה שניה, שנת תשפ״א –

Copyright © 2020 by Rabbi Zev Hofstedter
Second edition © 2021

ISBN 978-1-60091-788-2

All rights reserved.

No part of this book may be reproduced in any form
without written permission from the copyright holder.
The rights of the copyright holder will be strictly enforced.

Book layout by:

VIVIDESIGN
SRULY PERL | 845.694.7186
mechelp@gmail.com

Distributed by:

Israel Bookshop Publications
501 Prospect Street
Lakewood, NJ 08701
Tel: (732) 901-3009
Fax: (732) 901-4012
www.israelbookshoppublications.com
info@israelbookshoppublications.com

Printed in Bulgaria

Distributed in Israel by:
Tfutza Publications
P.O.B. 50036
Beitar Illit 90500
972-2-650-9400

Distributed in Europe by:
Lehmanns
Unit E Viking Industrial Park
Rolling Mill Road,
Jarrow, Tyne & Wear NE32 3DP
44-191-406-0842

Distributed in Australia by:
Gold's Book and Gift Company
3-13 William Street
Balaclava 3183
613-9527-8775

Distributed in South Africa by:
Kollel Bookshop
Ivy Common
107 William Road, Norwood
Johannesburg 2192
27-11-728-1822

TABLE OF CONTENTS

מאמר הכנה לקבלת התורה
By Hagaon Harav Yitzchok Sorotzkin *shlit"a* .... **xxi**

CHAPTER ONE
The Mitzvah of *Sefiras Haomer* 3

1. The Basic Rules of *Sefirah* 4

The Obligation to Count 49 Days / Counting at Night / An Individual Obligation / Hearing the *Brachah* from Someone Else / A Woman's Obligation / Children of *Chinuch* Age / A Child Who Becomes Bar Mitzvah during *Sefirah* / An *Onen* / A *Ger* / Counting the *Omer* in the Presence of Filth or Immodesty

2. The Procedure for Counting the *Omer* 9

Reciting the *Brachah* / Counting while Standing / Supporting Oneself on an Object / An Interruption between the *Brachah* and the Counting / Counting Orally / Understanding the Count / Counting in an Unusual Manner / Using Cardinal Numbers / Beginning with the Word "*Hayom*" / "*Baomer*" or "*Laomer*" / When to Insert "*Baomer*" or "*Laomer*" when Counting the Weeks / The Obligation to Count Days and Weeks / A Mistake in the Count / Grammatical Considerations / Reciting *Tefillos* after the Count

3. The Time for the Mitzvah 17

Counting at Nightfall / The Second Night of Pesach in *Chutz La'Aretz* / Counting during *Bein Hashemashos* / *Tzeis Hakochavim* of Rabbeinu Tam / Davening *Maariv* Immediately after *Shekiah* / Davening *Maariv* before Sunset / *Maariv* before Sunset on Erev Shabbos / A Person Who Will Daven

Maariv Later at Night / Kiddush and Havdalah in Shul / Counting during *Seudah Shelishis* / Counting the *Omer* with the Congregation / Arriving Late to *Maariv* / Counting in the Morning / Counting until *Alos Hashachar*

4. Missed Days and Situations of Uncertainty 24

If a Person Neglects to Count at Night / A Person Who Is Uncertain if He Counted at Night / A Missed Day / A Person Who Counted Incorrectly / Reciting *Sefirah* for the Congregation after Missing a Day / A Person Who Is Uncertain if He Counted Correctly / Applying the Principle of "*Sfek Sfeika*" / Counting after *Shekiah* / Counting for the Previous Day after *Kabbalas Shabbos* and *Maariv* / Reciting the *Brachah* when One Expects to Miss a Day / Traveling to Another Time Zone

5. Mental Intent in *Sefiras Haomer* 30

The Intent to Fulfill the Mitzvah of *Sefiras Haomer* / Informing Someone Else of the Correct Count / Inadvertent Counting before *Shekiah* / Stating the Count in a Different Language / Citing the Number without the Week / Inquiring About the Day / Helping a Child Count or Correcting Someone Else / Reading the Day's Count while Learning / Invoking the Name of Lag Baomer / Hearing the *Shaliach Tzibbur*'s *Brachah* / Reciting the *Brachah* with the Correct Count in Mind / If a Person Had the Wrong Count in Mind / Correcting an Error / Changing One's Count Erroneously / If a Person Cannot Ascertain the Correct Day to Count

6. Activities Prohibited before *Sefirah* 37

Beginning a Prohibited Activity before Counting *Sefirah* / Definition of a Meal / A *Shomer* or a Regular *Minyan* / Designating a *Shomer* after Nightfall / Counting *Sefiras Haomer* during a Permitted Meal / Counting *Sefiras Haomer* after Beginning a Prohibited Meal / Abstaining from Other Activities / Abstaining from *Melachah* at Night during *Sefiras Haomer* / The Duration of the *Minhag* / The Practical Implications of the *Minhag* / The Definition of *Melachah* with Respect to the *Minhag*

CHAPTER TWO

Halachos and *Minhagim* of the *Sefirah* Period 47

1. Weddings and Engagements 48

The Prohibition to Marry during *Sefirah* / A First Marriage / If the Prohibition Is Violated / Celebrating an Engagement / *Sheva Brachos*

2. Dancing and Music 49

The Prohibition of Dancing / Dancing at a *Seudas Mitzvah* or *Hachnassas Sefer Torah* / Dance Lessons / Listening to Music / Recorded Music / Music without Instruments / Music Lessons and Professional Musicians / Hearing

Music Involuntarily / Music for Purposes Other than Enjoyment / Recorded Stories for Children / Singing Lively Songs / Playing Music for a Person Who Is Ill / Music and Dancing on Chol Hamoed / Music and Dancing when Haircuts Are Permitted / Listening to Music throughout the Year / Music and Dancing on the Night of Lag Baomer

3. Reciting *Shehecheyanu* and Other Forms of Festivity...........53

Reciting *Shehecheyanu* / Creating an Opportunity to Recite *Shehecheyanu* / New Garments / Scenarios in Which *Shehecheyanu* May Certainly Be Recited / Moving to a New House / Home Renovations / Trips and Swimming / Social Events / A *Seudas Mitzvah*

4. Cutting Hair...56

The Prohibition to Cut Hair / Haircuts for Women / Shaving for Work or Business / Cutting a Child's Hair / Haircuts and Shaving for the Participants in a *Bris Milah* / A Bar or Bas Mitzvah / A *Pidyon Haben* / A Chassan / Shaving for a Date or Engagement Party / Attending a Wedding while Observing the Halachos of *Sefirah* / Haircuts for Medical Reasons / Haircuts at the Conclusion of *Aveilus* / A Person Who Would Be Permitted to Cut His Hair on Chol Hamoed / The Arizal's Stringency / Cutting Another Person's Hair / Haircuts on Lag Baomer and Rosh Chodesh / Combing Hair / Bathing in Hot Water / Trimming Nails

5. When to Observe the *Sefirah* Restrictions 61

The Sephardic Custom / The Ashkenazic Custom / Common Ashkenazic Custom in Eretz Yisrael and *Chutz La'Aretz* / Combining the Leniencies or Stringencies of the Different Customs / Divergent Customs in One Community / Choosing a Custom / The Custom of a Married Woman / Attending a Wedding while Observing the Mourning Restrictions / Concluding a Wedding or Haircut That Began on Lag Baomer / Haircuts on Erev Shabbos before Rosh Chodesh Sivan or the *Shloshes Yemei Hagbalah* / When Rosh Chodesh Iyar Falls on Shabbos

6. Lag Baomer...67

The Significance of Lag Baomer / *Tachanun* / Allowing an *Avel* to Lead the Davening / *Tzidkascha* / *Lamnatzeiach* and *Kel Erech Apayim* / Fasting on a *Yahrtzeit* or Wedding Day / *Tziduk Hadin*, *Hespedim*, and *Hakamas Matzeivah* / *Sefiras Haomer* on Lag Baomer / Weddings / Haircuts and Shaving / Added Festivity / Visiting Meron / Lighting Candles or a Fire / Cutting the Hair of a Three-Year-Old Boy ("*Upsheren*")

7. Halachos Pertaining to *Tefillah* from Pesach
to Shavuos..71

Omitting *Mashiv Haruach U'morid Hageshem* at *Mussaf* on Pesach / Announcing the Omission of *Mashiv Haruach* / *Tefillas Tal* / An Individual

Who Davens Late / The Custom to Recite *"Morid Hatal"* / If *"Mashiv Haruach U'morid Hageshem"* Is Erroneously Recited / Realizing an Error during the *Brachah*'s Conclusion / Omitting *"Hashem Sefasai Tiftach"* in a Repetition of the *Shemoneh Esrei* / A Country Where Rain Is Needed after Pesach / Correcting an Error *Toch K'dei Dibbur* / If a Person Is Uncertain if He Has Erred / If a Person Has Omitted a *Tefillah* / If an Uncertainty Arises after Davening Has Ended / A Strategy to Avoid Repeating *Shemoneh Esrei* in a Case of Uncertainty / Omitting *"Vesein Tal U'matar Livrachah"* on Pesach / A Drought after Pesach / *"Vesein Tal U'matar"* in the Summer Months / Correcting the Error *Toch K'dei Dibbur* / *Av Harachamim* / When Rosh Chodesh Iyar Falls on Shabbos / *Kel Malei Rachamim* / *Pirkei Avos* / Disparities in the *Parshas Hashavua* between Eretz Yisrael and Other Countries / Traveling between Eretz Yisrael and *Chutz La'Aretz* during These Weeks / Compensating for a Missed *Parshah* / The Fasts of Behab / Reciting *Mi Shebeirach* for Those Who Fast / Accepting the Fasts of Behab / *Selichos* and Reading *"Vayechal"* / *Aneinu* / A *Seudas Mitzvah* / Pesach Sheni / Reciting *Lamnatzeiach* and *Kel Erech Apayim* on Pesach Sheni / Eating Matzah / *Hespedim* / *Tachanun* in the Month of Sivan / Fasting during Sivan

CHAPTER THREE
The Halachos of *Chadash* 87

1. What Is *Chadash*? 88
The Prohibition of *Chadash* / The Determining Factor / Grain of Unknown Status / Grain as a Minority Ingredient / Utensils Used for Cooking or Baking *Chadash*

2. *Chadash* in *Chutz La'Aretz* 90
The Prohibition in *Chutz La'Aretz* / Proximity to Eretz Yisrael / Grain Belonging to a Non-Jew / Defending the Lenient Practice / The Situation in America Today / *Chadash* in Eretz Yisrael

3. Applications of *Chadash* Today 93
The Five Species of Grain / Winter Crops and Spring Crops / Rye and Spelt / Oats and Barley / Winter Wheat and Spring Wheat / Products Subject to Potential *Chadash* Issues / Verifying the Status of a Product

CHAPTER FOUR
The Yom Tov of Shavuos 99

1. General Halachos of Shavuos 100
Davening *Maariv* after *Tzeis Hakochavim* / *Tosefes Yom Tov* / Lighting Yom

Tov Candles / Immersing in the *Mikveh* / *Maariv* of Shavuos / Preparing for Yom Tov on Shabbos / *Seudah Shelishis* on Erev Yom Tov / Marital Relations on Shavuos / Learning throughout the Night / The Prohibition to Fast / The *Tefillos* of Shavuos Morning / *Krias HaTorah* / *Akdamus* / Reading the *Aseres Hadibros* / Standing for the *Aseres Hadibros* / The *Haftarah* of Shavuos Morning / Standing during the *Haftarah* / *Megillas Rus* / The *Brachah* on Reading the *Megillah* / Reading the *Megillah* Multiple Times / *Krias HaTorah* on the Second Day of Shavuos / *Yizkor* / Holding a *Hachnassas Sefer Torah* on Shavuos / *Isru Chag* / Omitting *Tachanun* after Shavuos

2. Learning throughout the Night on Shavuos 108
Studying Torah throughout the Night / Optional but Important / Learning the *Tikkun* / Learning on the Second Night of Shavuos / Reciting *Brachos* on Food and Drink / The *Shiur Ikul* / A Change of Location (*Shinui Makom*) / Eating and Drinking after *Alos Hashachar*

3. *Netilas Yadayim* after a Sleepless Night 113
The Obligation of *Netilas Yadayim* / Washing before *Alos Hashachar* / Continuing to Learn after *Alos Hashachar* / A Person Who Has Slept for Part of the Night / *Netilas Yadayim* after Sleeping in the Morning / *Netilas Yadayim* for a Person Who Sleeps before *Shacharis*

4. Reciting the *Brachah* on *Tzitzis* 117
Reciting the *Brachah* on *Tzitzis* on the Morning of Shavuos / One Who Did Not Hear the *Brachah*

5. *Birchos HaTorah* 119
Reciting *Birchos HaTorah* / Learning before *Birchos HaTorah* / Reciting the *Brachos* after a Daytime Nap / The Definition of *Sheinas Keva* / Waking Up during the Night to Learn / Sleeping in the Morning before *Shacharis*

6. *Birchos Hashachar* 123
Reciting *Birchos Hashachar* on the Morning of Shavuos / *Birchos Hashachar* before Dawn / Reciting *Birchos Hashachar* before *Chatzos* / Reciting the *Brachos* after Sleeping in the Morning

7. Eating Dairy on Shavuos 125
Eating Dairy Products on Shavuos / Serving Dairy and Meat Meals / Eating Meat after Milk / Eating Meat after Hard Cheese / Serving a *Milchig* Yom Tov *Seudah* / Waiting between Meat and Milk / Eating Dairy after a Nap / Meat and Dairy at the Same Table / Preparing for or Participating in a *Milchig* Meal while *Fleishig* / Washing Drinking Glasses between *Fleishig* and *Milchig* Meals / Eating *Milchig* Foods after Kiddush / The *Brachah* on Cheesecake

8. Other *Minhagim* of Shavuos..132
Adorning Shuls and Homes with Greenery / The *Muktzeh* Status of Plants / Moving Plants on Shabbos or Yom Tov / Moving a Vase of Flowers / Placing Flowers in Water on Shabbos or Yom Tov / Inhaling the Scent of Fragrant Branches and Leaves / Placing Trees in Shuls and Homes / Plants and *Chukos Hagoyim* / Avoiding Theft while Collecting Flowers / Dancing on Shavuos

CHAPTER FIVE
Shivah Asar B'Tammuz..139

1. Halachos of the Fast..140
A Public Fast / A Mandatory Fast / The Five Tragedies Commemorated by the Fast / The Duration of the Fast / Rising before *Alos Hashachar* to Eat or Drink / Fasting for Children / The Final Three Fasts of Childhood / A Bar Mitzvah on a Postponed Fast / A Broken Fast / Fasting for *Baalei Simchah*

2. Exemptions from the Fast..143
Pregnant and Nursing Women / A Woman after Birth / Fasting in a Case of Illness / A Minor Ailment on a Postponed Fast / Taking Antibiotics / Fasting in Spite of an Exemption / Swallowing a Pill / When Fasting Affects One's Work

3. General Halachos of Shivah Asar B'Tammuz..147
The Differences between Shivah Asar B'Tammuz and Tishah B'Av / Bathing in Hot Water / Pious Conduct / Music, Haircuts, and New Garments / Celebrating a Wedding or *Sheva Brachos* on the Night before the Fast / Brushing Teeth / When a Fast Day Conflicts with Shabbos / Meat and Wine after the Fast

4. Halachos Pertaining to *Tefillah* on a Fast Day..149
Aneinu / If the *Shaliach Tzibbur* Omits *Aneinu* / Reciting *Aneinu* while Fasting / *Selichos* / *Avinu Malkeinu* / *Krias HaTorah* / Receiving an *Aliyah* if One Is Not Fasting / *Krias HaTorah* at *Minchah* / Reciting *Aneinu* at *Minchah* / If *Aneinu* Is Omitted / Omitting *Aneinu* when One Is Exempt from Fasting

CHAPTER SIX
The Period of the Three Weeks 155

1. From Shivah Asar B'Tammuz until Rosh Chodesh Av........156
The Onset of the Period of Mourning / Engagements and Weddings /

Dancing / Playing Musical Instruments / Listening to Music / Singing / Singing or Playing Music to Calm Children / Music for Children / A *Seudas Mitzvah* / Cutting Hair and Shaving / Giving a Haircut to a Child / Cutting Hair for a *Bris, Pidyon Haben* or Bar Mitzvah / An *Upsheren* / Cutting Hair for a Shidduch Date / Cutting Hair to Fulfill the Mitzvah of Tefillin / Hair Removal for Women / Cutting Nails / Swimming / Optional Recitations of *Shehecheyanu* / Reciting *Shehecheyanu* when Required / Satisfying a Need for a New Fruit / Purchasing a New Fruit or Garment / Wearing New Clothes That Do Not Warrant *Shehecheyanu* / The *Brachah* of *Hatov Vehameitiv* / Exercising Caution / Mourning for the *Beis Hamikdash* during the Day

2. Halachos of the Nine Days 163

The Onset of the Nine Days / Minimizing Joy / Purchasing Articles That Engender Joy / New Clothes / Gifts / Browsing in a Store / Buying Sefarim / Conducting Business / Conducting Renovations for Business Purposes / Purchasing, Leasing, or Moving into a New Home / Non-Essential Home Renovations / Essential Renovations / Gardening / Purchases or Construction for a Mitzvah / Engagements / Conducting a Court Case with a Non-Jew / Cutting Nails / Air Travel / End-of-Year Photographs / Swimming

3. Laundering Garments 170

Laundering Garments during the Nine Days / Ironing / Items Subject to the Prohibition / Laundering an Item to Be Used after Tishah B'Av / Using a Washing Machine / Instructing a Non-Jew to Launder Garments / Removing a Stain / Turning on a Washing Machine before Rosh Chodesh / Soaking a Stained Garment / Shining Shoes / Washing and Setting a Sheitel / Washing and Polishing Floors / A Person Who Lacks Clean Clothes / Laundering for a Mitzvah / Giving Garments to a Non-Jewish Cleaner / Laundering Garments for a Non-Jew / Laundering Children's Clothes / Washing Additional Garments / Exception to Laundering Garments for after Tishah B'Av / Doing Laundry for Health Reasons / Leniencies for a Mourner

4. Wearing New or Freshly Laundered Clothing 176

Wearing Freshly Laundered Garments / Using Clean Bedsheets, Towels, and Tablecloths / Undergarments and Socks / Preparing Garments before the Nine Days / Clean Clothes for Children / A Person Who Did Not Prepare Clothing before the Nine Days / A Guest / Wearing Clean Garments for a Mitzvah / Wearing New Garments / Pressed Garments / Wearing Shabbos Finery on Shabbos Chazon / Removing One's Shabbos Clothes Immediately after Shabbos / Wearing Fresh Clothes at a *Bris Milah* / A Bar Mitzvah / An *Aufruf* / Wearing Fresh Clothes for a Shidduch

5. Sewing, Purchasing, and Mending Garments 182
Making New Garments / Hiring a Non-Jew to Fashion Garments / Making Garments for Others / Mending a Garment / Arranging the Threads on a Loom / Buying Clothing / Buying *Tzitzis* / Footwear for Tishah B'Av / Purchasing Clothing at a Discounted Price / Purchasing or Sewing Non-Clothing Items / Eyeglasses / Returns and Exchanges

6. Abstaining from Meat and Wine 185
Meat and Wine during the Nine Days / The Onset of the Prohibition / *Shechitah* / Selling Meat / Poultry / Foods Cooked with Meat / Parve Foods Cooked in *Fleishig* Utensils / A Small Quantity of Meat in Parve Food / Grape Juice / Beer and Whiskey / Diluted Wine / Artificial Grape Flavor / Meat and Wine on Shabbos / *Seudah Shelishis* and *Melaveh Malkah* / Sampling Shabbos Foods on Erev Shabbos / Drinking Wine at Havdalah / Reciting *Birkas Hamazon* with Wine / A *Seudas Mitzvah* / Wine at a *Bris Milah* / A *Bris Milah* after the Eighth Day / Celebrating a *Siyum* / When a *Siyum* May Be Held / Participating in the Celebration of a *Siyum* / Partaking of a *Seudah* without Attending the *Siyum* / Singing at a *Seudas Mitzvah* / A Bar Mitzvah / *Chanukas Habayis* / Children / Eating Meat during Illness or after Birth / A Person with a Dairy Allergy

7. Bathing and Showering 193
Bathing during the Nine Days / Bathing in Cold Water / Bathing for Medical Reasons / Bathing for a Mitzvah / *Tevilah* for a Man on Erev Shabbos / *Tevilah* before Davening / Immersion for a *Sandak* before a *Bris* / Showering before *Tevilah* / Bathing to Remove Dirt or Perspiration / Bathing in Lukewarm Water / Using Soap or Shampoo / Using a Wet Washcloth / Bathing Children / Erev Shabbos on Rosh Chodesh Av / Bathing on Erev Shabbos Chazon / When Tishah B'Av Falls on Shabbos / Cutting Nails / Applying Creams and Fragrances

CHAPTER SEVEN
Erev Tishah B'Av 201
1. The Halachos of Erev Tishah B'Av 201
Omitting *Tachanun* at *Minchah* / *Seudas Mitzvah* on Erev Tishah B'Av / Pleasure Strolls / Learning Torah after *Chatzos* / Learning Topics of Sorrow in Depth / Fasting on Erev Tishah B'Av

2. *Seudah Hamafsekes* 204
The Final Meal before the Fast / Meat and Wine Are Prohibited / Beverages / The Limit of One Cooked Dish / Two Versions of a Dish or Two Foods

Cooked in a Single Pot / Foods Generally Cooked Together / A Cooked Dish Generally Consumed with Other Foods / Pasteurized Foods / Foods That Are Edible when Uncooked / Uncooked Fruits and Vegetables / Hard-Boiled Eggs / The Preferable Practice / Dipping the Bread in Ashes / The Final Meal for a Person Exempt from the Fast / Sitting on the Floor / Wearing Leather Shoes / Avoiding the Formation of a *Zimun* / A Meal Prior to the *Seudah Hamafsekes* / *Seudah Hamafsekes* on Shabbos

3. After the *Seudah Hamafsekes* 210
Eating and Drinking after the Meal / Declaring the Intent to Continue Eating / Accepting the Fast Verbally / The Onset of the Fast / When the Other Restrictions Take Effect

4. When Erev Tishah B'Av Falls on Shabbos 212
The Final Meal before the Fast / Eating Meat / Eating at the Table and *Bentching* with a *Zimun* / Singing *Zemiros* / A *Seudah* for a *Bris Milah* / An *Aufruf* / A Stipulation at the End of *Seudah Shelishis* / Observing the Laws of Tishah B'Av after *Shekiah* / Removing Leather Shoes after Reciting *Barchu* / The Prohibition of *Hachanah* / *Maariv* after *Tzeis Hakochavim* / *Zemiros* before *Maariv*

CHAPTER EIGHT
The Laws of Tishah B'Av 219
1. Fasting 220
The Obligation to Fast / The Duration of the Fast / Pregnant and Nursing Women / Fasting while Ill / Resuming the Fast after an Interruption / A Woman after Childbirth / Eating Ordinary Quantities of Food / Breaking the Fast to Avoid Becoming Ill / Swallowing Pills / Involvement in Communal Affairs / The Elderly / Reciting Havdalah before Breaking the Fast / Rinsing the Mouth / Children on Tishah B'Av / A Child Who Reaches Adulthood on a Postponed Fast / Washing for Bread / Donning Tefillin before Eating / If the Fast Is Broken in Error

2. Washing and Anointing 226
The Prohibition to Wash / Washing to Remove Dirt / Washing an Object / *Netilas Yadayim* / Washing after Relieving Oneself / Washing All the Fingers / Washing Only until the Knuckles / *Birkas Kohanim* and Washing for Bread / Immersing in a *Mikveh* / Performing the *Hefsek Taharah* / *Tevilah* before Davening / Washing the Face / Using a Wet Towel / Entering a Body of Water / Soaking One's Feet and Cleaning a Wound / The Prohibition of *Sichah* / Anointing for a Purpose Other than Pleasure / Insect Repellent or Sunscreen / Exception for a Kallah / Children

3. Wearing Shoes..232
The Prohibition to Wear Shoes / Non-Leather Shoes / Shoes with Leather Components / Shoes Made of Synthetic Leather / Wearing Leather Shoes for a Long Walk / Wearing Leather Shoes in the Company of Non-Jews / Standing on Leather / Leather Orthotics / Reciting the *Brachah* of *She'asah Li Kol Tzorki* / Children

4. Learning Torah..234
The Prohibition to Learn Torah / Topics That Evoke Sorrow / Learning Relevant Halachos / Learning *Mussar* / Learning *Al Derech Pshat* / Thinking About Torah / Recording Torah Thoughts in Writing / Giving Halachic Rulings / Teaching Torah to Children / Reciting Torah Passages in Davening / Reciting *Krias Shema* after the *Zman* / Reciting *Tehillim* / Reading Other Material

5. General Conduct on Tishah B'Av..239
Greeting Others / Responding to a Greeting / Giving a Gift / Walking in Public Places / The Prohibition of Marital Relations / Marital Relations when the Ninth of Av Falls on Shabbos / Altering One's Sleeping Arrangements / Minimizing Pleasurable Activities / Sitting on the Floor / Sitting on a Low Chair / When a Regular Chair May Be Used / Standing for a Rav or Elderly Person / Holding a Child

6. Work and Business Dealings..243
Working on Tishah B'Av / Working after *Chatzos* / Writing / Food Preparation / Conducting Business / Forms of Prohibited Work / Instructing a Non-Jew to Perform *Melachah* / Preventing a Loss / Business Dealings after *Chatzos* / Working on Tishah B'Av when the Fast Is Postponed

CHAPTER NINE
Tefillos and *Minhagim* of Tishah B'Av..249

1. The Night of Tishah B'Av..249
The Order of Davening / Removing the *Paroches* / Dimming the Lights / Sitting on the Floor / A Mournful Melody / Reciting a *Brachah* on *Megillas Eichah* / Reading Along in an Undertone / A Woman's Obligation / Reciting the *Pasuk* of "*Hashiveinu*" Aloud / Reciting *Uva Letzion* and Kaddish / *V'yehi Noam* and *Vayiten Lecha*

2. The Day of Tishah B'Av..252
Kinnos / Davening at *Neitz Hachamah* / Sitting in One's Regular Place / *Shacharis* on Tishah B'Av / *Tachanun*, *Selichos*, and *Avinu Malkeinu* /

Krias HaTorah / Reciting *Kinnos* without Distraction / The Conclusion of *Shacharis* / Reading *Eichah* after *Kinnos* / A Mourner during the First Three Days of *Shivah* / Visiting a Cemetery / *Tziduk Hadin* at a *Levayah* / Preparing Food after *Chatzos* / Returning the *Paroches* to Its Place / *Shir Shel Yom* / Washing Hands before *Minchah* / Torah Reading and *Haftarah* / *Bentching Gomel* and Receiving an *Aliyah* for a Bar Mitzvah / *Nacheim* / Reciting *Nacheim* when One Is Not Fasting / *Nacheim* in *Birkas Hamazon* / Inserting *Aneinu* in the *Shemoneh Esrei* / *Aneinu* for the *Shaliach Tzibbur* / The Conclusion of *Minchah*

3. *Tzitzis* and Tefillin..258

Wearing *Tzitzis* on Tishah B'Av / Grasping the *Tzitzis* during *Shacharis* / Tefillin / The Sephardic Custom / Wearing a *Tallis* and Tefillin at *Minchah* / Designating a *Shomer*

4. A *Bris* on Tishah B'Av..260

The Timing of a *Bris* / Lighting Candles / *Besamim* / Drinking the Wine / Reciting *Shehecheyanu* / Wearing Shabbos Clothes / Wearing a *Tallis* / A *Bris* when the Fast Has Been Postponed / Davening *Minchah* at the Earliest Possible Time / A *Bris* That Has Been Delayed / Reciting Havdalah / Delaying the *Seudah* until Nightfall / A *Pidyon Haben*

CHAPTER TEN

Tishah B'Av on Sunday...267

1. Halachos Pertaining to Shabbos..267

Torah Study / Leisure Activities / Marital Relations / *Av Harachamim* and *Tzidkascha* / *Seudah Hamafsekes* / Singing at *Seudah Shelishis* / Other Practices of Mourning / Taking a Pill on Shabbos to Prepare for the Fast

2. Halachos Pertaining to Motzaei Shabbos..........................270

Reciting *Baruch Hamavdil* / The Passages of *L'Dovid* and *Lamnatzeiach* / *Atah Chonantanu* / The Passages of *V'yehi Noam* and *Vayiten Lecha* / Havdalah / The *Brachah* of *Borei Meorei Ha'eish* / Deriving Benefit from the Flame / The *Brachah* of *Borei Meorei Ha'eish* for Women / The *Brachah* on *Besamim* / Havdalah before Eating on Tishah B'Av / Listening to Havdalah on Tishah B'Av / Havdalah for a Woman on Tishah B'Av / Havdalah for a Child / Leniencies when the Fast Is Postponed

3. Halachos Pertaining to Sunday Night................................274

The Passage of *Atah Chonantanu* / Havdalah / Drinking Water before Havdalah / *Kiddush Levanah* / Activities Prohibited after Tishah B'Av

CHAPTER ELEVEN
Motzaei Tishah B'Av 279

1. The Conclusion of the Fast 279
Breaking the Fast / Eating and Drinking before *Maariv* / Havdalah on Sunday Night / When to Recite *Kiddush Levanah*

2. Restrictions on Motzaei Tishah B'Av 281
Meat and Wine / Bathing, Haircuts, Laundering Garments, and Wearing Freshly Laundered Clothing / Marital Relations / Reciting *Shehecheyanu* / Music

3. Exceptions to the Prohibitions 282
A *Seudas Mitzvah* / A Woman after Birth / Reciting *Birkas Hamazon* with a *Kos* / Extenuating Circumstances / *Kavod* Shabbos / Preparing for Shabbos on Thursday Night

4. Conduct after a Postponed Fast 284
Meat and Wine / The Other Prohibitions / Havdalah on Sunday Night

CHAPTER TWELVE
Zecher L'churban in a Home 289

1. The Basic Obligation 289
An Unfinished Patch on a Wall / Eretz Yisrael and the Diaspora / One *Zecher L'churban* for a Home / The Measurement of an *Amah* / The Shape of the Unfinished Patch

2. Parameters of a *Zecher L'churban* 290
An Unplastered Area / Wallpaper / A Cement Wall / Painting the Square Black or Hanging a Sign / The Placement of the *Zecher L'churban* / A House with Two Entrances

3. Places Requiring a *Zecher L'churban* 292
Residential Homes / Public Buildings / A Home Purchased from a Non-Jew / A Home Purchased from a Jew / A Home Intended for Sale or a Rental / A Rented Home

CHAPTER THIRTEEN
Other Halachos Commemorating the *Churban* 297

1. Limitations at a *Seudah* 297
Omitting a Dish / A Meal with Guests / Shabbos and Yom Tov Meals / Omitting an Insignificant Dish / Leaving an Empty Space on the Table / The Contemporary Practice / Fancy Dishes / *Al Naharos Bavel*

2. Music 299
Playing or Listening to Music / While Drinking Wine / Listening to Music at a Set Time / Playing Music for Income / Singing to Praise or Thank Hashem / Music at a Wedding or *Seudas Mitzvah* / Using Music to Lift One's Spirits / Exercise and Driving / Singing to Put Children to Sleep / A Musical Ring Tone or Door Chime

3. Halachos Pertaining to a Wedding 302
Placing Ashes on a Chassan's Head / The Placement of the Ashes / Removing the Ashes before the *Chuppah* / Breaking a Cup / Using an Intact Glass / Using a Glass / Breaking a Dish at the *Tenaim* / Head Adornments for a Chassan and Kallah

4. Other Forms of Mourning 304
Omitting a Piece of Jewelry / Omitting Jewelry on Shabbos and Yom Tov / Jewelry Worn on a Daily Basis / Dressing Ostentatiously in Public / Enjoyment without Happiness / Filling One's Mouth with Laughter

CHAPTER FOURTEEN
The Halachos of *Kriah* 309

1. Rending One's Garments for Yerushalayim and the *Makom Hamikdash* 309
The Obligation to Perform *Kriah* / Tearing *Kriah* upon Seeing the Old City Today / Tearing *Kriah* at the Site of the *Beis Hamikdash* / Performing *Kriah* from Afar / The Kosel Hamaaravi / Seeing Both the Old City and the *Makom Hamikdash* / *Kriah* for Women / *Kriah* for Children / Performing *Kriah* Once in 30 Days

2. The Procedure for *Kriah* 312
How to Tear the Garment / Tearing a Garment Next to the Heart / Tearing the Outermost Garment / Wearing an Old Garment / Tearing the Same Garment Twice / Repairing the Tear

3. Exemptions from Performing *Kriah* 314
Shabbos and Yom Tov / Erev Shabbos and Erev Yom Tov / Chol Hamoed / Days When *Tachanun* Is Omitted / A Person Who Has Seen the Locations within the Past 30 Days / A Child who Turns Bar or Bas Mitzvah / A Person Who Forgot to Perform *Kriah* / A Resident of Yerushalayim / Transferring Ownership of One's Clothing

INDEX 317

ישיבת סלבודקה "כנסת ישראל"

THE JERUSALEM KOLLEL

TORAH SCHOLARSHIP FOR THE JEWISH COMMUNITY WORLDWIDE

RABBI YITZCHAK BERKOVITS
ROSH KOLLEL

יצחק שמואל הלוי ברקוביץ
ראש הכולל

בס"ד ירושלם ת"ו, ארבעים למטמונים תש"פ

עברתי על חלקים נכבדים מספרו של הרה"ג ר' זאב הופשטטר שליט"א *קיצור הלכות ספירת העומר ובין המצרים* ומצאתיו מעשה ידי אומן. אם כי מדובר בהמון פרטים ופרטי פרטים, הדברים מסודרים באופן מופתי המקל גם על הלימוד על מנת לרכוש ידע בהלכות אלו, וגם לחפש את ההלכה למעשה לעת מצא.

כמיטב הבנתי ההלכות מדוייקות, מה גם כי לכל הלכה בית אב, מקורות משו"ע ונו"כ ועד לפוסקי זמננו.

ויה"ר שהרב המחבר שליט"א ימשיך לזכות את הרבים בספריו רבי התועלת מתוך בריאות הנפש ובריאות הגוף, וכדרכה של המשפחה הכבודה המזכה את ציבור לומדי התורה בקנין התורה, ההלכה והמוסר בסדר גודל שלא ידע כלל ישראל כמוהו למשך דורות.

הכו"ח לכב' המחבר ולכב' העוסקים בלימוד ההלכה למעשה,

יצחק ברקוביץ

SANHEDRIA HAMURCHEVET 140 JERUSALEM, ISRAEL 97707

בס"ד

Rabbi Michel Steinmetz
Rav of
K'hal Toldos Yakov Yosef
D'chasidei Square
of Brooklyn

נחמן יחיאל מיכל שטיינמעץ
דומ"ץ דק"ק תולדות יעקב יוסף
דחסידי סקווירא בארא פארק
בעמח"ס שו"ת משיב נבונים על ד' חלקי שו"ע,
שפתי נבונים בירור הלכות על סדר השו"ע,
באר נבונים על התורה ומועדים

4716 17th Avenue • Brooklyn, N.Y. 11219 • Tel. 718.853.3744 • Fax: 718.436.3566

[חתימה וחותמת]

HAGAON HARAV YITZCHOK SOROTZKIN *shlit"a*,
Rosh Yeshivah of Telshe and Lakewood Mesivta

הכנה לקבלת התורה

ויסע משה את ישראל מים סוף ויצאו אל מדבר שור וילכו שלשת ימים במדבר ולא מצאו מים (שמות טו, כב).

בב"ק דף פ"ב א' דתניא וילכו שלשת ימים במדבר ולא מצאו מים דורשי רשומות אמרו אין מים אלא תורה שנאמר (ישעיה נה) הוי כל צמא לכו למים כיון שהלכו ג' ימים בלא תורה נלאו עמדו נביאים שביניהם ותקנו להם שיהיו קורין בשבת וקורין בשני וקורין בחמישי כדי שלא ישהו שלשה ימים בלא תורה, ויש לתמוה והלא זה היה קודם מתן תורה כשעדיין לא נצטוו על תלמוד תורה וא"כ למה נתבעו על ביטול תורה, ועוד צ"ב דהנה כשהיו במצרים וכן לפני שנסעו מים סוף ג"כ לא עסקו בתורה ומ"מ לא נתבעו על ביטול תורה ולמה כשנסעו מים סוף נתבעו על ביטול תורה.

ונראה דאיתא בספרים שכלל ישראל יצאו ממצרים בפסח ובימים שבין פסח לעצרת הכינו עצמם לקראת קבלת התורה, והנה הרמב"ן בפרשת בשלח כתב שבמרה ניתן להם מקצת פרשיות של תורה שיתעסקו בהם להרגילם ולנסות אותם אם יקבלו אותם בשמחה ובטוב לבב, ויסוד הדבר עפימש"כ האבני אליהו על סדר התפלה דבעינן לקבל את התורה בלב שמח [ועיין מש"כ בזה בגבורות יצחק פורים ענין כב] ולכך נתן להם קצת מצוות שיתעסקו בהם לנסות אותם אם יקבלו אותן בשמחה ובטוב לב דאם יקבלו אותן בשמחה הרי זה מורה שמוכנים לקבל התורה בשמחה. והנה רבנו ירוחם בנתיב החמישי חלק רביעי כתב דמצוות ספירה הוא לשמחת התורה כדאיתא במדרש כשאמר להם משה תעבדון את האלקים על ההר הזה אמרו לו מתי אמר להם לסוף נ' יום ומרוב שמחתם שהיו ממתינים אותו מעמד היו מונין אותו כך וכך כחתן המונה יום הכנסת כלתו לחופה ולכן אנו מונין אותו עתה זכר להם, הרי שכלל ישראל ספרו למתן תורה מרוב שמחתם שמקבלים את התורה וזה היתה הכנתם לקבל התורה מרוב שמחה. והנה החינוך במצוה ש"ו כתב דשורש ספירת העומר להראות בנפשנו החפץ הגדול אל קבלת התורה הנכסף ללבנו כי המנין מראה לאדם כי כל ישעו וכל חפצו להגיע אל הזמן ההוא, וזה היתה הכנתם לקבל התורה דלקבלת התורה צריך להיות בכיסופין שזה כל ישעו וחפצו.

והנה רש"י הביא המכילתא ויסע משה הסיעם בעל כרחם שעטרו מצרים סוסיהם בתכשיטי זהב וכסף ואבנים טובות והיו ישראל מוצאים אותם בים לפיכך הוצרך להסיעם

בעל כרחם, והנה הכלי יקר כתב לפי שעסקו בביזת היום יותר מהראוי מאז היו בלתי ראויים לקבלת התורה כי כבר אמר להם הקב"ה תעבדון את האלהים על ההר הזה דהיינו קבלת התורה והם היו עסוקים בביזת הים ולא אמרו נלכה ונרוצה לקבל התורה, והיינו דהי' חסר בשמחתם וכיסופם לקבל התורה שאם היה להם רוב כיסופין ושמחה לקבל התורה לא היו עוסקים בביזת הים ומשיאין עצמן מלרוץ לקבל התורה. וכמש"כ האור החיים בפרשת כי תבוא שאם היו מרגישים שמחת הטוב היו משתגעין ומתלהטים אחרי' ולא הי' נחשב בעיניהם כל כסף וזהב שבעולם כלום. והנה הרמב"ן בפרשת יתרו (יט א-ב) כתב דכתיב בחודש השלישי לצאת בני ישראל מארץ מצרים ביום הזה באו מדבר סיני והיה ראוי שיאמר הכתוב ויסעו מרפידים ויחנו במדבר סיני בחדש השלישי אבל בעבור היות ביאתם במדבר סיני שמחה להם ויו"ט ומעת צאתם מארץ מצרים נכספים אליו כי ידעו ששם יקבלו התורה כי משה הגיד להם תעבדון את האלקים על ההר הזה בעבור זה התחיל הפרשה בחדש הזה כי ביום שהתחיל החודש באו לשם, והנה כתיב ויסעו מרפידים ויבואו מדבר סיני והיה ראוי שיאמר ויחנו במדבר סיני אבל כתיב ויבואו מדבר סיני לומר כי מיד שבאו אל מדבר סיני חנו במדבר בראותם ההר מנגד ולא המתינו עד שיכנסו בו אל מקום טוב לחנות שם אבל חנו במדבר או בחורב שהוא מקום חורב שממה לפני ההר וזה טעם ויחנו במדבר ויחן שם ישראל נגד ההר, והנה עיין באור החיים הקדוש שהפסוקים בא לומר עיקרי ההכנה לקבלת התורה שבאמצעותם נתרצה ה' להנחילם התורה יעו"ש בדבריו, ולפימש"כ הרמב"ן נראה דעיקר ההכנה לקבלת התורה החשק והכיסופין והשמחה רבה לקבל התורה וכלל ישראל הכינו עצמם לקבלת התורה על ידי שספרו למתן תורה להגביר החשק והכיסוף למתן תורה והתרגלו עצמם לעסוק בתורה בשמחה וטוב לב.

ולפי המבואר נראה דזה היתה התביעה על כלל ישראל כשנסעו מים סוף שלשת ימים בלי מים דאף שלא היו מצווין במצוות ת"ת מ"מ היו צריכים להכין עצמם לקבלת התורה שכל ישעם וחפצם להגיע לקבלת התורה וירבה שמחתם לקבל התורה וכיון שהיו עסוקים בביזה והיו להם כסוף וחפץ לתענוגי עוה"ז ולא מהרו לילך אל המדבר לקבלת התורה לא היו ראוים לקבלת התורה, והנה כלל ישראל הלכו ג' ימים במדבר בלי כיסופין לתורה ובלי הרגשת השמחה של קבלת התורה, כ"א שנתחזקו בהן החשק לעושר ותענוגי עוה"ז וע"ז נלאו לקבל התורה שהתורה הי' מר להם ע"ז ניתן להם במרה מקצת פרשיות של תורה שיתעסקו בהם להרגילם ולנסות אם יתעסקו בהם בשמחה וטוב לב. ולפי"ז הרי אתי שפיר ג"כ מ"ט לא נתבעו על ביטול תורה לפני קריעת ים סוף, ולפי המבואר אתי שפיר דבאמת כיון שלא נצטוו על ת"ת לא נתבעו על ביטול תורה כי אם התביעה היתה ע"ז שעסקו בביזת הים והיה להם בקשת ותשוקה לעוה"ז ולא הי' להם הכיסופין לקבלת התורה וע"ז לא היו ראויין לקבלת התורה.

והנה בתנחומא ר"פ נח ביאר דאע"ג שכלל ישראל אמרו נעשה ונשמע על תורה

שבכתב מפני שאין בה יגיעה וצער והיא מעט הוצרכו שיכפו עליהם הר כגיגית לקבל
תורה שבע"פ לפי שאין לומד אותה אלא מי שאוהב הקב"ה בכל לבו ובכל נפשו ובכל
מאודו שנאמר ואהבת את ה' אלקיך בכל לבבך ובכל נפשך ובכל מאדך, ומנין אתה אומר
שאין אהבה זו אלא תלמוד ראה מה כתיב אחריו והיו הדברים האלה אשר אנכי מצוך
היום על לבבך ואיזה זה תלמוד שהוא על הלב, ללמדך שפרשה ראשונה של ק"ש אין
בה פירוש מתן שכרה בעוה"ז כמש"כ בפרשה שניה והיה אם שמוע תשמעו וגו' ונתתי
מטר ארצכם בעתו זה מתן שכר עוסקי מצות שאין עוסקין בתלמוד, ובפ' שניה כתיב בה בכל
לבבכם ובכל נפשכם ולא כתב בכל מאדכם ללמדך שכל מי שאוהב עושר ותענוג אינו
יכול ללמוד תורה שבע"פ לפי שיש בה צער גדול ונדוד שינה ויש מבלה ומנבל עצמו
עליה ע"כ, הרי דכלל ישראל בשעת קבלת תורה לא רצו לקבל תורה שבע"פ מפני
שאהבו עושר ותענוג והיה חסר באהבתם לתורה, ונראה דשורש הדבר שהיה להם אהבת
עושר ותענוגים היתה משום שעסקו בביזת הים ובשביל רוב כסף וזהב שהושפע להם
היה הסיבה שנולד בהם חמדת הממון ואהבת התענוגים, ומשו"ה כאשר כלל ישראל
עסקו בביזת הים לא היו ראויין לקבלת התורה, דלקבל התורה בעיין שלא יהא לאדם
אהבת העושר ותענוגים וכשהיה להם אהבת העושר ותענוגים לא היו ראויין לקבלת
התורה ונתבעו ע"ז אע"פ שעדיין לא נצטוו על לימוד התורה.

והנה בפרשת יתרו (יט א) בחדש השלישי לצאת בני ישראל מארץ מצרים ביום הזה
באו מדבר סיני ופירש"י שלא היה צריך לכתוב אלא ביום ההוא מהו ביום הזה שיהיו
דברי תורה חדשים עליך כאילו היום ניתנו, וכבר הקשו שזה היתה קודם מתן תורה
וא"כ איך שייך הך ענין כאילו היום ניתנו, אולם בחידושי מרן רי"ז הלוי תהלים ביאר
מאי דכתיב שש אנכי על אמרתך כמוצא שלל רב עפ"מ שאמרו חז"ל בכל יום יהיו
בעיניך כחדשים, וזה שאמר דוד שכ"כ הם בעיניו כחדשים עד שהוא שש עליהם תמיד
כמוצא שלל רב כי אינו דומה השמחה שאח"כ להשמחה שבשעת מציאה שאז השמחה
גדולה מאד, וזהו שאמר כי השמחה על ד"ת הם אצלו כמו שעכשיו מצא את השלל רב
כי הם תמיד אצלו כחדשים ושש עליהם כשעת מציאה, וזהו דכתיב כמוצא שלל רב
ולא כעל שלל רב, כי ד"ת הם תמיד כשעת מציאה ע"כ, ולפי"ז נראה דהנה כבר הבאנו
לדברי הרמב"ן שבמרה ניתן להם מקצת פרשיות שיתעסקו בהם לנסות אותן אם יקבלו
אותן בשמחה וטוב לב, וכיון שאמרו חז"ל שהשמחה צריך להיות כמוצא שלל רב איכלל
בהנסיון לראות אם ישמחו במקצת הפרשיות שעסקו בהם כמוצא שלל רב וע"ז כתיב
בתורה שכלל ישראל שמחו בתורה כמוצא שלל רב כי היו אצלם כחדשים וששו עליהם
כשעת מציאה והיו ראויין לקבלת התורה.

CHAPTER ONE

The Mitzvah of *Sefiras Haomer*

1. The Basic Rules of *Sefirah*
2. The Procedure for Counting the *Omer*
3. The Time for the Mitzvah
4. Missed Days and Situations of Uncertainty
5. Mental Intent in *Sefiras Haomer*
6. Activities Prohibited before *Sefirah*

CHAPTER ONE

The Mitzvah of *Sefiras Haomer*

Introduction: The mitzvah of *sefiras haomer* begins on the second night of the holiday of Pesach, the night of the 16th of Nissan. The Torah teaches this to us in the *pasuk* (*Vayikra* 23:15), "*Usefartem lachem mimacharas haShabbos* – You shall count for yourselves on the day after Shabbos." *Chazal* explain that the word "Shabbos" in this *pasuk* does not refer to the Shabbos day but rather to the first day of Pesach; thus, the phrase "on the day after Shabbos" denotes the second day of Pesach. The Torah commands us to count "*sheva Shabbosos temimos* – seven full weeks"; thus, the mitzvah is to count each of the 49 days leading up to the holiday of Shavuos.[1]

During the era of the *Beis Hamikdash*, when the *korban omer* was offered on Pesach and the *korban shtei halechem* was brought on Shavuos, the mitzvah of *sefiras haomer* was *mid'oraisa*. Today, however, since these *korbanos* are no longer offered, there is a dispute among the Rishonim as to whether the mitzvah is still *mid'oraisa* or it applies only *mid'rabbanan*. The majority opinion is that the obligation to count the days of the *omer* is *mid'rabbanan*.[2] There are several important implications of the status of this mitzvah, which will be discussed in the following sections.

---

1. מנחות דף סה:.
2. ראה תוס' מנחות דף ס"ו. ד"ה זכר, רא"ש סוף פסחים סי' מ', שו"ת הרשב"א הובא בב"י סי' תפ"ט. ועי' ר"ן סוף פסחים הוב"ד בב"י שם שכ' דרוב המפרשים הסכימו דהשתא דליכא הבאה וקרבן, אינו אלא מדרבנן זכר למקדש. וכ"פ השו"ע סי' תפ"ט ס"ב. ועי' ביה"ל סי' תפ"ט ס"א ד"ה לספור העומר.

Introduction ~ 3

1. The Basic Rules of *Sefirah*

1. **The Obligation to Count 49 Days:** The mitzvah of *sefiras haomer* is to begin counting the days of the *omer* period from the second night of Pesach. We are required to count every one of the 49 days between Pesach and Shavuos.[3]

2. **Counting at Night:** *Lechatchilah*, one should recite each day's count at nightfall, which is when the new day begins (see section 3 below for more details). However, the obligation can be fulfilled throughout the night, and a person may therefore recite the *brachah* on counting *sefirah* at any time during the night.[4] See section 4 below regarding a person who did not recite the count at night.

3. **An Individual Obligation:** The *pasuk* describes the mitzvah of *sefiras haomer* with the words "*Usefartem lachem* – You shall count *for yourselves.*" *Chazal* infer from this phrase that the mitzvah of *sefiras haomer* is an individual obligation rather than a communal one.[5] The exact meaning of this concept is the subject of some discussion among the *poskim*. One possible interpretation is that the Torah simply means to distinguish the mitzvah of *sefiras haomer* from other requirements, such as the counting of the *shemittah* and *yovel* years, which are obligatory only for *beis din*. Another interpretation, though, is that the *pasuk* means to convey that every individual must perform the mitzvah personally, rather than merely hearing the count being recited by someone else. In the case of many other mitzvos, such as the requirement of Kiddush, this is an acceptable way to fulfill the mitzvah, due to the principle

---

3. גמ' שם. שו"ע שם ס"א.
4. שו"ע שם ומ"ב סק"ד.
5. גמ' שם.

of *shomea k'oneh* (i.e., hearing another person's recitation is tantamount to actually pronouncing the words).[6]

Lechatchilah, in light of this dispute, every individual should recite the count on his own. Nevertheless, if a person listens to someone else count the *omer* with the intention of thereby fulfilling his obligation (and the person reciting the count intended to be *motzi* him), even though it is proper for him to repeat the count personally, he should not recite the *brachah*.[7]

4. **Hearing the *Brachah* from Someone Else:** The discussion cited above relates to the actual counting of the *omer*. All *poskim* agree, however, that a person may fulfill his obligation to recite the *brachah* on *sefiras haomer* by hearing it recited by another person, as is the case with regard to all *birchos hamitzvos*. Nevertheless, the *minhag* is for the *brachah* to be recited by every individual, rather than for the *shaliach tzibbur* to recite it on behalf of the entire congregation.[8]

There are certain instances, however, when the principle of *shomea k'oneh* is employed regarding the *brachah*. When a person is in doubt as to whether he has an obligation to count the *omer*, the principle of *safek brachos lehakel* dictates that he should not recite the *brachah*. In that case, he should certainly hear the *brachah* recited by someone else in order to fulfill his obligation, and he should then personally recite the count.[9]

5. **A Woman's Obligation:** The mitzvah of *sefiras haomer* is a *mitzvas aseh shehazman grama* (a positive mitzvah that is in effect only at a specific time), and women are therefore

---

6. עי' מ"ב שם סק"ה. ועי' בביה"ל ד"ה ומצוה על כל אחד ואחד.
7. עי' ביה"ל שם.
8. מ"ב שם. (וראה מ"ב סי' ח' ס"ק י"ג, ועי' שיח הלכה סי' ח' אות כ"ח.)
9. שעה"צ סק"ה.

The Basic Rules of Sefirah 5

exempt from the obligation.[10] Nevertheless, many women opt to observe the mitzvah and receive reward for it, as they do with other time-related mitzvos. Some *poskim* maintain that although women are technically exempt from the mitzvah, they have voluntarily assumed the obligation.[11] The Rema's ruling, which is the normative halachah for Ashkenazim, is that a woman who wishes to perform a time-related mitzvah is permitted to recite the *brachah* on the mitzvah;[12] therefore, an Ashkenazic woman would recite the *brachah* on the daily count. Some *poskim* maintain, however, that the common practice is for women to refrain from counting *sefirah*, and that even if a woman wishes to perform the mitzvah, she should not recite the *brachah*, since she is likely to forget a day at some point.[13] Some authorities would remind the women in their households to count *sefirah*,[14] while others did not require the women to count *sefirah* at all.[15]

If an Ashkenazic girl is engaged to a Sephardic boy and their wedding is scheduled during the period of *sefirah*, she should consult a Rav regarding whether she should recite the *brachah* upon counting the *omer* before her marriage and, if so, if she should continue reciting the *brachah* until the conclusion of *sefirah*.

6. **Children of *Chinuch* Age:** A boy who has reached the age of *chinuch* – which means, in this context, that he understands

---

10. רמב״ם פ״ז הל׳ תמידין ומוספין הכ״ד.
11. מ״ב סק״ג בשם המ״א. וראה מנחת חינוך מצוה ש״ו סק״ד.
12. סי׳ י״ז ס״ב וסי׳ תקפ״ט ס״ו.
13. מ״ב סי׳ תפ״ט שם. וראה לשון השלחן שלמה שממנו הביא המ״ב דין זה, שכ׳ בודאי יטעו ביום אחד ולא יודעים הדין (והמ״ב לא העתיק מילים אלו "ולא יודעים הדין"), משמע שהטעם הוא שאינן יודעות שאם יחסרו יום אחד שאינן מברכות, ולכן אין להם להתחיל שבודאי יעבור כמה פעמים על איסור ברכה לבטלה, ולא מפני שמסתבר שבעתיד תפסיד יום אחד מהספירה ולכן יש טעם שלא להתחיל לברך על מצוה זו.
14. בבית הגרי״י קנייבסקי זצ״ל הובא בארחות רבינו ח״ב עמוד צ״ד.
15. בבית הגרשז״א זצ״ל הובא בהליכות שלמה פי״א הערה 35.

the basic concept of the mitzvah and is capable of counting *sefirah* – is obligated to perform the mitzvah.[16] An adult is permitted to teach the *brachah* on *sefiras haomer* to such a child and to pronounce Hashem's Name for that purpose; this does not constitute a *brachah levatalah*.[17]

In order to be subject to the obligation of *chinuch* for this mitzvah, a child must be old enough to remain awake until nightfall and count *sefirah* every day for a period of 49 days. A child who is accustomed to going to bed earlier is not obligated in this mitzvah and therefore is not required to stay awake for that purpose.[18]

If a child at the age of *chinuch* forgets to count one of the days of the *omer*, he should not recite the *brachah* on subsequent nights, just as an adult who forgets to count one day may not continue reciting the *brachah*.[19]

7. **A Child Who Becomes Bar Mitzvah during *Sefirah*:** Most *poskim* maintain that a boy who celebrates his bar mitzvah during the period of *sefirah* may continue reciting the *brachah* after his 13th birthday if he remembered to count all of the previous days, even though his performance of the mitzvah until that point was required only for *chinuch*.[20] Nevertheless, since there is a minority opinion that he should not recite the *brachah*, any such case should be referred to a Rav for a practical ruling.

8. **An *Onen*:** In general, an *onen* is exempt from all mitzvos. Nevertheless, some *poskim* allow an *onen* to perform the

---

16. שע"ת סי' תפ"ט סק"כ.
17. שו"ע סי' רט"ו ס"ג.
18. חוט שני שבת ח"ד עמוד שע"ז.
19. תשובת הגרח"ק שליט"א הובא בגליון מים חיים.
20. עי' שע"ת שם, מנחת חינוך מצוה ש"ו סק"ו, שו"ת כת"ס או"ח סי' צ"ט, ערוה"ש סי' תפ"ט סט"ו ושו"ת הר צבי ח"ב סי' ע"ו. וכן פסקו הגרשז"א זצ"ל הובא בהליכות שלמה פי"א ס"י, והגר"ש וואזנער זצ"ל בקובץ מבית לוי ניסן עמוד פ"ה. וראה מועדים וזמנים ח"ד סי' רפ"ח-רפ"ט.

mitzvah of *sefiras haomer* because it is a mitzvah that takes only a few moments to perform. These authorities suggest that the mourner should omit the *brachah* when he counts as an *onen*. A person who follows this ruling will be permitted to continue reciting the *brachah* on subsequent nights.[21]

If a mourner had the status of an *onen* only at night, he should count *sefirah* on the following day, omitting the *brachah*, and should then resume reciting the *brachah* on subsequent nights. If he was an *onen* both at night and during the day and therefore missed an entire day of *sefirah* (assuming that he did not follow the opinion that permits an *onen* to recite the count without reciting the *brachah*), he should omit the *brachah* throughout the remainder of the *sefirah* period.[22]

9. **A Ger:** If a non-Jew becomes a *ger* in the middle of the *sefirah* period, he should count *sefirah* for the remainder of the period without reciting the *brachah*.[23]

10. **Counting the *Omer* in the Presence of Filth or Immodesty:** If a person is unable to recite the *brachah* due to the presence of excrement, urine, a foul odor, or an improperly dressed woman, and that situation will remain unchanged for the duration of that night, he should count the *omer* without reciting the *brachah*.[24]

---

21. עי' שו"ת נודע ביהודה או"ח מהדו"ק סי' כ"ז והעתיקו הגרע"א בהגהותיו, ובביה"ל ס"ח ד"ה בלא ברכה.
22. עי' שע"ת שם ובביה"ל שם.
23. שע"ת שם, ערוה"ש סט"ו (דלא כשו"ת חס"ל תנינא סי' נ"ו). ואם נעשה גר ביום א' וספר היום בלא ברכה יכול להמשיך לספור עם ברכה, שע"ת שם, וכה"ח סי' תפ"ט ס"ק צ"ה.
24. עי' ביה"ל סי' תפ"ח ס"ב ד"ה שמע ט' תקיעות שצידד שלא מצאנו שאסור לקיים מצוה במקום מטונף, ומ"מ סיים בצ"ע. ועי"ש מה שהביא אח"כ מהמטה אפרים. וראה הליכות שלמה תפילה פ"כ ס"ק ל"ו.

2. The Procedure for Counting the *Omer*

1. **Reciting the *Brachah*:** Before reciting the count, a person recites the *brachah* on the mitzvah of counting the *omer*. This *brachah* concludes with the words "*asher kideshanu bemitzvosav vetzivanu al sefiras haomer.*"[25] See section 4 below for a discussion of various situations in which the *brachah* is not recited. The *brachah* of *shehecheyanu* is *not* recited on the mitzvah of *sefiras haomer*.[26]

2. **Counting while Standing:** One must stand while performing the mitzvah of *sefiras haomer*. This is derived from the *pasuk* (*Devarim* 16:9) that states that the counting of the *omer* begins "*mehachel chermeish bakamah*" – literally, "after the sickle begins cutting the standing grain," implying that one must stand while performing the mitzvah.[27]

    One must stand for the recitation of the *brachah* as well[28] (as is the case with all *birchos hamitzvos*[29]). *B'dieved*, if a person recited the count while sitting, he has fulfilled his obligation and is not required to repeat it.[30]

3. **Supporting Oneself on an Object:** Leaning on an object is halachically equated with sitting;[31] therefore, one may not lean on anything while reciting the *brachah* or counting the *omer*.[32]

---

25. שו"ע סי' תפ"ט ס"א.
26. עי' באר היטב סי' תפ"ט סק"ה. וראה ס' ספירת העומר פ"ד ס"ק י"ב שהאריך בזה והביא י"ד טעמים מהפוסקים למה אין מברכים שהחיינו, עי"ש.
27. רמב"ם פ"ז תו"מ הכ"ג, רא"ש פסחים פ"י סי' מ"א, שו"ע סי' תפ"ט ס"א, וסי' תקפ"ה ס"א וט"ז סק"א.
28. מ"ב סק"ו.
29. שעה"צ סק"ז. וראה ב"י ריש סי' ח'.
30. מ"ב שם.
31. ראה סי' קמ"א ס"א לענין קה"ת, וסי' תכ"ב ס"ז לענין קריאת הלל, וסי' תקפ"ה ס"א לענין שופר.
32. מ"ב סי' תקפ"ה סק"ב. ועי' בשעה"צ שם סק"ב.

If necessary, it is permitted to support one's weight slightly on something. However, leaning heavily on something, to the extent that one would fall if it were removed, is considered as sitting. Nevertheless, a person who is elderly or ill and must support himself in such a manner (or must sit) is permitted to do so.[33]

4. **An Interruption between the *Brachah* and the Counting:** It is prohibited to interrupt between the *brachah* and the counting. If a person speaks about something related to the *sefirah* (e.g., he asks another person which day to count), he will not be required to repeat the *brachah*; however, if the interruption is unrelated to the *sefirah*, the *brachah* must be repeated before the recitation of the count. *Lechatchilah*, one should avoid even a silent delay that is longer than the span of *toch k'dei dibbur*.

5. **Counting Orally:** The mitzvah of *sefiras haomer* requires an oral recitation of the count. The obligation cannot be fulfilled by counting the *omer* mentally.[34] Similarly, a person who puts the day's count in writing (e.g., making note of the day of the *omer* in a letter to a friend or jotting it down to inform someone else of the correct day) does not fulfill the mitzvah by doing so, even if he deliberately intends to fulfill the mitzvah in that fashion.[35] Nevertheless, there is a minority opinion among the *poskim* that the mitzvah is indeed fulfilled through writing the count; thus, a person who writes the day of the *omer* should not recite the *brachah* afterward before counting

---

33. פשוט שהרי בדיעבד יוצא בישיבה. וראה מ"ב סי' צ"ד סק"כ לענין תפילה.
34. דקימ"ל הרהור לאו כדיבור, עי' סי' מ"ז ס"ד. ועי' שע"ת סי' תפ"ט סק"ו, וביה"ל שם ס"א ד"ה מונה והולך.
35. עי' שע"ת שם בשם הברכ"י שהכותב בראשי תיבות לא יצא, אבל השע"ת עצמו מסיק שאפי' פירט בכתב היום כך וכך, לא יצא. וכ"פ בערוך השלחן ס"ט.

orally. Therefore, *lechatchilah* one should refrain from writing the day of *sefirah* before actually counting the *omer*.[36]

6. **Understanding the Count:** It is permissible to count the *omer* in any language; however, in order to fulfill the mitzvah, a person must understand the words he is pronouncing. If a person merely recites the formula of *sefirah* without comprehending what he is saying, it is not considered an act of counting. Therefore, even if a person recites the *sefirah* in *lashon hakodesh*, he will not fulfill the mitzvah unless he understands what he has said.[37]

7. **Counting in an Unusual Manner:** There is a debate among the *poskim* regarding whether one can fulfill the mitzvah by pronouncing the combination of Hebrew letters that represent the number of the day, such as reciting the words "*hayom beis*" instead of "*hayom shnei yamim*" on the second night.[38] If a person counts in this fashion, he should repeat the count without repeating the *brachah*.[39]

If, instead of reciting the count in the normal fashion, a person recites a particular formula that yields the number of the day – for instance, on the 39th day he says "*hayom arbaim chaser achas*" ("today is forty minus one") – he has fulfilled the mitzvah.[40] Some *poskim* limit this to a case in which the person uses this specific formula – a multiple of ten, minus one day – since we find that the Torah itself sometimes expresses numbers in this manner. Any other formula, though, such as identifying the day as one less than any other number (e.g., "today is nine minus one"), two less than a multiple of ten (e.g., "today is forty minus two"), or the sum of any two

---

36. עי' שו"ת רע"א סי' כ"ט - ל"ב, ועי' שו"ת כת"ס יו"ד סי' ק"ו.
37. מ"ב סק"ה ובשעה"צ סק"ו.
38. עי' שע"ת סק"ו.
39. ביה"ל ס"א ד"ה מונה והולך.
40. מ"ב ס"ק י"א.

numbers (e.g., "today is ten plus one") would not be a valid form of counting.[41]

8. **Using Cardinal Numbers:** The days of *sefirah* should be counted using cardinal numbers rather than ordinal numbers. Thus, on the first night one recites the words "*hayom yom echad*" ("today is one day"),[42] on the second night one recites "*hayom shnei yamim*" ("today is two days"), and so forth. The count should not be phrased as "today is the first day," "today is the second day," and the like. Some authorities rule that a person who recites the words "*hayom yom rishon*" ("today is the first day") on the first night of the *omer* has not fulfilled his obligation.[43]

9. **Beginning with the Word "*Hayom*":** In order to fulfill the mitzvah, one must begin the count with the word "*hayom*" (or an equivalent phrase in a different language, such as the words "today is"). If a person merely recites the number of the day but does not use the word "*hayom*," he has not fulfilled his obligation.[44]

10. **"*Baomer*" or "*Laomer*":** Some conclude the recitation of the daily count with the word "*baomer*,"[45] while others use the word "*laomer*."[46] Both versions are valid, and one may fulfill the mitzvah by reciting either one. In fact, even if a person omits this part of the recitation altogether and does not state explicitly that he is counting the days of the *omer* – e.g., he recites simply, "*Hayom shnei yamim* – Today is two days," he has fulfilled his obligation.[47] Chassidim and others who daven

---

41. הליכות שלמה פי״א סק״ו והערה 16.
42. שו״ע תפ״ט ס״א.
43. חזו״א הובא בארחות רבינו ח״ב עמוד צ״ד.
44. מ״ב סק״כ.
45. רמ״א תפ״ט ס״א.
46. נוסח האריז״ל והשל״ה הובא בבאר היטב ושע״ת סק״ח.
47. מ״ב סק״ח.

in *nusach* Sephard generally use the word *"laomer,"* which is based on Kabbalah, whereas many who daven *nusach* Ashkenaz use the word *"baomer."*

11. **When to Insert *"Baomer"* or *"Laomer"* when Counting the Weeks:** There are divergent customs regarding how to formulate the counting of the *omer* when we begin counting the weeks. The Sephardic custom is to recite the number of days followed by the word *"laomer"* or *"baomer"* and then to recite the count of the weeks.[48] Ashkenazim, on the other hand, customarily count both the days and the weeks before reciting this word.[49]

12. **The Obligation to Count Days and Weeks:** The mitzvah of *sefiras haomer* calls for a person to count both the days and the weeks of the *omer* period.[50] Therefore, on the seventh day one recites the words, *"Hayom shivah yamim she'heim shavua echad* – Today is seven days, which are one week," and on the eighth day one declares, *"Hayom shemonah yamim she'heim shavua echad v'yom echad* – Today is eight days, which are one week and one day."[51] However, the Rishonim debate whether it is necessary to count both the total number of days and the number of weeks in order to fulfill the mitzvah. Some Rishonim maintain that after the completion of the first week, it is necessary only to count the number of full weeks that have elapsed, along with the number of individual days in the current week. Thus, for instance, on the eighth day one would declare simply that it is "one week and one day," and it would not be necessary to cite the count of eight days as well. Other Rishonim, meanwhile, rule that it is necessary to count the

---

48. עי׳ כה״ח סי׳ תפ״ט ס״ק ל״ד.
49. עי׳ מקראי קדש פסח ח״ב סוסי׳ ס״ד, ועי׳ מועדים וזמנים ח״ז סי׳ רל״א.
50. גמ׳ מנחות דף סו., שו״ע שם.
51. שו״ע שם וכדעת הרא״ש והטור.

weeks only at the conclusion of each full week, and that one should count *only* the total number of days at any other time.[52]

If a person does not recite the full formula of *sefiras haomer* on any given night during this period, but he satisfies one of these two opinions, he may continue reciting the *brachah* throughout the remainder of the *omer* period. Thus, on any day from the eighth day onward, if a person counts the number of weeks and intervening days but neglects to count the full number of days (e.g., he states simply that "today is one week and one day," omitting the count of eight days), he has fulfilled the mitzvah *b'dieved*. Likewise, if a person recites only the full number of days and omits the number of weeks at any time in the middle of a week of the *omer*, he has fulfilled his obligation *b'dieved* and may recite the *brachah* on subsequent nights.[53] However, at the conclusion of a week, such as on the seventh or fourteenth day, if a person counts only the number of weeks and not the total number of days, he is not considered to have fulfilled the mitzvah.[54]

Some *poskim* maintain that it is also insufficient to count only the total number of days, without mentioning the number of weeks, at the conclusion of a week (e.g., stating only "today is seven days" on the seventh night of the *omer*, without adding that it is also one week). Other *poskim* disagree and maintain that this is a valid fulfillment of the mitzvah. A person who has counted in this fashion should recite the count again, in the standard form, without repeating the *brachah*. If, however, he fails to do so, he may continue reciting the *brachah* prior to the count on subsequent nights.[55]

---

52. ראה טור ובי"י ריש סי' תפ"ט.
53. מ"ב סק"ט.
54. מ"ב סק"ז, ועי' שעה"צ ס"ק י"א. אמנם ראה ביה"ל להלן ס"ח ד"ה יספור בדעת הט"ז וסיים שם בצ"ע למעשה.
55. עי' מ"ב סק"ז ושעה"צ סק"ט.

13. **A Mistake in the Count:** If a person errs in the count of either the days or weeks, it is considered a complete omission of the count.[56] The halachah therefore follows the guidelines presented in the previous paragraph: In the middle of a week, he has fulfilled his obligation as long as one of the two figures he identified was correct – either the total number of the days or the number of weeks and additional days.[57] (The incorrect count is ignored, even though it contradicted the correct count.) The halachah regarding an error at the conclusion of a week is likewise the same as in the paragraph above.

14. **Grammatical Considerations:** The words *"shavua"* and *"shavuos"* are masculine nouns (*zachar*). Therefore, the masculine forms of the number should be used with reference to the weeks, e.g., one should recite the phrases *"shavua echad"* and *"shnei shavuos"* rather than *"shavua achas"* and *"shtei shavuos."* Nevertheless, if a person uses the feminine forms of the numbers, he has fulfilled his obligation.[58]

From the second through the tenth day, we use the word *"yamim,"* the plural of the word *"yom,"* in reference to the days. Beginning on the 11th day, we revert to using the singular form, *"yom,"* in keeping with the grammatical rules of *lashon hakodesh*. If a person used the word *"yamim"* instead of *"yom,"* he has fulfilled his obligation.

For the numbers above 20, one should recite the unit's digit first. For example, the number 21 is expressed as *"echad v'esrim"* (literally, "one and twenty"). If a person inverts the order and pronounces the ten's digit first (e.g., *"esrim v'echad"*), he has nonetheless fulfilled his obligation.[59]

---

56. מ"ב ס"ק ל"ה.
57. עי' מ"ב ס"ק ל"ח.
58. מ"ב סק"ט.
59. שם.

15. **Reciting *Tefillos* after the Count:** After the counting of the *omer*, it is customary to recite a *tefillah* for the *Beis Hamikdash* to be rebuilt.[60] Some also recite *perek* 67 of Tehillim, which begins with the words "*Lamnatzeiach b'neginos mizmor shir.*"[61] Some authorities cite a custom to recite other *tefillos*, such as "*Ana B'koach*" and "*Ribbono shel Olam,*" at this time,[62] while others are opposed to the practice.[63] Every individual should follow his own *minhag*. Similarly, some recite *Leshem Yichud* before the *brachah*,[64] while some *poskim* oppose this custom.[65] Generally, those who daven *nusach* Sephard recite these *tefillos*, while they are omitted in *nusach* Ashkenaz.

In some siddurim, the *tefillah* of *Leshem Yichud* includes the words "*lekayeim mitzvas aseh shel sefiras haomer k'mo shekasuv baTorah* – to fulfill the positive mitzvah of counting the *omer* as it is written in the Torah." Some *poskim* recommend omitting these words, since this statement may violate the prohibition of *bal tosif*, according to the authorities who maintain that the mitzvah is only *mid'rabbanan* today.[66] Other *poskim* justify the phrase, explaining that it indicates a mitzvah *d'rabbanan* that is based on what is written in the Torah.[67]

---

60. מ"ב סק"י, ועי' שעה"צ ס"ק ט"ו.
61. מ"ב שם.
62. שו"ע הרב סי' תפ"ט סי"א.
63. ראה חק יעקב סי' תפ"ט ס"ק י"א, ומעשה רב סי' ס"ט. וראה ערוך השלחן סי' תפ"ט ס"ו.
64. יסוד ושורש העבודה שער תשיעי פ"ח, כה"ח שם סק"ז.
65. שו"ת נודע ביהודה מהדו"ק יו"ד סי' צ"ג, חק יעקב שם ס"ק י"א.
66. שו"ת אור לציון ח"ג פל"ז סי' ב', תשובות והנהגות ח"א סי' ש"י. וראה מש"כ בביכורי יעקב סי' תרנ"ח סוסק"א לענין מצות לולב בזה"ז בירושלים.
67. הליכות שלמה שם ס"ב.

3. The Time for the Mitzvah

1. **Counting at Nightfall:** The Torah states (*Vayikra* 23:15) that the seven weeks of *sefiras haomer* must be *"temimos"* (complete). Therefore, we recite *sefiras haomer* immediately after *Maariv*, at nightfall, in order to count each day as soon as it begins.[68] For the same reason, it is customary in many congregations to count the *omer* even before the recitation of *Aleinu*.[69] Some congregations, however, have the custom to count after *Aleinu*.[70] (A person should follow the practice of the *minyan* with which he is davening.) Nevertheless, even when davening *Maariv* after *tzeis hakochavim*, we do not recite *sefirah* before *Maariv*, since the mitzvos of *Krias Shema* and *Shemoneh Esrei* are more frequently observed (*"tadir"*) and therefore take precedence over the mitzvah of counting the *omer*.[71]

2. **The Second Night of Pesach in *Chutz La'Aretz*:** In *chutz la'Aretz* on the second night of Pesach, some customarily wait until the conclusion of the Seder to begin counting *sefiras haomer*. The rationale for this practice is that counting the *omer* before the Seder would be a contradiction to the Yom Tov itself, since the Torah calls for the counting to begin after the first Yom Tov of Pesach. (This is somewhat comparable to the practice of omitting the *brachah* on sitting in the sukkah on Shemini Atzeres.) Many chassidim observe this custom due to its sources in Kabbalah.[72] (There are divergent *minhagim* as to when exactly the count should be recited during the

---

68. שו״ע סי׳ תפ״ט ס״א.
69. מ״ב סק״ב.
70. עי׳ מעשה רב סי׳ ס״ט, כה״ח סי׳ תפ״ט ס״ק ק״ב, כדי לא להפסיק בסדר התפילה.
71. ביה״ל שם ד״ה אחר תפילת ערבית. ועי׳ שו״ת אגרות משה או״ח ח״ד סי׳ צ״ט.
72. עי׳ ברכ״י סי׳ תפ״ט אות ה׳, ועי׳ יסוד ושורש העבודה שער תשיעי פרק ח׳, ועוד. (אמנם ראה

Seder; some count the *omer* after the fourth cup of wine, while others wait until after the *piyutim*.) However, those who do not have a family tradition to observe this *minhag* must count immediately after *Maariv*.[73]

3. **Counting during *Bein Hashemashos*:** As noted above, *sefiras haomer* should be performed at night after *tzeis hakochavim*, which is the beginning of the new halachic day. Technically, since many *poskim* maintain that the mitzvah of counting the *omer* is only *d'rabbanan* today, it can be fulfilled during the period of *bein hashemashos*. Nevertheless, it is proper to wait until *tzeis hakochavim*.[74] Many congregations, though, daven *Maariv* shortly after *shekiah* and count with a *brachah* and there is justification for this practice.[75] Some *poskim* maintain that a person who counted the *omer* during *bein hashemashos* should repeat the count after *tzeis hakochavim*, albeit without reciting the *brachah*.[76] A person who counted during *bein hashemashos* and did not repeat it later may still continue counting the *omer* and reciting the *brachah* on subsequent nights.

4. ***Tzeis Hakochavim* of Rabbeinu Tam:** The time of *tzeis hakochavim* varies in different locations. Since most *poskim* maintain that the mitzvah of *sefiras haomer* is only *d'rabbanan* today, even if a person follows the stringent view

---

כה"ח שם סק"ו שכתב שעפ"י הסוד צריך לספור תיכף אחרי ערבית וכו' ואם יאחרנה גורם לתת אחיזה לחיצונים.)

73. עי' מ"א סי' תפ"ט סק"ט שהקשה מ"ש משמיני עצרת ועי"ש תירוצו, וכמו"כ עי' בחק יעקב שם סק"ב, הרי שנקטו להלכה שמברכים וסופרים אחרי מעריב. ועי' בברכי יוסף שם שהקשה על המנהג לקיים המצוה אחרי הסדר שהרי אסור לאכול סעודה לפני קיום המצוה. וראה ערוך השלחן סי' תפ"ט סי"א.

74. שו"ע שם ס"ב ובמ"ב ס"ק י"ד, והטעם משום דאין נכון להכניס עצמו לספק לכתחילה. ועי' גם שו"ע שם ס"ג ובמ"ב ס"ק ט"ז. ובענין זמן ביהש"מ עי' ביה"ל שם ס"ב ד"ה וכן ראוי לעשות.

75. דלא גרע ממש"כ בביה"ל ס"ג ד"ה מבעוד יום, ואף עדיף.

76. מ"ב סק"ט בשם הא"ר לחוש להפוסקים שסוברים דספירה בזמן הזה דאורייתא. וראה גם ביה"ל ס"א ד"ה לספור.

of Rabbeinu Tam concerning the time of *tzeis hakochavim* for *mitzvos d'oraisa*, such as Shabbos and Yom Kippur, there is no need for him to wait until the *zman* of Rabbeinu Tam in order to count the *omer*. On the contrary, it is better to count with the congregation after *Maariv* rather than delaying the *sefirah* until a later hour.[77] Nevertheless, a person who follows Rabbeinu Tam's view with respect to *mitzvos d'rabbanan* as well should wait until the *zman* of Rabbeinu Tam before counting the *omer*.[78]

5. **Davening *Maariv* Immediately after *Shekiah*:** If a person davens *Maariv* immediately after *shekiah*, prior to *tzeis hakochavim*, yet he wishes to be stringent and to recite *sefiras haomer* after *tzeis hakochavim* (as explained in paragraph 3 above), he should nonetheless count the *omer* along with the congregation without reciting the *brachah*, with the mental stipulation that if he remembers to count again later in the evening, he will not have fulfilled the mitzvah by counting with the congregation. After *tzeis hakochavim*, he should recite the *brachah* and repeat the count. By employing this strategy, he will be able to rest assured that even if he forgets to count later in the evening, he will have fulfilled the mitzvah by counting with the congregation at *Maariv*.[79]

In order to make use of this stipulation and recite the *brachah* later in the evening, it is imperative to have the explicit intent *not* to fulfill the mitzvah together with the congregation. It is not sufficient merely to count the *omer* without the positive intent of fulfilling the mitzvah.[80]

6. **Davening *Maariv* before Sunset:** Some congregations daven

---

77. שו"ת מנחת יצחק ח"ו סי' מ"ה וח"ט סי' נ"ה, ואם רוצה להחמיר יספר אח"כ בביתו בלא ברכה.
78. שם ח"ט סי' נ"ה. ועי' שו"ת דברי יציב ח"ב סי' רט"ו.
79. שו"ע שם ס"ג, מ"ב ס"ק ט"ז.
80. רמ"א שם ס"ג, מ"ב ס"ק י"ז ובשעה"צ ס"ק כ"ג.

Maariv after *plag hamincha*.[81] There is a halachic basis to permit this practice, provided that the participants maintain a consistent davening schedule in this respect. That is, it would not be permissible to daven *Minchah* during the period between *plag* and *shekiah* on some days, and to daven *Maariv* during the same period on other days.[82] Certainly, one may not daven both *Minchah* and *Maariv* during the period between *plag hamichah* and *shekiah* on the same day.[83]

A person who davens *Maariv* during this period should refrain from counting *sefiras haomer* until nightfall. (It is advisable to set up some sort of reminder for oneself, since it is easy to forget to count the *omer*.) If a person erroneously recited the count during this time, he should repeat it at night; according to some *poskim*, he may even recite a *brachah* at that time.[84] Other *poskim* maintain that while the count itself should be repeated, the *brachah* should not be recited.[85] Nevertheless, if a congregation has the practice of reciting *sefiras haomer* after *Maariv* even before sunset, there is no need to protest, since there is a halachic basis for their actions. The individual himself, however, should not count along with them. If a person who davens in such a *minyan* is concerned that he may forget to count the *omer* later in the evening, it is permissible for him to count along with them without reciting the *brachah*, making the same mental stipulation described in paragraph 5 above; he may then recite the *brachah* and repeat the count after nightfall.[86]

---

81. כשיטת רבי יהודה שזמן מנחה עד פלג המנחה וזמן מעריב מפלג המנחה ואילך, עי׳ ברכות דף כ״ו. וכו׳, שו״ע סי׳ רל״ג ס״א ובמ״ב שם.
82. שם, ועי׳ מ״ב סי׳ רל״ג סק״ו-י״ג.
83. עי׳ מ״ב שם ס״ק י״א וי״ג.
84. שו״ע סי׳ תפ״ט ס״ב ובמ״ב ס״ק י״ב-י״ג.
85. שו״ע הרב סי׳ תפ״ט סי״ב, כה״ח שם ס״ק ל״ט.
86. עי׳ ביה״ל סי׳ תפ״ט ס״ג ד״ה מבעוד יום, ושעה״צ ס״ק י״ז.

7. ***Maariv* before Sunset on Erev Shabbos:** On Erev Shabbos, all authorities agree that one may daven *Kabbalas Shabbos* and *Maariv* after *plag haminchah*, even before *shekiah*.[87] (This is true even for a person who regularly davens *Minchah* at that time of day on an ordinary weekday.) Nevertheless, even in this case, *sefiras haomer* must be recited at night.[88] According to many *poskim*, it is preferable to refrain from counting the *omer* even during *bein hashemashos* on Shabbos.[89] (Some *poskim* state, though, that it is common to rely on counting the *omer* during *bein hashemashos* on Shabbos.[90])

8. **A Person Who Will Daven *Maariv* Later at Night:** In principle, a person may count *sefirah* immediately after nightfall (see paragraph 1 above), even if he has not yet davened *Maariv* (and even on Motzaei Shabbos).[91] Nevertheless, due to the principle of "*tadir kodem*" (the more frequent practice must be performed first), the standard practice is to count the *omer* only after *Maariv*.[92] If a person does not habitually attend a later *minyan* and is able to daven *Maariv* at *tzeis hakochavim*, he should certainly do so.[93] If a person is not able to daven *Maariv* at *tzeis hakochavim* – e.g., he is unable to join a *minyan* until later in the evening – the *poskim* disagree as to whether he should count *sefirah* immediately at *tzeis hakochavim* or he should wait to recite it after *Maariv*. Some *poskim* maintain that if a person habitually attends a later *minyan* (e.g., after a *shiur*) he should delay *sefiras haomer* until

---

87. עי' מ"ב סי' רס"ז סק"ג.
88. מ"ב סי' תפ"ט ס"ק י"ח.
89. כמבואר במ"ב שם שלפי משנ"כ בס"ק ט"ז הרי מדובר בסעי' זה לענין ביה"ש"מ.
90. ערוך השלחן שם ס"ז.
91. מ"ב ס"ק י"ח.
92. ביה"ל ס"א ד"ה אחר תפילת ערבית.
93. פשוט. ובפרט דלכמה פוסקים יש ענין "תמימות" בכל יום ויום בנפרד, שו"ע הרב שם ס"ג, חיי אדם כלל קל"א ס"ב, וראה ביה"ל ס"ח ד"ה סופר, "דהאי תמימות תהיינא קאי אכל יומא שהתחיל לספור מבערב".

The Time for the Mitzvah ~ 21

after *Maariv* so that it will be preceded by *Krias Shema* and *Shemoneh Esrei*.[94] Other *poskim*, meanwhile, argue that when a person plans to daven *Maariv* later at night, the principle of "*tadir kodem*" is not applicable at all, and he should count the *omer* immediately at nightfall.[95] Nevertheless, even these *poskim* acknowledge that there are grounds for delaying the performance of the mitzvah until after *Maariv*, since it is likely that a person will forget *sefiras haomer* if he is required to count at nightfall in solitude.[96] (According to this opinion, an individual who plans to daven in solitude, and who will not be davening immediately after nightfall, should recite *sefiras haomer* at the beginning of the night. The *poskim* cited previously, however, would maintain that he should wait until after *Maariv*.)

9. **Kiddush and Havdalah in Shul:** In a congregation where Kiddush is recited in shul on Friday night and on the night of Yom Tov, *sefiras haomer* should be recited after Kiddush.[97] Nevertheless, if a member of such a congregation returns home before reciting *sefirah*, he should count the *omer* before his private recitation of Kiddush, since he is not permitted to begin a *seudah* before *sefirah*.[98] (This is true only if the time to count *sefirah* has arrived; if a person has accepted Shabbos early, he may begin his *seudah* even before counting *sefirah*, as will be explained below in section 6.)

In a congregation where Havdalah is customarily recited in shul, it should be preceded by *sefiras haomer*.[99] Even when the

---

94. עי' שו"ת אגר"מ או"ח ח"ד סי' צ"ט.
95. עי' שו"ת מנח"י ח"ט סי' נ"ה, ועי' שו"ת שבה"ל ח"ו סי' נ"ג.
96. שו"ת שבה"ל שם. ועי' מנח"י שם.
97. שו"ע שם ס"ט. ובמ"ב ס"ק ל"ט שכל מה שנוכל להקדים קדושת היום יש לנו להקדים.
98. מ"ב שם.
99. שו"ע שם. ובמ"ב סק"מ דאפוקי יומא מאחרין ליה כל מה דאפשר. ועי' שו"ת אגר"מ או"ח ח"ד סי' צ"ט.

eighth day of Pesach falls on Motzaei Shabbos, and Kiddush and Havdalah are recited together, *sefiras haomer* should be recited first.[100]

Similarly, in a congregation where the passages of *Vayiten Lecha* are recited on Motzaei Shabbos after *Maariv*, *sefiras haomer* should be performed first.[101]

10. **Counting during *Seudah Shelishis*:** If a person recited *sefiras haomer* during *seudah shelishis* (e.g., he was afraid that he would forget to recite it later), he may still recite *retzei* in *birkas hamazon*.[102]

11. **Counting the *Omer* with the Congregation:** There is a special *inyan* to fulfill the mitzvah of *sefiras haomer* together with the congregation.[103] Therefore, one should not step outside the shul after *Shemoneh Esrei* or leave shul early and count in solitude.

12. **Arriving Late to *Maariv*:** If a person arrives late to *Maariv* and finds the congregation about to begin *Shemoneh Esrei*, he should recite *Shemoneh Esrei* with the congregation and then recite the *brachos* of *Krias Shema* afterward. The authorities debate when a person should count the *omer* in such a scenario. On the one hand, it is important to count the *omer* together with the congregation; however, in this case it would entail reciting the count prior to the *brachos* of *Krias Shema*, which have the status of *tadir*. Similarly, if a person arrives in shul and finds the congregation finishing *Shemoneh Esrei* (at the last *minyan* of the evening), the same question would apply: Should he recite *sefiras haomer* with

---

100. שו"ע שם ובמ"ב ס"ק מ"ג.
101. מ"ב ס"ק מ"א.
102. עי' מ"ב סי' רס"ג ס"ק ס"ז בשם המ"א שנסתפק לענין מי שאמר ברוך המבדיל באמצע סעודת שלישית, ומ"מ לענין ספירת העומר אי"ז תרתי דסתרי ויכול עדיין לומר רצה, תשובת הגרנ"ק שליט"א הובא בגליון מים חיים.
103. של"ה הוב"ד בבאר היטב סי' תפ"ט סק"כ, והיינו כשמתפללין מעריב בזמנו.

The Time for the Mitzvah ∽ 23

the congregation, or should he daven *Maariv* first due to the frequency of its observance? Some *poskim* rule that a person in these situations should count the *omer* along with the congregation,[104] while others maintain that the principle of "*tadir*" always takes precedence over counting *sefirah* with the congregation (unless a person fears that he will forget to count the *omer* altogether if he does not count along with the congregation).[105]

13. **Counting in the Morning:** Some congregations have the custom to recite *sefirah* again in the morning after *Shacharis*, in case anyone forgot to count at night.[106] This is the *minhag* in many communities in Eretz Yisrael.

14. **Counting until *Alos Hashachar*:** If a person did not count the *omer* at the beginning of the night, he may fulfill the mitzvah at any time until *alos hashachar*.[107] (See section 4 below regarding a person who neglected to count the *omer* during the night altogether.) At any point, if a person remembers that he did not yet count the *omer*, it is preferable for him to do so without delay.[108]

4. Missed Days and Situations of Uncertainty

Introduction: There is much discussion among the Rishonim regarding whether the mitzvah of *sefiras haomer* can be fulfilled during the daytime. Some Rishonim equate the mitzvah of *sefiras haomer* with the *ketziras haomer* (the harvesting of the wheat to be

---

104. עי' שו"ת מנחת יצחק ח"ט סי' נ"ו אות ב'.
105. עי' תשובות והנהגות ח"א סי' ש"י וח"ב סי' רמ"ח.
106. כף החיים שם סק"פ.
107. שו"ע שם ס"א.
108. פשוט דשיהוי מצוה לא משהינן וזריזין מקדימין.

used for the *korban omer* in the *Beis Hamikdash*), which is supposed to be performed at night. Nevertheless, even regarding that mitzvah, there are conflicting indications in the Mishnah regarding whether the harvest is valid if it is performed during the day.[109]

The Rishonim also debate another important issue concerning *sefiras haomer*: the implication of the concept of *temimos* – the requirement for the counting of the *omer* to consist of seven complete weeks. One possibility raised by the Rishonim is that this principle means that all 49 days of *sefiras haomer* constitute a single unit. If this is the case, then a person who misses even one day of *sefirah* will not be capable of fulfilling the mitzvah and will not be permitted to recite the *brachah* on subsequent nights. Some Rishonim, however, maintain that each day of *sefirah* is considered a distinct mitzvah, and therefore a person should continue reciting the *brachah* even if he has omitted a day.

This section will discuss the halachic ramifications of these two discussions.

1. **If a Person Neglects to Count at Night:** As was noted in the previous section, *lechatchilah* one should count *sefirah* at the beginning of the night, but the mitzvah may be fulfilled at any time during the night. If a person neglects to count during the night altogether, the Rishonim debate whether the mitzvah can be fulfilled during the following day.[110] In light of the various views on this subject, a person in this situation should count *sefirah* during the day without reciting the *brachah*,[111] and he may then continue reciting the *brachah* on subsequent nights.[112]

---

109. מנחות דף ע"א. ותוס' מגילה דף כ: ד"ה כל הלילה.
110. עי' תוס' מנחות דף סו. ד"ה זכר בשם הבה"ג שנקט דגם היום כשר לספירת העומר, ודעת ר"ת שזמנה רק בלילה, ועי' תוס' מגילה דף כ: ד"ה כל הלילה. ועי' שעה"צ סי' תפ"ט ס"ק מ"ג.
111. שו"ע סי' תפ"ט ס"ז וכדנקט הרא"ש פסחים פ"י סי' מ"א, לחוש לדעת המחמירים.
112. מ"ב ס"ק ל"ד, והטעם משום דיש כאן ספק ספיקא, ספק שמא ספירה כשר ביום ואת"ל פסול, שמא אין הימים מעכבים זא"ז, והוא עפ"י התרה"ד סי' ל"ז, ועי' שעה"צ ס"ק מ"ה.

2. **A Person Who Is Uncertain if He Counted at Night:** The same halachah applies to a person who is unsure if he counted *sefirah* at night. If he realizes this during the day, he should count at that point without reciting the *brachah*, and he may then continue reciting the *brachah* on the following nights.[113]

3. **A Missed Day:** Some Rishonim maintain that every day of the *sefiras haomer* period is considered an independent mitzvah. According to this view, even if a person forgets to count one day, he may continue reciting the *brachah* on subsequent nights. Other Rishonim explain the principle of "*temimos*" to mean that the entire *sefirah* period is considered a single unit that must be complete; therefore, if a person misses even a single day, it will be impossible for him to fulfill the mitzvah.[114] Since this is a matter of dispute, a person who misses a day of the *omer* is nonetheless required to continue counting on subsequent nights, in keeping with the view that each day is a separate mitzvah; at the same time, since there is a view among the Rishonim that he will no longer be able to fulfill the mitzvah, he may not recite the *brachah*.[115] It is preferable for a person in this situation to hear the *brachah* from someone else, and for both to have in mind for him to thereby be *yotzei* his obligation to recite the *brachah*.[116]

This halachah applies to any person who misses a day of *sefirah*, regardless of whether it was due to negligence or a result of circumstances beyond his control (the halachic concept of *oness*).[117]

---

113. ביה"ל ס"ז ד"ה שכח.
114. עי' תוס' מנחות דף סו. סוף ד"ה זכר, רא"ש פסחים פ"י סמ"א, ר"ן סוף פסחים, טור סוף סי' תפ"ט בשם הגאונים. ועי' פמ"ג סי' תפ"ט א"א ס"ק י"ג שהקשה למ"ד דהוי מצוה אחת ולכן אם דילג אינו מברך, למה מברכים בכל לילה, ונשאר בצ"ע.
115. שו"ע שם ס"ח.
116. מ"ב ס"ק ל"ז.
117. פשוט. וראה ערוך השלחן סי' תפ"ט סט"ו, כף החיים שם ס"ק צ"ג.

4. **A Person Who Counted Incorrectly:** If a person realizes at night that he counted the wrong number on the previous night, he is considered to have missed the previous day. Therefore, for the duration of the *sefirah* period he should continue counting without reciting the *brachah*.[118]

5. **Reciting *Sefirah* for the Congregation after Missing a Day:** In many communities the Rav (or another distinguished person) recites *sefiras haomer* aloud, along with the *brachah*, before it is recited by the congregation. If the Rav has missed a day and will suffer great embarrassment if he is unable to recite the *brachah*, it is permitted for him to recite the count publicly along with the *brachah*. This situation is considered a *shaas hadchak* (a case of extenuating circumstances), in which it is justified to rely on the Rishonim who permit reciting the *brachah* even if one has omitted a day.[119]

6. **A Person Who Is Uncertain if He Counted Correctly:** If a person is uncertain if he missed a day or if he counted the correct day on a previous night, he may continue reciting the *brachah*.[120] This is due to the principle of "*sfek sfeika* – a twofold doubt," since there are two possible reasons to permit him to recite the *brachah*: First, it is possible that he did not actually miss a day or count incorrectly, and second, even if he did neglect to count correctly on a previous night, the halachah might follow the view of the Rishonim who permit reciting the *brachah* even after one has missed a day.[121]

---

118. מ"ב ס"ק ל"ה.
119. שו"ת שבט הלוי ח"ג סי' צ"ו וח"ד סי' קנ"ז. ובס' קובץ הלכות עמוד 45 הובא בשם הגר"ש קמינצקי שליט"א שיכול לבקש מאחד בציבור שלא לברך ושהוא יוציאו עם הברכה.
120. שו"ע שם עפ"י התרה"ד.
121. שם ובמ"ב ס"ק ל"ח. ואף שמבואר במ"ב סי' רט"ו סק"ו שלענין ספק ברכה לבטלה גם היכא דאיכא ס"ס אמרינן ספק ברכות להקל, עי' ס' שיח הלכה סי' ו' אות י"ב בשם הגרשז"א זצ"ל שאם יש גם רוב דיעות שסוברים שיש לברך, נקטינן, בהצטרף עוד ספק, שיש לברך. וראה הליכות שלמה פי"א הע' 24.

Missed Days and Situations of Uncertainty ~ 27

7. **Applying the Principle of "*Sfek Sfeika*"**: The principle of "*sfek sfeika*" (as explained in the previous paragraph) applies in any situation where there is a halachic uncertainty or dispute regarding *sefiras haomer* and thus one was obligated *lechatchilah* to repeat the *sefirah* without a *brachah*. In any such case, if the person forgets to repeat *sefiras haomer*, he is nevertheless permitted to recite the *brachah* on subsequent nights. For example, if a person forgets to declare the number of days or the number of weeks, or if he cites only one of the two correctly but he recites an incorrect count for the other, he is required *lechatchilah* to repeat *sefirah* without reciting the *brachah* (see above, section 2, paragraph 12). *B'dieved*, though, if he does not do so, he may continue reciting the *brachah* on subsequent nights.[122]

8. **Counting after *Shekiah***: The *poskim* debate whether the above rule applies to a person who realizes only after sunset, but before *tzeis hakochavim* – i.e., during *bein hashemashos* – that he has forgotten to count *sefirah*. *Bein hashemashos* is a time of halachic uncertainty; it is a *safek* as to whether it is part of the day or night, and therefore it is questionable whether a person who counts *sefirah* for the preceding day only after *bein hashemashos* has begun – without a *brachah*, of course – may continue reciting the *brachah* on subsequent nights.[123] There is no clear consensus among the *poskim* on this issue; some maintain that he should no longer recite the *brachah*,[124] while others permit the *brachah* to be recited on subsequent nights.[125] There is greater justification to continue

---

122. מ"ב שם. ובאם טעה בימים ביום דמשלם שבוע, עי' מ"ב סק"ז, ועי' ביה"ל ס"ח ד"ה יספור.
123. עי' שע"ת סק"ב.
124. כף החיים שם ס"ק פ"ג.
125. עי' שו"ת מנחת יצחק ח"ט סי' נ"ז. וכ"פ הגרשז"א זצ"ל הוב"ד בהליכות שלמה שם ס"ו, והגר"ש וואזנר זצ"ל בקובץ מבית לוי עניני ניסן אות ו'.

reciting the *brachah* if one counted *sefirah* within 13 minutes after *shekiah*.[126]

9. **Counting for the Previous Day after *Kabbalas Shabbos* and *Maariv*:** If a person accepts Shabbos before *shekiah* and then realizes that he forgot to count *sefirah* on Friday, he may recite the count for Friday (without reciting a *brachah*), and he may then continue reciting the *brachah* on subsequent nights. Even though he has already accepted Shabbos and davened *Maariv*, it is still considered to be the daytime with respect to *sefiras haomer*.[127]

10. **Reciting the *Brachah* when One Expects to Miss a Day:** Even if a person anticipates that he will be unable to count a particular day during the period of *sefirah* (e.g., he has a surgery scheduled and knows that he will be unable to count that day), many *poskim* maintain that he should nonetheless begin counting with a *brachah*.[128] (After the missed day, he should count the remaining days of the *omer* without reciting the *brachah*.)

11. **Traveling to Another Time Zone:** If a person travels to a different time zone and realizes that he neglected to count *sefirah* before his departure, he must recite the count prior to nightfall in his new location. Therefore, if a person travels to the east and does not count before nightfall in his new location, he will be considered to have missed a day, even if

---

126. כן הכריע הגרי"ש"א זצ"ל הוב"ד בהלכות חג בחג פ"ו הערה 14.
127. עי' ש"ך יו"ד סי' קצ"ו סק"ד, ועי' שערי תשובה שם בשם המחזיק ברכה בשם הזרע אמת. ועי' שו"ת אגר"מ או"ח ח"ד סי' צ"ד אות ג' שנקט לבסוף להלכה שיכול עדיין לספור (אבל משמע שמי שמיקל לפעמים בשאר ימים לספור אחר פלג אינו יכול לספור בכה"ג).
128. עי' הליכות שלמה שם ס"ט, שו"ת קובץ תשובות ח"ג סי' פ"ג, קובץ מבית לוי ח"ג עמוד ל"ו אות ח'. ועי' מ"ב סק"ג משנ"ב בשם השלחן שלמה בענין נשים שבנידו"ד ג"כ לא יתחיל לברך, אבל לפימש"כ לעיל שהמעיין בש"ש יראה שכוונתו שישכחו יום א' ולא ידעו שלא לברך אח"כ. ועי' שע"ת ריש סי' קנ"ח שהביא לענין נט"י בשם הריטב"א בחולין שכתב שמי שנטל ידיו ובירך ענט"י על דעת לאכול ואח"כ נמלך מלאכול לא הוי ברכה לבטלה. ועי' בס' ספירת העומר פ"ד סק"א שהאריך בשם הפוסקים בזה ובענין אם דילג האם נחשב למפרע שכל הברכות שבירך הוי ברכות לבטלה.

Missed Days and Situations of Uncertainty 29

in his previous location night has not yet fallen. Similarly, if a person travels to the west, he may count the day of the *omer* for as long as night hasn't fallen in his new location, even if it is already nightfall at his previous location.[129]

5. Mental Intent in *Sefiras Haomer*

Introduction: One of the basic principles in the fulfillment of a mitzvah is *"mitzvos tzrichos kavanah"* – i.e., when a person performs a mitzvah, he must have the *kavanah* (mental intent) to fulfill a commandment of Hashem. There is a dispute among the Amoraim in the Gemara as to whether a mitzvah is invalidated when it is performed without this intent.[130] The practical halachah on this issue is the subject of a dispute among the Rishonim.[131] All authorities agree that the intent to fulfill the mitzvah is necessary *lechatchilah*; however, they debate whether the absence of *kavanah* renders the mitzvah invalid. The *Shulchan Aruch* rules that a mitzvah performed without this intent is indeed rendered invalid.[132] However, the later *poskim* are in disagreement as to whether this ruling applies only to mitzvos *d'oraisa* or also to mitzvos *d'rabbanan*.[133]

This question has various ramifications regarding the mitzvah of *sefiras haomer*. Either possible ruling may have both stringent and lenient applications with respect to this mitzvah. If a mitzvah *d'rabbanan* can be fulfilled without *kavanah*, then if a person counts

---

129. עי' במקראי קודש פסח ח"ב סי' ס"ג אות ג' מה שנסתפק בזה, ועי"ש בהררי קודש הערה 2. וכן דעת הגר"ש וואזנער זצ"ל הובא בקובץ מבית לוי ח"ג עמוד ל"ז (וראה שו"ת באר משה ח"ז סי' קפ"ט [לענין יום הוסת] דאזלינן תמיד בתר המקום שנמצא עכשיו).

130. ר"ה דף כ"ח.-כח:.

131. דעת הרמב"ם פ"ב שופר ה"ד לפסוק דמצוות צריכות כוונה, וכ"פ הרמב"ן מלחמות ר"ה וכן דעת הרא"ש. ודעת הרשב"א ר"ה דף כח: לפסוק דמצוות א"צ כוונה, וכן דעת ר' שמואל הובא בר' יונה בברכות דף יב. ועי' בטור סוף סי' ס' וסוף סי' תקפ"ט בשם הגאונים.

132. שו"ע סי' ס' ס"ד וסי' תקפ"ט ס"ח.

133. עי' מ"ב סי' ס' סק"י ועי"ש בביה"ל ד"ה וכן הלכה. ועי' שעה"צ סי' תר"צ ס"ק מ"א.

without the intent to fulfill the mitzvah, he is nevertheless considered to be *yotzei* and is not required to repeat the count. At the same time, this will mean that if a person inadvertently counts *sefirah* by telling someone else the day of the *omer*, even if he did not intend to fulfill the mitzvah by doing so, he will nonetheless have discharged his obligation and will not be permitted to recite the *brachah* before formally counting *sefirah*. Conversely, if the halachah follows the opposite view, and even a mitzvah *d'rabbanan* cannot be fulfilled without *kavanah*, then there is no need for concern that one may inadvertently fulfill the mitzvah without intending to do so. In any event, if a person expressly intends not to fulfill the mitzvah, he will certainly not be *yotzei*.[134]

1. **The Intent to Fulfill the Mitzvah of *Sefiras Haomer*:** When a person recites *sefiras haomer*, he should have the express intent to fulfill the mitzvah commanded to us by Hashem. Nevertheless, if a person did not have this mental intent, he is presumed to have fulfilled the mitzvah; however, in order to satisfy the dissenting opinion, he should repeat the *sefirah* (without repeating the *brachah*). This is not necessary, however, if he recited *sefiras haomer* in the context of *Maariv*, since it is assumed that when a person counts *sefirah* in the usual manner, it is with the intent of performing the mitzvah.[135] Furthermore, if a person recites the *brachah* before counting *sefirah*, it is likewise considered an indication that he had the necessary mental intent.[136]

2. **Informing Someone Else of the Correct Count:** After *shekiah* on any night of the *omer* period, if a person is asked which day it is, he should not respond with a full sentence identifying the day (e.g., "Today is two"), since he will then not be permitted to recite the *brachah* on that night's *sefirah*.[137]

---

134. ב"י סי' תקפ"ט, ובסי' תפ"ט בשם תשו' הרשב"א.
135. עי' מ"ב סי' ס' סק"י.
136. ביה"ל שם.
137. שו"ע סי' תפ"ט ס"ד.

Mental Intent in Sefiras Haomer ∽ 31

(He will be permitted, however, to continue reciting the *brachah* on subsequent nights.) There is a twofold rationale for this ruling. First, according to the authorities who maintain that *kavanah* is not necessary to fulfill a mitzvah *d'rabbanan*, the speaker will have unintentionally fulfilled his mitzvah by identifying the day's count. Furthermore, even according to the view that there is no distinction between a mitzvah *d'oraisa* and a mitzvah *d'rabbanan* in this respect, in this case we must also take into consideration the opinions that maintain that *kavanah* is not vital for the fulfillment of any mitzvah, due to the severity of the transgression of reciting a *brachah* in vain.[138] Nevertheless, even if a person "counts" in this fashion, he must still repeat *sefiras haomer* formally, albeit without a *brachah*.[139] If a person forgets to count the *omer* formally but knows that he told someone else the day of the *omer*, which may have been a fulfillment of his obligation, he is permitted to recite the *brachah* on subsequent nights, due to the principle of *sfek sfeika* as explained in section 4 above.

When a person wishes to tell someone else the day of the *omer* prior to his own counting, he should either tell him only the previous day's count[140] or have express intent not to fulfill the mitzvah with his response.[141]

3. **Inadvertent Counting before *Shekiah*:** The above halachah applies any time after *shekiah*, even before nightfall.[142] However, if a person states the day of the *omer* to someone else *before shekiah*, even if he has davened *Maariv* after *plag haminchah*, it is of no concern and he may still recite

---

138. מ"ב שם ס"ק כ"ב ובשעה"צ ס"ק כ"ו. וראה מ"ב סי' ס' סק"י.
139. ביה"ל ס"ד ד"ה אינו יכול.
140. שו"ע שם.
141. מ"ב סי' תפ"ט ס"ק כ"ב.
142. מ"ב שם ס"ק י"ט.

the *brachah* when he counts *sefirah* later in the evening.[143] Nevertheless, some *poskim* suggest that it is preferable *lechatchilah* to avoid stating the day of the *omer* even before sunset, during the period after *plag haminchah*.[144]

If a person is meticulous about never counting *sefirah* before *tzeis hakochavim*, it is questionable if he is automatically considered to have the express intention not to fulfill the mitzvah prior to that time. If that is the case, then he would be permitted to make a full statement of the day of the *omer* even after *shekiah*, and would still be permitted to recite the *brachah* upon counting after nightfall.[145]

4. **Stating the Count in a Different Language:** Even if a person makes a full statement of the day of the *omer* in English or any language, he will not be permitted to recite the *brachah* later in the evening, since the mitzvah of counting *sefirah* can be fulfilled in any language. It is also not sufficient for a person to avoid mentioning the word "*omer*" expressly in his statement, since one can be *yotzei* without using the words "*laomer*" or "*baomer*." Nevertheless, if a person is asked the day of the *omer* and responds only with a number, without prefacing it with the words "today is" or any other such phrase, he is not considered to have performed the mitzvah and therefore is permitted to recite the *brachah*.[146]

5. **Citing the Number without the Week:** Once the seventh day of the *omer* has arrived, the *poskim* discuss whether a person who tells someone else the number of days but does not mention the count of weeks will be prohibited to recite the *brachah*. Some authorities maintain that when he omits the

---

143. ביה"ל שם.
144. שו"ע הרב סי' תפ"ט סט"ו וכה"ח סי' תפ"ט ס"ק נ"ב.
145. עי' ביה"ל ד"ה שאם יאמר לו, וסיים בצ"ע למעשה.
146. מ"ב סק"כ-כ"א.

Mental Intent in Sefiras Haomer

number of weeks, it is considered as if he expresses the intent to avoid fulfilling the mitzvah, and therefore he may recite the *brachah* when counting later in the evening. Other *poskim* maintain that this line of reasoning is valid only on the last day of each respective week (the seventh day, the fourteenth day, and so forth), when counting the weeks is an indispensable component of the mitzvah. In the middle of a week of the *omer*, though, when one fulfills the mitzvah *b'dieved* even without counting the weeks, these *poskim* maintain that one might fulfill the mitzvah merely by informing someone else of the number of the day, and therefore the *brachah* should be omitted.[147]

6. **Inquiring About the Day:** If one person turns to someone else and asks if it is a specific day of the *omer* (e.g., he says, "Is today two days?"), and the other person answers in the affirmative without repeating the actual number, neither person has fulfilled the mitzvah, and both are permitted to recite the *brachah*.[148]

7. **Helping a Child Count or Correcting Someone Else:** If a person counts *sefirah* aloud for a child to repeat after him, it is questionable whether it is considered a fulfillment of the mitzvah. Therefore, unless he has express intent not to fulfill the mitzvah with this act, he should not recite the *brachah* upon counting later in the evening.[149] (However, he should repeat the *sefirah* itself.) The same is true if a person overhears someone else counting incorrectly and corrects him by stating the actual day of the *omer*. (As above, this is true only if he presented it as a full statement, beginning with the words "today is" or the like.)

---

147. עי׳ מ״ב ס״ק כ״ב ובשעה״צ ס״ק כ״ח.
148. עי׳ כף החיים שם ס״ק ס״א. קובץ מבית לוי ניסן עמוד פ״ד אות ז׳.
149. עי׳ מ״ב סי׳ ס׳ סק״ט, ובביה״ל שם ד״ה לצאת.

8. **Reading the Day's Count while Learning:** After *shekiah*, if a person reads aloud from the *Shulchan Aruch* or any other sefer and reads a statement that reflects the actual count of that day (beginning with the word *hayom*), it is questionable if he is permitted to recite the *brachah* upon formally counting.[150]

9. **Invoking the Name of Lag Baomer:** On the 33rd night of the *omer*, if a person mentions that tonight is Lag Baomer but does not mean to actually identify the count (e.g., he is simply noting that there will be a bonfire that night), he certainly has not fulfilled the mitzvah and must still recite the *brachah*. If he does not count again later in the evening, he is considered to have missed the day and may not recite the *brachah* on subsequent nights.[151]

10. **Hearing the *Shaliach Tzibbur*'s *Brachah*:** It is not necessary for a person to have the express mental intent that he will recite the *brachah* on his own, rather than fulfilling his obligation by hearing the *brachah* of the *shaliach tzibbur*. Even though a person can fulfill his obligation by hearing the *brachah* recited by someone else (which is not the case regarding the actual counting of the *omer*), the common practice is for every individual to recite the *brachah* on his own. Therefore, it is considered as if the listeners had the express intent *not* to fulfill their obligations.[152]

11. **Reciting the *Brachah* with the Correct Count in Mind:** When reciting the *brachah*, one should preferably be aware

---

150. עי' כף החיים שם ס"ק כ"ט.
151. עי' כף החיים שם סק"ל, ועי' שו"ת אור לציון ח"ג פט"ז סי' ד', הגריש"א זצ"ל הובא בהלכות חג בחג פ"ו הערה 1.
152. הגרשז"א זצ"ל בהליכות שלמה פי"א ס"ג ובדבר הלכה סק"ד דלא צריך לחוש למש"כ בשו"ע הרב שם סי"ד, שאם לא כיון שלא לצאת א"א לברך אח"כ (ויש לעי' ממש"כ הרב שם סי"ד, והוא כסברא הנזכר דכוונה לחזור ולספור הוי ככוונה שלא לצאת ולכאורה סתר את עצמו.) מיהו עי' לשון הביה"ל ס"ג ד"ה ואפילו דמשמע שלעולם צריך כוונה להדיא שלא לצאת. ומ"מ בזמננו שכולם נוהגים לברך לעצמם הוי סתמא כמכוין להדיא שלא לצאת ואפשר שגם השו"ע הרב יודה, עי' הליכות שלמה שם הערה 11.

of the number of the day.[153] If a person recites the *brachah* without being aware of the correct count – e.g., if he intended to listen to someone else count and then to repeat after him – he is *yotzei*. Nevertheless, after reciting the *brachah*, *lechatchilah* one should not wait (even in silence) longer than the span of *toch k'dei dibbur* (the amount of time required to pronounce 3-4 words) before counting.[154]

12. **If a Person Had the Wrong Count in Mind:** If a person either begins or concludes the *brachah* with the incorrect count in mind, or even if he recites the entire *brachah* with the incorrect day in mind, he will nonetheless be *yotzei* if he actually recited the correct count.[155] Conversely, even if a person recites the *brachah* with the correct count in mind, but then recited the wrong day, he must repeat the count along with the *brachah*, unless he corrects his error within the span of *toch k'dei dibbur*.[156]

13. **Correcting an Error:** When a person corrects himself within *toch k'dei dibbur* after he has counted inaccurately, it is not necessary for him to repeat the word *hayom*, even *lechatchilah*. For example, if a person erroneously recites the words "*hayom arbaah yamim laomer* – today is four days of the *omer*" on the fifth day, but then he quickly corrects himself and says "*chamishah yamim laomer*," he is *yotzei*.[157]

Even if a person had the wrong day in mind while he recited the *brachah*, he can still fulfill the mitzvah by correcting his *sefirah* within the span of *toch k'dei dibbur*.[158]

---

153. מ״ב סי׳ תפ״ט ס״ק כ״ט ובשעה״צ ס״ק ל״ז.
154. שו״ע שם ס״ה ובמ״ב שם.
155. שו״ע שם ס״ו ובביה״ל ד״ה או איפכא.
156. מ״ב ס״ק ל״ב.
157. שם.
158. שם ובשעה״צ ס״ק מ״א.

14. **Changing One's Count Erroneously:** If a person counts correctly but then mistakenly believes that he has erred, and he alters his count within *toch k'dei dibbur* to an incorrect number, the *poskim* debate whether his initial counting is uprooted and he is considered not to have fulfilled the mitzvah.[159] The accepted ruling in such a case is that the person should count again (without a *brachah*) but *b'dieved* if he did not reverse his error, he may continue reciting the *brachah* on subsequent nights.[160]

15. **If a Person Cannot Ascertain the Correct Day to Count:** If a person is unsure as to the specific day of the *omer* and he has no way to verify the correct day, he should state the count of every day that he believes might be correct; however, he should not recite the *brachah*.[161]

6. Activities Prohibited before *Sefirah*

Introduction: In general, the halachah prohibits beginning a *seudah* shortly before the time for an obligatory mitzvah arrives. This is a *gezeirah d'rabbanan* that is intended to prevent a person from forgetting a mitzvah that he is required to observe. This rule applies equally to mitzvos *d'oraisa* and to mitzvos *d'rabbanan* and takes effect half an hour before the earliest time the mitzvah can be performed. If a person violates this law and begins a meal during this prohibited time period, the halachah distinguishes between mitzvos *d'oraisa* and *d'rabbanan*.

---

159. עי' מ"ב סי' מ"ו סק"כ שמוכח דתיקון תכ"ד מהני רק כשהוא למעליותא (ואין להקשות ממש"כ שם בדין הראשון כשרצה לסיים פוקח עורים שהביא ב' דיעות ובסי' ר"ט סק"ו סתם דיצא ידי ברכת בשמים, דשאני התם שהרי נקט הבשמים בידיו, ראה שיח הלכה סי' מ"ו אות י'), וכ"מ ממ"ב סי' נ"ט סק"ט. אמנם, עי' דעת תורה סי' קי"ד בהג"ה שדן בזה ומה שהביא מהרמב"ם עפ"י הגמ' ברכות דף יב., ועי' גם בפרישה סי' נ"ט סוסק"ג ובפר"ח שם סק"ב דאמרינן תוכ"ד לגריעותא, אבל מהמ"ב הנ"ל מוכח דלא פסקינן כן. וראה שו"ת שבט הלוי ח"ו סי' ט"ז. וראה הליכות שלמה תפילה פ"ח סי"ג.

160. הליכות שלמה שם ס"ה.

161. עי' שו"ת אבנ"ז יו"ד סי' רמ"ח אות ג' ועי' מקראי קודש פסח ח"ב סי' ס"ז.

If the mitzvah that must be performed is a mitzvah *d'oraisa*, one must interrupt the meal in order to perform the mitzvah. For a mitzvah *d'rabbanan*, though, it is permitted to delay the performance of the mitzvah until after the conclusion of the meal, provided that there will be sufficient time remaining to fulfill the mitzvah. If a person begins a meal at a time when it is permitted to do so – i.e., more than half an hour before the time for the performance of the mitzvah – he is not obligated to interrupt his meal even for a mitzvah *d'oraisa*, provided that he will have sufficient time to perform the mitzvah after the meal has concluded.

Similarly, the halachah prohibits going to sleep (*sheinas keva*) before the performance of a mitzvah, as well as beginning certain types of activities, as will be explained below.[162]

1. **Beginning a Prohibited Activity before Counting *Sefirah*:** During the days of *sefiras haomer*, it is prohibited to begin a *seudah* or any other prohibited activity or to go to sleep at any time within a half hour prior to *tzeis hakochavim*. This prohibition remains in effect until one has performed the mitzvah of *sefiras haomer*. Even if a person intends to count *sefirah* later in the night, he may not begin any of the prohibited activities at an earlier time. (See paragraph 2 below regarding the definition of a "meal" with respect to this halachah, and paragraph 7 for the parameters of other forbidden activities.) Although these activities are prohibited due to the obligations of *Krias Shema* and *Maariv* as well, this halachah will have bearing on a person who has already davened *Maariv* and hasn't yet counted *sefirah*, such as someone who has davened *Maariv* after *plag haminchah* but will count *sefirah* after *tzeis hakochavim* (as discussed above in section 3).[163]

    Although the mitzvah of *sefiras haomer* can be fulfilled

---

162. שבת דף ט:, ועי' שו"ע סי' רל"ב ס"ב וסי' רל"ה ס"ב.

163. רמ"א סי' תפ"ט ס"ד ובמ"ב ס"ק כ"ג.

after *shekiah* (see section 3, paragraph 3), the prohibition to begin a meal or any other forbidden activity takes effect only half an hour prior to *tzeis hakochavim*.[164] It is also prohibited to engage in Torah study before counting *sefirah*; however, this prohibition takes effect only at *tzeis hakochavim* itself.[165]

2. **Definition of a Meal:** This prohibition applies to a *seudah* – a halachic "meal" defined as the consumption of more than the volume of a *kebeitzah* of bread or baked mezonos products. Mezonos foods that have been cooked, such as pasta, may be consumed in any quantity; however, one should refrain from eating a complete meal.[166]

The prohibition also includes drinking more than the volume of a *kebeitzah* of intoxicating beverages. It is permissible to consume any quantity of other beverages.[167]

3. **A *Shomer* or a Regular *Minyan*:** It is permissible to begin a *seudah* even during the prohibited time frame if a *shomer* is appointed to remind one to perform the mitzvah. This dispensation applies to the mitzvos of *Krias Shema* and *tefillah* as well.[168] The *shomer* may not participate in the meal; however, a group of people who eat together may serve as *shomrim* for each other, since it can be assumed that they will remind each other to count *sefirah*. At a large *seudah*, such as the festive meal celebrating a *bris milah* or *pidyon haben*, when a large group of people participate in a lengthy meal together and sometimes become intoxicated, it is not sufficient to appoint a *shomer*.[169]

---

164. שעה"צ ס"ק כ"ט. אמנם בשו"ע הרב שם סי"ז כ' מבין השמשות.
165. מ"ב סי' רל"ה ס"ק י"ז.
166. שו"ע סי' רל"ב ס"ג ובמ"ב ס"ק ל"ד.
167. מ"ב שם ס"ק ל"ה.
168. רמ"א סי' רל"ב ס"ב, ובמ"ב שם ס"ק כ"ט, ובמ"ב סי' רל"ה ס"ק י"ז וי"ח וסי' תפ"ט ס"ק כ"ג.
169. מ"ב סי' רל"ב שם.

Activities Prohibited before Sefirah ~ 39

According to some *poskim*, a person who regularly davens at a specific *minyan* at a fixed time is likewise permitted to begin a meal even during the time frame when it is ordinarily prohibited.[170] In order for this dispensation to be applicable, the person must daven regularly at the same time in a specific shul.[171] However, other *poskim* argue that attending a set *minyan* makes it permissible only to engage in Torah study but does not suspend the prohibition of commencing a meal.[172]

4. **Designating a *Shomer* after Nightfall:** According to some *poskim*, the dispensation to begin a meal if one designates a *shomer* (or regularly davens in a fixed *minyan*) applies only to a meal that begins prior to *tzeis hakochavim*. These *poskim* maintain that it is prohibited to begin a *seudah* after *tzeis hakochavim* under any circumstances.[173] The authorities who permit relying on a *shomer* (or a regular *minyan*) after nightfall to delay reciting *Krias Shema* or davening would likewise permit for *sefiras haomer*. Therefore, if a person typically relies on one of these dispensations regarding the mitzvah of *Krias Shema* and *Maariv*, he may do the same for *sefiras haomer*.[174]

5. **Counting *Sefiras Haomer* during a Permitted Meal:** If a *seudah* has commenced at a permitted time – i.e., more than half an hour before *tzeis hakochavim* – one need not interrupt the meal at *tzeis hakochavim* to count *sefirah*. It is permitted

---

170. ערוך השלחן סי׳ רל״ב סט״ז. וכדמצאנו בשו״ע סי׳ פ״ט ס״ו לענין לימוד לפני התפילה. ועי׳ שו״ת אגר״מ או״ח ח״ד סי׳ צ״ט אות א׳. ועי׳ שעה״צ סי׳ רל״ה ס״ק י״ט.
171. שש״כ פנ״ו ס״ג וס״ק י״ב.
172. דעת הגריש״א זצ״ל הובי׳ בשבות יצחק ח״ב פכ״ג לחלק בין לימוד וסעודה.
173. עי׳ מ״א סי׳ רל״ב ס״ק ט״ו וסי׳ תפ״ט ס״ק י״א ומ״ב סי׳ תפ״ט ס״ק כ״ג.
174. עי׳ שו״ת אגר״מ שם. ועי׳ הליכות שלמה פי״א ס״א שכ׳ נוהגין המדקדקין להחמיר שלא להתחיל לאכול ולהתעסק במלאכה כשהגיע זמן ספירת העומר ואין סומכין בזה על העמדת שומר. ועי״ש סק״א. ויש שמחלקים בין שומר פרטי לקריאת שמע או מנין קבוע, ששומר פרטי מועיל אפי׳ אחר צה״כ אבל קריאת שמע או מנין קבוע מועיל רק לענין סמוך, עי׳ חוט שני שבת ח״ד עמוד שע״ו ומיישב בזה דברי המ״ב ס״ק י״ח.

to delay the performance of the mitzvah until after the conclusion of the meal.[175]

This halachah is often relevant on *leil* Shabbos, when many people accept Shabbos early and begin their *seudos* more than half an hour before nightfall. In this scenario, it is not necessary to interrupt the Shabbos meal in order to recite *Krias Shema* and count *sefiras haomer* at nightfall; the mitzvos may be delayed until the conclusion of the meal. (Nevertheless, one may choose to perform both mitzvos immediately at nightfall to avoid forgetting them at a later time.) When performing the two mitzvos, one should recite *Krias Shema* first (due to its status of *tadir*) and then count *sefirah*.

6. **Counting *Sefiras Haomer* after Beginning a Prohibited Meal:** If a person has begun a meal within half an hour of *tzeis hakochavim* in violation of the halachah (and he has not designated a *shomer*, nor does he attend a regular *minyan*), the general rule is that he must interrupt his meal immediately to perform a mitzvah *d'oraisa* but that he may wait until the conclusion of the meal to perform a mitzvah *d'rabbanan*.[176] There is a dispute as to whether the mitzvah of *sefiras haomer* is *mid'oraisa* or *d'rabbanan* today (as explained in the introduction to Chapter One). Although many *poskim* maintain that it is only a mitzvah *d'rabbanan*, some authorities rule nonetheless that a person in this situation should interrupt his meal to perform the mitzvah immediately, since it is a brief and easy mitzvah.[177]

7. **Abstaining from Other Activities:** The halachos that govern the performance of a prohibited *melachah* within half an hour before *tzeis hakochavim* are identical to the laws concerning

---

175. רמ"א סי' תפ"ט ס"ד.
176. שו"ע סי' רל"ה ס"ב ורמ"א סי' תפ"ט שם.
177. מ"ב סי' תפ"ט ס"ק כ"ה.

Activities Prohibited before Sefirah ∾ 41

a meal.[178] A *melachah* is defined in this context as a time-consuming task that generally cannot be interrupted.[179] There is a difference of opinion among the *poskim* regarding whether one may begin a time-consuming task that can be interrupted easily.[180] Minor chores are certainly permitted during this time. See the following paragraphs regarding an additional custom that entails abstaining from *melachah*.

8. **Abstaining from *Melachah* at Night during *Sefiras Haomer*:** Aside from the halachah discussed in the previous paragraph, which is a general prohibition that applies whenever it will be necessary to perform a mitzvah, there is a *minhag* to refrain from engaging in *melachah* at night specifically during the period of *sefiras haomer*. One reason for this custom is the fact that the students of Rabi Akiva died around the time of *shekiah*, and the people were therefore occupied with their burials and did not engage in work during the evenings. Furthermore, since the Torah uses the phrase "*sheva Shabbosos*" both regarding the period of *sefiras haomer* and with respect to *shemittah*, when it is prohibited to work the land, the restriction on work is applied to *sefiras haomer* as well. (This is not directly derived from the *pasuk*; it is a *remez* that is used as a basis for the *minhag*.)[181]

9. Although the prohibition to begin a meal or other prohibited activity within half an hour before nightfall applies only to men, this *minhag* to refrain from *melachah* applies equally to women.[182]

10. **The Duration of the *Minhag*:** There is a practical difference

---

178. שו"ע סי' רל"ב ס"ב. מ"ב סי' תפ"ט ס"ק כ"ד.
179. עי' שו"ע סי' רל"ב ס"ב ובמ"ב סק"ט ובביה"ל שם ד"ה לבורסקי.
180. עי' ביה"ל שם. ובמקום צורך יש להקל.
181. טור סוסי' תצ"ג, שו"ע שם ס"ד ומ"ב ס"ק י"ט.
182. טור ושו"ע שם. ומש"כ "נהגו הנשים" אינו דוקא לנשים כמש"כ המ"ב שם ס"ק י"ח. ובשו"ע הרב שם ס"ט ובקיצור שו"ע סי' ק"כ ס"י כתבו שנשים ספרדיות יש לשבות ממלאכה כל הלילה.

between the two rationales presented for this *minhag*. According to the explanation that the period of *sefiras haomer* is equated with the *shemittah* year, one need abstain from *melachah* after *shekiah* only until the actual counting of the *omer*. According to the view that the custom originated with the deaths of Rabi Akiva's students, though, one should abstain from *melachah* for the approximate amount of time that the burials would have required.[183]

11. **The Practical Implications of the *Minhag***: In practical terms, since men are prohibited to engage in *melachah* until they count *sefirah* in any event, this custom creates only three additional stringencies (aside from the fact that it applies to women): First, *melachah* is prohibited beginning at *shekiah*, instead of only half an hour prior to *tzeis hakochavim* (however, these two time frames are identical in some locales). Second, a person must abstain from *melachah* for the amount of time that would be required to perform a burial, not merely until after he has counted *sefirah*. Finally, the dispensation for someone who has appointed a *shomer* or who regularly davens in a fixed *minyan* would not permit this *minhag* to be waived.

Some *poskim* rule that this *minhag* does not reflect the accepted practice and should be observed only if it is one's family tradition.[184]

12. **The Definition of *Melachah* with Respect to the *Minhag***: With regard to this *minhag*, the prohibited *melachah* is defined, as above, as any form of time-consuming work.[185] Household chores such as cooking, baking, and folding laundry are permitted,[186] but sewing is prohibited.

---

183. מ"ב ס"ק י"ט ובשעה"צ ס"ק ט"ז ומאידך בטור כ' עד שחרית.
184. עי' חק יעקב סי' תצ"ג ס"ק י"ב. ועי' בהליכות שלמה פי"א הערה 50 שכ' שבבית הגרשז"א זצ"ל לא נמנעו הנשים מלעשות מלאכה כלל.
185. עי' כף החיים סי' תצ"ג ס"ק נ"ד בשם אחרונים דדוקא מלאכה גמורה וארוכה.
186. הליכות שלמה שם סי"ג וקובץ מבית לוי ניסן עמוד פ"ח.

CHAPTER TWO

Halachos and *Minhagim* of the *Sefirah* Period

※

1. Weddings and Engagements
2. Dancing and Music
3. Reciting *Shehecheyanu* and Other Forms of Festivity
4. Cutting Hair
5. When to Observe the *Sefirah* Restrictions
6. Lag Baomer
7. Halachos Pertaining to *Tefillah* from Pesach through Shavuos

CHAPTER TWO

Halachos and *Minhagim* of the *Sefirah* Period

Introduction: The period between Pesach and Shavuos was the time of a historic tragedy, when 24,000 students of Rabi Akiva passed away.[1] This tremendous calamity was the impetus for the *minhag* to observe certain halachos of mourning during this time of year. Most *poskim* maintain that the deaths of Rabi Akiva's students occurred only during part of this period, and the mourning practices are therefore observed only for part of the period of *sefirah*. There are, however, several opinions regarding the specific time frame during *sefirah* when these halachos of mourning should be observed.[2]

There is a common misconception that the mitzvah of counting the *omer* itself is related to the passing of Rabi Akiva's students. This is not the case; the tragedy of their deaths simply coincided with the period of *sefiras haomer*, and the halachos of mourning were therefore enacted during the same time of year.

These halachos have the status of a *minhag* rather than a rabbinic prohibition, since *Chazal* did not institute an actual *gezeirah* concerning these practices.

---

1. יבמות דף סב:.
2. טור וב"י סי' תצ"ג. (ועי' בערוך השלחן סי' תצ"ג ס"א שעיקרי ימי הגזרות בשנות המאות שעברו בצרפת ובאשכנז היו בימים אלו).

1. Weddings and Engagements

1. **The Prohibition to Marry during *Sefirah*:** The *minhag* is to refrain from getting married during the period of *sefiras haomer*. This is one of the restrictions observed due to the tragic deaths of the students of Rabi Akiva.[3] It is prohibited to hold a wedding even without music and dancing.

2. **A First Marriage:** The custom not to marry applies even to a man who has never married or had children, and who is therefore obligated in the mitzvah of *peru u'revu*.[4] It is permitted, however, to remarry one's former spouse, which is considered a less joyous event.[5]

3. **If the Prohibition Is Violated:** If a couple violates the *minhag* and marries during the period of *sefirah*, no penalty is imposed by the *beis din* or the Rav even if they have the authority to do so, since marriage is a mitzvah. (Penalties may be imposed, however, on people who violate the other restrictions observed during this period.)[6]

4. **Celebrating an Engagement:** It is permissible to celebrate an engagement.[7] A "*vort*" or "*tenaim*" may be held, even if a full *seudah* is served. However, it is prohibited to dance at these celebrations, even without music.[8] (See section 2 below.)

5. ***Sheva Brachos*:** A *seudas sheva brachos* may be held during the period of *sefirah* (i.e., if the wedding took place either before

---

3. שו״ע סי׳ תצ״ג ס״א.
4. מ״ב סי׳ תצ״ג סק״א, ועי׳ שעה״צ סק״א. ועי׳ בשו״ע יו״ד סי׳ שצ״ב ס״ב שמותר לאבל לישא אשה אם לא קיים פר״ו או שאין לו מי שישמשנו, ועי׳ במ״ב סי׳ תקנ״א ס״ק י״ד.
5. מ״ב סי׳ תצ״ג שם.
6. שו״ע סי׳ תצ״ג ס״א ובמ״ב סק״ד. ועי׳ שו״ת אגר״מ או״ח ח״א סי׳ קנ״ט.
7. שו״ע שם.
8. מ״ב סק״ג.

or on Rosh Chodesh, depending on one's personal custom, or on Lag Baomer). It is permissible for any guest to attend such a *seudah*. Some *poskim* even permit music and dancing[9] (see section 2 below).

6. The halachos regarding holding or attending a wedding on Rosh Chodesh, on Lag Baomer, or after Lag Baomer, and whether a person may make or attend a wedding after Lag Baomer if his personal *minhag* is to observe the halachos of *aveilus* during that time, will be discussed below in section 5.

2. Dancing and Music

1. **The Prohibition of Dancing:** It is prohibited to dance during the period of *sefirah*, even without music.[10]

2. **Dancing at a *Seudas Mitzvah* or *Hachnassas Sefer Torah*:** The *poskim* debate whether it is permissible to dance at a *seudas mitzvah* such as a bar mitzvah, *bris milah*, or *siyum*. (It is certainly prohibited to dance at an engagement party; see above, section 1, paragraph 4.) Some permit dancing at a *seudas mitzvah* even if music is played[11] while others prohibit it.[12] It is prohibited to dance at any event that is not an actual *seudas mitzvah*, even one that is held for the purpose of a mitzvah, such as a fundraising dinner.[13] According to some *poskim*, a *hachnassas sefer Torah* should not be scheduled during the period of *sefirah*; however, it is permitted during the *Shloshes Yemei Hagbalah* (the three days immediately

---

9. שו"ת אגר"מ או"ח ח"ב סי' צ"ה.
10. מ"ב שם.
11. עי' שו"ת אגר"מ או"ח ח"א סי' קנ"ט.
12. עי' שו"ת מנחת יצחק ח"א סי' קי"א בשם הדעת קדושים, הליכות שלמה פי"א סי"א וס"ק כ"ו. וכן דעת הגר"ש וואזנער זצ"ל הוב"ד בס' בין פסח לשבועות פי"ג סק"ג במילואים.
13. שו"ת מנח"י שם.

prior to Shavuos).¹⁴ Some *poskim*, however, permit celebrating a *hachnassas sefer Torah* during the *sefirah* period, even with music and dancing.¹⁵

3. **Dance Lessons:** One must refrain from participating in dance lessons during *sefirah*.¹⁶

4. **Listening to Music:** The *minhag* is to refrain from listening to music even if one does not dance along with it.¹⁷ This custom must be observed even by children who have reached the age of *chinuch*.¹⁸

5. **Recorded Music:** The prohibition of listening to music includes both live and recorded music.¹⁹

6. **Music without Instruments:** Listening to recorded singing that is not accompanied by instruments is the subject of a debate among the *poskim*. Some authorities permit it,²⁰ while others draw a distinction between rousing, joyous songs that can lead to dancing, which are prohibited, and uplifting songs or pieces of *chazzanus*, which are permitted.²¹ Some authorities take an even more stringent position and prohibit listening to any recorded songs, even those that are sung without instrumental accompaniment, since they consider the recording itself to be akin to a musical instrument. Nevertheless, these *poskim* note that there are grounds for leniency, especially for a person who is in low spirits and

---

14. הליכות שלמה שם הערה 57.
15. הגריש"א זצ"ל הובא בהלכות חג בחג פ"ז הערה 36.
16. הליכות שלמה שם הערה 51.
17. ערוך השלחן סי' תצ"ג ס"ב. וכן עמא דבר. ועי' בשו"ת מנחת יצחק ח"א סי' קי"א שהוא נלמד קל וחומר מריקוד דאסור כ"ש לשמוע כלי זמר. ועי' שו"ת אגר"מ או"ח ח"ג סי' פ"ז ויו"ד ח"ב סי' קל"ז.
18. שו"ת אגר"מ או"ח ח"ד סי' כ"א אות ד'.
19. שו"ת אגר"מ או"ח ח"א סוף סי' קס"ו, שו"ת שבט הלוי ח"ח סי' קכ"ז אות ב', ועוד.
20. שו"ת אגר"מ שם.
21. הגרשז"א זצ"ל בהליכות שלמה שם סי"ד והערה כ"ב, ועי"ש הערה 54 דאין להתיר בשופי רק כשקיימת סיבה לכך.

Chapter Two: *Halachos and Minhagim of the Sefirah Period*

feels the need to listen to music in order to lift his mood.[22] Many *poskim* prohibit listening to a capella music due to its resemblance to actual music produced by instruments. One should consult with a Rav regarding whether such recordings may be equated with ordinary recorded singing (which some authorities permit playing during *sefirah*, as above).

7. **Music Lessons and Professional Musicians:** All *poskim* prohibit participating in music lessons or playing musical instruments for one's enjoyment. The *poskim* are in dispute regarding whether a person may play or practice music for his income; some rule that it is permitted,[23] while others prohibit this.[24]

8. **Hearing Music Involuntarily:** If a person is in an environment where music is being played, such as a workplace or waiting room, he is not required to leave the area in order to avoid hearing the music. Nevertheless, he should avoid paying attention to the music and enjoying it.[25] Similarly, if a person hears music when his telephone call is placed on hold, he is not required to disconnect the call.

9. **Music for Purposes Other than Enjoyment:** A person who is afraid that he may fall asleep while driving is permitted to listen to music to keep himself awake. Similarly, it is permissible to listen to music while exercising in order to keep pace or for similar purposes.[26]

10. **Recorded Stories for Children:** It is permissible to play recordings of stories for children even if the recordings

---

22. עי' שו"ת שבט הלוי שם.
23. שו"ת אגר"מ או"ח ח"ג סי' פ"ז.
24. קובץ מבית לוי ח"ג עמוד ל"ט. ועי' שו"ת מנח"י שם.
25. הליכות שלמה שם הערה 51. ויש לעיין במי שיש לו בפלפון צלצול של מוסיקה משמחת, האם צריך לשנותו.
26. הגר"ש קמינצקי שליט"א בקובץ הלכות פ"ט סי"ג.

Dancing and Music ~ 51

contain some background music.[27] This is permitted even for children who are of the age of *chinuch*.

11. **Singing Lively Songs:** Some *poskim* even prohibit singing lively, joyous songs, except at a *seudas mitzvah* (or an engagement party, where it is permissible to sing as long as one does not dance as well). These authorities permit singing only slow, uplifting songs.[28] Other *poskim* disagree and maintain that even lively, joyous songs may be sung as long as they will not lead to dancing.[29]

12. **Playing Music for a Person Who Is Ill:** One may play music for a person who is ill or depressed and is therefore permitted to listen to music.[30]

13. **Music and Dancing on Chol Hamoed:** Some *poskim* permit music and dancing on Chol Hamoed Pesach, and the common practice is to be lenient in this regard.[31] Nevertheless, the prohibitions to dance and listen to music remain in effect at other festive times, such as on Isru Chag, Rosh Chodesh, Erev Shabbos after midday, and Motzaei Shabbos.[32]

14. **Music and Dancing when Haircuts Are Permitted:** During the portion of the *sefirah* period when the halachos of mourning are not in effect and it is permissible to take haircuts (as per the various customs outlined in section 5 below), it is questionable whether dancing and music are

---

27. הליכות שלמה שם הערה 53.
28. ראה הליכות שלמה שם סי״ד ובהערות לשם וסי״ח ובהערות לשם.
29. הגריש״א זצ״ל הובא בהלכות חג בחג פ״ז הערה 34.
30. הליכות שלמה שם הערה 54.
31. הגריש״א זצ״ל הובא בהלכות חג בחג פ״ז הערה 95 (אמנם משמע שם שרק התיר בצירוף המנהג שנוהגים יותר מל״ג יום), הלכות פסח להגר״ש איידער זצ״ל פכ״ט ס״ק ע״ז. אבל עי׳ בפמ״ג סי׳ תצ״ג מ״ז סק״ב שנקט לאסור ריקודים של רשות. וראה גם הליכות שלמה שם סט״ו שלמעשה לא התיר ריקודים של רשות.
32. פשוט, דלא מצאנו בפוסקים להתיר.

likewise permitted.³³ Some *poskim* suggest a stringent position to permit music and dancing only on Lag Baomer.³⁴ However, the common practice in *chutz la'Aretz* is to permit listening to music at any time when cutting hair is permitted.

15. **Listening to Music throughout the Year:** The halachos concerning playing musical instruments and listening to music throughout the year, which may be prohibited in order to commemorate the *churban*, will be discussed in Chapter Thirteen.

16. **Music and Dancing on the Night of Lag Baomer:** Some *poskim* rule that those who refrain from taking haircuts until the morning of Lag Baomer (as will be explained below in section 5) should likewise refrain from dancing or listening to music at night.³⁵ However, the common practice in Eretz Yisrael is to permit music and dancing on the night of Lag Baomer in honor of the *yahrtzeit* of Rabi Shimon bar Yochai.³⁶

3. Reciting *Shehecheyanu* and Other Forms of Festivity

1. **Reciting *Shehecheyanu*:** In general, festivity should be minimized during this time. Nevertheless, the *brachah* of *shehecheyanu* should be recited if there is reason for it.³⁷

2. **Creating an Opportunity to Recite *Shehecheyanu*:** The *poskim* debate whether it is permissible *lechatchilah* to enter

---

33. עי' שעה"צ סי' תצ"ד סק"ד. ועי' הלכות חג בחג פ"ז הערה 37.
34. הליכות שלמה שם סט"ו ס"ק כ"ג.
35. שו"ת שבט הלוי ח"ח סי' קס"ח אות ה'.
36. עי' הליכות שלמה שם הערה 58. אמנם, יתכן שרק שירים לכבודו של ר' שמעון מותר ולא סתם לשמע מוזיקה בבית.
37. מ"ב סי' תצ"ג סק"ב.

into a situation that warrants reciting *shehecheyanu*, such as purchasing a new fruit.[38] Some *poskim* permit this,[39] while others rule that one should not initiate such a situation.[40]

3. **New Garments:** Many people refrain from reciting *shehecheyanu* on new articles of clothing during this time. Since this halachah is not mentioned by earlier *poskim*, contemporary authorities debate whether this practice has the status of a *minhag* or if it is baseless and can be ascribed to confusion with the halachos of *bein hametzarim*, and therefore it can be disregarded.[41] Indeed, many *poskim* maintain that the halachah concerning the purchase of new clothing is the same as that which governs purchasing new fruits, and both are permitted when there is occasion to do so.[42] Nevertheless, a person should be stringent in this regard if this *minhag* is his family tradition. Even if a person has the custom to refrain from reciting *shehecheyanu* on a new article of clothing, though, he may still purchase a garment and delay wearing it until Lag Baomer or Shavuos, since the *brachah* is recited when the item is first worn, not when it is purchased.[43] It is certainly permitted to purchase articles of clothing on which *shehecheyanu* is never recited. Note: It is important to distinguish between the laws of *sefiras haomer* and the halachos governing the Nine Days (beginning on Rosh

---

38. לשון המ״ב שם "אם נזדמן לו איזה ענין שצריך לברך עליו שההחיינו יברך".
39. דעת הגרח״ק שליט״א הוב״ד בס׳ בין פסח לשבועות פט״ז סק״א. וראה הליכות שלמה פי״א הערה 53.
40. הגרנ״ק שליט״א הוב״ד בחוט שני שבת ח״ד עמ׳ שע״ט.
41. עי׳ ס׳ בין פסח לשבועות פט״ז הערה א׳-ב׳ שהאריך טובא בשם הרבה פוסקים בענין זה.
42. כדנראה מדברי המ״ב שם, כה״ח סי׳ תצ״ג סק״ד וכן הורה הגרשז״א זצ״ל הוב״ד בהליכות שלמה שם, אמת ליעקב סי׳ תצ״ג הערה 466, ועי׳ ס׳ בין פסח לשבועות שם.
43. דלא גרע מימי בין המצרים (משבעה עשר בתמוז עד ר״ח) שמותר לקנות בגד חדש אם אינו לובשו, עי׳ כה״ח סי׳ תקנ״א ס״ק פ״ח. אמנם בלקט יושר או״ח (עמוד 97-98 ד״ה ואמר) שממנו מקור לחומרא זו, משמע שאסור לקנות אלא בל״ג בעומר.

Chodesh Av), when it is prohibited to purchase clothing of any kind.

4. **Scenarios in Which *Shehecheyanu* May Certainly Be Recited:** Even for those who follow the stringent custom and avoid reciting *shehecheyanu* during the period of *sefirah*, there are certain occasions when it is certainly permitted to recite the *brachah*. One may recite *shehecheyanu* on Shabbos whenever there is an occasion to do so. Likewise, the *brachah* may be recited at a *bris milah* or upon purchasing clothing for a chassan and kallah (i.e., a garment which requires no altering and would thus warrant *shehecheyanu* upon purchasing) who will be married on or after Lag Baomer.[44]

5. **Moving to a New House:** According to those who permit reciting *shehecheyanu* during *sefirah*, it is also permissible to move to a new home.[45] Some *poskim* state that it is preferable to move on Lag Baomer, or if necessary, after Lag Baomer.[46]

6. **Home Renovations:** It is permissible to perform any type of renovation during this period. This includes even work whose purpose is merely to enhance or beautify the home.[47] It should be noted that the halachah is different for the Nine Days, as will be explained below in Chapter Eight.

7. **Trips and Swimming:** It is permissible to go on a trip or excursion during this time.[48] There is no prohibition to swim in a pool, lake, or ocean.[49]

8. **Social Events:** Social gatherings and communal dinners are

---

44. עי' ס' בין פסח לשבועות שם ס"ה'-ו'. ומש"כ לקנות בגדים לחתן וכלה היינו אפי' אם יברך בשעת הקנייה ולא לבישה כגון שא"צ שום תיקון.

45. דעת הגרי"ש א זצ"ל והגרח"ק שליט"א הוב"ד בס' הלכות חג בחג פ"ז הערה 26.

46. שו"ת שבט הלוי ח"י סי' קל"ה אות ג'. והיינו אפי' אם לא מברכים שהחיינו אלא הטוב והמטיב משום דלא מסמנא מלתא. ולצורך רב עד ר"ח אייר.

47. ראה הלכות חג בחג שם.

48. עי' ס' בין פסח לשבועות פט"ז סי"ב וס"ק ט"ו.

49. ארחות רבינו ח"ב עמוד צ"ה בשם הגרייי"ק זצ"ל.

permitted as long as there is no music or dancing.[50] However, some *poskim* prohibit organizing a particularly festive event.[51]

9. **A *Seudas Mitzvah*:** It is permissible to hold a *seudas mitzvah* in honor of a *bris milah*, a *pidyon haben*, a bar mitzvah (even if it is not on the boy's actual birthday), a *siyum*, or a *vort*. See section 2 above for a discussion of whether music and dancing are permitted at such an event.

4. Cutting Hair

1. **The Prohibition to Cut Hair:** It is prohibited to take a haircut during *sefirah*.[52] It is also prohibited for a man to shave his facial hair.[53] However, it is permissible to trim a mustache that interferes with eating.[54] Some *poskim* maintain that it is permissible to trim a mustache under any circumstances, and that it is not included in the prohibition of cutting hair.[55]

2. **Haircuts for Women:** Many *poskim* rule that a woman should refrain from cutting her hair unless she must do so to maintain a favorable appearance for her husband, for reasons of modesty, or for *tevilah*.[56] Some *poskim* maintain, though,

---

50. שו"ע הרב סי' תצ"ג ס"א (וכתב שם שלא יהיה שמחות יתירות) וערוך השלחן סי' תצ"ג ס"ב.
51. עי' שו"ת אגר"מ אבהע"ז ח"א סי' צ"ח בענין חתן וכלה שבאו לעירם אחר סיום השבע ברכות ורוצים לעשות שמחה לאוהביהם וקרוביהם בעירם, ומתחילה צידד להחמיר ורק לבסוף סיים להתיר מפני שהדרך שעושין שמחה כזו כשבאים ונחשב כסעודת מצוה.
52. שו"ע סי' תצ"ג ס"ב.
53. פשוט דאין חילוק בין גילוח הראש והזקן. וכן מבואר בשו"ת אגר"מ או"ח ח"ד סי' ק"ב ומעוד פוסקים שדנו להתיר לצורך פרנסה.
54. שו"ע סי' תקנ"א סי"ב וכ"ש הכא.
55. וכמו לענין חוה"מ, עי' מ"ב סי' תקל"א ס"ק כ"א, ואף שלכאורה מסברא היינו מדמין מהלכות בין המצרים הנ"ל וא"כ אינו מותר אלא אם מעכב האכילה, מ"מ לפי מש"כ הביה"ל ריש סי' תצ"ג בשם הפמ"ג שכל מה שמותר בחוה"מ התירו בספיה"ע יש להתיר גזיזת השפם בכ"ג, תשובת הגריש"א זצ"ל והגרנ"ק שליט"א הוב"ד בגליון מים חיים.
56. עי' שו"ת אגר"מ יו"ד ח"ב סי' קל"ז אות ב'. וראה פמ"ג סי' תקנ"א מ"ז ס"ק י"ג ובמ"ב שם ס"ק ע"ט.

that the prohibition of cutting hair does not apply to women at all.[57] This ruling is followed by Sephardim.[58] All *poskim* permit waxing or shaving for women.[59]

3. **Shaving for Work or Business:** Some *poskim* rule that it is permitted for a man to shave during *sefirah* if his work environment makes it necessary and he might suffer a loss if he refrains from doing so.[60] Other *poskim*, however, rule stringently even in this case.[61] It should be emphasized that it is permissible to shave only if it is reasonable to assume that the failure to do so will cause an actual loss. In the modern workplace, with its liberal attitudes concerning dress and behavior, it is questionable if this leniency still applies.

4. **Cutting a Child's Hair:** It is questionable whether the prohibition of cutting hair applies to children.[62] Unless there is a pressing need, one should be stringent in this respect and refrain from giving a haircut to a child who has reached the age of *chinuch*.[63] (With regard to this halachah, this is defined as the age at which the child can understand the concept of *sefiras haomer* and the idea that we are supposed to mourn the calamity that took place during this time.) It is permissible to cut the hair of a child younger than the age of *chinuch*.[64]

---

57. עי' שו"ת אור לציון ח"ג פי"ז ס"ג.
58. דאפי' באבל דעת השו"ע יו"ד סי' ש"צ ס"ה דמותר אחר השבעה.
59. הגרשז"א זצ"ל והגר"ש ואזנר זצ"ל הוב"ל בס' בין פסח לשבועות פ"ט סי"א.
60. שו"ת אגר"מ או"ח ח"ד סי' ק"ב לאפוקי משבוע שחל בו ת"ב שאסור מדינא שאין להתיר אפי' במקום הפסד.
61. הגרי"ש זצ"ל הוב"ד בהלכות חג בחג פ"ז הערה 65.
62. עי' שו"ע סי' תקנ"א סי"ד שאסור לגדולים לספר לקטנים ועי"ש במ"א ס"ק ל"ח ובמ"ב ס"ק פ"א בטעם הדבר ורצ"ע אם שייך כאן ובפרט דגם שם הביא המ"ב ס"ק פ"ב שאין להחמיר אלא בשבוע שחל בו ת"ב ולא מי"ז בתמוז. ובחול המועד אין איסור לספר הקטנים כדאיתא סי' תקל"א ס"ו.
63. כן מבואר בהליכות שלמה פי"א סט"ז ובהערות לשם שיש דין חינוך על זה, וכן דעת הגרי"ש זצ"ל הוב"ד בהלכות חג בחג פ"ז הערה 58. ועי' שו"ת אור לציון ח"ג פי"ז שאין איסור לקטנים.
64. כן נראה, ואפי' לפני ת"ב יש צד להתיר עי' מ"ב סי' תקנ"א ס"ק פ"א ובשעה"צ ס"ק צ"א. אמנם, יש שמביאים ראי' לאסור לקטן אף שלא הגיע לחינוך ממה שמובא מהאריז"ל שמותר לעשות חלקה בל"ג בעומר, מיהו יש לדחות ראי' זו.

Cutting Hair ~ 57

5. **Haircuts and Shaving for the Participants in a *Bris Milah*:** When a *bris milah* is held, the father, *mohel*, and *sandak* are permitted to take haircuts and to shave. (This is not permitted for the *kvatter*.)⁶⁵ The haircuts may be performed even on the day prior to the *bris*, close to *shekiah*. If the *bris* will be held on a Shabbos, the participants may cut their hair at any time on Friday, even in the morning (but not on Thursday).⁶⁶ If the *bris* will be held on a Sunday, it is questionable whether haircuts may be performed on the preceding Friday.⁶⁷ If it cannot be delayed until the day of the *bris* itself, a Rav should be consulted.

6. **A Bar or Bas Mitzvah:** It is questionable whether a boy may take a haircut on the day of his bar mitzvah. The same question applies to the father of a bar mitzvah boy.⁶⁸ Some *poskim* rule that a bar mitzvah boy should preferably be given a haircut before his 13th birthday, when he still has the status of a child, but that if he did not do so, he may take a haircut on the day of his bar mitzvah. However, these authorities do not permit the boy's father to take a haircut.⁶⁹

   A girl may not take a haircut in honor of her bas mitzvah.⁷⁰ (However, Sephardim permit this.)

7. **A *Pidyon Haben*:** When a *pidyon haben* is held, neither the father nor the *kohen* is permitted to take a haircut or shave.⁷¹

8. **A *Chassan*:** A chassan is permitted to take a haircut and shave on the day before his *aufruf*.⁷²

---

65. רמ"א סי' תצ"ג ס"ב ובמ"ב ס"ק י"ב.
66. מ"ב ס"ק י"ג.
67. עי' הגהו' חת"ס על השו"ע סי' תצ"ג ס"ב, ועי' כף החיים סי' תצ"ג ס"ק ל"ז.
68. עי' שו"ת רבבות אפרים או"ח ח"א סי' של"ז.
69. הליכות שלמה שם סט"ז ובהערות לשם.
70. שם ס"ק כ"ה.
71. דעת הגרי"ש א' זצ"ל והגרנ"ק שליט"א הוב"ד בס' סידור פסח כהלכתו פי"ב סי"ב.
72. שע"ת סק"ז בשם הדגו"מ.

9. **Shaving for a Date or Engagement Party:** One may not take a haircut or shave before a date or in honor of an engagement party.[73]

10. **Attending a Wedding while Observing the Halachos of *Sefirah*:** If a person who observes the mourning restrictions of *sefirah* after Lag Baomer attends a wedding at that time (as will be discussed in the next section), he is permitted to take a haircut and shave in honor of the wedding if he would otherwise not attend. However, if he is aware of the impending wedding before the period of *sefirah* begins, it is preferable for him to alter his *minhag* for that particular year and observe the restrictions during the first part of the *sefirah*, until Lag Baomer, instead of keeping to his usual practice.[74] See the next section for further details.

11. **Haircuts for Medical Reasons:** It is permissible to shave or cut one's hair for medical reasons[75] (e.g., because of a skin rash or to perform a medical procedure).

12. **Haircuts at the Conclusion of *Aveilus*:** An *avel* may take a haircut at the conclusion of *shloshim* even during *sefirah*. (A person who is mourning the loss of a parent should wait until someone tells him that he needs a haircut, and preferably should wait until after three months have passed.) It is preferable for the *avel* to perform *hataras nedarim* before having a haircut.[76]

13. **A Person Who Would Be Permitted to Cut His Hair on Chol Hamoed:** Any person who would be permitted to take a haircut during Chol Hamoed (e.g., someone who was in jail or in captivity, or who arrives on land after a sea voyage; see

---

73. תשובת הגריש״א זצ״ל הוב״ד בגליון מים חיים.
74. עי׳ שו״ת אגר״מ או״ח ח״ב סי׳ צ״ה.
75. ערוך השלחן סי׳ תצ״ג ס״ג.
76. שע״ת שם.

Cutting Hair 59

Kitzur Halachos: Yom Tov and Chol Hamoed, Chapter Eight, section 4, paragraph 6) may have his hair cut during *sefirah* as well.[77]

14. **The Arizal's Stringency:** The Arizal maintains that a person should refrain from cutting his hair between Pesach and Erev Shavuos even for a *bris* or in any of the other permissible situations discussed above.[78] Many chassidim and Sephardim follow this ruling. It is questionable whether the Arizal includes conducting weddings in this stringency.[79]

15. **Cutting Another Person's Hair:** It is permissible to cut the hair of another person, who is permitted to take a haircut at that time, even during one's personal observance of *sefirah*.[80]

16. **Haircuts on Lag Baomer and Rosh Chodesh:** See section 5 below regarding taking a haircut on Lag Baomer or Rosh Chodesh.

17. **Combing Hair:** It is permissible to comb hair even if some hairs will certainly be detached in the process.[81]

18. **Bathing in Hot Water:** One need not refrain from bathing or showering in hot water during these days.[82]

19. **Trimming Nails:** Trimming nails is permitted during the *sefirah* period.[83]

---

77. ביה"ל סי' תצ"ג ס"ב ד"ה נוהגים בשם הפמ"ג. וראה שו"ת אגר"מ או"ח ח"ב סי' צ"ו מה שתמה ע"ז.
78. שע"ת סק"ח וכף החיים שם ס"ק י"ג.
79. עי' שו"ת מנחת אלעזר ח"ד סי' ס', ושו"ת דברי יואל ח"א סי' כ"ו.
80. תשובת הגרשז"א זצ"ל והגרנ"ק שליט"א הוב"ד בגליון מים חיים.
81. ראה מ"ב סי' תקנ"א סק"כ וכ"ש הכא.
82. פשוט.
83. עי' מ"ב שם דנחלקו הפוסקים לענין שבוע שחל בו ת"ב אבל לענין ספירת העומר עמא דבר להתיר. וכ"כ בכף החיים שם ס"ק ט"ז.

5. When to Observe the *Sefirah* Restrictions

Introduction: As explained at the beginning of this chapter, since the students of Rabi Akiva passed away during the period between Pesach and Shavuos (which is known as the period of *sefiras haomer* due to the mitzvah that is observed every day during these weeks), various mourning customs were instituted at this time of year. Based on a Midrash, many Rishonim maintain that the deaths of Rabi Akiva's students spanned only 34 days or, according to some opinions, 33 days during this period. Nevertheless, there is a divergence of opinion regarding precisely when their deaths took place and, by extension, when the mourning practices should be observed. Some authorities maintain that the restrictions should be observed during the first 33 or 34 days of the *sefirah* period, while others maintain that the deaths took place specifically on the 33 days between Pesach and Shavuos when *Tachanun* is recited (i.e., every day except the seven days of Pesach, the six other Shabbosos of this period, the two days of Rosh Chodesh Iyar, and the single day of Rosh Chodesh Sivan). According to this opinion, the 16 days when *Tachanun* is omitted are not subject to the restrictions of *sefirah*, which are observed on the remaining 33 days of the period. Another opinion is to subtract the first 16 days and begin the customs of mourning from Rosh Chodesh Iyar and continue for 33 days.[84] As a result of this dispute, there are various *minhagim* with respect to when the laws of *sefirah* should be observed. The details of these *minhagim* and their applications in various scenarios are discussed in this section.

1. **The Sephardic Custom:** The Shulchan Aruch follows the opinion of the Rishonim who maintain that Rabi Akiva's students passed away during the first 34 days of the *sefirah*

---

84. עי' טור ב"י ודרכי משה סי' תצ"ג.

period, and that therefore the mourning restrictions should be observed at that time. Due to the principle of *"miktzas hayom kekulo* – a small portion of the day is considered like the entire day," it is sufficient to observe the restrictions through the *beginning* of the 34th day; therefore, the prohibitions of haircuts and weddings come to an end on the morning of the 34th day of the *omer*.[85] If the 34th day is on Shabbos, the Shulchan Aruch permits taking a haircut on Friday in honor of Shabbos.[86]

2. **The Ashkenazic Custom:** The Rema lists several customs that are commonly observed among Ashkenazim.

    - The first custom is similar to the Sephardic practice cited by the Shulchan Aruch, with one notable difference: The Ashkenazic custom permits weddings and haircuts as early as the morning of the 33rd day of *sefirah* (Lag Baomer).[87] Some *poskim* rule that one may take a haircut even on the night of Lag Baomer; however, many of these *poskim* prohibit holding a wedding on that night unless the 33rd day of the *omer* is Erev Shabbos and it is too burdensome to schedule a wedding on a Friday.[88] Nevertheless, other authorities argue that if the prohibition to take a haircut does not include the night of Lag Baomer, then it is certainly permissible to hold a wedding as well.[89] According to this custom, if the 33rd day of the *omer* falls on Sunday, one may take a haircut on the preceding Friday in honor of Shabbos.[90]

    - Another custom is to exclude the first 16 days of *sefirah* and

---

85. שו"ע סי' תצ"ג ס"ב.
86. שם.
87. רמ"א שם ס"א וס"ב.
88. מ"ב ס"ק י"א ובשעה"צ ס"ק י"ב.
89. שו"ת אגר"מ או"ח ח"א סי' קנ"ט ושו"ת מנח"י ח"ד סי' פ"ד.
90. רמ"א שם ס"ב. אבל אין להסתפר במוצ"ש, הליכות שלמה פי"א ס"ק ל"א והגריש"א זצ"ל הובא בס' בין פסח לשבועות פ"י סק"כ.

to begin the mourning restrictions after Rosh Chodesh Iyar and to continue until Shavuos. On Lag Baomer haircuts are permitted during the daytime.[91]

- A third custom is likewise to observe the latter portion of *sefirah*, albeit without including the *Shloshes Yemei Hagbalah* (the three days immediately prior to Shavuos) in the period of mourning. To extend the period of mourning for a full 33 days, the mourning restrictions are also observed on both days of Rosh Chodesh Iyar and continue until the morning of the third day of Sivan, which counts as a full day due to the principle of *"miktzas hayom kekulo."*[92]

- A fourth custom is to observe the *sefirah* restrictions from the beginning of the *sefirah* period until Rosh Chodesh Sivan, but to suspend the practices on Rosh Chodesh Iyar and Lag Baomer.[93]

3. **Common Ashkenazic Custom in Eretz Yisrael and *Chutz La'Aretz*:** In *chutz la'Aretz* the prevalent custom is to observe the *minhagim* of mourning either from the beginning of *sefirah* until Lag Baomer or from Rosh Chodesh Iyar until the *Shloshes Yemei Hagbalah*. In Eretz Yisrael, however, the common custom is to observe the restrictions from the beginning of the *sefirah* period until Rosh Chodesh Sivan (excluding Rosh Chodesh and Lag Baomer). As noted in section 4 above, according to Kabbalah one should refrain from taking a haircut at any time between Pesach and Erev Shavuos.[94] (If Shavuos falls on Sunday, one may take a haircut on Erev Shabbos.[95])

---

91. רמ״א שם ס״ג.
92. מ״ב ס״ק ט״ו.
93. שם. ועי׳ שו״ת אגר״מ שם שביאר כל המנהגים.
94. שע״ת סק״ח.
95. כף החיים סי׳ תצ״ג ס״ק י״ג.

When to Observe the Sefirah Restrictions ∽ 63

4. **Combining the Leniencies or Stringencies of the Different Customs:** One may not combine the leniencies of two different customs, such as by taking a haircut on or before Rosh Chodesh Iyar and then cutting one's hair again after Lag Baomer.[96] On the other hand, it is permissible to adopt the stringencies of two different customs and to observe the halachos of mourning from Pesach until Erev Shavuos, or until Rosh Chodesh Sivan, or until the *Shloshes Yemei Hagbalah* (excluding Lag Baomer). Although it is generally considered foolish for a person to observe conflicting stringencies, that principle does not apply to the mourning restrictions of the *sefirah* period, since a person may observe multiple stringencies simply because he is not certain which *minhag* is correct. Nevertheless, a person who does not have an established *minhag* is not required to follow the stringencies of all the opinions; he may simply choose the custom he wishes to follow.[97]

5. **Divergent Customs in One Community:** Although the halachah generally requires all the residents of a single community to observe the same *minhag*,[98] this halachah does not apply today, since our communities generally consist of an assortment of individuals from diverse backgrounds with their own individual *minhagim*.[99]

6. **Choosing a Custom:** According to some *poskim*, even a person who has an established *minhag* in his family is permitted to change his practice from year to year.[100] Moreover, some authorities maintain that a person may choose to observe

---

96. רמ"א שם ס"ג.
97. מ"ב ס"ק י"ז.
98. רמ"א שם.
99. עי' שו"ת אגר"מ שם, שו"ת מנח"י שם.
100. עי' שו"ת אגר"מ שם. אמנם, ראה מכתבים ומאמרים ח"ו איגרת תרנ"ז שדעת הגרא"מ שך זצ"ל שאין כדאי לעשות כן.

two different customs regarding the calculation of the 33 days even in the same year, one with regard to the prohibition on haircuts and the other with regard to refraining from holding a wedding.[101]

7. **The Custom of a Married Woman:** A married woman should adopt her husband's custom regarding which mourning period to observe.[102] A woman should change her custom only after her marriage and not when she is engaged. If a couple gets married during the period of *sefirah* (i.e., on Lag Baomer) and the wife's family observes a different custom from that of her new husband (i.e., she only began from Rosh Chodesh and her husband is finishing after Lag Baomer), according to some authorities she should not change her practice until the following year.[103] A Rav should be consulted for a final ruling.

8. **Attending a Wedding while Observing the Mourning Restrictions:** The *poskim* debate whether it is permitted to attend a wedding at a time when one is observing the *sefirah* restrictions, e.g., if a wedding is held after Lag Baomer. Some *poskim* rule that a guest may attend a wedding even while he is observing the mourning practices of *sefirah* (and it is not even necessary to change his *minhag* for that year) because it is the act of getting married that is prohibited, which applies only to the chassan and kallah themselves. The other guests at a wedding, according to these *poskim*, are considered to be attending a *seudas mitzvah*, which is permitted during the *sefirah*; therefore, they are permitted even to listen to the music and participate in the dancing.[104] However, some *poskim* rule that a guest who is still observing the restrictions

---

101. שו״ת אגר״מ שם. וכן עי׳ שו״ת מנחת יצחק שם.
102. שו״ת אגר״מ או״ח ח״א סי׳ קנ״ח.
103. עי׳ שו״ת מנחת יצחק ח״ד סי׳ פ״ג. ויש לעיין בדעת האגר״מ שם.
104. שו״ת אגר״מ או״ח ח״א סי׳ קנ״ט, הליכות שלמה פי״א סי״ט, וכ״ה דעת הגריש״א זצ״ל הוב״ד בהלכות חג בחג פ״ז הערה 92.

of *sefirah* should attend only the *chuppah* and the beginning of the *seudah* and should leave the wedding before the music and dancing begin.¹⁰⁵

9. **Concluding a Wedding or Haircut That Began on Lag Baomer:** The *poskim* debate whether a person who observes the *sefirah* restrictions after Lag Baomer and chooses to marry on Lag Baomer itself may continue the *seudah*, dancing, and music into the night. Some *poskim* permit this,¹⁰⁶ while others maintain that the dancing and music should conclude before nightfall.¹⁰⁷

If a person who observes the *sefirah* restrictions after Lag Baomer is in the middle of a haircut when the night after Lag Baomer begins, he may complete the haircut in order to preserve his dignity (i.e., due to *kavod habriyos*).¹⁰⁸

10. **Haircuts on Erev Shabbos before Rosh Chodesh Sivan or the *Shloshes Yemei Hagbalah*:** As was discussed in paragraph 2 above, the Ashkenazic custom is to permit cutting hair on Erev Shabbos in honor of Shabbos when Lag Baomer falls on Sunday.¹⁰⁹ (Music and dancing, however, are not permitted on that day.) The *poskim* debate whether the same leniency applies when Rosh Chodesh Sivan or the beginning of the *Shloshes Yemei Hagbalah* falls on Sunday, for those who observe the customs of mourning until that time. Some *poskim* permit taking a haircut on the preceding Erev Shabbos;¹¹⁰ however, others prohibit it.¹¹¹

11. **When Rosh Chodesh Iyar Falls on Shabbos:** It is permitted

---

105. עי' שו"ת מנחת יצחק ח"ד סי' פ"ד, קובץ מבית לוי עמוד ע"ה אות ב'.
106. שו"ת אגר"מ אבהע"ז ח"א סי' צ"ז.
107. שו"ת מנחת יצחק שם.
108. ארחות רבינו ח"ב עמוד צ"ו בשם החזו"א, וכן הובא בס' בין פסח לשבועות פ"י ס"ז.
109. רמ"א שם ס"ב.
110. עי' פמ"ג סי' תצ"ג א"א סק"ה. וכ"פ הגרשז"א זצ"ל הוב"ד בהליכות שלמה שם סכ"ד והערה 94.
111. דעת הגרמ"פ זצ"ל והגריש"א זצ"ל הוב"ד בס' בין פסח לשבועות פ"י ס"ק כ"ב.

to take a haircut or hold a wedding on Erev Shabbos when Rosh Chodesh Iyar falls on Friday and Shabbos, since the confluence of Rosh Chodesh and Shabbos lends a twofold *kedushah* to the day. (This halachah is relevant to those who begin observing the mourning customs of *sefirah* immediately after Pesach.)[112] The *poskim* debate whether a person who observes the custom to abstain from haircuts on Rosh Chodesh, based on Rabi Yehudah HaChasid's *tzavaah*, must abstain on Rosh Chodesh Iyar as well. Some maintain that this custom is not relevant to this situation,[113] while others argue that the custom remains in force.[114]

6. Lag Baomer

Introduction: The 33rd day of *sefiras haomer* ("Lag Baomer") has the status of a semi-Yom Tov: *Tachanun* is omitted, haircuts and weddings are permitted, and certain dimensions of festivity are introduced into the day. There are several reasons for the significance of this day: It is variously identified as the day when the epidemic that took the lives of Rabi Akiva's students came to an end,[115] the day of the *yahrtzeit* of Rabi Shimon bar Yochai,[116] and the date when Rabi Akiva conferred *semichah* on his five remaining students, which ensured the continuation of the transmission of the Torah.[117] The halachos and customs that pertain to this day are discussed below.

1. **The Significance of Lag Baomer:** The 33rd day of *sefiras*

---

112. מ״ב סי׳ תצ״ג סק״ה.
113. דעת הגרמ״פ זצ״ל הוב״ד בס׳ בין פסח לשבועות פ״י סק״ח.
114. דעת הגריי״ק זצ״ל הוב״ד שם סק״ז.
115. מהרי״ל הוב״ד בדרכ״מ סי׳ תצ״ג סק״א. שו״ע ורמ״א סי׳ תצ״ג ס״ב. ועי׳ בפר״ח סי׳ תצ״ג ס״ב שהקשה שמחה זו למה ומה בכך שפסקו למות הרי לא נשאר מהם וכולם מתו ואפשר שהשמחה על התלמידים שהוסיף אח״כ.
116. חיי אדם כלל קל״א סי״א, ערוך השלחן סי׳ תצ״ג ס״ה, כף החיים סי׳ תצ״ג ס״ק כ״ו.
117. כה״ח שם.

haomer, which falls out on the 18ᵗʰ of Iyar, has the status of a festive semi-holiday (see introduction above) with certain specific halachos and customs. We commonly refer to this day as Lag Baomer, a reference to the fact that it is the 33ʳᵈ day of the *omer*, represented by the letter combination *lamed gimmel*.

2. **Tachanun:** *Tachanun* is omitted at *Shacharis* and *Minchah* on Lag Baomer,[118] as well as at *Minchah* on the day preceding Lag Baomer.[119]

3. **Allowing an *Avel* to Lead the Davening:** Even though *Tachanun* is omitted, it is technically permissible for an *avel* to serve as the *shaliach tzibbur* since *Hallel* is not recited.[120] Nevertheless, it is customary in many communities for an *avel* to refrain from leading the davening when *Tachanun* is not recited.

4. **Tzidkascha:** When Lag Baomer falls on Motzaei Shabbos, *Tzidkascha* is omitted at *Minchah* on Shabbos, as is the practice whenever *Tachanun* would be omitted on a weekday.[121]

5. **Lamnatzeiach and Kel Erech Apayim:** The practice of most Ashkenazim is to recite both the passage of *Lamnatzeiach* (*perek* 20 of *Tehillim*, which is recited at *Shacharis* between *Ashrei* and *Uva Letzion*) and *Kel Erech Apayim* (which is recited on Monday and Thursday before *Krias HaTorah*), even though *Tachanun* is omitted.[122] Sephardim omit *Lamnatzeiach* (and *Kel Erech Apayim*) on any day when *Tachanun* is not recited.[123] Some chassidim follow the practice of Sephardim.

6. **Fasting on a *Yahrtzeit* or Wedding Day:** It is prohibited to

---

118. רמ"א שם, וסי' קל"א ס"ו.
119. מ"ב סק"ט, וסי' קל"א ס"ק ל"ג.
120. מ"ב סי' תרע"א ס"ק מ"ד.
121. כמבואר בשו"ע סי' רצ"ב ס"ב.
122. רמ"א סי' קל"א ס"א וסי' תכ"ט ס"ב ומ"ב סי' קל"א ס"ק ל"ה. ועי' פמ"ג סי' תצ"ג א"א סק"ג.
123. פר"ח סי' קל"א ס"א.

fast on Lag Baomer, even for the *yahrtzeit* of a parent.[124] It is questionable whether a *chassan* and *kallah* should fast if it is the day of their *chuppah*.[125] One should consult a Rav if such a situation arises.

7. ***Tziduk Hadin, Hespedim,* and *Hakamas Matzeivah*:** We do not recite *tziduk hadin* for a *niftar* on Lag Baomer, unless the deceased was an *adam gadol*.[126] Likewise, *hespedim* (eulogies) are delivered only for an *adam gadol*.[127] A *hakamas matzeivah* should not take place on Lag Baomer because it is usually accompanied by a *hesped*.[128]

8. ***Sefiras Haomer* on Lag Baomer:** See Chapter One, section 2, paragraph 7, regarding what should be done if a person identifies the day as "Lag Baomer" in the daily count (i.e., he recites the words "*hayom Lag Baomer*," rather than stating the actual number of the day). See Chapter One, section 5, paragraph 9, regarding whether a person may recite the *brachah* on *sefiras haomer* if he has told someone else after *shekiah* that "today is Lag Baomer."

9. **Weddings:** Ashkenazic custom permits holding a wedding on Lag Baomer. (Sephardic custom permits weddings only on the 34th day of *sefirah*.) This is true even for those who observe the *sefirah* restrictions during the period following Lag Baomer.[129] Most authorities permit weddings only during the daytime on Lag Baomer and not during the previous night, even after nightfall.[130] Some authorities, however, rule that a wedding may

---

124. רמ"א סי' תקס"ח ס"ט.
125. עי' מ"ב סי' תקע"ג סק"ז. וראה הליכות שלמה פי"א סכ"ב.
126. רמ"א סי' ת"כ ס"ב ובמ"ב שם סק"ד.
127. עי' ביה"ל סי' תקמ"ז ס"ג ד"ה שמותר.
128. שו"ת מנחת יצחק ח"ג סי' נ"א-נ"ב ועי"ש שיש חולקים.
129. רמ"א סי' תצ"ג ס"א, ס"ב וס"ג וביה"ל שם ד"ה יש נוהגין.
130. רמ"א שם ס"ב ומ"ב ס"ק י"א.

Lag Baomer 69

be held even on the night of Lag Baomer.[131] (See above, section 5, paragraph 2.) If the need arises for a wedding to be held on the night of Lag Baomer (i.e., when it cannot take place during the day for technical reasons), one should consult a Rav. (Note: In many parts of the world, where the night begins very late at that time of year, it would be impractical to hold a wedding after nightfall on Lag Baomer in any event, due to the late hour.)

See section 5, paragraph 9, regarding whether a person who celebrates a wedding on Lag Baomer but still observes the *sefirah* restrictions after Lag Baomer must stop the music and dancing before nightfall.

10. **Haircuts and Shaving:** Ashkenazic custom permits taking a haircut and shaving on Lag Baomer even for those who continue observing the restrictions of *sefirah* after Lag Baomer.[132] (The Sephardic custom, however, is to refrain from these practices until the 34th day of the *omer*.) There are different opinions among the *poskim* regarding whether it is permissible to take a haircut on the night of Lag Baomer or only during the day.[133] A person who does not have an established custom should consult a Rav.

11. **Added Festivity:** It is customary to engage in added festivities on Lag Baomer because Rabi Akiva's students ceased to die and in honor of the *yahrtzeit* of Rabi Shimon bar Yochai.[134]

12. **Visiting Meron:** There is a *minhag* on Lag Baomer to visit the *kever* of Rabi Shimon bar Yochai and his son Rabi Elazar in Meron.[135] It should be noted, however, that some *poskim*

---

131. שו"ת אגר"מ או"ח ח"א סי' קנ"ט.
132. רמ"א שם ס"א, ס"ב וס"ג. ועי' ביה"ל שם. אמנם, עי' כה"ח שם ס"ק י"ג עפ"י האריז"ל.
133. עי' רמ"א שם ס"ב ובמ"ב ס"ק י"א.
134. רמ"א שם, חיי אדם כלל קל"א דין י"א, ערוה"ש שם ס"ה.
135. שע"ת סי' תקל"א סק"ז בשם פע"ח.

objected to transforming a visit to the *kever* of Rabi Shimon bar Yochai into a joyous occasion.[136]

13. **Lighting Candles or a Fire:** There is a custom to light candles or a fire in honor of the *yahrtzeit* of Rabi Shimon bar Yochai.[137]

14. **Cutting the Hair of a Three-Year-Old Boy ("*Upsheren*"):** For those who delay cutting a boy's hair until he is three years old, many have the custom to give the child his first haircut specifically on Lag Baomer.[138] There are different views as to whether (and for how much time) one should postpone the child's haircut after his birthday or cut his hair before the full three years have passed in order to observe this custom. A person should follow his family's custom, and in the absence of an established *minhag*, a Rav should be consulted.

7. Halachos Pertaining to *Tefillah* from Pesach to Shavuos

1. **Omitting *Mashiv Haruach U'morid Hageshem* at *Mussaf* on Pesach:** We discontinue the recitation of "*mashiv haruach u'morid hageshem*" during *Mussaf* on the first day of Pesach; the words are still recited at *Maariv* and *Shacharis*.[139] If a person erroneously omits these words in *Maariv* or *Shacharis* on the first day of Pesach, even if he does not insert the phrase "*morid hatal*," he has still fulfilled his obligation and is not obligated to repeat the *Shemoneh Esrei*.[140]

---

136. עי' שו"ת חת"ס יו"ד סי' רל"ג, ועי' שו"ת שו"מ מהדו"ה סי' ל"ט.
137. ס' ארץ ישראל להגרי"מ טוקצינסקי סי' י"ח ס"ג. וראה טעמי המנהגים אות תרי"ו ותר"יז.
138. שע"ת שם בשם פע"ח שכן נהג האריז"ל שהלך לקבר רשב"י ור"א בימים ההם לגלח בנו בשמחה ובמשתה.
139. שו"ע סי' קי"ד ס"א.
140. מ"ב סק"ג.

2. **Announcing the Omission of *Mashiv Haruach*:** Those who recite the words "*morid hatal*" in the *Shemoneh Esrei* during the summer (which is generally the practice of *nusach* Sephard, as well as *nusach* Ashkenaz in Eretz Yisrael) should announce the words "*morid hatal*" before the silent *Shemoneh Esrei* of *Mussaf*. When this is done, the congregants should omit the words "*mashiv haruach u'morid hageshem*" in their silent *Shemoneh Esrei*, and instead recite the phrase "*morid hatal*." Those who do not recite the words "*morid hatal*" in the summer months (which is the general practice of *nusach* Ashkenaz outside Eretz Yisrael) do not have the option of announcing before *Mussaf* that the congregation should recite "*morid hatal*"; however, it is also not appropriate for them to announce that the recitation of "*mashiv haruach u'morid hageshem*" should cease, since one should never state that a blessing (i.e., the rain) should stop. Therefore, in such communities the congregation should recite the words "*mashiv haruach u'morid hageshem*" in the silent *Shemoneh Esrei* at *Mussaf*, but the passage should be omitted by the *shaliach tzibbur* in his repetition of the *Shemoneh Esrei*. This omission by the *shaliach tzibbur* is essentially a signal to the congregation to cease reciting the phrase in their subsequent *tefillos*.[141] A person should follow the custom of the congregation with which he is davening.

3. ***Tefillas Tal*:** There are different customs as to whether *Tefillas Tal* is recited before the silent *Shemoneh Esrei* or before *chazaras hashatz*. In congregations in which the words "*morid hatal*" are recited in the silent *Shemoneh Esrei* at *Mussaf*, it is customary to recite *Tefillas Tal* before the silent *Shemoneh Esrei*.[142]

---

141. רמ"א שם ס"ג, מ"ב סק"ג.
142. עי' שו"ת הר צבי ח"א סי' נ"ה וארחות רבינו ח"א עמוד ס"ג.

4. **An Individual Who Davens Late:** In a congregation in which the practice is for *"mashiv haruach u'morid hageshem"* to be recited in the silent *Shemoneh Esrei* of *Mussaf*, if an individual begins his silent *Mussaf* after the *shaliach tzibbur* has begun his repetition and has omitted the phrase, the individual should follow suit and refrain from including it in his silent *Mussaf*. If a person is davening at home and is uncertain whether the *shaliach tzibbur* has already reached that point in his repetition in shul, he should omit the words.[143]

5. **The Custom to Recite "*Morid Hatal*":** It is the custom among those who follow *nusach* Sephard to insert the words *"morid hatal"* in the *Shemoneh Esrei* during the summer months. Among those who follow *nusach* Ashkenaz, there are divergent *minhagim*. The Rema states that the Ashkenazic custom is not to recite the words;[144] however, many people nonetheless have an established custom to recite this phrase, especially in Eretz Yisrael. Although a person who omits the words *"morid hageshem"* in the *Shemoneh Esrei* during the winter has not fulfilled his obligation, a person who customarily recites the phrase *"morid hatal"* in the summer need not repeat the *Shemoneh Esrei* if he omits it, as long as he did not recite the words *"morid hageshem"* in its place.[145]

6. **If "*Mashiv Haruach U'morid Hageshem*" Is Erroneously Recited:** If a person erroneously recites the words *"morid hageshem"* in any *Shemoneh Esrei* after *Mussaf* of the first day of Pesach, he must return to the beginning of the *brachah* and recite it correctly. If he returns to the words *"rav lehoshia"* and then concludes the *brachah* correctly, he is *yotzei b'dieved*.[146]

---

143. מ"ב ס"ק ט"ז.
144. רמ"א שם. וראה שעה"צ ס"ק ט"ז.
145. שו"ע שם ס"ג.
146. מ"ב ס"ק י"ט.

If he realizes his error only after concluding the *brachah*, he must return to the beginning of the *Shemoneh Esrei*.[147]

7. **Realizing an Error during the *Brachah*'s Conclusion:** In the above case, if the person realizes his mistake immediately after he has recited the Name of Hashem at the conclusion of the *brachah*, he should say the words *"lamdeini chukecha"* and return to the beginning of the *brachah*. If he has already recited the word *"mechayeh,"* he must return to the beginning of the *Shemoneh Esrei* instead.[148]

8. **Omitting *"Hashem Sefasai Tiftach"* in a Repetition of the *Shemoneh Esrei*:** When a person makes an error that requires him to return to the beginning of the *Shemoneh Esrei*, he need not repeat the line beginning *"Hashem sefasai tiftach,"* which introduces the *Shemoneh Esrei*.[149] Some *poskim* maintain that this line is omitted only if he realized his error in the middle of his previous *Shemoneh Esrei*; however, if a person realizes his error after completing the *Shemoneh Esrei* in its entirety, he should repeat the passage of *"Hashem sefasai tiftach"* when he begins the *Shemoneh Esrei* anew.[150]

9. **A Country Where Rain Is Needed after Pesach:** Even in countries where rain is needed after Pesach, a person who erroneously recites the words *"morid hageshem"* must return to the beginning of the *Shemoneh Esrei*.[151] When a person is required to repeat *Shemoneh Esrei* for this reason in such a locale, he should have in mind that it should be considered a *tefillas nedavah*.[152] Even in countries in the southern hemisphere such as Australia, where the seasons

---

147. שו"ע שם ס"ד.
148. מ"ב סק"כ.
149. מ"ב ס"ק כ"א.
150. שו"ת אגר"מ ח"ה סי' כ"ד אות ח', הגרח"ק שליט"א באשי ישראל שאילה קס"ט.
151. שו"ע שם, ועי' ביה"ל ד"ה ואפילו.
152. ביה"ל שם.

are the opposite of those in the northern hemisphere and the winter begins after Pesach, many authorities maintain that the recitation of "*morid hageshem*" should be discontinued on Pesach as it is in the north.[153] Most communities have an established practice in this regard, and one should follow the local *minhag*.

10. **Correcting an Error *Toch K'dei Dibbur*:** According to many *poskim*, a person who erroneously recites "*morid hageshem*" must return to the beginning of the *brachah* even if he has corrected his error within the span of *toch k'dei dibbur*, since the incorrect recitation still stands.[154] Some authorities disagree and maintain that he is not required to repeat the *brachah*.[155]

11. **If a Person Is Uncertain if He Has Erred:** If a person is uncertain if he erroneously recited "*morid hageshem*" after the first day of Pesach, it is assumed that he has maintained his previous habit until 30 days have elapsed since the change was implemented. After 30 days have elapsed, it can be presumed that he has grown accustomed to the new form of the *Shemoneh Esrei*. Therefore, within 30 days of the first day of Pesach, a person who is in this situation is required to repeat the *Shemoneh Esrei*; after 30 days have elapsed, he can assume that he has davened correctly.[156] Even within the first 30 days, if a person is unsure if he omitted the phrase "*mashiv haruach u'morid hageshem*" but knows that he has already davened correctly 90 times, he should not repeat the *Shemoneh Esrei*,

---

153. עי' שו"ת הר צבי ח"א סי' נ"ו, שו"ת מנחת יצחק ח"ו סי' קע"א, אור לציון ח"ב פ"ז אות ל', תשובות והנהגות ח"א סי' צ"ח. ומאידך בשו"ת שבט הלוי ח"א סי' כ"א וח"ג סי' צ"א נקט להפוך הזמנים.
154. הליכות שלמה תפילה פ"ח סי"ג, אור לציון פ"ז אות כ"ט, שו"ת שבה"ל ח"ו סי' ט"ו ושכן מוכח מהרמ"א שם ס"ד. ועי' תשובות והנהגות ח"ב סי' מ"ב.
155. דעת הגריש"א זצ"ל הובא באשי ישראל פכ"ג ס"ק ק"ח.
156. שו"ע שם ס"ח.

since some authorities maintain that it is the recitation of 90 *tefillos*, rather than the passage of 30 days, that establishes a new habit.[157]

12. **If a Person Has Omitted a *Tefillah*:** The presumption that one has davened correctly does not take effect unless one has davened every *tefillah*. If a person has missed a *tefillah* and then finds himself in a position of uncertainty, many *poskim* maintain that he cannot rely on this presumption unless an additional *tefillah* was davened to compensate for the missed *tefillah*.[158] A Rav should be consulted for a final ruling. If a person erred during this time but repeated the *Shemoneh Esrei* to correct his error, the passage of 30 days or 90 *tefillos* will still be sufficient to establish this presumption.[159]

13. **If an Uncertainty Arises after Davening Has Ended:** If a person knows that he intended to omit the phrase "*mashiv haruach u'morid hageshem*" when he first began the *Shemoneh Esrei*, but he becomes uncertain afterward if he davened correctly, the halachah will depend on when the uncertainty arose. If he became uncertain as soon as he finished, he must repeat *Shemoneh Esrei*; however, if the uncertainty arose only a while later, he may presume that he davened correctly even if it is still within the first 30 days after Pesach.[160]

14. **A Strategy to Avoid Repeating *Shemoneh Esrei* in a Case of Uncertainty:** To avoid being required to repeat the *Shemoneh Esrei* in a case of uncertainty, one may simply recite the words "*mechayeh meisim Atah rav lehoshia, morid hatal*" a full 90 times. Once this has been done, a person is entitled to presume that he has established the habit of omitting the words "*mashiv*

---

157. עי' מ"ב ס"ק ל"ז.
158. עי' מ"ב שם, שהרבה אחרונים מפקפקים בדברי הט"ז. ומ"מ השו"ע הרב ס"י פסק כהט"ז, וראה גם כה"ח סק"נ.
159. הליכות שלמה פ"ח הערה 94, ורק צריך להוסיף על מנין צ' פעמים.
160. מ"ב ס"ק ל"ח.

haruach u'morid hageshem."¹⁶¹ For those who do not say "*morid hatal*," it is questionable whether it is sufficient to recite the words "*mechayeh meisim Atah rav lehoshia mechalkel chaim*" (i.e., the words of the *brachah* without the insertion of "*mashiv haruach u'morid hageshem*") 90 times.¹⁶²

15. **Omitting "*Vesein Tal U'matar Livrachah*" on Pesach:** At *Maariv* on the first night of Chol Hamoed Pesach, the recitation of "*vesein tal u'matar livrachah*" in the weekday *Shemoneh Esrei* is likewise discontinued.¹⁶³ Nevertheless, an announcement should not be made for the congregation to recite the words "*vesein brachah*," since that would imply that we do not desire rain.¹⁶⁴

16. **A Drought after Pesach:** In a country where rain is needed after Pesach, even if it is experiencing a drought, the phrase "*vesein tal u'matar*" is not recited in the *brachah* of *barech aleinu*. Instead, it should be included in the *brachah* of *shema koleinu*.¹⁶⁵

17. **"*Vesein Tal U'matar*" in the Summer Months:** If a person erroneously includes the words "*vesein tal u'matar*" in the *Shemoneh Esrei*, the halachah varies based on when he realizes his error. If he realizes it only after he has finished the *Shemoneh Esrei*, meaning that he has already recited the passage of "*yiheyu leratzon*" at the conclusion of *Elokai netzor*, even if he has not yet taken the three steps backward at the conclusion of the *Shemoneh Esrei*, he must repeat the entire *Shemoneh Esrei*. If he has not yet recited that passage, he should return to the *brachah* of *barech aleinu*. If he realizes his error before concluding the *brachah* of *barech aleinu*, he

---

161. שו"ע ס"ט. ולכתחילה יש לאמרה ק"א פעמים, מ"ב ס"ק מ"א בשם החת"ס.
162. רמ"א ס"ט, מ"ב ס"ק מ"ג.
163. שו"ע סי' קי"ז ס"א.
164. מ"ב סי' תפ"ח ס"ק י"ב.
165. שו"ע סי' קי"ז ס"ב.

should return to the beginning of the *brachah*.¹⁶⁶ If he realizes his error immediately after reciting the Name of Hashem, he should say the words "*lamdeini chukecha*" and return to the beginning of the *brachah*.¹⁶⁷

18. **Correcting the Error *Toch K'dei Dibbur*:** If a person recites the words "*vesein tal u'matar*" and then immediately corrects himself by saying the words "*vesein brachah*" within the span of *toch k'dei dibbur*, he is *yotzei* and may continue the *Shemoneh Esrei*. If a person does not correct this error within the span of *toch k'dei dibbur*, he must return to the beginning of the *brachah*. Nevertheless, *b'dieved*, if a person merely returned to the words "*vesein brachah*" instead of repeating the *brachah* from the beginning, he was *yotzei*.¹⁶⁸

19. ***Av Harachamim*:** In general, the Ashkenazic custom is to recite the *tefillah* of *Av Harachamim* on Shabbos before *Mussaf*, except on *Shabbos Mevarchim* or on a day when *Tachanun* would be omitted if it were a weekday. Nevertheless, since *Av Harachamim* was composed in response to the many terrible massacres that occurred during the *sefirah* period in the year 4856 (1096), it is recited during *sefirah*¹⁶⁹ even on *Shabbos Mevarchim* of the month of Sivan and even on a Shabbos when a *bris* takes place.¹⁷⁰

20. **When Rosh Chodesh Iyar Falls on Shabbos:** When Rosh Chodesh Iyar falls on Shabbos, *Av Harachamim* is omitted.¹⁷¹ There are divergent customs regarding whether the *tefillah* should be recited on the *Shabbos Mevarchim* prior to Rosh

---

166. שו"ע שם ס"ג ומ"ב ס"ק י"ד.
167. חיי אדם כלל כ"ד סי"ד.
168. ביה"ל שם ס"ג ד"ה אם שאל.
169. רמ"א סי' רפ"ד ס"ז, ובמ"ב שם ס"ק י"ח.
170. במ"ב ס"ק י"ח עפ"י המ"א. אמנם, להנוהגים עפ"י הגר"א א"א כדאיתא במעשה רב אות קל"ח והובא בלוח א"י.
171. שם.

Chodesh Iyar. A person should follow the custom of his congregation.

21. **Kel Malei Rachamim:** *Hazkaras neshamos* (*Kel Malei Rachamim*) is not recited on *Shabbos Mevarchim* even during the period of *sefirah*.[172]

22. **Pirkei Avos:** It is customary to recite *Pirkei Avos* after *Minchah* every Shabbos during this time of the year, from the Shabbos after Pesach through the Shabbos prior to Rosh Hashanah.[173] (Many Sephardim have the *minhag* to recite *Pirkei Avos* only until Shavuos.) When Shavuos coincides with Shabbos, *Pirkei Avos* is not recited; when Shavuos falls on Motzaei Shabbos, it is recited as usual on the previous day.[174] The general custom is to recite one *perek* on each Shabbos.[175]

23. **Disparities in the *Parshas Hashavua* between Eretz Yisrael and Other Countries:** When the 22nd day of Nissan falls on Shabbos, it is Isru Chag in Eretz Yisrael and the regular *parshas hashavua* (either *Parshas Shemini* or, during a leap year, *Parshas Acharei Mos*) is read; however, in *chutz la'Aretz* this Shabbos is the eighth day of Pesach and the Torah reading for Yom Tov is read instead. This results in a discrepancy between the *parshas hashavua* that is read in Eretz Yisrael and that which is read in *chutz la'Aretz*, which continues over the following weeks until the *parshiyos* of *Behar* and *Bechukosai*. (These *parshiyos* are split over two weeks in Eretz Yisrael while they are read on a single Shabbos in other countries, so that the *parshiyos* become synchronized again on the following week.) In a leap year, the weekly Torah readings remain out of sync until the *parshiyos* of *Mattos* and *Masei*.

---

172. מ״ב שם ס״ק י״ז.
173. רמ״א סי׳ רצ״ב ס״ב. ועי׳ בלבוש סי׳ תצ״ג ס״ד הטעם משום שיש תוכחה ומוסר וזה הכנה לקבלת התורה.
174. מ״ב סי׳ תצ״ד ס״ק י״ז.
175. כף החיים סי׳ רצ״ב ס״ק כ״ג.

24. **Traveling between Eretz Yisrael and *Chutz La'Aretz* during These Weeks:** A resident of *chutz la'Aretz* who is visiting Eretz Yisrael or a resident of Eretz Yisrael who is visiting *chutz la'Aretz* may receive an *aliyah* and serve as *baal korei* even though the *parshas hashavua* is different in their respective places of residence.[176] Regarding the mitzvah of *shenayim mikra v'echad targum*, a *ben Eretz Yisrael* who is visiting *chutz la'Aretz* is not required to repeat the *parshah* that he read on the previous week, while a *ben chutz la'Aretz* who is visiting Eretz Yisrael should recite *shenayim mikra v'echad targum* for both *parshiyos*. When he returns to *chutz la'Aretz*, he will not be required to repeat the *parshah* that he read in Eretz Yisrael.

25. **Compensating for a Missed *Parshah*:** A *minyan* of *bnei chutz la'Aretz* who are temporarily residing in Eretz Yisrael should compensate for the *parshah* they miss (i.e., the *parshah* read in Eretz Yisrael on the 22nd of Nissan, which they observed as the eighth day of Pesach) by reading the entirety of that *parshah* during the first *aliyah* on the following Shabbos, along with three *pesukim* from the *parshah* of the week. Alternatively, at *Minchah* on the Shabbos of the eighth day of Pesach, some continue *leining* until the end of the *parshah* during the third *aliyah* of the Torah reading. (This situation is common in yeshivos for students from outside Eretz Yisrael or communities with young couples from *chutz la'Aretz* temporarily residing in Eretz Yisrael.) An individual visiting Eretz Yisrael for a Shabbos when the *parshiyos* are not synchronized is not obligated to hear the *parshah* read in *chutz la'Aretz*. Rather, he listens to the *parshah* that is read where he davens.

26. **The Fasts of Behab:** There is a *minhag* to fast on the first or second Monday of Iyar (see paragraph 27 below), followed

---

176. יו״ט שני כהלכתו פ״ט סט״ז בשם הגרשז״א זצ״ל.

by the Thursday of the same week and then the subsequent Monday, in order to atone for any transgressions committed over Pesach. These days are commonly known as בה״ב (pronounced "Behab"), an acronym that represents the respective days of the week on which it is observed. (The letter *beis* represents Monday, the second day of the week, while the *heh* represents Thursday, the fifth day of the week. Thus, "Behab" indicates that the fasts are observed on a Monday, a Thursday, and another Monday.) These fasts are not observed immediately after Pesach because fasting is prohibited during the month of Nissan.[177]

27. **Reciting *Mi Shebeirach* for Those Who Fast:** It is customary to recite a *mi shebeirach* in shul after *Krias HaTorah* on the Shabbos before the first day of Behab, for those who take it upon themselves to fast.[178] (If there is a *bris milah* or an *aufruf*, then the *mi shebeirach* is recited at *Minchah*.[179])

When Rosh Chodesh falls on Shabbos, the *mi shebeirach* is recited on the following Shabbos and thus the fasts of Behab begin two days after that, on the second Monday of the month and not the first.[180]

28. **Accepting the Fasts of Behab:** A person who wishes to observe the fasts of Behab must accept the fast at *Minchah* on the day before, since the fast does not have the status of a *taanis tzibbur*. However, responding *amen* to the *mi shebeirach* with the intention to fast is also considered an acceptance of the fast, with a notable difference: A person who accepts the fast verbally must perform *hataras nedarim* if he wishes to renege on his commitment to fast, whereas a person who

---

177. טור ושו״ע סי׳ תצ״ב.
178. מ״ב סי׳ תצ״ב סק״ג.
179. שם. מיהו עי׳ שו״ת אגר״מ או״ח ח״א סי׳ ק״ו שבמקומינו שאין מפטירין לחתן שוש אשיש אומרים המי שברך בשחרית.
180. פמ״ג סי׳ תצ״ב מ״ז סק״א, ושערי אפרים שער י׳ סמ״ו.

accepts it by responding *amen* to the *mi shebeirach* is not required to do so.[181]

29. **Selichos** and **Reading "Vayechal"**: Some congregations recite *Selichos* on the days of Behab.[182] *Selichos* may be recited even if there are not ten men in the congregation who are fasting.[183] However, the portion of "*Vayechal*" may not be read from the Torah at *Shacharis* and *Minchah* unless there are ten people who are fasting.[184] Nowadays, when most people do not observe the fast, the passage of "*Vayechal*" is read only at *Minchah* (if ten people are fasting) even if ten people who are fasting are present at *Shacharis*.[185]

30. **Aneinu**: If ten people are fasting, the *shaliach tzibbur* should recite the passage of "*aneinu*" in *chazaras hashatz* after he concludes the *brachah* of *goel Yisrael*.[186] Those who are fasting should recite *aneinu* in the *brachah* of *shomea tefillah* at *Minchah*, as on an ordinary fast day.

31. **A Seudas Mitzvah**: If a *bris, pidyon haben*, or other *seudas mitzvah* takes place on one of the days of Behab, even a person who always observes the fast may eat at the *seudah*. There is no need to perform *hataras nedarim* for this purpose.[187] (However, a person who accepted the fast verbally at *Minchah* on the preceding day might be obligated to perform *hataras nedarim*.[188]) If a person feels unwell during the fast and wishes

---

181. מ"ב שם. מיהו יש מחמירים בזה עי' מ"ב סי' תקס"ב ס"ק ל"ט. ועי' בביה"ל שם ס"ב ד"ה שרגיל.
182. שו"ע סי' תקס"ו ס"ד ובמ"ב סי' תצ"ב שם.
183. מ"ב סי' תצ"ב סק"ה.
184. רמ"א סי' תצ"ב ובמ"ב סק"ו. אמנם עי' מ"ב סי' תקס"ו סק"י שבזמננו שרק יחידים מתענים יקראו בשחרית פרשת השבוע ורק במנחה יקראו ויחל.
185. מ"ב סי' תקס"ו סק"י וערוה"ש סי' תקס"ו ס"ד.
186. מ"ב שם סק"ט.
187. מ"ב סי' תצ"ב סק"ה.
188. עי' מ"ב סי' תקס"ח ס"ק כ"א.

to eat, he must first perform *hataras nedarim*.[189] Even if a person knows that he will attend a *seudas mitzvah*, he is not permitted to break his fast prior to the *seudah*, but he may continue eating after it has concluded.[190]

32. **Pesach Sheni:** The 14th day of Iyar is known as Pesach Sheni. In the era of the *Beis Hamikdash*, a person who was unable to offer the *korban Pesach* on the 14th day of Nissan (because he was ritually impure or far away from Yerushalayim) was obligated to bring the *korban* on the 14th day of Iyar.[191] The *minhag* in most congregations is to omit *Tachanun* on this day.[192] However, *Tachanun* is recited at *Minchah* on the previous day.[193]

When Pesach Sheni falls on a Behab fast day, some congregations omit *Selichos* and *Avinu Malkeinu*.[194]

33. **Reciting *Lamnatzeiach* and *Kel Erech Apayim* on Pesach Sheni:** On Pesach Sheni, *Lamnatzeiach* is recited between *Ashrei* and *Uva Letzion*. The *tefillah* of *Kel Erech Apayim* is likewise recited before the Torah reading if it is a Monday. See paragraph 36 below.

34. **Eating Matzah:** Many people have the custom to eat some matzah on Pesach Sheni.[195]

---

189. שעה״צ סי׳ תצ״ב סק״ז.
190. מ״ב סי׳ תקס״ח ס״ק י״ח.
191. במדבר ט׳, ט׳-י״ב. פסחים דף צ״ג.
192. שע״ת סי׳ קל״א ס״ק י״ט, שערי אפרים שער י׳ סכ״ז, ערוך השלחן סי׳ קל״א סי״ב, כף החיים סי׳ קל״א ס״ק צ״ט. אמנם אי אמירת תחנון בפסח שני לא הובא בטור שו״ע רמ״א ומ״ב. ומפורש בפמ״ג סי׳ קל״א מ״ז ס״ק ט״ו שאומרים תחנון. והנהגת החזו״א היה לאמר כמו שהובא בכמה ספרים.
193. הליכות שלמה פי״א ס״ק כ״ט.
194. שם ס״ר. ויש שאומרים סליחות אבל מקצרים ויש שאומרים סליחות מלא ורק שלא מתענים.
195. עי׳ שו״ת רבבות אפרים או״ח ח״ג סי׳ של״א. ועי״ש ח״ב סי׳ קכ״ט אות ל״ט על מנהג החסידות לאכול מצה בליל ט״ו אייר.

35. **Hespedim**: *Hespedim* (eulogies) should not be delivered on Pesach Sheni.[196]

36. ***Tachanun* in the Month of Sivan:** *Tachanun* is omitted on every day from Rosh Chodesh Sivan through the day after Shavuos.[197] (In some congregations, it is omitted throughout the six days following Shavuos as well.) This is considered a festive period because Moshe Rabbeinu instructed Klal Yisrael on the second day of Sivan to prepare for *Kabbalas haTorah*, and the *Shloshes Yemei Hagbalah* begin on the third day of Sivan.[198] However, *Lamnatzeiach* is still recited between *Ashrei* and *Uva Letzion*, and the *tefillah* of *Kel Erech Apayim* is recited before the Torah reading (except in congregations where these *tefillos* are customarily omitted whenever *Tachanun* is not recited).[199]

37. **Fasting during Sivan:** Fasting is prohibited from Rosh Chodesh Sivan until Isru Chag of Shavuos.[200]

---

196. שערי אפרים שער י׳ סי׳ ז׳.
197. רמ״א סי׳ תצ״ד ס״ג.
198. מ״ב סי׳ תצ״ד סק״ח.
199. כמבואר ברמ״א סי׳ תכ״ט ס״ב ובמ״ב שם סק״ח.
200. שו״ע סי׳ תצ״ד ס״ג ובמ״ב סק״ו-ז׳.

CHAPTER THREE

The Halachos of *Chadash*

❦

1. What Is *Chadash*?
2. *Chadash* in *Chutz La'Aretz*
3. Applications of *Chadash* Today

CHAPTER THREE

The Halachos of *Chadash*

Introduction: It is prohibited *mid'oraisa* to consume any of the five species of grain from the new year's crop until the *korban omer* has been offered on the 16th of Nissan. Any grain that took root after the 16th of Nissan is considered *"chadash"* (new grain) and is prohibited for consumption until the 16th of Nissan of the following year. Grain that took root prior to the 16th of Nissan is considered *"yashan"* (old grain), as it is rendered permissible by the current year's *korban* even if it was harvested long after Pesach.[1] In contemporary times, since the *Beis Hamikdash* has been destroyed and we can no longer offer the *korban omer*, the prohibition of *chadash* remains in effect until the conclusion of the 16th day of Nissan.[2] In *chutz la'Aretz*, the prohibition ends only after the 17th of Nissan. There is a dispute among the halachic authorities regarding whether the prohibition is still *d'oraisa* or it has been reduced to the level of *d'rabbanan*. The final halachah is to rule that the prohibition of *chadash* is considered *d'oraisa* even today; however, the opinions that view it as *d'rabbanan* may be combined with other factors to permit leniency in certain cases, as will be explained below.

1. ויקרא כ"ג, י"ד. מתני' מנחות דף ע.
2. מתני' מנחות דף סח. ובסוכה דף מא.

Introduction ~ 87

1. What Is *Chadash*?

1. **The Prohibition of *Chadash*:** Any of the five species of grain (wheat, barley, spelt, oats, or rye) that took root after the 16th of Nissan are forbidden for consumption until after the 16th of Nissan of the following year. This prohibition still applies today, when we no longer offer the *korban omer*. In the era of the *Beis Hamikdash*, when the *korban omer* was offered on the 16th of Nissan, the new grain became permissible immediately after the *korban* was brought. Today, however, the prohibition remains in effect until the conclusion of the day. In *chutz la'Aretz*, where the 16th of Nissan is observed as Yom Tov Sheni, the grain is prohibited until the conclusion of the 17th day of Nissan.[3] This prohibition is known as "*chadash*," which refers to the new crop. When the grain becomes permitted at the beginning of the 17th or 18th of Nissan, it is referred to as "*yashan*," or the old crop.

These halachos do not pertain to other grains such as corn, rice, buckwheat, and the like.

2. **The Determining Factor:** The status of *chadash* or *yashan* is determined by the date when the crop takes root, not when it is planted or harvested. Any grain that takes root prior to the 16th of Nissan will become permitted and will be considered *yashan* even if it continues to grow and is harvested much later. On the other hand, grain that is planted before the 16th of Nissan but does not take root until afterward will be prohibited for consumption until the following Pesach.[4] Therefore, all grain must be planted at least two weeks before

---

3. שו"ע או"ח סי' תפ"ט ס"י וביו"ד סי' רצ"ג ס"א. ובענין אם איסור קצירת תבואה לפני ט"ז נוהג בזה"ז עי' שו"ת שבט הלוי ח"ח סי' רל"א.

4. מתני' מנחות דף ע:, טור ושו"ע יו"ד סי' רצ"ג ס"ג.

the 16th of Nissan in order to allow it to take root in time to be considered *yashan*.[5]

3. **Grain of Unknown Status:** When it cannot be determined when a particular crop was planted, the *poskim* permit the consumption of the grain on the basis of a *sfek sfeika* (a twofold uncertainty): The grain might be from the previous year's crop, and even if it is from the current crop, it is possible that it took root prior to the 16th of Nissan.[6] However, if the majority of a crop is usually planted after Pesach (as is common with barley and oats), this leniency does not apply.[7] Of course, if a product is purchased before the harvest season, one can be certain that the grain is from the previous year's crop. See section 2 below regarding other possible leniencies. It should be noted that the aforementioned leniency of *safek* is not common nowadays, since kashrus agencies can usually determine and provide the source information of products containing grain. (An individual's lack of knowledge does not constitute a *safek* if he can simply make a phone call and find out.)

4. **Grain as a Minority Ingredient:** The prohibition of *chadash* applies to any food containing any of the five species of grain. Even a food that contains grain as a minority ingredient is prohibited. This is true even if the grain is less than one sixtieth of the volume of the entire food.[8]

5. **Utensils Used for Cooking or Baking *Chadash*:** Any food that is considered *chadash* and that was cooked or baked in a utensil is viewed as having imparted flavor to the utensil,

---

5. דלא כש"ך סי' רצ"ג סק"ב שכתב ג' ימים, עי' נקודות הכסף שם ובחי' רע"א על הש"ך שם ובשו"ת נודע ביהודה מהדו"ק יו"ד סי' פ"ז. ובשעת הדחק יש לסמוך על ג' ימים, עי' שו"ת מנחת יצחק ח"ו סי' מ"ג. אמנם לחומרא נקטינן כשיעור ג' ימים, ראה מ"ב סי' של"ו ס"ק ל"ג. ועי' שו"ת שבט הלוי ח"ז סי' צ"ד אות ו'.

6. רמ"א יו"ד סי' רצ"ג ס"ג. ועי' חי' רע"א שם שתמה דשם ספק חד הוא.

7. רמ"א שם ובש"ך שם סק"ג ובמ"ב סי' תצ"ג ס"ק מ"ה.

8. ט"ז יו"ד סי' רצ"ג סק"א משום דהוא דבר שיש לו מתירין ולפעמים אף משום מעמיד.

What Is Chadash? 89

which therefore takes on the prohibited status of *chadash*. If the food was not known definitely to be *chadash*, one may use the vessel for other foods without kashering it. Furthermore, even if the food was definitely *chadash*, one may use the vessel after 24 hours have elapsed even without kashering it, due to the other reasons for leniency that are customarily taken into account, which will be explained below.[9] In any event, after the 17th of Nissan, when all grain from the new year's crop becomes permitted, any utensils that have absorbed the flavor of *chadash* likewise become permitted.[10]

2. *Chadash* in *Chutz La'Aretz*

Introduction: There is a dispute among the *Tannaim* regarding whether *chadash* is prohibited on a *d'oraisa* level or only on a *d'rabbanan* level outside Eretz Yisrael.[11] The *Amoraim* debate this matter further, but the final ruling is that the prohibition is considered *d'oraisa* even in *chutz la'Aretz*.[12] Nevertheless, since some authorities consider the prohibition in *chutz la'Aretz* to be only rabbinic in nature, and other authorities maintain that the prohibition was reduced to a rabbinic level even in Eretz Yisrael after the destruction of the *Beis Hamikdash*, these opinions may sometimes be combined with other lenient factors to permit the consumption of *chadash*, as will be explained below. Furthermore, although the halachah is that the prohibition of *chadash* applies equally to grain belonging to Jews and non-Jews alike, there is a dissenting view that maintains that the prohibition does not apply to grain acquired from a non-Jew. This view is likewise sometimes

---

9. מ"ב סי' תפ"ט ס"ק מ"ח.
10. שו"ת שבט הלוי ח"י סי' קפ"ג אות ב'.
11. מתני' קידושין דף לו: ולז., ערלה פ"ג מ"ט.
12. מנחות דף סח:.

combined with other factors to permit the consumption of *chadash*, as will be explained.

1. **The Prohibition in *Chutz La'Aretz*:** The prohibition of *chadash* applies even to grain grown outside Eretz Yisrael.[13] The prevalent view is that the prohibition is *d'oraisa* even in *chutz la'Aretz*.[14]

2. **Proximity to Eretz Yisrael:** Some authorities maintain that the prohibition of *chadash* in *chutz la'Aretz* applies only in places that are in close proximity to Eretz Yisrael.[15] However, the majority of *poskim* disagree with this ruling.[16]

3. **Grain Belonging to a Non-Jew:** According to one opinion, the prohibition of *chadash* does not apply to grain that belongs to a non-Jew.[17] Nevertheless, the accepted ruling is to prohibit all new grain, regardless of who has owned it.[18]

4. **Defending the Lenient Practice:** In previous years, the common practice in Europe was to adopt a lenient approach to the laws of *chadash*. Earlier *poskim* explain that it was extremely difficult to obtain *yashan* flour in Europe for many years, and bread and grain foods were a staple of the people's diet and their primary beverage was beer, which is made from grain. Therefore, it was considered a *shaas hadchak* (a time of extenuating circumstances), which justified relying on the minority opinions that the prohibition does not apply in *chutz la'Aretz*, or at least in areas far from Eretz Yisrael, or to

---

13. שו"ע או"ח סי' תפ"ט ס"י ויו"ד סי' רצ"ג ס"ב.
14. עי' ביה"ל סי' תפ"ט ס"י ד"ה אף בזמן הזה.
15. שיטת רבינו ברוך (הובא בשו"ת הרא"ש כלל ב' ס"א). ועי' מ"א סוסי' תפ"ט.
16. עי' ביה"ל שם.
17. כן נקט הב"ח יו"ד סי' רצ"ג להלכה הובא בט"ז יו"ד סי' רצ"ג סק"ב ובש"ך שם סק"ו. וראה שו"ת בית הלוי ח"ג סי' נ"ב.
18. שו"ע יו"ד סי' רצ"ג ס"ב. ועי' בט"ז שם וסק"ד וש"ך שם, ובביאור הגר"א סק"ב. (וראה ערוך השלחן סי' רצ"ג סי"ג-ט"ו שיש צד לומר שהוא רק מדרבנן.)

grain that belongs to a non-Jew.[19] Since the majority of *poskim* dispute these opinions, it is preferable not to rely on these considerations. This is merely an explanation that justifies the lenient approach adopted by many communities, and one need not object against those who practice this leniency.[20]

5. **The Situation in America Today:** For many decades, the aforementioned justification for leniency has not been applicable in North America. Today, *yashan* flour and grain products are generally obtainable in abundance. Although the halachos of *chadash* were almost unheard of in North America in the post-war era, this was not due to the arguments for leniency discussed in the previous paragraph. Rather, it was because there was always a surplus of wheat, and therefore all flour on the market could be assumed to be *yashan*. In recent decades, however, they began selling surplus wheat to other countries rather than storing it, which gave rise to the real possibility that wheat products on the market might be *chadash*. Consequently, it is difficult to justify relying on the lenient approach today. Indeed, many companies, bakeries, and stores ensure that their products are made with *yashan* ingredients. Nevertheless, most kashrus organizations still do not require the products they certify to adhere to the halachos of *chadash*. Therefore, a *hechsher* does not signify that a product is *yashan* unless it is specifically indicated as such. See section 3 below for practical considerations.

6. ***Chadash* in Eretz Yisrael:** In Eretz Yisrael, none of the lenient arguments cited above are applicable. Consequently, *chadash* is definitely prohibited for consumption. Nevertheless, the issue is less relevant in Eretz Yisrael, since the planting season for grain is in the winter and all grain is therefore typically

---

19. עי' ט"ז יו"ד סי' רצ"ג סק"ד. אמנם בנקודות הכסף שם ודגו"מ שם תמהו עליו.
20. מ"ב סי' תפ"ט ס"ק מ"ה ובביה"ל שם ד"ה אף.

yashan by the time it is harvested. However, any flour or other grain products imported to Eretz Yisrael may be *chadash* and subject to the restrictions above. On a practical note, any products or establishments bearing a reputable *hechsher* in Eretz Yisrael are certified for *chadash* as well.

3. Applications of *Chadash* Today

Introduction: It was explained in the previous sections that the laws of *chadash* apply today even in *chutz la'Aretz* and even to grain that belongs to non-Jews. The leniencies that were relied upon in previous generations due to extenuating circumstances cannot be applied today. Furthermore, we can no longer presume grain in America to be *yashan*. In Eretz Yisrael there are no leniencies whatsoever regarding the laws of *chadash*, but the fact that grain is planted in the winter makes it safe to assume that all Israeli products are *yashan*. Nevertheless, imported products containing the five grains are in abundance and are likely to be *chadash*. This section highlights which grains and products can pose an issue of *chadash*, so one can be aware of the need to verify with the kashrus agency certifying a product whether it is *chadash* or *yashan*. A *hechsher* on a product in *chutz la'Aretz* does not automatically indicate that it is *yashan* unless it is explicitly stated, while a *hechsher* on a product in Eretz Yisrael (that is manufactured in Eretz Yisrael) is certified for *yashan*. This section is not intended as a comprehensive list of products subject to the laws of *chadash*; such a list can be obtained from kashrus organizations.

1. **The Five Species of Grain:** Any food containing flour from any of the five species of grain (wheat, barley, spelt, oats, or rye) or any derivative of those grains (such as barley malt) may be subject to the prohibition of *chadash*, even if the grain is only a minority ingredient.

2. **Winter Crops and Spring Crops:** In the northern hemisphere,

there are two planting seasons for grain. One crop of grain is known as the winter crop, while the other is the spring crop. The winter crop is planted before the winter and harvested in the early summer; thus, any grain from the winter crop is certainly *yashan*. The spring crop is planted in the spring, usually after Pesach, and harvested at the end of the summer. All spring grains must be considered *chadash* and prohibited until after the 17th of Nissan. Therefore, the "*chadash* season" for these crops extends from around August or September (when a spring crop is normally harvested) until Pesach.

3. **Rye and Spelt:** In North America, rye and spelt are winter crops and therefore always *yashan*. However, one should not make the mistake of assuming that rye bread is always *yashan*, since rye bread contains wheat flour as well. Rye and spelt products that are imported from elsewhere in the world may be *chadash*.

4. **Oats and Barley:** Oats and barley in North America are usually spring crops and therefore must be assumed to be *chadash* until the Pesach that follows the harvest. Many products contain malt, which is derived from barley and therefore may be *chadash*. If one sees malt in a product's ingredient list, he should contact the kashrus agency certifying the product. Regarding beer, one should not assume that since it is mass produced it is probably *yashan*; rather, he should consult a kashrus agency.

5. **Winter Wheat and Spring Wheat:** Winter wheat and spring wheat produce different types of flour and therefore have different commercial uses. Spring wheat produces high-gluten flour, including durum flour, while winter wheat produces low-gluten flour. Winter wheat is always *yashan*, whereas spring wheat is *chadash*. (Note: Even if a product states that it is made with winter wheat, it may still contain a small percentage of spring wheat.)

6. **Products Subject to Potential *Chadash* Issues:** Many non-wheat products might include flour or malt and therefore may be subject to the prohibition of *chadash*. Some examples of such items include soups, cornflake crumbs, spices, candies, baking spray, and coated foods such as French fries.

7. **Verifying the Status of a Product:** For a product that contains one of the five grains, kashrus agencies can provide either a purchase date or a package date with which consumers can determine whether it contains *chadash*. When kashrus agencies provide a purchase date, it means that any products bought prior to that date can be assumed to be *yashan*. Any products purchased after that date might be *chadash*. A package date refers to the date printed on the item itself, which can be used to assess whether the product might contain *chadash*. A product bearing a package date that is later than the date provided by the kashrus agency might contain *chadash*. Note: The package dates used by many companies are coded. Kashrus agencies can advise how to decipher the codes.

CHAPTER FOUR

The Yom Tov of Shavuos

1. General Halachos of Shavuos
2. Learning throughout the Night on Shavuos
3. *Netilas Yadayim* after a Sleepless Night
4. Reciting the *Brachah* on *Tzitzis*
5. *Birchos HaTorah*
6. *Birchos Hashachar*
7. Eating Dairy on Shavuos
8. Other *Minhagim* of Shavuos

CHAPTER FOUR

The Yom Tov of Shavuos

Introduction: The Yom Tov of Shavuos is celebrated on the sixth day of Sivan. The Torah identifies this holiday as the 50th day from the beginning of *sefiras haomer*, as the *pasuk* states, *"Shivah shavuos tispar lach ... v'asisa chag Shavuos laHashem* – You shall count seven weeks for yourself ... and you shall observe the holiday of Shavuos for Hashem" (*Devarim* 16:9-10; see also *Vayikra* 23:16 and *Bamidbar* 28:26). The day of Shavuos itself is not included in the mitzvah of counting the *omer*; the final count is recited on the 49th day, the day before Shavuos. Shavuos is also known as *"zman matan Toraseinu"* since it commemorates the giving of the Torah at Har Sinai. Therefore, many halachos and *minhagim* of Shavuos are associated with its significance as the day when the Torah was given.

The halachos governing the performance of *melachah* and the observance of *simchah* and *kavod* are identical to the laws that pertain to other Yamim Tovim. These halachos are described in detail in *Kitzur Halachos: Yom Tov and Chol Hamoed*.

In addition to the standard halachos pertaining to a holiday, there is a unique prohibition to draw blood on Erev Shavuos. This prohibition is based on the Gemara's teaching (*Shabbos* 129b) that the time prior to the giving of the Torah is considered a time of danger, since a person might choose not to accept the Torah. A medical procedure may be performed in a life-threatening situation, but any procedures that are not urgent should be postponed. See *Kitzur Halachos: Pesach*, Chapter Eight, section 5, for more details.

1. General Halachos of Shavuos

1. **Davening *Maariv* after *Tzeis Hakochavim*:** The Yom Tov of Shavuos is celebrated at the conclusion of the period of *sefiras haomer*. In order to fulfill the requirement to count 49 complete days of the *omer* (that the days of the *omer* should be "*temimos*"), the halachah stipulates that one should daven *Maariv* on the night of Shavuos after *tzeis hakochavim*, to avoid encroaching on the 49th day of the *omer* period.[1] Although some authorities maintain that it is permissible to daven *Maariv* even before *tzeis hakochavim*, and only Kiddush must be delayed until nightfall,[2] the accepted practice is to delay *Maariv* as well.[3] (On the first night of Pesach and Sukkos, it is permissible to daven *Maariv* before *tzeis hakochavim* as long as Kiddush is recited after *tzeis hakochavim*.)

2. ***Tosefes Yom Tov*:** Although we daven *Maariv* only after *tzeis hakochavim*, the halachos of "*tosefes Yom Tov*" (adding to the Yom Tov) still apply. Therefore, every individual should accept Yom Tov prior to *shekiah*.[4] The halachos of *tosefes Yom Tov* are identical to the halachos of *tosefes Shabbos*.[5]

3. **Lighting Yom Tov Candles:** In general, there are divergent *minhagim* regarding the time when candles are lit on any Yom Tov. Some women light the candles for Yom Tov before *shekiah*, as they do on Erev Shabbos, whereas others light after *tzeis hakochavim* (see *Kitzur Halachos: Yom Tov and Chol Hamoed*, Chapter One, section 3). There is a dispute among

---

1. שו"ע סי' תצ"ד ומ"ב סק"א.
2. עי' דעת תורה סי' תצ"ד ס"א בשם המשאת בנימין. וראה ס' אשי ישראל פמ"ג ס"ק מ"ב.
3. כמוש"כ המ"ב שם, וכן עמא דבר.
4. עי' שו"ת בנין שלמה תיקונים והוספות סי' כ'. אמנם ראה העמק דבר פרשת אמור פסוק כ"א, וראה שו"ת אז נדברו חי"ד סי' מ'.
5. עי' מ"ב סי' רס"א ס"ק י"ט.

the *poskim* as to whether a woman who generally lights Yom Tov candles before *shekiah* should do so on Erev Shavuos as well. A woman's act of lighting candles ushers in the holiday on the level of a communal acceptance of Yom Tov (in contrast to an individual's acceptance of *tosefes Yom Tov*, which does not have this effect); furthermore, many women recite the *brachah* of *shehecheyanu* when they light candles for Yom Tov (see *Kitzur Halachos: Yom Tov and Chol Hamoed*, Chapter One, section 3, for a discussion of the practice of reciting *shehecheyanu* on the Yom Tov candles). Due to these factors, some *poskim* maintain that lighting the candles for Shavuos might be akin to davening *Maariv* or reciting Kiddush before *tzeis hakochavim*, which is viewed as a violation of the principle of *temimos*. Therefore, some authorities rule that the candles for Shavuos should be lit only after *tzeis hakochavim*;[6] however, other *poskim* take the position that lighting the Yom Tov candles does not render the 49 days of *sefirah* incomplete, and that a woman should maintain the same practice on Shavuos as on other Yamim Tovim.[7] A woman should follow the custom of her husband's family in this regard. If they do not have an established *minhag*, she should consult a Rav.

4. **Immersing in the *Mikveh*:** One should immerse in the *mikveh* on Erev Shavuos.[8] See *Kitzur Halachos: Yom Tov and Chol Hamoed*, Chapter One, section 1, paragraph 4.

5. ***Maariv* of Shavuos:** The standard *Maariv* for Yom Tov is recited on the night of Shavuos. In the *brachah* of *Atah bechartanu* and in the passage of *Yaaleh V'yavo*, the phrase "*es yom chag haShavuos hazeh, zman matan Toraseinu* – this day of the festival of Shavuos, the time of the giving of our Torah"

---

6. לוח א״י להגרי״מ טוקיצינסקי.
7. הגרשז״א זצ״ל הובא בהליכות שלמה פי״ב ס״ב וסק״ב.
8. באר היטב סי׳ תצ״ד סק״ז.

General Halachos of Shavuos 101

is inserted to identify the holiday.[9] Likewise, the standard Kiddush for Yom Tov is recited on Shavuos, with the same phrase inserted as the description of Shavuos. The *brachah* of *shehecheyanu* is recited after Kiddush. (In *chutz la'Aretz*, the *brachah* is recited on both nights of Yom Tov.) When the first night of Shavuos falls on Motzaei Shabbos, the passage of *Vatodieinu* is inserted in the *Shemoneh Esrei*, and Havdalah is combined with Kiddush. The details of these halachos can be found in *Kitzur Halachos: Yom Tov and Chol Hamoed*, Chapter Five, section 1.

6. **Preparing for Yom Tov on Shabbos:** When Shavuos falls on Motzaei Shabbos, it is forbidden to prepare for Yom Tov on Shabbos, due to the prohibition of *hachanah*. After *tzeis hakochavim*, women should make sure to recite the formula "*baruch hamavdil bein kodesh l'kodesh*" before preparing for the nighttime meal or performing any *melachos* that are permitted on Yom Tov. On Shabbos afternoon, it is permissible to take a nap in preparation for staying awake throughout the night, but one should not make a verbal statement of this intention.[10] See *Kitzur Halachos: Yom Tov and Chol Hamoed*, Chapter Two, section 4, for further details regarding the halachos that pertain to preparing for the following day when Yom Tov falls immediately after Shabbos, or for the second day of Yom Tov in *chutz la'Aretz*.

7. **Seudah Shelishis on Erev Yom Tov:** Regarding fulfilling the mitzvah of *seudah shelishis* when Yom Tov will begin after Shabbos, see *Kitzur Halachos: Yom Tov and Chol Hamoed*, Chapter One, section 1.

8. **Marital Relations on Shavuos:** It is proper to abstain from marital relations on the night of Shavuos, unless it is a *leil*

9. שו"ע סי' תצ"ד ס"א.
10. עי' מ"ב סי' ר"צ סק"ד וע"יש בשע"ת סק"ב.

tevilah.[11] On the second night of Shavuos in *chutz la'Aretz*, relations are permitted.[12]

9. **Learning throughout the Night:** The *minhag* of remaining awake throughout the night of Shavuos and the halachos of *netilas yadayim* and *birchos hashachar* on the following morning will be discussed in the following sections.

10. **The Prohibition to Fast:** It is prohibited to fast on Shavuos, even for a *taanis chalom* (if one has had a disturbing dream). This is unlike the halachah with respect to Shabbos and other Yamim Tovim, when a *taanis chalom* is permitted.[13]

11. **The *Tefillos* of Shavuos Morning:** On the morning of Shavuos (as well as on the second day of Shavuos in *chutz la'Aretz*), the complete *Hallel* is recited.[14] A person who recites only the abridged version of *Hallel*, which is recited on Rosh Chodesh and the latter days of Pesach, is not *yotzei*. The details of these halachos are discussed in *Kitzur Halachos: Yom Tov and Chol Hamoed*.

12. ***Krias HaTorah*:** Two *sifrei Torah* are used for the Torah reading on the morning of Shavuos. The reading from the first *sefer Torah* is drawn from the Torah's description of the giving of the Torah in *Parshas Yisro*, including the *Aseres Hadibros* (*Shemos* 19-20). This Torah reading is divided into five *aliyos*. The second *sefer Torah* is used for the *aliyah* of *maftir*, for which we read the passage in *Parshas Pinchas* (*Bamidbar* 28) dealing with the *korbanos* of Shavuos, beginning with the words "*u'vayom habikkurim*."[15]

---

11. מ״ב סי׳ תצ״ד סק״א.

12. שע״ת סי׳ תצ״ד סק״ז. ועי׳ בכף החיים סי׳ תצ״ד ס״ק י״ד. ועי׳ בכה״ח שם ס״ק י״ג שהביא מהכנה״ג לפרוש בשלושת ימי הגבלה וכמו בזמן מתן תורה, ומ״מ מסיק שם שבודאי אין איסור בתשמיש בימים אלו ואפי׳ עפ״י הקבלה.

13. מ״ב שם ס״ק י״א בשם המ״א סי׳ תר״י סק״א (ושאני שבועות עפ״י הגמ׳ פסחים דף סח: דהכל מודים בעצרת דבעינן נמי לכם, מאי טעמא, יום שניתנה בו תורה הוא), באר היטב סי׳ תצ״ד סק״ח.

14. שו״ע שם ס״א.

15. שם.

General Halachos of Shavuos 103

13. **Akdamus:** It is customary for *Akdamus Milin* to be recited on the first day of Shavuos prior to *Krias HaTorah*. *Akdamus* is read after the *kohen* is called for the first *aliyah*, before he recites the *brachah*.[16] (The *sefer Torah* is opened and then covered before the recitation of *Akdamus*.[17]) *Akdamus* is not followed by Kaddish; instead, the *kohen* recites the *brachah* immediately and the Torah reading begins.

14. **Reading the *Aseres Hadibros*:** The *Aseres Hadibros* are read with the *taam elyon*. This is a different version of the *trop*, in which each of the commandments is read as a single, distinct *pasuk*, in contrast to the way the *pesukim* are actually divided in the Torah.[18] This reading also changes the vowelization of some of the words.

15. **Standing for the *Aseres Hadibros*:** In some communities it is customary for the congregation to stand during the reading of the *Aseres Hadibros*. This is not obligatory and may even be halachically problematic, since it may create the erroneous impression that these *pesukim* are more important than other portions of the Torah;[19] however, this custom is referenced by earlier *poskim*,[20] and many authorities offer resolutions for the aforementioned halachic objection.[21] Some *poskim* suggest that the congregation should begin standing slightly before the *Aseres Hadibros* in order to avoid creating the impression that these *pesukim* are more significant than others.[22] A person who is davening with a *minyan* where everyone else stands for

---

16. מ"ב סק"ב. ויש לעיין מה הדין אם טעה הכהן ואמר ברכו. ואם כבר התחיל הברכה בודאי צריכים לקרות התורת עם הכהן אלא דיש לעיין אם האם עלייתו או ג' פסוקים יש להפסיק לקרות אקדמות לפני הלוי.
17. פמ"ג סי' תצ"ד מ"ז סק"א.
18. מ"ב סק"ג ובביה"ל ד"ה מבחודש השלישי.
19. עי' שו"ת הרמב"ם סי' רס"ג. ועי' כה"ח שם סק"ל.
20. סידור בית יעקב להיעב"ץ סדר יום א של שבועות. וראה שערי אפרים שער ז' סל"ז.
21. שו"ת אגר"מ או"ח ח"ד סי' כ"ב, הגרשז"א זצ"ל הוב"ד בהליכות שלמה פי"ב ס"ח וסק"ח.
22. עי' תשובות והנהגות ח"א סי' קמ"ד.

the *Aseres Hadibros* should certainly follow the congregation's practice.[23]

16. **The *Haftarah* of Shavuos Morning:** The *haftarah* read on the morning of Shavuos is the passage in *Sefer Yechezkel* dealing with the "*maaseh merkavah*."[24] In some congregations, it is customary to call up the Rav or a *talmid chacham* to read this *haftarah*.[25]

17. **Standing during the *Haftarah*:** Some have the custom to stand respectfully when they recite this *haftarah* quietly along with the *baal korei*.[26] (One should recite the *haftarah* quietly when the *baal korei* reads from a Tanach but when it is read from a *klaf* one should just listen.)

18. ***Megillas Rus*:** The Ashkenazic custom is to read *Megillas Rus* on Shavuos.[27] Various explanations have been advanced for this custom. Some suggest that the story of the *megillah* demonstrates that Torah is acquired through suffering,[28] while others maintain that it is read on Shavuos because this holiday is the date of both the birth and the death of Dovid Hamelech, and the *megillah* traces Dovid's lineage.[29] A third explanation is that the *megillah* describes the conversion of Rus, and the entire Jewish nation likewise "converted" when the Torah was given to them.[30]

In *chutz la'Aretz*, *Megillas Rus* is read on the second day of

---

23. שו"ת אגר"מ שם.
24. שו"ע שם.
25. מ"ב סק"ד.
26. מ"ב שם.
27. רמ"א סי' ת"צ ס"ט.
28. מ"ב סי' ת"צ ס"ק י"ז.
29. שע"ת סי' תצ"ד סק"ז בשם הבכ"ש.
30. עי' כף החיים סי' ת"צ סק"פ.

General Halachos of Shavuos ~ 105

Shavuos.[31] If a resident of *chutz la'Aretz* is spending Shavuos in Eretz Yisrael and will not be able to daven with a *minyan* on the second day of Yom Tov, he should hear the reading of the *megillah* on the first day.

19. **The *Brachah* on Reading the *Megillah*:** There is a difference of opinion among the *poskim* regarding whether the *brachah* of *al mikra megillah* should be recited when *Megillas Rus* is read from a *klaf*.[32] In most congregations, there is an established *minhag* in this regard.

20. **Reading the *Megillah* Multiple Times:** A *baal korei* who has already read *Megillas Rus* in one *minyan* may read it again for another congregation and may even recite the *brachah* again (where it is customary to recite it).[33]

21. The reading of *Megillas Rus*, followed by the recitation of *Kaddish Yasom*, should take place before the *sifrei Torah* are removed from the *aron*.[34]

22. **Krias HaTorah on the Second Day of Shavuos:** On the second day of Shavuos in *chutz la'Aretz*, two *sifrei Torah* are used once again for the Torah reading. The passage beginning with the words "*kol habechor*" in *Parshas Re'eh* (*Devarim* 15), which discusses the Yamim Tovim, is read from the first *sefer*.[35] On an ordinary day of Yom Tov, this passage is divided into five *aliyos*. When the second day of Shavuos falls on Shabbos and it is necessary to read seven *aliyos*, the Torah reading begins earlier in the *parshah*, with the *pasuk* beginning with

---

31. מ"ב שם. ועי' בפמ"ג סי' ת"צ א"א סק"ח בטעם הדבר כי עיקר התורה ניתנה בו' סיון ועוד שביום א' ערים בלילה ומרבים בפיוטים ולכן דוחין ליום ב'.
32. עי' רמ"א סי' ת"צ ס"ט ובמ"ב ס"ק י"ט. ועי' עמק ברכה עמוד נ"א בענין חסרות ויתרות. ועי' גם שו"ת שבט הלוי ח"ב סי' קמ"ז אות ג'. ועי' תשובות והנהגות ח"א סי' שכ"ג בענין ברכת שהחיינו.
33. הליכות שלמה שם ס"ט ובהערות שם.
34. עי' שש"כ פנ"ח ס"ק ק"ו בשם הגרשז"א זצ"ל שביאר האיך קוראין לפני התורה והרי קרה"ת תדיר.
35. שו"ע סי' תצ"ד ס"ב.

the words "*aser te'aser*" (*Devarim* 14).[36] The Torah reading for *maftir* is identical to that of the first day, and the *haftarah* is read from the passage in *Sefer Chavakuk* that begins with the words "*v'Hashem b'heichal kadsho.*"[37] Many communities have the custom to recite the *piyut* of *Yetziv Pisgam* after the first *pasuk* of the *haftarah*.[38]

23. **Yizkor:** On the second day of Shavuos, *Yizkor* is recited before *Mussaf*. In *chutz la'Aretz*, *Yizkor* is always recited after the reading of the *parshah* of "*Kol Habechor*," which discusses giving *tzedakah*, as it is customary to donate *tzedakah* in order to bring merit to the deceased.[39] In Eretz Yisrael, *Yizkor* is recited on the first day of Yom Tov. When *Yizkor* is recited, the passage of *Av Harachamim* is likewise included in the davening, even though it is Yom Tov. On the first day of Shavuos in *chutz la'Aretz*, where *Yizkor* is not recited, *Av Harachamim* is likewise omitted.[40] The *piyut* of *Kah E-li*, which is recited before *Mussaf* on a standard Yom Tov, is omitted on any day when *Yizkor* is recited. Consequently, this *piyut* is not recited on Shavuos in Eretz Yisrael, but it is recited in *chutz la'Aretz* in many communities on the first day of Yom Tov.

24. **Holding a *Hachnassas Sefer Torah* on Shavuos:** The holiday of Shavuos is considered an appropriate time for a *hachnassas sefer Torah*, as the *poskim* state that donating a *sefer Torah* to a shul on Shavuos is akin to offering the special *korban minchah* of Shavuos in the era of the *Beis Hamikdash*.[41]

25. **Isru Chag:** On Isru Chag, the day after Shavuos, *Tachanun* is

---

36. מ"ב שם סק"ה.
37. שו"ע שם.
38. מ"ב סק"ב.
39. מ"ב ס"ק י"ז.
40. מ"ב שם.
41. שע"ת שם סק"ז בשם הברכ"י בשם העו"א.

General Halachos of Shavuos 107

omitted and there is a prohibition to fast.[42] This prohibition includes a chassan and kallah on the day of their wedding.[43] Likewise, one should not fast on Isru Chag even for the *yahrtzeit* of a parent.[44] It is customary to eat and drink slightly more than usual on Isru Chag.[45] (See also *Kitzur Halachos: Yom Tov and Chol Hamoed*, Chapter One, section 2.)

26. **Omitting *Tachanun* after Shavuos:** Some communities have the *minhag* to omit *Tachanun* throughout the six days following Shavuos, since the *korbanos* of Shavuos could still be offered during those days during the era of the *Beis Hamikdash*.[46] (Even in *chutz la'Aretz*, the six days should be counted from after the first day of Yom Tov.[47])

In Eretz Yisrael, many people have a custom to visit the Kosel at some point during these six days if they were unable to go there on Shavuos itself, in order to commemorate the mitzvah of *aliyah l'regel*.[48] (See *Kitzur Halachos: Yom Tov and Chol Hamoed*, Chapter One, section 1, paragraph 6, regarding the applications of the mitzvah of *aliyah l'regel* nowadays.)

2. Learning throughout the Night on Shavuos

Introduction: The Zohar (*Parshas Emor*) mentions a custom to stay awake and engage in Torah study throughout the night on Shavuos.

---

42. שו"ע ורמ"א שם ס"ג ומ"ב סק"ו.
43. מ"ב סי' תקע"ג סק"ז.
44. שו"ע הרב סי' תכ"ט סי"ז.
45. רמ"א סי' תכ"ט ס"ב.
46. עי' בשע"ת סי' קל"א סק"ז ומ"ב ס"ק ל"ו.
47. הליכות שלמה שם סט"ז וס"ק כ"ה.
48. וכן נהג הגרשז"א זצ"ל (לעת זקנותו כשלא היה לו כח ללכת בחג עצמו) הובא בהליכות שלמה שם הערה 79.

This custom is based on a Midrash that relates that Bnei Yisrael had to be awakened from their sleep on the morning of *Kabbalas haTorah*. In order to make amends for this lapse, a custom was instituted to remain awake throughout the night of Shavuos every year in order to prepare ourselves to receive the Torah. The Arizal is quoted as teaching that a person who engages in Torah study throughout the night of Shavuos and does not sleep at all is guaranteed that he will live out the year and that no harm will befall him. The *Shelah HaKadosh* (Shavuos) relates that Rav Yosef Karo, the author of the *Beis Yosef* and *Shulchan Aruch*, spent the entire night of Shavuos immersed in Torah study, and in that merit he was granted *gilui Shechinah* (a Divine revelation). This demonstrates the great significance of his act of engaging in Torah study throughout the night.

The observance of this practice requires a person to be aware of how to contend with the obligations of *netilas yadayim* and reciting *birchos haTorah* and *birchos hashachar*, mitzvos that are typically observed when one awakens in the morning. The details of these halachos are discussed below.

1. **Studying Torah throughout the Night:** The custom of engaging in Torah study throughout the night of Shavuos dates back to the era of the Tannaim. This custom has been practiced for hundreds of years by most learned people.[49]

2. **Optional but Important:** Although this custom has been practiced by most learned people and is observed in most communities today, it is not an obligatory *minhag*; no prohibition is transgressed by a person who sleeps on the night of Shavuos.[50] Nevertheless, a person should not relate to this *minhag* lightly, as it is observed by most communities.

---

49. מ"א תחילת סי' תצ"ד ומ"ב סק"א.
50. פשוט בכל הפוסקים דלא נמצא בשום אחד מהם שיכתוב שחייב לנהוג כן אלא רק מצטטים את הזוהר והמ"א. (ואולי מפני שמתחילה לא נתפשט כן רק אצל הלומדים כדאיתא במ"א או מפני שמעולם לא נתקבל כמנהג חובה). ובבית בריסק לא היו מקפידים על המנהג להיות ניעור כל ליל שבועות, ראה ספר עובדות והנהגות לבית בריסק ח"ב עמוד ע"ט.

A person should exert himself to stay awake throughout the night even if he finds it difficult.[51]

3. **Learning the *Tikkun*:** There is an established order of learning for this night, known as the *tikkun leil Shavuos*, which spans the entire Torah and is based on the Zohar and Arizal.[52] Many *poskim* recommend learning the *tikkun* on the night of Shavuos,[53] while others recommend studying Torah *shebaal peh* (Gemara or *mishnayos*) if one can do so.[54] In general, a person should study the material with which he will make the best use of his time.

4. **Learning on the Second Night of Shavuos:** Most Ashkenazim do not observe the practice of learning throughout the night on the second night of Shavuos. (In some Sephardic communities, this custom is observed on the second night as well.[55])

5. **Reciting *Brachos* on Food and Drink:** It is only natural to partake of food or drink over the course of the night in order to maintain one's energy and wakefulness. When doing so, a person should be aware of the halachos governing the recitation of *brachos* on intermittent snacks of this nature. After a person recites a *brachah rishonah*, it remains in effect as long as he has not experienced a *hesech hadaas* (mental diversion) *and* he remains in the same location.[56] As long as those two criteria have been met, it is not necessary to repeat a *brachah rishonah* if one wishes to continue eating or drinking. A *brachah acharonah*, on the other hand, may be recited only

---

51. עי' הליכות שלמה שם הערה 13.
52. שער הכוונות ענין חג השבועות דף פ"ט, ועי' של"ה שבועות ועי' כף החיים סי' תצ"ד סק"ו-ז'.
53. פמ"ג א"א תחילת סי' תצ"ד, דרך החיים דיני חג השבועות ס"ב, יסוד ושורש העבודה שער ט' פ"י, כף החיים סק"ז-ט'.
54. חק יעקב סי' תצ"ד סק"א, שו"ע הרב סי' תצ"ד ס"ג. ועי' מקראי קדש פסח ח"ג סי' ל"ד.
55. עי' כף החיים שם סק"י.
56. רמ"א סי' קע"ח ס"ב.

within the "*shiur ikul*," the length of time until the body begins to digest the food one has consumed, which is presumed to have passed when a person begins to feel slightly hungry or thirsty again.[57] Some *poskim* maintain that once the *shiur ikul* has passed, the *brachah rishonah* must also be repeated before a person resumes eating or drinking, even if he has not recited a *brachah acharonah*. Nevertheless, the accepted halachah is that it is not necessary to repeat a *brachah rishonah* as long as one hasn't experienced a *hesech hadaas*.[58] Nonetheless, *lechatchilah* one should avoid such a situation. Therefore, if a person finishes eating or drinking and does not have a specific intent to continue at a particular time, even if he is certain that he will eat or drink again later in the night, he should recite a *brachah acharonah* (provided that he consumed the requisite quantity of food or drink within the span of time that warrants reciting a *brachah acharonah* – i.e., he has drunk a *reviis* of a beverage within the span of time in which a *reviis* can be drunk, or he consumed a *kezayis* of food within the span of *k'dei achilas pras*). He should then recite a *brachah rishonah* again when he resumes eating or drinking.

6. **The *Shiur Ikul*:** The *shiur ikul*, when the digestive process begins and it is no longer possible to recite a *brachah acharonah*, is reached when a person begins to feel slightly hungry or thirsty again. This can be difficult to gauge; therefore, *poskim* estimate it to be 72 minutes after the consumption of food.[59] If a person consumes only a small quantity of light food or drink, some *poskim* rule that the *shiur* is presumed to be half an hour.[60]

---

57. שו"ע סי' קפ"ד ס"ה.
58. עי' מ"ב סי' קפ"ד ס"ק י"ז. מיהו צ"ע ממש"כ לעיל שם סק"י. ועי' בשו"ת מנחת יצחק ח"ה סי' ק"ב מש"כ ליישב.
59. מ"ב שם סק"כ.
60. כף החיים סי' קפ"ד ס"ק כ"ט.

7. **A Change of Location (*Shinui Makom*):** As mentioned above, a person who changes his location is required to recite a *brachah rishonah* again before eating or drinking. A change of location (*shinui makom*) is defined as going from indoors to outdoors or vice versa. For example, after stepping outdoors for some fresh air, one must recite a *brachah rishonah* again before continuing to drink.[61] It makes no difference if a person knows while reciting a *brachah* that he will change his location afterward; even in that scenario, he will still be required to repeat the *brachah rishonah*. The *brachah rishonah* on a beverage or a food requiring *borei nefashos* must be repeated even if a person brings his drink or food along with him when he steps outdoors, unless he was already on his way out when he recited the *brachah* indoors.[62] It is questionable if the *brachah rishonah* for mezonos foods or the *shivas haminim* (the seven species of fruits associated with Eretz Yisrael) must likewise be repeated after a *shinui makom*; therefore, a person who has been eating such foods should not recite a *brachah* again even after changing his location. However, *lechatchilah* one should avoid a change of location after reciting the *brachah rishonah* on these foods.[63] Moving to another room or floor within the same building does not constitute a *shinui makom*; however, *lechatchilah* a person should have in mind while reciting the *brachah* that he plans to move to a different part of the building.[64] (Note: There are scenarios in which it is questionable if stepping outside constitutes a *shinui makom*, such as if a person exits to a balcony or a private yard. These situations are the subject of debate among the *poskim* and are beyond the scope of this work.)

---

61. שו"ע ורמ"א סי' קע"ח ס"א-ב'.
62. עי' שו"ע שם ס"ד ובמ"ב שם ס"ק מ"ב. ועי' בשו"ת אגר"מ ח"ב סי' נ"ז.
63. שו"ע ורמ"א שם ס"ה ובמ"ב ס"ק מ"ה.
64. שו"ע שם ס"א ובמ"ב ס"ק י"ב ובביה"ל ד"ה בבית אחד.

8. **Eating and Drinking after *Alos Hashachar*:** After *alos hashachar*, it is prohibited to eat even a small quantity of food. Drinking water, tea, or coffee is permitted if necessary.[65]

3. *Netilas Yadayim* after a Sleepless Night

Introduction: It is questionable whether a person is obligated to perform *netilas yadayim* in the morning after remaining awake throughout the night. In order to better understand this, a brief introduction is necessary.

The requirement to perform *netilas yadayim* in the morning is actually a function of two separate obligations. One is the requirement to remove the *ruach raah* (spirit of impurity) that comes to rest on a person's hands during the night. This impurity has the potential to endanger a person if it is not removed through the washing process. However, according to most opinions, the *brachah* of *al netilas yadayim* does not relate to this aspect of the obligation; if one were performing *netilas yadayim* only to remove *ruach raah*, the *brachah* would not be recited.

There is another reason to perform *netilas yadayim* in the morning, though: There is a mitzvah *d'rabbanan* to wash one's hands before davening, and this obligation requires the recitation of a *brachah* as well. The rationale for this mitzvah is the subject of a dispute among the Rishonim. One view maintains that since the *neshamah* leaves a person while he is asleep and returns when he wakes up in the morning, every person is considered like a new creation when he rises in the morning and therefore must offer thanks to Hashem for creating him to serve Him. According to this view, the mitzvah of *netilas yadayim* is akin to the ritual hand washing performed by *kohanim* before they begin the

---

65. שו"ע סי' פ"ט ס"ג ובמ"ב שם ס"ק כ"א-כ"ג.

avodah in the *Beis Hamikdash*, as its purpose is to prepare a person to serve Hashem. A second opinion among the Rishonim maintains that the purpose of the mitzvah of *netilas yadayim* is to cleanse the hands in preparation for davening, since a person often touches covered parts of his body while he is asleep, and he is not permitted to daven until his hands have been cleansed. There is a practical difference between these two opinions: According to the first view, a person fulfills the mitzvah of *netilas yadayim* by washing his hands immediately upon awakening, and he may recite the *brachah* of *al netilas yadayim* at that time. However, according to the second opinion, if a person's hands will become unclean again before he davens *Shacharis* (i.e., while getting dressed), he cannot recite the *brachah* upon the initial washing of his hands in the morning. In order to satisfy both opinions, it is proper to delay reciting the *brachah* until the last time one performs *netilas yadayim* before davening.

It is questionable whether any of these rationales for *netilas yadayim* are applicable to a person who has not slept at night. With regard to the *ruach raah* that must be removed by washing one's hands, the *poskim* debate whether this *ruach raah* comes about only if one has slept or it is a function of the night itself and rests upon the hands even of a person who has remained awake. Nevertheless, since the removal of *ruach raah* does not trigger a requirement to recite a *brachah*, this does not create halachic complications, since a person can simply wash his hands three (or four) times in case he is indeed obligated to wash. The actual mitzvah of *netilas yadayim*, which requires an accompanying *brachah*, presents a more complex issue, since it is forbidden to recite a *brachah* unless one has an actual obligation to perform the mitzvah.

In principle, the question of whether to recite a *brachah* depends on the precise rationale for the mitzvah of *netilas yadayim*. According to the first view cited above, that the mitzvah results from becoming a new creation in the morning, the requirement of *netilas yadayim* is always in force, even if one remained awake throughout the night, and therefore the *brachah* should be recited. This is based on the halachic principle of "*lo plug*" (literally, "we do not differentiate"), which calls for certain halachos to be observed even if a situation arises in which the rationale technically does not apply. The second opinion, however, maintains that the requirement to wash in preparation for davening applies only if a person's hands are actually unclean; therefore, if a person has not slept at night and therefore has no reason to assume that he has touched a covered part of his body, he will have no obligation to perform this mitzvah. Thus, according to this opinion, one may not recite the *brachah* on *netilas yadayim* after remaining awake throughout the night.

1. **The Obligation of *Netilas Yadayim*:** One who has remained awake all night is subject to a *safek* whether he is obligated in the mitzvah of *netilas yadayim*, and thus it is questionable whether he may recite a *brachah* after washing.[66] Refer to the introduction for an explanation. The accepted practice (for Ashkenazim) is for a person to deliberately render his hands unclean after a sleepless night by tending to his bodily needs before davening. By doing this, a person will incur the obligation to wash his hands even according to the second opinion cited above (in the introduction), and he will therefore have a definite obligation to recite the *brachah* of *al netilas yadayim* (as well as the *brachah* of *asher yatzar*).[67]

2. **Washing before *Alos Hashachar*:** If a person performs the mitzvah of *netilas yadayim* prior to *alos hashachar* (daybreak), it may be necessary for him to wash again. This is due to the requirement to wash one's hands in order to remove *ruach raah* (a spirit of impurity), since some authorities maintain that the *ruach raah* descends upon one's hands only at *alos hashachar*. Therefore, if a person goes through the process of relieving himself, washing his hands, and reciting the *brachah* of *al netilas yadayim* (as explained in the previous paragraph)

---

66. שו״ע סי׳ ד׳ סי״ג, ועי׳ מ״ב ס״ק כ״ח ובביה״ל שם ד״ה ויטלם בלא ברכה.
67. מ״ב שם סק״ל וסי׳ תצ״ד סק״א. ובאם צריך דוקא עשיית צרכיו ומ״ר או שיכול לחכך בראש וליגע במקומות המכוסים, עי׳ ס׳ אשי ישראל פ״ב ס״ק צ״ט.

before *alos hashachar*, he may be required to wash again, albeit without reciting the *brachah*, after *alos hashachar*. The accepted practice is indeed to wash again at *alos hashachar*, and to refrain from reciting the *brachah*.[68]

3. **Continuing to Learn after *Alos Hashachar*:** When *alos hashachar* arrives, a person who is still learning is not required to interrupt his studies in order to wash his hands to remove the *ruach raah*. He should simply make sure to wash his hands when he leaves his seat.[69]

4. **A Person Who Has Slept for Part of the Night:** According to the authorities who maintain that *netilas yadayim* is required only if one has actually slept, the requirement is triggered only by *sheinas keva* – substantial sleep that shares the characteristics of ordinary nighttime slumber. A person who has merely dozed briefly during the night (which is defined as *sheinas arai* – a casual or temporary sleep) does not incur the obligation to wash. If a person sleeps in a sitting position (even for a long period of time), it is considered *sheinas arai* and does not create an obligation to perform *netilas yadayim*. (See below, section 5, paragraph 4.) If a person sleeps a *sheinas keva* and then rises in the middle of the night to learn and washes his hands to remove the *ruach raah*, the requirement for him to perform *netilas yadayim* in the morning will still be subject to the same halachic dispute cited above. Therefore, in order to recite the *brachah* of *al netilas yadayim*, he must still render his hands unclean in the morning by tending to his bodily needs.[70]

5. ***Netilas Yadayim* after Sleeping in the Morning:** If a person

---

68. שו"ע ורמ"א שם סי"ד, מ"ב ס"ק ל"א-ל"ג ובביה"ל שם ד"ה ויטלם בלא ברכה.
69. הליכות שלמה פי"ב ס"ד. אמנם יש להעיר מלשון שו"ע הרב סי' ד' סי"ג. ועי' תשובות והנהגות ח"א סי' ד' וח"ב סי' ב'. עו"כ בהליכות שלמה שם שא"צ לדקדק שלא לגעת בנקבים שבגוף, ומאידך ראה ס' אשי ישראל פ"ב הערה צ"ו בשם הגרח"ק שליט"א שטוב ליזהר שלא יגע בנקבים.
70. מ"ב סי' ד' ס"ק כ"ז ובביה"ל שם ד"ה כל הלילה.

sleeps in the morning after davening (in a manner that meets the criteria for *sheinas keva*), he is required to wash his hands three (or four) times each in order to remove the *ruach raah*. This halachah follows the authorities who maintain that *ruach raah* descends upon the hands even during a daytime nap. The *brachah* of *al netilas yadayim* is not recited.[71]

6. **Netilas Yadayim for a Person Who Sleeps before Shacharis:** If a person remains awake throughout the night and goes to sleep before *Shacharis*, he should perform *netilas yadayim* and recite the *brachah* when he awakens to daven.

4. Reciting the *Brachah* on *Tzitzis*

1. **Reciting the *Brachah* on *Tzitzis* on the Morning of Shavuos:** Another halachic complication that arises when a person remains awake throughout the night is the question of whether to recite the *brachah* on *tzitzis* (i.e., on the *tallis katan*). This is based on the following: There is a dispute among the Rishonim as to whether the mitzvah of *tzitzis* is in effect only during the daytime hours or the obligation applies at any time of the day or night. According to the second view, there is a different limitation on the mitzvah of *tzitzis*: It applies only to a garment typically worn during the day, while a garment designated as nightwear is not required to be equipped with *tzitzis* even if worn by day. According to the first opinion, even if a person remained awake throughout the night and did not remove his *tzitzis*, he is not considered to have been observing the mitzvah during the nighttime hours and therefore is required to recite the *brachah* on wearing *tzitzis* in the morning (after the *zman* of *misheyakir*). According

---

71. שו"ע ורמ"א סי' ד' סט"ו.

to the second opinion, however, since the mitzvah of *tzitzis* applies during the night as well, a person who remained awake throughout the night has continuously fulfilled the mitzvah and therefore is not required to repeat the *brachah*. The accepted practice is to refrain from repeating the *brachah* in the morning, due to the principle of *safek brachos lehakel*.

2. This halachic quandary presents a problem only for an unmarried man who does not don a *tallis gadol*. A married man recites a *brachah* upon donning a *tallis gadol* every morning in any event, and that *brachah* relates to the *tallis katan* as well; therefore, there is no need for him to make any special accommodation for a *brachah* on his *tallis katan* on the morning of Shavuos. An unmarried man, on the other hand, who does not wear a *tallis gadol*, generally recites a *brachah* when putting on his *tallis katan*. In light of the issue discussed here, he should make sure to hear the *brachah* recited by someone else on a *tallis gadol* and should have in mind to fulfill his own obligation, in case he is indeed required to recite the *brachah* in the morning. (If a man recites the *brachah* on behalf of everyone in the shul, it can be assumed that he has the intent to be *motzi* everyone who hears his *brachah*, and there is no need to ask him to have a particular person in mind.)[72]

3. **One Who Did Not Hear the *Brachah*:** If one misses the opportunity to hear the *brachah* recited by others, he may ask someone else for his *tallis* as a *matanah al menas lehachzir* (a gift on the condition that it is returned) and put it on briefly after reciting a *brachah*, while having his own *tallis katan* in mind during the *brachah* as well. It is not sufficient to "borrow" a *tallis*, since the *brachah* is not recited on a borrowed *tallis*. Another solution is to don a different *tallis*

---

72. שו"ע סי' ח' סט"ז ובמ"ב שם ס"ק מ"ב וסי' תצ"ד סק"א.

katan in the morning, which likewise creates an obligation to recite a *brachah*.

5. *Birchos HaTorah*

1. **Reciting *Birchos HaTorah*:** Yet another issue faced by a person who remains awake throughout the night is the question of whether to recite *birchos haTorah* in the morning. Some *poskim* rule that the *brachos* should not be recited, because there has been no *hesech hadaas* (diversion of attention) from the mitzvah of Torah study since the *brachos* that were recited the previous morning. These authorities contend that just as the *brachos* need not be repeated when one learns Torah after nightfall, even though it is considered the start of a new halachic day, there is also no reason to repeat the *brachos* in the morning. Other *poskim*, however, consider *birchos haTorah* analogous to *birchos hashachar*, which are recited daily irrespective of whether one has slept at night. (See below regarding the *brachos* of *hamaavir sheinah* and *Elokai neshamah*.) There is no conclusive ruling on this matter. Therefore, a person who has learned throughout the night on Shavuos must hear the *brachos* from someone who has slept. (The listener must have the intent to fulfill his obligation by hearing the *brachos*, and the person who recites the *brachos* must likewise have in mind to be *motzi* him. A person who recites these *brachos* for the entire congregation is automatically presumed to have in mind everyone who is listening to him.) After hearing the *brachos*, every individual should recite the *pesukim* that follow *birchos haTorah*. If a person cannot find someone else to be *motzi* him (i.e., he has missed the public recitation of the *brachos* for the congregation and he cannot find another individual who can recite the *brachos* for him), he should have the intent to fulfill

his obligation while reciting the *brachah* of *ahavah rabbah* (or *ahavas olam*) before *Krias Shema*. A person who employs this option is required to engage in some minimal Torah learning immediately after davening.[73] If a person has slept on Erev Shavuos in a manner that meets the criteria of *sheinas keva* (as is common, especially when Erev Shavuos falls on Shabbos; see below for the definition of *sheinas keva*), some *poskim* maintain that he may recite *birchos haTorah* himself.[74]

2. **Learning before *Birchos HaTorah*:** There is a further debate among the *poskim* as to whether it is prohibited to engage in Torah study after *alos hashachar* if one has not yet heard *birchos haTorah*. Some authorities indeed maintain that a person must stop learning at *alos hashachar* until he has fulfilled *birchos haTorah*.[75] Others rule that since on a practical level a person is not permitted to recite the *brachos* himself, due to the dissenting opinion, he may continue learning until he has the opportunity to hear them recited by someone else.[76]

3. **Reciting the *Brachos* after a Daytime Nap:** There is a dispute among the Rishonim as to whether a person who sleeps during the day, as many people tend to do after spending the entire night of Shavuos awake, is required to recite *birchos haTorah* again. This dispute relates only to a person who experiences *sheinas keva*; a casual nap that is categorized as *sheinas arai* certainly does not warrant repeating the *brachos*.[77] In practice, it is accepted that the *brachos* should not be repeated; however, if a person wishes to recite the *brachos*

---

73. מ"ב סי' מ"ז ס"ק כ"ח.
74. מ"ב שם בשם רע"א. (אמנם הגרח"ק שליט"א בשם החזו"א [הוב"ד בס' אשי ישראל פ"ו סכ"ז הערה ע"ה] נקט שאין לברך דכל שינת יום נחשב עראי.) ויש להעיר, שאם ישן שינת קבע ביום, הרי לכתחילה מורין לו שיכוין באהבת עולם במעריב לצאת ברכת התורה וא"כ שוב אין לו ממה נפשך לברך בבקר.
75. שו"ת שבט הלוי ח"י סי' ע"ז אות ב'.
76. חזו"א דינים והנהגות פ"א אות ט"ו, מנחת שלמה סי' צ"א אות א', ועי' קובץ תשובות ח"א סי' ט'.
77. שו"ע סי' מ"ז סי"א.

after a daytime sleep, he may rely on the many authorities who rule that one should do so.[78] Although it is generally considered proper to avoid entering a situation in which the halachah is subject to dispute, sleeping on Shabbos and Yom Tov is an exception to this rule and is permitted *lechatchilah*.[79] Nevertheless, a person who sleeps during the day (in a manner considered *sheinas keva*) should have the intent to be *yotzei* the *birchos haTorah* with the recitation of the *brachah* of *ahavas olam* at *Maariv*.[80] (He should then make sure to learn after davening in order for the *brachah* to take effect.) If a person awakens from an afternoon nap and intends to learn before *Maariv*, it is recommended that he mentally pronounce the words of the *brachos* before doing so.[81]

4. **The Definition of *Sheinas Keva*:** A person is considered to be engaging in *sheinas keva* only if he sleeps in a bed. If a person sleeps while sitting on a chair and resting his head on a table or *shtender*, it is certainly considered *sheinas arai* and may not warrant the recitation of *birchos haTorah*. The *poskim* debate whether it is considered *sheinas keva* if a person sleeps on a bed or couch without changing into nightclothes; some maintain that it is considered *sheinas keva* as long as a person sleeps while lying down,[82] while others rule that it is considered *sheinas arai* if one hasn't changed into sleepwear.[83] Even if a person changes his clothes and sleeps in a bed, it is still considered *sheinas arai* if he sleeps for less than half an hour.[84]

---

78. מ"ב ס"ק כ"ה.
79. מנחת שלמה ח"א סי"ח, תשובות והנהגות ח"א סי"ד.
80. מ"ב ס"ק י"ג.
81. כף החיים סי' מ"ז ס"ק כ"ה.
82. שו"ת מהרש"ם ח"ג סי' של"ז, וכן דעת הגריש"א זצ"ל הוב"ד בשבות יצחק תפילה עמוד מ"ז-מ"ט.
83. דעת החזו"א הובא בארחות רבינו ח"ג עמוד ר"י, וכן דעת הגרשז"א זצ"ל הובא בהליכות שלמה תפילה פ"ו סק"ג ובשבות יצחק שם.
84. הליכות שלמה שם ס"ב. (אמנם לשון האורחות רבינו שם הוא שאם פשט בגדיו בלילה אפי' ישן מעט צריך לברך.)

Birchos HaTorah 121

5. **Waking Up during the Night to Learn:** In general, if a person sleeps for part of the night and then gets up to learn, he must recite *birchos haTorah* if his sleep qualified as *sheinas keva*. If he has engaged only in *sheinas arai*, he should not recite *birchos haTorah*, and he should make sure to hear the *brachos* from someone else after *alos hashachar*.[85] However, if a person wakes up before *chatzos* (halachic midnight), even after *sheinas keva*, it is questionable whether he is required to recite *birchos haTorah*.[86] It is preferable to refrain from placing oneself in this particular situation; therefore, a person who feels the need to take a short nap (longer than half an hour) after the nighttime *seudah* in order to have the strength to learn through the night should preferably avoid lying down. (If he must lie down in order to nap, he should at least not change into nightclothes.)

If a person sleeps for part of the night (in a manner that qualifies as *sheinas keva*), recites *birchos haTorah* before learning, and then goes back to sleep, he is not obligated to repeat the *brachos* when he wakes up, even if he began his second period of sleeping before *alos hashachar*. Nevertheless, it is permissible to repeat the *brachos* if he wishes to do so, since some *poskim* rule that there is indeed a requirement to repeat them.[87] (See paragraph 3 above.)

6. **Sleeping in the Morning before *Shacharis*:** If a person stays awake throughout the night and then goes to sleep before davening, he should recite *birchos haTorah* before *Shacharis*.[88]

---

85. עי' שו"ע שם סי"ג ובמ"ב וביה"ל שם.
86. עי' ערוך השלחן סי' מ"ז סכ"ג. אבל מסתימת המ"ב שם סק"ח משמע שצריך לברך (וכן משמע מהאורחות רבינו שם).
87. מ"ב ס"ק כ"ט.
88. אם הלך לישון לפני עלות השחר בודאי יברך, וגם אם הלך לישון אחרי עה"ש לדעת רע"א הוב"ד במ"ב שם ס"ק כ"ח, יש לברך. (מיהו דעת הגרח"ק שליט"א [הוב"ד בס' אשי ישראל פ"ו סכ"ז הערה ע"ה] שאין לברך.)

6. *Birchos Hashachar*

1. **Reciting *Birchos Hashachar* on the Morning of Shavuos:** *Birchos hashachar*, the series of *brachos* recited every morning, are general *brachos* of praise to Hashem for the wonders of the world. Since these *brachos* do not relate specifically to an individual's personal benefits, they must be recited even by a person who has been awake throughout the night.[89] However, some *poskim* contend that a person who has not slept at night should omit the *brachos* of *Elokai neshamah* and *hamaavir sheinah*, since these two *brachos* are recited in the singular form and therefore relate to an individual's personal benefit. (For instance, the *brachah* of *Elokai neshamah* refers to "*neshamah shenasata bi* – the soul that You have placed within me," and the *brachah* of *hamaavir sheinah mei'einai* states that Hashem "removes sleep from *my* eyes.") Many authorities disagree and view these *brachos* as similar to the rest of the *birchos hashachar*, which are not considered personal *brachos*. Nevertheless, the accepted halachah is that a person should adopt the stringent position and hear these *brachos* from someone who slept at night, rather than reciting them himself.[90] If a person cannot find someone else to be *motzi* him (i.e., he missed the *brachos* being recited in shul), many *poskim* permit him to recite them himself.[91]

2. ***Birchos Hashachar* before Dawn:** It is permissible to recite *birchos hashachar* before *alos hashachar*; however, some authorities rule that the *brachah* of *hanosein lasechvi vinah* should not be recited before *alos hashachar*. *Lechatchilah*, a

---

89. עי' שו"ע ורמ"א סי' מ"ו ס"ח.
90. מ"ב סי' מ"ו ס"ק כ"ד.
91. ערוך השלחן סי' מ"ו סי"ג, ועי' כף החיים שם ס"ק מ"ט דעת הרבה פוסקים ודעת האריז"ל, ולכן המנהג אצל הספרדים לברכם.

person should follow this opinion and refrain from reciting this particular *brachah* before dawn (unless he actually hears a rooster crow), but a person who recites it is considered to have been *yotzei* nonetheless.[92]

The passage in *Korbanos* describing the *korban tamid* may not be recited before *alos hashachar*.[93] However, the passages relating to the *kiyor* and the *terumas hadeshen* may be recited before daybreak.[94]

3. **Reciting *Birchos Hashachar* before *Chatzos*:** A person should not recite *birchos hashachar* prior to *chatzos* (halachic midnight), even if he has already slept in a manner that constitutes *sheinas keva*.[95]

4. **Reciting the *Brachos* after Sleeping in the Morning:** If a person remains awake throughout the night and then sleeps before *Shacharis*, it is certainly permissible for him to recite the *brachos* of *Elokai neshamah* and *hamaavir sheinah* upon awakening if he went to sleep before *alos hashachar*.[96] If he went to sleep only after *alos hashachar*, it is questionable whether he may recite those *brachos* upon awakening.[97] The accepted halachah is that a person should be *yotzei* the *brachos* by hearing them from someone else.[98]

---

92. שו"ע סי' מ"ז סי"ג ובמ"ב סי"ק ל"א ובביה"ל שם.
93. שו"ע שם.
94. מ"ב סי' א' ס"ק י"ז.
95. עי' מ"ב סי' מ"ז סק"ל ודוק.
96. מ"ב סי' מ"ו ס"ק כ"ד, ואפי' לא ישן אלא שיתין נשמין (שי"א שהוא חצי שעה) בתחילת הלילה יכול לברך.
97. עי' שו"ת מחזה אליהו סי' א' וסי' ב'. ועי' ס' אשי ישראל פ"ה ס"ק מ"ג שהאריך בזה.
98. הגרח"ק שליט"א הובא באשי ישראל שם.

7. Eating Dairy on Shavuos

Introduction: It is customary to eat dairy foods on Shavuos. Various explanations are offered for this practice:

We eat a *milchig* meal followed by a *fleishig* meal in order to trigger the halachic requirement to use a separate loaf of bread for each meal. These two loaves of bread serve to commemorate the *korban shtei halechem* (literally, the "offering of two breads") that was brought in the *Beis Hamikdash* on Shavuos.[99] (This is comparable to Pesach when we commemorate the *korban Pesach* and *korban chagigah*.)

The seven weeks of *sefiras haomer* are comparable to the seven clean days during which a *niddah* prepares to become pure. The consumption of dairy alludes to the fact that when a woman produces milk, she does not experience the menstrual flow that causes her to become a *niddah*. Furthermore, milk symbolizes Hashem's mercy while blood signifies Divine judgment.[100]

After *Kabbalas haTorah*, Bnei Yisrael were not immediately able to eat meat, since they had become bound by the halachos of *shechitah* and salting meat, and their cooking utensils had to be kashered. Consequently, they had no choice but to eat dairy at the time, and we eat dairy on Shavuos to commemorate that fact.[101]

The consumption of dairy alludes to the fact that the Torah is likened to milk and honey.[102]

After the sin of the Golden Calf, the angels demanded that the Torah be taken away from Bnei Yisrael and returned to them. Hashem

---

99. רמ"א סי' תצ"ד ס"ג.
100. מ"א סי' תצ"ד סק"ו עפ"י הזוהר.
101. מ"ב סי' תצ"ד ס"ק י"ב. ועי' מש"כ בליקוטי הלכות סוף מסכת חולין דלפי השיטות שהתורה ניתנה בשבת, הרי בלא"ה היה אסור הכל.
102. חק יעקב סי' תצ"ד סק"ט בשם הכל בו הובא במ"ב ס"ק י"ג. ועי' באר היטב סק"ח בשם השכנה"ג והשל"ה. ולטעם זה המנהג הוא לאכול גם דבש.

justified the Jewish people's possession of the Torah based on the fact that the angels had eaten meat and milk together, in violation of the Torah's laws, when they visited Avraham Avinu, whereas even the children of the Jewish people are careful to observe the laws requiring the separation of milk and meat.[103]

1. **Eating Dairy Products on Shavuos:** There is a *minhag* to eat dairy products on Shavuos. This custom is not obligatory, and thus one who does not eat dairy is not transgressing. Rather, this is a commendable practice. There are different ways in which this custom is observed, based on the various reasons that have been advanced for the practice.

2. **Serving Dairy and Meat Meals:** Some have the practice of serving a *milchig* meal accompanied by bread (some use bread that is itself dairy[104]), followed by a *fleishig* meal with a different loaf of bread. Since the halachah is that it is prohibited to use leftover bread from the dairy meal at the meat meal, this practice commemorates the *korban shtei halechem*, which consisted of two loaves of bread. The challos for these two meals should therefore be made with wheat flour.[105] This interpretation of the *minhag* is not satisfied by eating a *milchig* Yom Tov meal in lieu of a *fleishig* meal or by eating *milchig* mezonos foods followed by a *fleishig* meal. Furthermore, this practice is observed specifically on the first day of Shavuos, which was the day on which the *korban shtei halechem* was brought in the *Beis Hamikdash*.[106]

3. **Eating Meat after Milk:** If a family observes this practice and serves a *fleishig* meal after a *milchig* meal, it is necessary to remove the bread and all dairy products from the table and

---

103. תורת חיים ב״מ דף פו: וציין לו הדע״ת סי׳ תצ״ד.
104. והיינו כשיש סימן או שהוא מועט לסעודה אחת.
105. רמ״א שם, מ״ב ס״ק י״ד-ט״ו, וי״ז.
106. כמבואר כל זה ברמ״א שם.

then to change the tablecloth before the second meal begins. It is prohibited to use the same tablecloth for *fleishig* and *milchig* meals.[107]

In addition, a person must wash his hands and cleanse his mouth after eating dairy before he is permitted to eat meat.[108] Cleaning the mouth is accomplished by eating a food that is parve and taking a drink. (It is not actually necessary to swallow the liquid; it is sufficient merely to rinse the mouth.)[109]

Technically, it is permissible to eat meat immediately after eating dairy, as long as the procedure described above is followed: The bread must be removed, the tablecloth must be changed, and the participants in the meal must wash their hands and rinse their mouths. It is not even necessary to recite a *brachah acharonah* or to wait for any amount of time before beginning the *fleishig* meal.[110] Nevertheless, some *poskim* quote the Zohar as a basis for their ruling that a *brachah acharonah* must be recited and that one should wait an hour before eating meat.[111] Many have the custom to wait half an hour, rather than a whole hour, after eating dairy.[112] A person should observe any strictures that he usually follows when eating meat after dairy, since there are no special leniencies on Shavuos in the laws governing the separation between meat and milk.[113]

Even if a person waits half an hour before eating meat,

---

107. שו"ע יו"ד סי' פ"ט ס"ד.
108. שו"ע יו"ד שם ס"ב.
109. שו"ע שם ועי' ש"ך שם ס"ק י"א וי"ג.
110. כמבואר בשו"ע שם, ועי' מ"א סי' קצ"ו סק"א ובמ"ב שם סק"ט ובמ"א סי' תצ"ד סק"ו ובמ"ב שם ס"ק ט"ז.
111. זוהר פרשת משפטים והובא בב"י או"ח סי' קע"ג, ועי' לבוש או"ח סי' קע"ג ויו"ד סי' פ"ט, פר"ח יו"ד סי' פ"ט סק"ו, סק"ח וס"ק ט"ו, ועי' באר היטב או"ח סי' תצ"ד סק"ח בשם השכנה"ג והשל"ה, שו"ת מהרש"ם ח"ג סי' קכ"ו, ועוד. ועי' שו"ת אגר"מ או"ח ח"א סי' ק"ס.
112. עי' הליכות שלמה פי"ב הע' 49, ועי' תשובות והנהגות ח"ב סי' ש"צ.
113. פמ"ג סי' תצ"ד א"א סק"ו הוב"ד במ"ב ס"ק י"ז.

he is still required to wash his hands and cleanse his mouth before doing so. A person who waits a full hour before eating the meat meal need not clean his hands or mouth, unless he detects some dairy residue.[114]

4. **Eating Meat after Hard Cheese:** If a person eats hard cheese, he is certainly required to recite a *brachah acharonah* and must also wait a full six hours before eating meat.[115] This halachah pertains to cheese that has been aged for at least six months,[116] such as Parmesan cheese (even if it has been shredded into small pieces and sprinkled over a salad or the like). Cheddar cheese and Swiss cheese may also be considered to have been aged for six months, depending on the specific production process. Many *poskim* add that one must also wait six hours after eating cheese that has been aged for less than six months if it has a high fat content.[117] The halachic status of ordinary yellow cheese is subject to dispute; many *poskim* in Eretz Yisrael rule that the obligation to wait for six hours applies to this cheese as well, whereas many *poskim* in America rule leniently on this issue.

5. **Serving a *Milchig* Yom Tov *Seudah*:** Some observe the custom of eating dairy on Shavuos by serving a *milchig* Yom Tov *seudah*. Although this practice does not serve to commemorate the *korban shtei halechem*, it satisfies the other reasons cited above for eating dairy on Shavuos, and it is mentioned in the *poskim*.[118] Although it is a common practice to serve a dairy *seudah* and dispense with the *fleishig* meal altogether (perhaps because of the halachic complexities discussed above that pertain to eating a *fleishig* meal shortly

---

114. אמת ליעקב יו"ד סי' פ"ט הע' 37, תשובות והנהגות שם.
115. רמ"א יו"ד סי' פ"ט ס"ב.
116. ש"ך שם ס"ק ט"ו.
117. ערוך השלחן יו"ד סי' פ"ט סי"א.
118. עי' דרכי תשובה יו"ד סי' פ"ט ס"ק י"ט. ועי' שו"ת אגר"מ שם.

after a *milchig* one, or simply because it is difficult to eat two *seudos* within a short span of time), some *poskim* challenge this practice since a Yom Tov *seudah* should include meat.[119]

6. **Waiting between Meat and Milk:** If a *milchig seudah* is served on the second night of Yom Tov after a meat meal during the day, one must ensure that sufficient time has passed since the consumption of meat. (There are various customs in this regard: Some wait one hour between meat and milk, while others wait three hours, five and a half hours, or six hours.) This is a matter of particular concern on the second night since it is common for the daytime *seudah* on the first day of Shavuos to take place late in the day, in order to allow the men to sleep in the morning. The required waiting time before eating dairy is the same for a person who has eaten chicken[120] or even a parve food that was cooked with meat.[121] On the other hand, there is no obligation to wait before eating dairy if one has merely eaten parve foods cooked in a *fleishig* pot,[122] or even a sharp food that was cooked in a *fleishig* utensil or cut with a *fleishig* knife.[123]

The prohibition to eat milk after meat is in effect only until the required amount of time (e.g., six hours) has passed after the consumption of the meat itself. It is not necessary to wait until this amount of time has passed since the conclusion of the entire *fleishig* meal. Similarly, it is permissible to begin a meal that will later include *milchig* foods even while one is

---

119. עי׳ דרכי תשובה שם. ובענין מצות שמחה בלילה דעת השאגת אריה סי׳ ס״ח שאין מצות שמחה נוהגת בלילה, אבל דעת המ״א סי׳ תקמ״ו סק״ד וסי׳ תרצ״ו שיש מצוה בלילה, ועי׳ שע״ת סי׳ תקכ״ט. ומ״מ שמא הטעם לאלו שנוהגין לאכול סעודה שלימה אחת חלבי ובוחרין דוקא סעודת לילה הוא מפני צירוף דעת השאגת אריה.

120. שו״ע שם ס״א.

121. רמ״א שם ס״ג.

122. שם.

123. חי׳ רע״א יו״ד סי׳ פ״ט על הש״ך סקי״ט. ובענין מאכל חריף שנחתך בסכין חלבי לאכלו תוך שש שעות מאכילת בשר, ראה ספר הלכות בשר בחלב פ״י ס״נ ובהערות לשם.

still prohibited to eat dairy, as long as one does not actually serve the dairy foods themselves until the requisite amount of time has passed.[124]

As mentioned in paragraph 3 above, a *milchig* meal must be served on a tablecloth that was not used for *fleishig* food, and must be accompanied by challah that has not been on the table during a *fleishig* meal.

7. **Eating Dairy after a Nap:** Most *poskim* rule that even if a person sleeps after a *fleishig* meal, this does not permit him to begin eating dairy earlier than usual.[125] (Some *poskim* rule leniently regarding a person who has eaten chicken rather than meat and has slept for several hours in a manner that constitutes *sheinas keva*.[126])

8. **Meat and Dairy at the Same Table:** It is prohibited for a group of people to sit at the same table with some eating meat and others eating dairy, unless a *heker* (an object that serves as a reminder to avoid mixing their foods) is placed between them. In order to accomplish this, one may place an object on the table that is not ordinarily present, or the participants in the meal may use different tablecloths or placemats.[127] It is also prohibited for them to use the same loaf of challah.

9. **Preparing for or Participating in a *Milchig* Meal while *Fleishig*:** A person is permitted to cook and prepare for a *milchig* meal even if he has eaten meat and he hasn't yet waited for sufficient time to be permitted to eat dairy.[128] He may also join a *milchig* meal and eat parve foods, although it is possible

---

124. בדה"ש סי' פ"ט סק"ז (אמנם, לשון הדגו"מ משמע להיפוך).
125. עי' תשובות והנהגות ח"א סי' תל"א.
126. עי' בקובץ הלכות להגר"ע אויערבאך שליט"א עמוד ר"י ובהערות לשם בשם הגריש"א זצ"ל.
127. שו"ע יו"ד סי' פ"ח ס"א-ס"ב.
128. יד אפרים יו"ד סי' פ"ח.

that a *heker* should be employed. Nevertheless, many *poskim* rule that a *heker* is not necessary in this scenario.[129]

10. **Washing Drinking Glasses between *Fleishig* and *Milchig* Meals:** Drinking glasses used for a meal of one type (*fleishig* or *milchig*) should not be used for a meal of the other type without being washed.[130]

11. **Eating *Milchig* Foods after Kiddush:** There is a third practice mentioned by the *poskim* to fulfill the custom of eating dairy on Shavuos: Some people recite Kiddush and then partake of *milchig* foods, and then serve a *fleishig* bread meal for the Yom Tov *seudah* after a short break.[131] A person who follows this practice should make sure to eat at least a *kezayis* of mezonos foods after Kiddush, in order to satisfy the requirement of *Kiddush b'makom seudah*. The halachos discussed in paragraphs 3-4 above regarding eating meat after milk should be kept in mind as well.

12. **The *Brachah* on Cheesecake:** Since it is a common practice to serve cheesecake on Shavuos, it is important to be aware of the correct *brachah*. If the cake is made with a substantial layer of dough that is intended to make it more satiating or to improve its taste, the *brachah* of mezonos should be recited. On the other hand, if the cheesecake has a thin crust whose purpose is only to hold the cake together or to improve its texture, its *brachah* is *shehakol*.[132] For a cheesecake whose *brachah rishonah* is *borei minei mezonos*, one should recite the *brachah* of *al hamichyah* after eating it, provided that one has consumed a *kezayis* of the dough within the span of *k'dei achilas pras*. If a person has eaten only a *kezayis* of the cheese

---

129. עי׳ דרכ״ת סי׳ פ״ח ס״ק ט״ז.
130. רמ״א סי׳ פ״ח ס״ב.
131. עי׳ דרכ״ת סי׳ פ״ט ס״ק י״ט.
132. מ״ב סי׳ קס״ח ס״ק כ״ז וס״ק מ״ה.

Eating Dairy on Shavuos

portion of the cake within this span of time, he should recite *borei nefashos*, even though he recited the *brachah* of *borei minei mezonos* before partaking of it.[133] If a person eats only one *kezayis* containing both dough and cheese, the correct *brachah acharonah* is *borei nefashos*.[134]

8. Other *Minhagim* of Shavuos

1. **Adorning Shuls and Homes with Greenery:** There is a *minhag* to decorate shuls and homes with greenery in honor of Shavuos. This practice commemorates the fact that Har Sinai was covered with flora at the time of the giving of the Torah. (Since Bnei Yisrael were warned not to allow their animals to graze on the mountain [*Shemos* 34:3], we infer that Har Sinai was covered with lush greenery.)[135]

2. **The *Muktzeh* Status of Plants:** Flowers and other plants and branches that were prepared before Yom Tov are not *muktzeh* (even if the plants do not produce pleasant fragrances and are not edible for animals), since they were designated to serve as decoration before Yom Tov began.[136] Flowers or plants found outside on Yom Tov are *muktzeh* even if they have already been detached from the ground.

3. **Moving Plants on Shabbos or Yom Tov:** It is permissible to decorate one's house with plants and flowers and to move the greenery around on Yom Tov. However, if Shavuos begins on Motzaei Shabbos, decorating the house with plants on

---

133. עי' מ"ב סי' ר"ח ס"ק מ"ח. ועי' בשו"ת מנחת שלמה סי' צ"א אות ד'.
134. מ"ב סי' ר"י סק"א.
135. רמ"א סי' תצ"ד ס"ג ובמ"ב סק"י.
136. מ"ב סק"ט.

Shabbos would be considered *hachanah* and is therefore prohibited.[137]

4. **Moving a Vase of Flowers:** Some *poskim* maintain that flowers that have been placed in water and have not fully blossomed may be moved only very slowly, since shaking the vase may cause the flowers to blossom more rapidly.[138] A vase that contains flowers in full bloom, or that contains plants that will not blossom or grow, may be moved in an ordinary fashion. Such flowers or plants may even be removed from the water, since they are not subject to the *melachah* of *toleish* (detaching).[139]

5. **Placing Flowers in Water on Shabbos or Yom Tov:** It is prohibited to place flowers or any other plants that will grow in water on Shabbos and Yom Tov. This prohibition applies even if the plants have fallen out of a vase with water or were briefly removed from their water. A plant that does not grow may not be placed into water for the first time, due to the prohibition of *tircha*; however, it is permitted to return the plant to water in which it was previously placed. Even if a vase of water was prepared for the plant before Yom Tov, it may potentially be considered a prohibited act of *tircha* to place it in the water on Yom Tov.[140] There is a dispute among the *poskim* as to whether one may return flowers in full bloom to water in which they were previously placed.[141]

It is prohibited to add water to a vase on Shabbos;[142] however, this is permitted on Yom Tov.[143]

---

137. מ"ב שם.
138. הגרש"ז זצ"ל הובא דבריו בס' יד ליולדת. ועי' ארחות שבת פי"ט הערה קפ"ה.
139. ששכ"ה פכ"ו סכ"ו.
140. רמ"א סי' של"ו סי"א ובמ"ב ס"ק נ"ד.
141. ששכ"ה פכ"ו סכ"ו והערה צ"א.
142. מ"ב סי' של"ו ס"ק נ"ד.
143. שו"ע סי' תרנ"ד.

Other Minhagim of Shavuos ~ 133

6. **Inhaling the Scent of Fragrant Branches and Leaves:** In shuls where it is customary to pass around branches and leaves during davening for the congregants to inhale their fragrance, this should not be done during *Pesukei D'zimrah*, and certainly not during the *brachos* of *Krias Shema*, since it is prohibited to recite a *brachah* on a pleasant fragrance at those times. The fragrant plants should instead be passed around after *Shemoneh Esrei* so that the *brachah* (*borei atzei besamim* or *borei isvei besamim*) may be recited.[144]

7. **Placing Trees in Shuls and Homes:** Another *minhag* mentioned by *poskim* is the practice of placing actual trees in shuls and homes, to allude to the judgment on fruit trees that takes place on Shavuos and to remind us to daven for good fruit.[145] (Due to the prohibition of *bal tashchis*, an actual fruit tree should not be uprooted and used for this purpose.) Some authorities argue that this practice should be discontinued today, since non-Jews customarily place trees in their homes on their own holidays.[146] Others, however, defend this custom.[147]

8. **Plants and *Chukos Hagoyim*:** The authorities who initially opposed the custom of placing trees in a home or shul did not raise the same objection to the previously mentioned *minhag* (in paragraph 1) to use plants and flowers for decoration.[148] Nevertheless, some later *poskim* did call for the *minhag* of using plants or flowers for decoration to be abolished as well.[149]

---

144. מ"ב סק"י.

145. מ"א סק"ה הוב"ד במ"ב סק"י. (ויש לעיין למה לא נהגו להעמיד תבואה בחג הפסח ואולי מפני חשש חמץ.)

146. הגר"א הוב"ד במ"ב שם. ועי' חיי אדם סוף כלל קל"א. ועי' חכמת אדם כלל פ"ט ס"א.

147. דעת תורה למהרש"ם סי' תצ"ד ס"ג עפ"י הריב"ש מאחר שאינו חוקה להם אלא עושים מאיזה טעם ליכא משום ובחוקותיהם לא תלכו.

148. כמו שצטטו הפוסקים הנ"ל את דברי הגר"א, וכן נקט למעשה הגריש"א זצ"ל הוב"ד בהלכות חג בחג פ"ח הערה 24.

149. ערוך השלחן סי' תצ"ד ס"ו.

Every shul or community should follow its own established custom.

9. **Avoiding Theft while Collecting Flowers:** One must take care, and warn children, not to pick flowers or plants growing on public or municipal property, and certainly not to take plants or flowers from the private property of others. It is certainly improper to honor the day of *Kabbalas haTorah* with stolen items.

10. **Dancing on Shavuos:** Although dancing and clapping are generally prohibited on Shabbos and Yom Tov,[150] many yeshivos and congregations have the custom to dance on Shavuos. This is permitted since the dancing is in honor of the Torah.[151] (It should be noted that there is a halachic basis to permit dancing even on a regular Shabbos or Yom Tov, and those who have the custom to do so may rely on this.[152])

---

150. שו״ע סי׳ של״ט ס״ג.
151. עי׳ מ״ב סי׳ של״ט סק״ח. וראה גם מ״ב סי׳ תרס״ט סק״ה לענין שמחת תורה. ובשעה״צ שם סק״ה הוסיף שלכאורה ה״ה הדמותר לספק כף אל כף. ובטעם הדבר למה התירו לרקוד כתב הפמ״ג סי׳ של״ט א״א סק״א מפני שלאו דרך המשוררים (כלומר שריקוד לכבוד התורה הוא ענין ריקוד אחר לגמרי).
152. רמ״א סי׳ של״ט ס״ג ובמ״ב שם סק״י.

Other Minhagim of Shavuos 135

CHAPTER FIVE
Shivah Asar B'Tammuz

1. Halachos of the Fast
2. Exemptions from the Fast
3. General Halachos of Shivah Asar B'Tammuz
4. Halachos Pertaining to *Tefillah* on a Fast Day

CHAPTER FIVE
Shivah Asar B'Tammuz

Introduction: The *neviim* instituted four public fast days to be observed over the course of the year. These fast days are listed in the *pasuk* (*Zechariah* 8) that describes "*tzom harevii, v'tzom hachamishi, v'tzom hashevii, v'tzom ha'asiri* – the fast of the fourth [month], the fast of the fifth, the fast of the seventh, and the fast of the tenth." The fast of the fourth month is the 17th of Tammuz (as the month of Tammuz is the fourth month from Nissan), while the other fasts enumerated in this *pasuk* are the fasts of Tishah b'Av (the ninth day of Av, the fifth month of the year), Tzom Gedaliah (the third day of Tishrei, which is the seventh month from Nissan) and Asarah b'Teves (the tenth day of the tenth month).[1]

The objective of these fast days is for the Jewish people to be spurred to engage in *teshuvah*. Each of these days commemorates specific tragic events and thus reminds us of the calamities that befell our nation on account of our forefathers' sins. This is meant to lead us to realize that we have been guilty of the same sins and we have a duty to repent. Consequently, every person must make a reckoning of his deeds and engage in *teshuvah* on these fast days. Fasting alone does not fulfill the goal of the days; it is merely a means of prodding ourselves to repent. Abstaining from food and drink without contemplating one's deeds and the need for repentance would therefore be ignoring the purpose

---
1. ר"ה דף יח:

of the fast. (On the other hand, of course, a person is required to fast; one may not simply engage in *teshuvah* and skip the fast itself.)[2]

1. Halachos of the Fast

1. **A Public Fast:** The 17th of Tammuz is a public fast day. Every person is obligated to fast on this day in order to remind himself of the calamities that it commemorates and to be motivated to repent for his or her sins.[3]

2. **A Mandatory Fast:** This fast is mandatory[4] for all adult men and women.[5] The obligation to fast on Shivah Asar b'Tammuz begins at the age of 13 for a boy and at the age of 12 for a girl.[6]

3. **The Five Tragedies Commemorated by the Fast:** The fast of the 17th of Tammuz commemorates five tragic events: First, it was the date when the first *Luchos* were broken when Moshe Rabbeinu descended from Har Sinai. It was also the date when the *korban tamid* was discontinued toward the end of the era of the first *Beis Hamikdash*. Toward the end of the era of the second *Beis Hamikdash*, the walls of Yerushalayim were breached on the same date. Finally, the 17th of Tammuz was the day when a *sefer Torah* was burned by Apostamus, as well as when an idol was erected inside the *Beis Hamikdash*.[7]

Although the city walls were breached on the ninth of

---

2. שו"ע סי' תקמ"ט ס"א ובמ"ב סק"א.
3. שו"ע שם.
4. מדינא דגמ', ר"ה דף י"ח:, בזמן דליכא שמד אין חייבים להתענות, מ"מ כבר נהגו וקבלו כחובה ואין לשנות ואסור לפרוץ גדר, טור ושו"ע סי' תק"נ ס"א, ובמ"ב סק"א.
5. שו"ע שם.
6. עי' ביה"ל שם ד"ה הכל חייבים, שכתב בשם הפמ"ג, שאף אם לא הביאו שתי שערות חייבים, וזה סותר משנ"כ במ"ב סי' תרט"ז ס"ק י"ג בשם המ"א, ועי' בשו"ת שבט הלוי ח"ו סי' קכ"ב אות ב' שהעלה דדברי הפמ"ג כאן הוא רק מצד מנהג.
7. תענית דף כו., הובא במ"ב סי' תקמ"ט סק"ב.

Tammuz during the period of the first *Beis Hamikdash*, we do not fast on that date as well, since it would be too onerous for the Jewish people to observe two fast days in such close succession. The 17th of Tammuz, rather than the ninth, was chosen to commemorate this calamity because the later destruction is more significant.[8]

4. **The Duration of the Fast:** The fast of Shivah Asar b'Tammuz begins at *alos hashachar* (daybreak) unlike the fast of Tishah b'Av, which begins on the previous night.[9] The fast concludes at *tzeis hakochavim*.

5. **Rising before *Alos Hashachar* to Eat or Drink:** If a person wishes to wake up before daybreak in order to eat, he must have in mind before going to sleep that he will do so. If a person fails to have this intention, he is considered to have begun his fast upon retiring for the night.[10] A person who usually drinks after he wakes up in the morning is considered to have had the intention to drink even if he failed to make a mental stipulation to that effect; however, *lechatchilah* a person who wishes to drink in the morning should make sure to have the express intention to do so.[11] When eating before *alos hashachar*, one may not eat more than a *kebeitzah* of baked mezonos (or bread) within the final half hour before daybreak.[12]

6. **Fasting for Children:** The obligation of *chinuch* does not extend to fasting. Therefore, even if a child is old enough to understand the concept of fasting and mourning, he should

---

8. ר"ה יח: ותוס' שם ד"ה זה תשעה ובשו"ע סי' תקמ"ט ס"ב, ובמ"ב סק"ד.
9. שו"ע סי' תק"נ ס"ב. והטעם משום דבזמן דליכא שמד אין חיוב מדינא להתענות רק מפני שנהגו וקבלו עליהם, כנתבאר לעיל, ובשעה שקבלו לא קבלו שיהא בחומר של תשעה באב לפי שאין רוב הציבור יכולים לעמוד בה.
10. שו"ע סי' תקס"ד ס"א.
11. רמ"א סי' תקס"ד, ובמ"ב שם סק"ו.
12. מ"ב סי' פ"ט ס"ק כ"ז.

Halachos of the Fast ~ 141

not observe the fast, even for part of the day. A child should not even observe a *taanis shaos* (postponing his usual meal for an hour, which is the practice on Yom Kippur). Nevertheless, a child who has reached the age of *chinuch* should be served only basic foods and should refrain from eating delicacies.[13]

7. **The Final Three Fasts of Childhood:** Many have a custom for a child to observe the final three fasts prior to bar or bas mitzvah. This is not a recorded *minhag* and its observance is not mandatory.[14]

8. **A Bar Mitzvah on a Postponed Fast:** When the 17th of Tammuz falls on Shabbos, the fast is postponed to the following day. In this situation, it is questionable whether a child who becomes bar or bas mitzvah on the 18th of Tammuz, the day of the postponed fast, is obligated to observe the fast. Some *poskim* maintain that since the fast on the 18th of Tammuz takes the place of the obligation that ordinarily exists on the 17th, a person who was still a child on the 17th and was therefore exempt from fasting is likewise exempt on the 18th. Others maintain that when the fast is observed on the 18th, any person who is an adult on that day is obligated to fast.[15] If this situation arises, a Rav should be consulted for a practical ruling.

9. **A Broken Fast:** If a person erroneously breaks his fast during the day, he is not permitted to continue eating after he realizes his error. Instead, he must resume fasting for the remainder of the day.[16] Nevertheless, he is not obligated to observe a fast on

---

13. מ"ב סי' תק"נ סק"ה. וראה הליכות שלמה פי"ג הע' 10.
14. ראה הליכות שלמה פי"ג סק"ו והע' 11 בשם הגרשז"א זצ"ל.
15. נמצא בגדולי הפוסקים דעות שונות בזה, בשו"ת אבני נזר סי' תכ"ו, ועוד, נקטו שפטור, ובשו"ת מהרש"ם ח"ג סי' שס"ג, ועוד, נקטו שחייב. ועי' שו"ת שבט הלוי ח"ד סי' ע"ב וח"ו סי' ע"א, שו"ת אבן ישראל ח"ז סי' כ"ו (כ' לפטור מתענית ולחייבו באבילות), ועוד. וראה הליכות שלמה פי"ג הערה 10 שהגרשז"א זצ"ל צידד לומר שפטור.
16. מ"ב סי' תקמ"ט סק"ג.

a different day to compensate for his error (although he may decide of his own accord to do so for the sake of atonement).[17] A person who has erroneously broken his fast should still recite *Aneinu* in the *Shemoneh Esrei* of *Minchah*.[18] (However, a person who is not fasting, such as someone who is ill, should not recite *Aneinu*.[19])

10. **Fasting for *Baalei Simchah*:** A person who celebrates a *bris* is nonetheless required to fast. Likewise, a newlywed chassan and kallah must fast even during the week of *sheva brachos*.[20]

2. Exemptions from the Fast

1. **Pregnant and Nursing Women:** Pregnant and nursing women are not halachically obligated to fast.[21] (This is also the case on Tzom Gedaliah and Asarah b'Teves; however, the halachos pertaining to Tishah b'Av are different, as will be explained in Chapter Eight, section 1.) The recorded *minhag*, though, is for women to observe the fast even if they are pregnant or nursing, unless they suffer great discomfort[22] or feel weak as a result of the fast.[23] Notwithstanding this *minhag*, many *poskim* have ruled that pregnant and nursing women should not fast at all today, since we are weaker than the people of previous

---

17. מ"ב סי' תקס"ח סק"ח. ושאני תעניות יחיד מתעניות ציבור שבתענית יחיד מחוייב להתענות יום אחר כמוש"כ הרמ"א שם.
18. מ"ב שם סק"ג.
19. ביה"ל סי' תקס"ה ס"א ד"ה בין.
20. ביה"ל סי' תקמ"ט ד"ה חייבים להתענות, מ"ב סי' תק"נ ס"ק י"ב (אבל עי' שעה"צ סי' תרפ"ו ס"ק ט"ז בשם הגר"א).
21. רמ"א סי' תק"נ ס"א. משום שבשעה שרצו וקבלו עליהן להתענות הקילו לכתחילה עליהן. ועי' במ"ב סק"ג דמעוברת לענין זה מקרי משעה שהוכר הולד ואפשר דלאחר ארבעים יום הוי בכלל זה אם מרגשת צער אבל בבציר מהכי הויא לה ככל הנשים אם לא שמצטערת הרבה או מרגשת חולשה. ועי"ש בשעה"צ סק"ב.
22. רמ"א שם.
23. מ"ב סק"ה.

generations were, and fasting is more difficult today.[24] A Rav should be consulted for a conclusive ruling.

2. **A Woman after Birth:** It is questionable if a woman is exempt from fasting within the first 24 months after childbirth if she is not nursing. Although a woman in this situation is governed by the same halachos as a nursing mother regarding some issues, there is a dispute among the *poskim* regarding her obligation on a fast day.[25] A woman in this situation should consult a Rav. Within the first 30 days after childbirth, though, a woman is certainly exempt from fasting, even if she is not nursing.

3. **Fasting in a Case of Illness:** A person who is bedridden due to illness, such as a person suffering from a fever, is exempt from fasting even if there is no concern that it might endanger him. (A person in this situation is described in halachah as "*choleh kol haguf*" – literally, someone whose entire body is ailing.) This exemption does not apply, however, to someone who is merely suffering from pain or an ailment such as a headache.[26] If the fast might be detrimental to an individual's health, as is often the case for an elderly person, one is exempt from fasting.[27]

4. **A Minor Ailment on a Postponed Fast:** When the 17th

---

24. עי' ס' מנהג ישראל תורה סי' תק"נ שהביא כמה מרמ"ק לזה. ולענין א"י שמזג האויר קשה בתקופה זו, עי' הליכות שלמה פט"ז הע' 2 שדעת הגרשז"א זצ"ל שאין להם להתענות (אם מרגשת חולשה מעט מן הרגיל), וכן עי' חוט שני שבת ח"ד עמוד רס"א שדעתו כן. וכן נוהגים כמה רבנים להורות למעשה אף בחו"ל. ובפרט במינקת, אם ע"י הצום לא תהא לה מספיק חלב, שאין להתענות, עי' הליכות שלמה שם ס"ק ה'-ז' ובחוט שני שם עמוד רנ"ט. ועי' שם בחוט שני עמוד ר"ס שכ' שאם מחמירה לצום כשאינה מצטערת אך ע"י התעסקות בצרכי הבית תבוא לידי מצטערת יש לה להתעסק בצרכי הבית ולא להתענות.

25. עי' דעת תורה למהרש"ם סי' תק"נ ומסקנתו להקל. אמנם דעת הגרי"ש אלישיב זצ"ל הוב"ד בס' הלכות ומנהגי ביהמ"צ עמוד י"ז הערה 12 להחמיר. וראה חוט שני ח"ד שבת עמוד ר"ס. ואם מינקת רק במקצת ע"י חוט שני שאפי' רק מניקה פעם אחת ביום, יש להקל שדינה כמינקת.

26. מ"ב סק"ד. ועי' ביה"ל ד"ה מידהו עוברות.

27. כף החיים סי' תק"נ סק"ו.

of Tammuz falls on Shabbos and the fast is postponed to Sunday ("*nidcheh*"), the halachah is more lenient regarding an exemption from fasting. In this case, even a person who does not have the status of "*choleh kol haguf*" and is merely suffering from pain (which is described in halachah as "*michush*" or "*choli ketzas*") is exempt from fasting.[28]

5. **Taking Antibiotics:** A person who is taking a course of antibiotics for an illness which was classified as *choleh kol haguf* is exempt from fasting, even if the symptoms of his illness have subsided.[29]

6. **Fasting in Spite of an Exemption:** A person who is exempt from fasting is not permitted to choose to observe the fast.[30] A person in this situation should eat normal quantities of food (as the practice of eating in increments smaller than a *shiur* applies only on Yom Kippur[31]) and with normal frequency (i.e., he should not fast even for part of the day or delay meals).[32] Nevertheless, a person who is not fasting should preferably refrain from consuming meat or wine unless there is a need to do so.[33] A person who is exempt from fasting on Shivah Asar b'Tammuz is not required to make up the fast on a different day.[34]

7. **Swallowing a Pill:** A person who is required to fast because he does not have the status of *choleh kol haguf* but is suffering from a minor illness or pain (which warrants breaking the fast only if it is a *nidcheh*) is permitted to swallow a pill. He

---

28. חי' רע"א סי' תקנ"ט ס"ט הובא בביה"ל שם ד"ה ואינו משלים.
29. הוראת הגרמ"ש קליין שליט"א הובא בתורת המועדים סי' תק"נ סק"ז.
30. מ"ב סק"ד ושעה"צ סק"ג.
31. שו"ת קובץ תשובות סי' נ"ז ושו"ת שבט הלוי ח"ד סי' נ"ו.
32. עי' שו"ת אבני נזר או"ח סי' תק"מ ועי' מועדים וזמנים ח"ח סי' של"ה בשם הגרי"ז מה שאמר בשם הגר"ח.
33. מ"ב סק"ה.
34. עי' ביה"ל ד"ה אין להתענות.

may swallow the pill with his saliva; however, he may not swallow it with water, nor may he consume sweet medicinal syrups or flavored pills. If it is impossible to swallow the pill without liquid, he should add a substance with a foul taste to the water before swallowing it.[35] Some *poskim*, however, permit swallowing a pill with water, provided that one uses the smallest possible quantity of liquid.[36]

8. **When Fasting Affects One's Work:** The *poskim* are in dispute as to whether a person may engage in his ordinary activities if it will prevent him from completing the fast. For instance, if a person is involved in communal affairs and he knows that the work while fasting will cause him to become sick, or if he has a job and anticipates that while fasting and working he will become ill, it is not clear that he is permitted to go about his usual activities. Some *poskim* maintain that such a person is permitted to work, and if he feels ill, he will then be allowed to break his fast.[37] However, other *poskim* rule that a person is not permitted to work if it will cause him to have the need to break his fast.[38] Doctors and nurses may be exempt from fasting if it could affect their work or judgment.[39] A Rav should be consulted for a ruling in any such scenario.

---

35. עי' באה"ט סי' תקס"ז סק"ז וכף החיים סי' תקנ"ד ס"ק ל"ד. ועי' שו"ת אגר"מ או"ח ח"ג סוסי' צ"א.
36. עי' אמת ליעקב הערה 522 שכ' להרגיל עצמו כמה ימים קודם לבלוע בלא מים ואם אינו יכול מותר לקחת עם מעט מים פחות מכשיעור, ועי' תשובות והנהגות ח"ג סי' קנ"ו.
37. עי' שו"ת אגר"מ או"ח ח"ד סי' קי"ד.
38. דעת הגריש"א זצ"ל הובא בס' תורת המועדים סי' תק"נ סק"ז.
39. עי' הליכות שלמה פי"ג הערה 12.

3. General Halachos of Shivah Asar B'Tammuz

1. **The Differences between Shivah Asar B'Tammuz and Tishah B'Av:** On the fasts of Shivah Asar b'Tammuz, Tzom Gedaliah, and Asarah b'Teves, there is no prohibition to bathe, to anoint oneself with oil, to wear leather shoes, or to engage in marital relations. These fasts also begin in the morning (at *alos hashachar*) rather than on the night before, unlike the fast of Tishah b'Av.[40]

2. **Bathing in Hot Water:** Although it is technically not prohibited to bathe or shower on Shivah Asar b'Tammuz, the *minhag* is to refrain from bathing in hot water. It is permissible to wash one's hands, face, and feet in hot water or to bathe or shower in cold water.[41] When Asarah b'Teves falls on Erev Shabbos (which is not possible on Shivah Asar b'Tammuz or Tzom Gedaliah), it is permissible to bathe or shower in hot water for the sake of *kavod* Shabbos.[42]

   If a woman's *leil tevilah* falls on the night after the fast, she may perform the standard *chafifah* during the day, using hot water.

3. **Pious Conduct:** A pious person should preferably be stringent and observe the prohibitions of Tishah b'Av on Shivah Asar b'Tammuz as well. Thus, he should abstain from marital relations on the night prior to the fast (unless it is a *leil tevilah*) and should also avoid anointing himself. The only restriction

---

40. שו"ע סי' תק"נ ס"ב. והטעם משום דבזמן דליכא שמד אין התענית מדינא אלא שנהגו וקבלו עליהם ובשעה שקבלו עליהם לא קבלו שיהיו בחומר של תשעה באב לפי שאין רוב הציבור יכולים לעמוד בה.
41. שעה"צ סק"ח.
42. מ"ב סק"ו.

that should not be observed is the prohibition to wear leather shoes, which is a public display of mourning and will cause a person to be mocked.[43] (Technically, this stringency would also entail beginning the fast at sunset on the previous night, just as the fast of Tishah b'Av begins at night.[44] Nevertheless, this is a more difficult stringency to observe and the practice is almost unheard of; therefore, even a pious person is not expected to begin fasting until daybreak.[45])

4. **Music and Haircuts:** There may be grounds on Shivah Asar b'Tammuz as well as the other fast days to observe the halachos of mourning that pertain during the Nine Days (the period from Rosh Chodesh Av through Tishah b'Av).[46] Consequently, one should preferably refrain from listening to music or taking a haircut on all fast days.[47]

5. **Celebrating a Wedding or *Sheva Brachos* on the Night before the Fast:** There is a difference of opinion among the *poskim* regarding whether a wedding may be held on the night before the fast.[48] If this issue is relevant, one should consult a Rav for a final ruling. A *sheva brachos* held on the night prior to the fast should be on a smaller scale than usual. After the conclusion of the fast, however, a *sheva brachos* may be held in the normal fashion.[49]

6. **Brushing Teeth:** A person may not rinse his mouth or brush his teeth on Shivah Asar b'Tammuz unless he will suffer

---

43. מ״ב שם.
44. שעה״צ סק״ט.
45. הגרח״ק שליט״א הובא בתורת המועדים סי׳ תק״נ ס״ק י״ד.
46. ביה״ל סי׳ תקנ״א ס״ב ד״ה מראש חודש בשם הא״ר והפרמ״ג. אמנם, עי׳ בדע״ת ובשונה הלכות מש״כ בזה ועי׳ שיש כאן ט״ס.
47. ראה קיצור שו״ע סי׳ קכ״ב ס״א שכתב לאסור כלי זמר גם בעשרה בטבת. ומש״כ בפנים לענין תספורת לכאורה פשוט דה״ה. ומיהו יש לעיין לענין בגדים מכובסים וכיבוס גופא, ולא שמענו למנוע מזה.
48. עי׳ שו״ת אגר״מ או״ח ח״א סי׳ קס״ח ועי׳ הליכות שלמה פי״ג ס״א ובהערות לשם.
49. הליכות שלמה שם.

discomfort. If a person needs to cleanse his mouth, he should keep his head down while doing so to avoid swallowing water.[50] One may apply deodorant.

7. **When a Fast Day Conflicts with Shabbos:** If the 17th of Tammuz falls on Shabbos, the fast is postponed until Sunday.[51] (There is no prohibition of marital relations on that Shabbos.[52]) If a fast day falls on Friday (which is possible only on the fast of Asarah b'Teves), the fast is observed even though it is Erev Shabbos, and one may not eat or drink until *tzeis hakochavim* (after Kiddush).[53]

8. **Meat and Wine after the Fast:** After the conclusion of the fast, one may eat meat and drink wine. This is prohibited only after the conclusion of Tishah b'Av.

4. Halachos Pertaining to *Tefillah* on a Fast Day

1. ***Aneinu*:** In Ashkenazic congregations, *Aneinu* is not recited during the silent *Shemoneh Esrei* at *Shacharis*.[54] *Aneinu* is recited by the *shaliach tzibbur* during his repetition of the *Shemoneh Esrei* both at *Shacharis* and at *Minchah*. In both cases, it takes the form of an independent *brachah* between the *brachos* of *goel Yisrael* and *refaeinu*, concluding with the words "*baruch Atah Hashem ha'oneh l'amo Yisrael b'eis tzarah.*"[55]

---

50. עי' מ"ב סי' תקס"ז ס"ק י"א ובשו"ת מנחת יצחק ח"ד סי' ק"ט.
51. שו"ע סי' תק"ן ס"ג.
52. דלא מצאנו רק לענין ת"ב שחל בשבת שדנו הפוסקים אם תשמיש מותר.
53. רמ"א סי' תק"ט ס"ג. ואומרים עננו וקוראין ויחל שחרית ומנחה, ורק א"א תחנון ואבינו מלכנו במנחה לפי שהוא ע"ש (ולכן אם ערב ר"ח חל בע"ש מתפללים יו"כ קטן ביום חמישי שלפניו לפי שא"א וידויים וסליחות במנחה של ע"ש).
54. רמ"א סי' תקס"ה ס"ג ובמ"ב סק"י.
55. שו"ע סי' תקס"ו ס"א ובמ"ב סק"ב.

2. **If the *Shaliach Tzibbur* Omits *Aneinu*:** If the *shaliach tzibbur* omits the passage of *Aneinu* and realizes his error before concluding the *brachah* of *refaeinu*, he should immediately recite *Aneinu* and then repeat the *brachah* of *refaeinu*. If he realizes his error only after concluding the *brachah*, he should recite *Aneinu* during the *brachah* of *shema koleinu*, before the words "*ki Atah shomea*" (at the same point in davening at which an individual would recite it) and omit the concluding *brachah* of "*ha'oneh l'amo Yisrael b'eis tzarah*."[56]

3. **Reciting *Aneinu* while Fasting:** In order to recite *Aneinu*, the *shaliach tzibbur* must be fasting.[57] (It is also necessary for a *minyan* of people, or according to some opinions at least seven individuals within the congregation, to be fasting.[58]) If the only person who can serve as *shaliach tzibbur* is not fasting, he should recite *Aneinu* during the *brachah* of *shema koleinu*, omitting its concluding *brachah*. He should also recite the words "*b'yom tzom hataanis hazeh*" in place of "*b'yom tzom taaniseinu*."[59]

4. **Selichos:** *Selichos* are recited on the morning of a fast day after the chazzan's repetition of the *Shemoneh Esrei*.[60] (Even a person who is exempt from fasting should recite *Selichos*.) *Lechatchilah*, *Selichos* should be recited with a *minyan*; however, a person who is unable to daven with a *minyan* should recite *Selichos* as well, omitting the recitation of the *yud gimmel middos*.[61]

5. **Avinu Malkeinu:** It is customary to recite *Avinu Malkeinu* after *Selichos*. The common custom is to open the *aron kodesh*

---

56. שו״ע סי׳ קי״ט ס״ד ורמ״א שם ומ״ב ס״ק ט״ז.
57. שו״ע סי׳ תקס״ו ס״ה.
58. מ״ב סי׳ תקס״ו ס״ק י״ד, ושעה״צ ס״ק ט״ו.
59. מ״ב שם ס״ק י״ח.
60. שו״ע שם ס״ד.
61. מ״ב סי׳ תקס״ה ס״ק י״ג.

for this *tefillah*. Nevertheless, *Avinu Malkeinu* should be recited even if a *minyan* is not present and even if there is no *aron kodesh*.

6. ***Krias HaTorah***: There is a Torah reading on every fast day, even if the fast does not fall on a Monday or Thursday.[62] The portion of "*Vayechal*" (*Shemos* 32:11-14 and 34:1-10) is read, divided into three *aliyos*.

7. **Receiving an *Aliyah* if One Is Not Fasting:** A person who is not fasting (or who knows he will not complete the fast) should not be given an *aliyah*.[63] If he is called to the Torah, then he may accept the *aliyah* if it is a Monday or Thursday, when the Torah would be read even if it was not a fast day. On a different day of the week, he should not accept the *aliyah* unless he will suffer great embarrassment if it becomes publicly known that he is not fasting.[64] If the only *kohanim* in shul are not fasting, they should leave the shul before *Krias HaTorah* so that the *aliyah* of *kohen* can be given to a *levi* or *yisrael*.[65]

8. ***Krias HaTorah* at *Minchah***: At *Minchah*, after *Ashrei* and the Half Kaddish, the passage of *Vayechal* is read again. The Torah reading at *Minchah* is followed by the *haftarah* that begins with the words "*dirshu Hashem b'himatzo*" (*Yeshayah* 55:6-56:8). The *brachos* on the *haftarah* are recited by the person who receives the third *aliyah*.[66] In Sephardic congregations, no *haftarah* is read on a fast day.

9. **Reciting *Aneinu* at *Minchah***: The *tefillah* of *Aneinu* is recited during the silent *Shemoneh Esrei* at *Minchah*. It is incorporated

---

62. שו"ע שם ס"א.
63. שו"ע שם ס"ו ומ"ב סק"כ. וראה ערוה"ש סי' קל"ה סי"ד שאין לו לעשות הוצאה, הכנסה, הגבהה וגלילה.
64. מ"ב ס"ק י"ט-כ"א.
65. שו"ע ומ"ב שם.
66. רמ"א סי' תקס"ו ס"א.

Halachos Pertaining to Tefillah on a Fast Day ~ 151

in the *brachah* of *shema koleinu*, before the words "*ki Atah shomea.*" (The concluding *brachah* recited by the *shaliach tzibbur* is not recited by an individual.)[67]

10. **If *Aneinu* Is Omitted:** If a person forgets to recite the passage of *Aneinu* and realizes his error before reciting Hashem's Name at the conclusion of the *brachah* of *shema koleinu*, he should return to the passage of *Aneinu* and continue from there. If he realizes his error only after reciting the Name of Hashem, he should continue davening and insert the recitation of *Aneinu* at the end of the *Shemoneh Esrei*, before the passage of *yiheyu leratzon*.[68] (Even if he realizes his error after reciting the words "*baruch Atah Hashem*" but before concluding the *brachah*, he should not recite the words "*lamdeini chukecha*" and return to the middle of the *brachah*, as is done by a person who omits certain other insertions in the *Shemoneh Esrei*; rather, he should recite the concluding words of the *brachah* and wait until the end of the *Shemoneh Esrei* to insert the passage of *Aneinu*.) If he realizes his mistake after reciting the passage of *yiheyu leratzon*, he should not go back or repeat the *Shemoneh Esrei*.[69]

11. **Omitting *Aneinu* when One Is Exempt from Fasting:** A person who is exempt from fasting (e.g., a child or a person who is ill) should not recite *Aneinu*.[70] Nevertheless, if a person has erroneously eaten during the course of the fast, he should recite *Aneinu*, since he must continue fasting until the end of the day.[71]

---

67. שו"ע ורמ"א סי' תקס"ה ס"א.
68. שו"ע ס"ב ומ"ב סק"ו-ז' ושעה"צ סק"ה.
69. שו"ע שם.
70. ביה"ל ריש סי' תקס"ה.
71. מ"ב סי' תקס"ח סק"ג. ועי' שו"ת שבט הלוי ח"ה סי' ס' שמיישב הסתירה בין הביה"ל סי' תקס"ה ס"א למ"ב סי' תקס"ח סק"ג.

Chapter Five: *Shivah Asar B'Tammuz*

CHAPTER SIX

The Period of the Three Weeks

---

1. From Shivah Asar B'Tammuz until Rosh Chodesh Av
2. Halachos of the Nine Days
3. Laundering Garments
4. Wearing New or Freshly Laundered Clothing
5. Sewing, Purchasing, and Mending Garments
6. Abstaining from Meat and Wine
7. Bathing and Showering

CHAPTER SIX

The Period of the Three Weeks

Introduction: The three weeks between the 17th of Tammuz and the ninth of Av are known as "*bein hametzarim*" (the period between calamities). This term alludes to the calamitous events of this time of year, which began with the tragedies of the 17th of Tammuz and culminated with the destruction of the *Beis Hamikdash* on Tishah b'Av.[1] During this time of year, various halachos of mourning are observed, and the halachah requires us to minimize our feelings of joy and refrain from engaging in celebration. It is also customary to refrain from certain activities due to the negative mazel that affects Klal Yisrael at this time of year.

The degree of national mourning increases in its severity over the course of the period of *bein hametzarim*. From Shivah Asar b'Tammuz until Rosh Chodesh Av, we engage in mourning to a limited degree, but the halachos become more stringent with the arrival of Rosh Chodesh Av. The level of mourning increases further on the week of Tishah b'Av and then again on Erev Tishah b'Av, until the mourning reaches its climax on Tishah b'Av itself. The various stages of mourning and their accompanying halachos will be described in detail in this chapter.

---

1. על שם הכתוב "כל רודפיה השיגוה בין המצרים" (איכה א,ג) ופירש"י בשם מדרש אגדה שהוא בין י"ז בתמוז עד תשעה באב.

1. From Shivah Asar B'Tammuz until Rosh Chodesh Av

1. In general, the halachos of mourning that apply throughout the Three Weeks, beginning on Shivah Asar b'Tammuz until Rosh Chodesh Av, have the status of *minhagim* rather than full-fledged prohibitions. The majority of these *minhagim* are observed only by Ashkenazim.

2. **The Onset of the Period of Mourning:** There is a debate among the *poskim* regarding whether the halachos of the *bein hametzarim* period take effect on the night of the 17th of Tammuz or only on the following morning, when the fast begins.[2] The accepted practice is to begin observing all the halachos on the night prior to the fast; however, in extenuating circumstances one may consult a Rav to determine whether there are grounds for leniency in this respect.

3. **Engagements and Weddings:** The Ashkenazic custom is to refrain from conducting weddings throughout the Three Weeks, anytime from Shivah Asar b'Tammuz.[3] (Sephardim observe this prohibition only from Rosh Chodesh Av.[4]) Nevertheless, it is permitted to finalize an engagement and even to hold a celebratory *seudah* to mark the occasion.[5] (See section 2 below regarding an engagement party after Rosh Chodesh Av.)

---

2. עי' שו"ת אגר"מ או"ח ח"א סי' קס"ח שדן בזה ומסיק שיש להקל בלילה ולכן כתב להתיר בעת הצורך נישואין בליל שבעה עשר בתמוז. אמנם כמה פוסקים נוקטים להחמיר מהלילה בכל ההלכות, עי' ארחות רבינו ח"ב עמ' קכ"ז-קכ"ח בשם הגרי"י קנייבסקי זצ"ל, ועי' שו"ת שבה"ל ח"י סי' פ"א אות ב', ועי' מועדים וזמנים ח"ח סי' של"ח.

3. רמ"א סי' תקנ"א ס"ב.

4. מיהו בבן איש חי דברים אות ד' כתב שאע"ג דמדינא אין איסור בנישואין אלא מר"ח מ"מ נהגו לאסור מי"ז תמוז. ולמעשה, הדבר תלוי במנהג.

5. מ"ב ס"ק י"ט ובשעה"צ ס"ק כ"ו (וראה עוד מ"ב סי' תמ"ד ס"ק כ"ד ובשעה"צ שם וביה"ל שם, אמנם עי' במ"ב סי' רמ"ט סק"ט שכתב שסעודה שעושין בשידוכין אינו סעודת מצוה).

4. **Dancing:** It is prohibited to dance during the Three Weeks (even at an engagement party).[6]

5. **Playing Musical Instruments:** It is also prohibited to play musical instruments during the Three Weeks. A person who plays music for income or who works as a music teacher may continue to do so (e.g., for non-Jewish clients or students) until Rosh Chodesh Av.[7] A person may continue playing music after Rosh Chodesh Av as well if he will otherwise suffer a financial loss (e.g., if his student will replace him with a different instructor).

6. **Listening to Music:** It is also prohibited to listen to music during the period after Shivah Asar b'Tammuz. Listening to recorded instrumental music or recorded singing is subject to the same dispute cited above regarding *sefiras haomer* (Chapter Two, section 2; see there for additional details of the prohibition).

7. **Singing:** Some *poskim* maintain that one should even refrain from singing during the Three Weeks, with the exception of songs about the *churban* or those that cause feelings of sorrow.[8] Other *poskim* rule that it is permissible to sing in solitude, but that singing in a group is prohibited, unless it is done at a *seudas mitzvah*.[9] Singing *zemiros* on Shabbos is permitted even when Tishah b'Av falls on Shabbos.[10]

---

6. מ"ב סי' תקנ"א ס"ק ט"ז.

7. ביה"ל סי' תקנ"א ס"ב ד"ה ממעטים בשם הפמ"ג. (אמנם, ראה קיצור שו"ע סי' קכ"ב ס"א שבי"ז בתמוז עצמו אסור, והוא עפ"י הפמ"ג הוב"ד בביה"ל סי' תק"נ, והבאנו לעיל פרק ה' שי"א שהוא טעות.)

8. עי' הליכות שלמה פי"ד ס"ג וסק"ה והערה 8. ועי' תורת המועדים סי' תקנ"א ס"ה בשם הגרח"ק שליט"א.

9. דעת הגריש"א זצ"ל הובא בתורת המועדים שם. ובהליכות שלמה שם ס"ד שאסר שירה, כתב שבמסיבת תנאים יש למעט בשירי שמחה אבל אין לרקוד. ושם בסק"ו כתב על קבלת פני חתן הנהוג בישיבה שלא ישירו במחיאת כפים שלא לבוא לידי ריקוד.

10. שו"ת אגר"מ או"ח ח"ד סי' קי"ב ואפי' מי שאין רגיל לשיר בשבת.

8. **Singing or Playing Music to Calm Children:** One may sing or play music to calm small children.[11] It is also permissible for one to play music for someone who is ill or depressed.

9. **Music for Children:** Children who have reached the age of *chinuch* should also refrain from listening to music.

10. **A *Seudas Mitzvah*:** Many *poskim* maintain that it is prohibited to dance or play music at a *seudas mitzvah* (such as a *sheva brachos*, *bris*, or bar mitzvah) during this period.[12] One should consult a Rav to determine the appropriate conduct.

11. **Cutting Hair and Shaving:** It is prohibited to take a haircut or shave during the Three Weeks.[13] (For Sephardim, this prohibition is observed only during the week of Tishah b'Av.[14]) The prohibition applies to women as well; however, a woman may cut off excess hair if it is unattractive to her husband[15] (or for the purpose of a mitzvah such as *tevilah*). A mustache may be trimmed if it interferes with eating.[16] It is prohibited to take a haircut even for the purpose of *kavod* Shabbos.[17]

A Sephardic *bachur* is permitted to take a haircut or shave even if he learns in an Ashkenazic yeshivah.[18]

Some *poskim* rule that an Ashkenazic individual should not cut the hair of a Sephardic person during this time.[19]

---

11. אמת ליעקב הערה 508, הגריש"א זצ"ל הוב"ד בתורת המועדים עמוד קי"ג.
12. מדברי המ"ב ס"ק ט"ז משמע שאסור. וע"י כף החיים סי' תקנ"א סק"מ דשמא יש להתיר לפי מש"כ הרמ"א ס"ב דלצורך מצוה הכל שרי אלא שהביא שבא"ר אוסר ומסיק שתלוי במנהג המקום. וראה ארחות רבינו ח"ב עמוד קכ"ו שדעת הגרי"י קניבסקי זצ"ל לאסור. וכן נקט בשו"ת שבט הלוי ח"ג סי' קנ"ז. וע"י מועדים וזמנים ח"ח סי' של"ח.
13. רמ"א סי' תקנ"א ס"ד.
14. שו"ע שם סי"ב.
15. מ"ב ס"ק ע"ט. וע"י שו"ת אגר"מ יו"ד ח"ב סי' קל"ז.
16. שו"ע שם סי"ג ובמ"ב סק"פ.
17. ע"י מ"ב ס"ק ל"ב ובביה"ל ס"ג ד"ה וכן לכבוד שבת.
18. הליכות שלמה פי"ד ס"י.
19. הגרח"ק שליט"א הובא בתורת המועדים עמוד קי"ז. אמנם דעת הגרשז"א זצ"ל בהליכות שלמה שם ס"ח שמעיקר הדין מותר ורק לכתחילה אין נכון לעשות כן.

A person who will suffer financial loss if he does not shave during this period is permitted to do so until the week of Tishah b'Av.[20] It should be noted, though, that the modern workplace is very liberal and accepting of diversity in appearance, and this situation is very uncommon.

A barber may cut the hair of a non-Jewish customer even after Rosh Chodesh.

12. **Giving a Haircut to a Child:** The prohibition of haircuts extends to children as well.[21] Some authorities maintain that the prohibition to cut a child's hair is not for the purpose of *chinuch*; rather, it is meant to add to the mourning of the adults, who will naturally feel anguish at the sight of children growing their hair long as a sign of mourning.[22] According to this view, the prohibition applies even to children who have not yet reached the age of *chinuch*.[23] Some authorities rule that one may be lenient and any children, even those of *chinuch* age, may take haircuts until the beginning of the week of Tishah b'Av.[24] (See the introduction to the next section regarding when the laws of the week of Tishah b'Av take effect in a year when Tishah b'Av falls on a Shabbos or Sunday.) If there is a need to cut a child's hair during this period, a Rav should be consulted.

13. **Cutting Hair for a *Bris*, *Pidyon Haben* or Bar Mitzvah:** Before a *bris milah*, the parents of the infant, as well as the *mohel* and *sandak*, are permitted to take haircuts and shave. Many *poskim* permit this even after Rosh Chodesh Av, until

---

20. שו"ת אגר"מ או"ח ח"ד סי' ק"ב, הליכות שלמה פי"ד ס"ז.
21. שו"ע שם סי"ד.
22. וכדין מקרעין לקטן בשביל עגמת נפש של הרואים, יו"ד סי' ש"מ.
23. עי' מ"ב ס"ק פ"א ובשעה"צ ס"ק צ"א.
24. חיי אדם הובא במ"ב ס"ק פ"ב ודלא כהא"ר שדעתו להחמיר מי"ז תמוז.

the week of Tishah b'Av.[25] It is not permissible to take a haircut in honor of a *pidyon haben*.[26] It is questionable whether a boy is permitted to take a haircut in honor of his bar mitzvah. One should consult a Rav for a ruling on this issue.

14. **An *Upsheren*:** Some *poskim* permit holding an *upsheren* during this period;[27] however, others rule that it is prohibited.[28]

15. **Cutting Hair for a Shidduch Date:** A girl may have a haircut for shidduch purposes until the beginning of the week of Tishah b'Av; however, a boy should not cut his hair or shave even for the sake of appearing presentable on a date.[29]

16. **Cutting Hair to Fulfill the Mitzvah of Tefillin:** A boy whose hair has grown long and creates a *chatzitzah* for his tefillin may take a haircut.[30]

17. **Hair Removal for Women:** A woman may remove hair from her body if necessary (e.g., removing facial hair or hair from the legs).[31]

18. **Cutting Nails:** Cutting nails is permitted during this period.[32] See section 2 below regarding cutting nails after Rosh Chodesh Av.

19. **Swimming:** There is no prohibition to swim during this period.[33] See below (section 2, paragraph 20) regarding swimming during the Nine Days.

---

25. עי' פמ"ג מ"ז ס"ק י"ג, ועי' שעה"צ סק"ד. ועי' באר היטב סק"ג, שערי תשובה סק"ג וקיצור שו"ע סי' קכ"ב סט"ו. אמנם, עי' שו"ת שבט הלוי ח"י סי' פ"א סק"ז מש"כ שהמנהג להחמיר אפי' מי"ז ואילך.
26. שו"ת חת"ס או"ח סי' קנ"ח.
27. הגריש"א זצ"ל הובא בתורת במועדים עמוד קי"ח.
28. הגרח"ק שליט"א הובא שם.
29. עי' הליכות שלמה פי"ד סק"י והערה 23.
30. שם הערה 19.
31. קיצור הל' בין המצרים להגר"ש איידער זצ"ל בשם הגרמ"פ זצ"ל. הליכות שלמה פי"ד סק"ט. אמת ליעקב הערה 512 שאי"ז בכלל תספורת. ועי' שו"ת שבט הלוי ח"י סי' פ"א אות ח'.
32. שהרי לא נחלקו הפוסקים אלא לענין מר"ח ואילך, עי' מ"ב סי' תקנ"א סק"כ.
33. עי' הליכות שלמה שם ס"ה, אבל צריך ליזהר ממקום מסוכן.

20. **Optional Recitations of *Shehecheyanu*:** Many authorities rule that the *brachah* of *shehecheyanu* should not be recited throughout the period between Shivah Asar b'Tammuz and Tishah b'Av. Therefore, one should refrain from voluntarily entering a situation in which the *brachah* is required (e.g., eating a new fruit or wearing a new garment).[34] Nevertheless, since some authorities maintain that the halachah does not prohibit reciting this *brachah* during this time, the accepted practice is to permit reciting it on Shabbos and on Rosh Chodesh Av.[35] If a person recites the *brachah rishonah* on a new fruit and then realizes his error, it is questionable whether he should recite the *brachah* of *shehecheyanu* as well.[36]

21. **Reciting *Shehecheyanu* when Required:** The previous paragraph relates to reciting the *brachah* of *shehecheyanu* in a situation that can be avoided, such as eating a new fruit or wearing a new garment. It is permissible, however, to recite the *brachah* on a life-cycle event that occurs during this time, such as a *pidyon haben*, the birth of a girl, or a *bris* (for those who have the custom to recite the *brachah* at a *bris milah*).[37] Moreover, one may voluntarily incur the obligation to recite *shehecheyanu* if the opportunity will no longer exist after Tishah b'Av (or on Shabbos), such as if one obtains a new fruit that will not remain fresh.[38]

22. **Satisfying a Need for a New Fruit:** A pregnant woman who craves a fruit that would typically require the recitation of *shehecheyanu* is permitted to eat it; however, she should not

---

34. שו"ע שם סי"ז.
35. מ"ב ס"ק צ"ח ושעה"צ ס"ק צ"ט. ויש לעיין האם מותר ללבוש בגד חדש ולברך בערב שבת מפני שהוא לכבוד שבת או רק לאחר קבלת השבת. ובגליון מים חיים הביא שדעת הגרנ"ק שליט"א להתיר אף קודם קבלת שבת ושדעת הגרח"ק שליט"א להחמיר בדבר. ויש מחמירין לגמרי לענין בגד חדש ורק מקילים בפירות, עי' כה"ח ס"ק ר"ה.
36. עי' שערי תשובה ס"ק ל"ח. ויש לעיין מ"ש מדין חולה שנקט שאוכלים בלי שהחיינו.
37. שו"ע שם.
38. רמ"א שם סי"ז.

recite the *brachah* of *shehecheyanu*. Similarly, a person who is ill and would benefit from consuming such a fruit is permitted to eat it.[39]

23. **Purchasing a New Fruit or Garment:** Since *shehecheyanu* is recited only upon consuming a new fruit, it is permitted to purchase a new fruit if one does not consume it during this time.[40] Similarly, the *brachah* of *shehecheyanu* is usually recited when a new garment is worn for the first time, not when it is bought (unless it needs no alterations, in which case the *brachah* may be recited at the time of the purchase). Consequently, it is permissible to purchase new clothes during this period.[41] After Rosh Chodesh Av, however, it is prohibited to purchase garments of any kind, even those that do not warrant the recitation of *shehecheyanu*, as will be explained in section 5 below.

24. **Wearing New Clothes That Do Not Warrant *Shehecheyanu*:** Until Rosh Chodesh Av, it is permissible to purchase and wear new garments that do not require the recitation of *shehecheyanu*. Likewise, if a person does not customarily recite *shehecheyanu* on garments at all, he may purchase and wear new garments until Rosh Chodesh. However, it is preferable to refrain from wearing an important garment that will cause one to experience joy.[42]

25. **The *Brachah* of *Hatov Vehameitiv*:** There is no prohibition to recite the *brachah* of *hatov vehameitiv* during this period, even if the occasion that warrants the *brachah* would require the recitation of *shehecheyanu* under other circumstances. (For instance, certain occasions require the recitation of *hatov*

---

39. מ"ב ס"ק צ"ט. ויש לעיין למה כתב שאין לברך שהחיינו, ומ"ש ממצוה עוברת, ועי' מש"כ בהליכות שלמה שם הע' 7 בשם הגרשז"א זצ"ל ליישב.

40. כמבואר במ"ב ס"ק ק"א.

41. עי' מ"ב ס"ק מ"ה, כף החיים ס"ק פ"ח, הליכות שלמה שם ס"א וסק"א.

42. ערוך השלחן סי"ח.

vehameitiv because the joyous occasion is shared with family members such as a wife and children; however, an unmarried, childless man who experienced the same situation would recite *shehecheyanu* instead.)[43]

26. **Exercising Caution:** Due to the presence of evil spirits during the Three Weeks, one should not venture alone into an isolated area from the beginning of the fifth hour of the day until the tenth hour. Additionally, one should not hit a student or a child during this period.[44] Some *poskim* recommend postponing all serious medical procedures until after the Three Weeks if possible.[45]

27. **Mourning for the *Beis Hamikdash* during the Day:** One should mourn the *churban Beis Hamikdash* after *chatzos* every day during this period.[46]

2. Halachos of the Nine Days

Introduction: Beginning on Rosh Chodesh Av, a person should limit his happiness and joy, and the halachos of mourning are intensified. Technically, many of the halachic strictures of this period were enacted only during the week of Tishah b'Av; however, the Ashkenazic custom is to begin observing these halachos on Rosh Chodesh Av. The Sephardic custom, on the other hand, is to observe those restrictions only during the week of Tishah b'Av, which is known in halachic parlance as *shavua shechal bo* (literally, "the week when it [Tishah b'Av] takes place"). When Tishah b'Av falls on Shabbos or Sunday, the

---

43. שע"ת על השו"ע ס"ו, שו"ת אגר"מ או"ח ח"ג סי' פ' ד"ה ומכונית, אבל לא התיר מר"ח ואילך (ובלא"ה בד"כ אסור לקנות כלי שמחה מר"ח).
44. שו"ע שם סי"ח.
45. אמת ליעקב הערה 515. ועי' בתורת היולדת פמ"ח הערה כ' עפ"י המהרש"ם בדע"ת, שבחדר ניתוח שיש מזוזה אולי אין קפידא.
46. מ"ב ס"ק ק"ג עפ"י האריז"ל.

poskim debate whether the previous week has the status of *shavua shechal bo*; according to the view that the previous week is not considered *shavua shechal bo*, Sephardim are not required to observe any of the mourning restrictions of this period during such a year.[47] For the majority of halachos, *shavua shechal bo* has no implication for Ashkenazim. Nevertheless, there are certain leniencies that apply even to Ashkenazim until the *shavua shechal bo*, as will be explained in the following sections.

1. **The Onset of the Nine Days:** All the halachos that pertain to the Nine Days (as will be discussed below) come into effect on the night of Rosh Chodesh Av, at *shekiah*.[48]

2. **Minimizing Joy:** Beginning on Rosh Chodesh Av (until after Tishah b'Av), there is a general requirement to minimize one's happiness.[49]

3. **Purchasing Articles That Engender Joy:** During the Nine Days, one may not purchase any articles that engender enjoyment or happiness, such as nice dishes, furniture, home accessories, jewelry, or any luxury item.[50] A vendor who markets such items may sell them only to non-Jews.[51] Even an item that was ordered and paid for before Rosh Chodesh may not be received during this time.[52] If a rare opportunity arises to purchase such an item at a very low price, it might be permissible to take advantage of the sale.[53]

---

47. שו״ע ס״ד. ועי׳ בכה״ח ס״ק ע״ח בשם הבא״ח שהמנהג להקל.
48. מ״א סי׳ תקנ״א ס״ק כ״ו (והוב״ד במ״ב שם ס״ק נ״ו).
49. מתני׳ תענית דף כו׳: שו״ע סי׳ תקנ״א ס״א. ובמ״ב סק״א בשם המ״א דר״ל שאין שמחין בו כלל, ועי״ש בשעה״צ סק״א דלפי דברי תוס׳ ביבמות דף מג. אפשר דהיינו שיתמעט ממה שדרכו לנהוג בשאר הימים.
50. שו״ע שם ס״ב ובמ״ב ס״ק י״א. ועי׳ שעה״צ ס״ק י״ג.
51. שעה״צ סק״י.
52. שו״ת אגר״מ או״ח ח״ג סי׳ פ״ב.
53. מ״ב ס״ק י״א ושעה״צ סקי״ב. ועי׳ כה״ח ס״ק כ״א בשם הבא״ח דה״ה אם לא ימצא שוב לקנותו אחר ת״ב.

One may not purchase items that create happiness even if the *brachah* of *shehecheyanu* is not recited on such a purchase. (An item on which *shehecheyanu* is recited may not be purchased at any time from Shivah Asar b'Tammuz, as explained in section 1. A purchase that warrants the *brachah* of *hatov vehameitiv*, such as an item from which other people will benefit as well, is permitted until Rosh Chodesh.⁵⁴) Standard household items may be purchased even during the Nine Days.

Regular toys and crafts may be purchased for children; however, a *special* toy should not be purchased for children of *chinuch* age.

4. **New Clothes:** The halachah regarding the purchase of apparel is more stringent: Even basic articles of clothing, which do not foster any particular happiness, may not be purchased during the Nine Days. See section 5 for details.

5. **Gifts:** One should refrain from giving or receiving gifts that engender happiness.⁵⁵

6. **Browsing in a Store:** It is permissible to browse in a store ("window shopping") for items that one intends to purchase after Tishah b'Av.⁵⁶

7. **Buying Sefarim:** It is permissible to purchase sefarim during this period.⁵⁷ However, a significant purchase of sefarim that would create special happiness, such as an entire set of Shas, is questionable. Some *poskim* permit buying sefarim only for immediate use.⁵⁸

8. **Conducting Business:** There is a difference of opinion

---

54. שו"ת אגר"מ או"ח ח"ג סי' פ'.
55. שו"ת אגר"מ אבהע"ז ח"ד סי' פ"ד סק"א, הגריש"א זצ"ל הובא בתורת המועדים עמוד ק"כ.
56. שו"ת אגר"מ שם.
57. הליכות שלמה פי"ד הערה 26.
58. הגריש"א זצ"ל הובא בתורת המועדים עמוד קכ"א.

Halachos of the Nine Days ෴ 165

among the *poskim* regarding the halachah of conducting business during the Nine Days. Some authorities maintain that it is permitted to conduct business as usual, unless one deals in the sale of luxury items, which is prohibited as in paragraph 3 above. Other *poskim*, however, maintain that all business dealings should be kept to a minimum, and that a person should work only to the extent that is necessary for his livelihood, to prevent a financial loss, or if he encounters a rare opportunity for profit.[59] The common practice is to conduct business as usual during the Nine Days (with the exception of selling luxury items, as above), since the reality in contemporary times is that all business dealings may be considered necessary for one's livelihood.[60] Even if a person has sufficient funds in his possession, reducing his business activity for an extended period of time can negatively impact future business, such as losing a client, etc.

9. **Conducting Renovations for Business Purposes:** It is likely that one may carry out renovations for business purposes, such as to refurbish a house, apartment, or office that will be rented to a tenant.[61] See paragraph 11 below.

10. **Purchasing, Leasing, or Moving into a New Home:** It is prohibited to purchase or lease a home, or even to move into a new house, during the Nine Days (unless one has nowhere else to live). A person who does not have a wife or children and therefore would recite *shehecheyanu* upon entering a new house, rather than *hatov vehameitiv*, should refrain from moving in at any time during the Three Weeks. If a person will suffer a loss if he delays purchasing, renting, or moving into a new home, he is permitted to do so even during this period. A home may be placed on the market and potential buyers

---

59. שו"ע שם ועי' בב"י תחילת הסימן. מ"ב ס"ק י"א.
60. מ"ב שם.
61. כן צידד הגרח"ק שליט"א הובא בתורת המועדים עמוד קי"ט.

may be allowed to view it during the Nine Days. Similarly, it is permissible to inspect a home that one is considering purchasing.[62]

11. **Non-Essential Home Renovations:** It is prohibited to perform construction or home renovations that are not essential for one's living space, such as painting, wallpapering, building an extension to a home, or landscaping outdoor spaces.[63] Technically, if a person hires a non-Jewish contractor prior to Rosh Chodesh for a construction project and does not require him to work during the Nine Days (i.e., the contract allows enough time for the job to be completed even if he does not work during those days), he is not required to order the contractor to suspend his work during the Nine Days. Nevertheless, if it is possible to persuade the contractor to interrupt the work until after Tishah b'Av, it is preferable to do so, even if this will entail a small added charge.[64]

A person who works in construction or home renovations may perform work for non-Jewish clients during this time.

12. **Essential Renovations:** Any construction or repair work that is essential for one's living space – such as repairing the damage caused by a leak, extending one's home if it is too small, or repairing appliances – is permitted even during the Nine Days.[65] If a repair is not essential at the moment but the situation might result in a monetary loss if the problem is not fixed (for example, if a fence might collapse and the homeowner would then be required to pay for a replacement rather than performing a less expensive repair), it is permitted to perform the work. The rationale in this case is that

---

62. הליכות שלמה פי״ד הערה 71.
63. שו״ע ס״ב, ובמ״ב ס״ק י״ב.
64. מ״ב שם. ועי' משו״כ בשו״ת אגר״מ או״ח ח״ג סי' פ״ב.
65. מ״ב שם.

one's intent is only to avoid financial loss and not to create happiness.⁶⁶

13. **Gardening:** Planting or gardening for enjoyment is prohibited during the Nine Days.⁶⁷ It is permissible to perform gardening work that prevents damage, such as uprooting weeds or pruning tree branches. Employing a non-Jewish gardener on a contractual basis who is not required to work during these days is subject to the same halachah delineated above (paragraph 11) regarding a contractor. A Jew who works as a landscaper may provide service to non-Jewish clients, as above.

14. **Purchases or Construction for a Mitzvah:** According to Ashkenazic custom, all the above prohibitions are waived in the case of a mitzvah.⁶⁸ (Sephardic custom does not permit waiving any of these restrictions for a mitzvah.⁶⁹) Therefore, it is permissible to purchase items that foster happiness, as well as clothing or a sheitel,⁷⁰ for a wedding that will take place shortly after Tishah b'Av.⁷¹ Likewise, it is permissible to purchase tefillin (although it is prohibited to purchase *tzitzis*, which is considered a garment⁷²), to perform renovations in a shul (even non-essential work such as painting the building),⁷³ and to engage in the construction of a *mikveh* or a halachically required railing (*maakeh*).

15. **Engagements:** It is permissible to finalize an engagement during the Nine Days (and even on Tishah b'Av itself). One may

---

66. שו"ע שם ומ"ב ס"ק י"ג.
67. שו"ע שם.
68. רמ"א שם ס"ב.
69. כף החיים ס"ק ל"ג.
70. הגרש"א זצ"ל הובא בתורת המועדים עמוד קכ"א.
71. מ"ב ס"ק י"ד.
72. שו"ת אגר"מ או"ח ח"ג סי' פ'.
73. מ"ב ס"ק י"ב (וצ"ע למה צ"ל מצוה דרבים ותיפוק ליה דהוא בנין של מצוה כגון בית חתנות). ומש"כ בפנים שמותר לצבוע, פשוט הוא, וכ"ה באמת ליעקב הערה 507.

serve refreshments at an engagement party; however, a *seudah* (even without music or dancing) may not be held at any time after Rosh Chodesh. A *seudah* celebrating an engagement may not be held even on Shabbos.[74] (As discussed above in section 1, weddings are prohibited throughout the Three Weeks.)

16. **Conducting a Court Case with a Non-Jew:** The mazel of Klal Yisrael is considered to be weak during this time. Therefore, a court case against a non-Jew that has been scheduled after Rosh Chodesh Av should be postponed (until Elul if possible, or at least until after Tishah b'Av).[75]

17. **Cutting Nails:** There is a dispute among the *poskim* as to whether it is prohibited to cut one's nails during this time.[76] A woman is certainly permitted to cut her nails prior to *tevilah*, and anyone may cut their nails for *kavod* Shabbos.[77]

18. **Air Travel:** Some *poskim* maintain that it is preferable to avoid air travel during the Nine Days, due to the potential danger. This does not include traveling to Eretz Yisrael, traveling for a mitzvah purpose, or flying for business or medical needs.[78]

19. **End-of-Year Photographs:** Some *poskim* note that class photos or graduation pictures should not be taken during this period.[79]

20. **Swimming:** Swimming constitutes bathing and is thus prohibited during this period, see below section 7. (It is also common understanding to refrain from swimming and boating due to the potential danger.) Many *poskim* permit swimming for health reasons (see section 7, paragraph 3).

---

74. שו"ע שם ס"ב ובמ"ב ס"ק ט"ז.
75. שו"ע שם ס"א ובמ"ב סק"ב. ועי' כה"ח סק"א וסק"ג.
76. דעת הט"ז לאסור בשבוע שחל בו ודעת המ"א להתיר, הוב"ד בשעה"צ ס"ק כ"ז.
77. מ"ב סק"ב.
78. אמת ליעקב הערה 515. ועי' הליכות שלמה פי"ד סכ"ד והערה 74, ועי"ש הערה 76 שתלמידים מחו"ל הלומדים בישיבה בא"י עדיף להם ליסוע בימים אלו מלחזור מוקדם מישיבה לפני ר"ח.
79. הגריש"א זצ"ל הובא בתורת המועדים עמוד קי"ט.

3. Laundering Garments

1. **Laundering Garments during the Nine Days:** Laundering garments is prohibited during the Nine Days (or, according to Sephardic custom, during the week of Tishah b'Av),[80] since the activity creates the impression that one is being distracted from the required mourning of this period.[81]

2. **Ironing:** Ironing is likewise prohibited.[82]

3. **Items Subject to the Prohibition:** The prohibition of laundering during the Nine Days applies to all articles of clothing, including undergarments.[83] (In contrast to the halachah of wearing laundered garments where some permit, see section 4.) It is also forbidden to launder other types of items, such as tablecloths, bedsheets, and towels.

4. **Laundering an Item to Be Used after Tishah B'Av:** It is forbidden to launder or iron a garment even if it will not be worn until after Tishah b'Av. At the same time, there is also a prohibition to wear freshly laundered garments during the Nine Days, even if they were cleaned before Rosh Chodesh, as will be explained in the following section.[84]

5. **Using a Washing Machine:** Even though the advent of the washing machine has made laundering garments a quick and simple task, rather than the laborious, time-consuming chore of previous generations, all *poskim* rule that the prohibition to launder clothes during the Nine Days remains in effect today.

6. **Instructing a Non-Jew to Launder Garments:** It is forbidden to instruct a non-Jew (such as a cleaning lady) to launder

---

80. שו"ע ורמ"א סי' תקנ"א ס"ג. וכהיום אין חילוק בין א"י לשאר ארצות.
81. מ"ב ס"ק כ"א. וראה מ"ב ס"ק מ"ב.
82. שו"ע שם.
83. פשוט, שהרי הוא כמו הכלי פשתן המוזכר בשו"ע שם.
84. שו"ע שם.

170 ∽ Chapter Six: *The Period of the Three Weeks*

garments during the Nine Days.[85] Even if a non-Jewish employee decides to launder a Jew's garments on her own initiative, without being instructed to do so, it is preferable for her employer to tell her to refrain from doing laundry.[86]

7. **Removing a Stain:** According to some authorities, spot cleaning a stain is not included in the prohibition to launder garments.[87] However, other *poskim* rule that this is also prohibited.[88] Nevertheless, all authorities agree that one may brush dust off a garment or scratch off dirt.

8. **Turning on a Washing Machine before Rosh Chodesh:** The *poskim* debate whether it is permissible to begin a load of laundry just before the arrival of Rosh Chodesh Av (i.e., shortly before *shekiah*) if the machine will continue cleaning the clothes after sunset. Some *poskim* prohibit this[89] while others permit it.[90] It is certainly permissible to place wet clothes in a dryer.

9. **Soaking a Stained Garment:** One may soak a stained garment to prevent it from becoming permanently stained.[91]

10. **Shining Shoes:** It is prohibited to shine shoes during the Nine Days, except for the purpose of *kavod* Shabbos (for those who have the custom to wear clean clothes on Shabbos Chazon, as will be explained in the next section). However, one may use

---

85. עי' שערי תשובה ס"ק י"ז.
86. עי"ש דנכון ליזהר משום מראת העין. אמנם, י"ל דדוקא בזמנו שהכביסה היה נעשית בחוץ משא"כ בזמננו שנעשית בחדרי חדרים והרי מ"ע על איסור דרבנן מותרת בחדרי חדרים, אפשר דמותר. ועי' שעה"צ ס"ק מ"ד.
87. הליכות שלמה פי"ד סט"ו.
88. ארחות רבינו ח"ב עמוד קל"ב בשם הגרח"ק שליט"א.
89. לכאורה כן עולה מדברי השע"ת ס"ק י"ז. וכן נקט להלכה בקובץ מבית לוי הל' בין המצרים עמוד י"ד ושו"ת שבט הקהתי ח"א סי' קע"א, אבל כתבו שאם יסתיים לפני צה"כ מותר.
90. הגריש"א זצ"ל והגרח"ק שליט"א הובא בתורת המועדים עמוד קל"ד.
91. עי' שערי תשובה ס"ק י"ז שמשמע שבכה"ג אין איסור בשרייה. אמנם דעת הגריש"א זצ"ל הובא בתורת המועדים עמוד קל"ד שאסור אא"כ יתקלקל. ועי' שו"ת שבט הקהתי ח"א סי' קע"ב.

shoe polish to treat shoes if their color is fading, since this is not considered an act of cleaning the shoes.[92]

11. **Washing and Setting a Sheitel:** In principle, washing and setting a sheitel is akin to laundering or ironing a garment and is therefore prohibited.[93] Some *poskim* rule that it may be permitted to wash and set a sheitel in a case of need, since it is not actually considered a garment.[94] One may certainly comb a sheitel, just as it is permissible to comb hair.

12. **Washing and Polishing Floors:** Some authorities prohibit washing or shining floors during the Nine Days, unless it is in honor of Shabbos.[95] Other *poskim* do not consider washing floors to be included in the prohibition of laundering.[96] Even according to the lenient view, one may not polish a marble floor.[97]

13. **A Person Who Lacks Clean Clothes:** Before the week of Tishah b'Av, a person who has no clean garments to wear is permitted to launder a garment.[98] Some *poskim* permit laundering a garment even during the week of Tishah b'Av if one does not have a single garment to wear that isn't noticeably soiled or that does not have an unpleasant odor.[99]

14. **Laundering for a Mitzvah:** It is permissible to launder garments for a mitzvah, such as for a woman who needs white

---

92. עי' שו"ת אגר"מ או"ח ח"ג סי' פ'. וראה הליכות שלמה פי"ד סי"ז וס"ק כ"ג.
93. קובץ מבית לוי הל' בין המצרים עמוד נ'.
94. דעת הגרח"פ שיינברג זצ"ל, ועי' שו"ת רבבות אפרים ח"ו סי' רצ"א.
95. ארחות רבינו ח"ב עמוד קל"ג בשם החזו"א. הליכות שלמה פי"ד סכ"א, ומבואר שם שאם מלוכלך ממש מותר אף לצורך חול.
96. דעת הגריש"א זצ"ל הובא בתורת המועדים עמוד קל"ה, מועדים וזמנים ח"ח סי' של"ח.
97. עי' שו"ת אגר"מ או"ח ח"ג סוף סי' פ'.
98. מ"ב ס"ק כ"ט.
99. עי' שו"ת אור לציון ח"ג פכ"ז דלא גרע ממי שהתלכלך גופו בטיט שמותר לרחצו בת"ב. וכ"ה דעת הגרח"ק שליט"א הובא בתורת המועדים עמוד קל"ה.

undergarments or a clean sheet for the *shivah nekiim*.[100] It is questionable whether it is permissible to launder garments for *kavod* Shabbos. However, a person who does not have a clean Shabbos garment or tablecloth may launder such an item or have it dry cleaned.[101] This dispensation does not apply to bedsheets.[102] A person who is catering a *seudas mitzvah* during the Nine Days is permitted to wash tablecloths if necessary.[103]

15. **Giving Garments to a Non-Jewish Cleaner:** One may give garments to a non-Jewish cleaner before Rosh Chodesh Av even if the garments will be laundered after Rosh Chodesh, or even during the week of Tishah b'Av. However, it is forbidden to give a garment to a non-Jewish cleaner after Rosh Chodesh. If one instructs the cleaner to launder the garments only after Tishah b'Av, there is a dispute among the *poskim* as to whether it is permitted to give garments to them after Rosh Chodesh.[104]

16. **Laundering Garments for a Non-Jew:** Technically, the halachah does not permit a Jewish woman to launder the garments of non-Jews (e.g., as an employee at a dry cleaning establishment) during this period, unless it is clear to an observer that the garments are not owned by Jews. This is due to the concern of *maris ayin* (the appearance of wrongdoing), since an onlooker might mistakenly believe that the woman is washing her own garments or those of another Jew. Today, however, when garments are laundered behind closed doors, where the process is not observed by the public, it is likely that the concern of *maris ayin* no longer exists and this is permitted.[105]

---

100. רמ"א שם ס"ג.
101. עי' מ"ב ס"ק ל"ב.
102. מ"ב ס"ק ל"ג.
103. שו"ת שבט הלוי ח"י סי' פ"ג.
104. עי' רמ"א שם ובמ"ב ס"ק ל"ד.
105. עי' שו"ע שם ס"ה ובמ"ב ס"ק מ"ב ובשעה"צ ס"ק מ"ד.

Laundering Garments ∽ 173

It is problematic for a Jewish-owned dry cleaning business to remain open during the Nine Days, even to service non-Jewish customers, since the public will notice that the business is operating. The only way to permit this is for the owners to find a way to publicize that they will accept only garments that belong to non-Jews for laundering during this time. A Rav should be consulted for guidance. A Jewish-owned laundromat, where customers wash their own clothes, may remain open during the Nine Days.

17. **Laundering Children's Clothes:** The prohibition to launder clothes applies to children's clothing as well.[106] (Some authorities maintain that children's garments may be laundered until the beginning of the week of Tishah b'Av.[107]) It is permissible to launder cloth diapers (a dispensation that is generally irrelevant today) or other articles of clothing worn by small children who soil their clothes constantly.[108] Some authorities permit laundering any garments worn by children until the age of three.[109] Other *poskim* take an even more lenient position and permit laundering the clothes of children who are of the age when they still soil their clothes while playing.[110]

    Some authorities rule that if a child does not have clean clothes to wear, it is preferable to purchase new garments rather than laundering his existing clothes.[111] Other *poskim* maintain that there is no difference.[112]

---

106. שו״ע שם סי״ד.
107. מ״ב ס״ק פ״ב בשם החה״א.
108. רמ״א שם סי״ד. ומש״כ בפנים שאר בגדים של קטנים שדרכם להתלכלך תמיד, הוא דעת הגרמ״פ זצ״ל הוב״ד בקיצור הלכות ביהמ״צ להגר״ש איידער זצ״ל ובשו״ת רבבות אפרים ח״ג סי׳ שמ״ז.
109. חיי אדם כלל קל״ב דין י״ח. ועי׳ לשון הלבוש סי׳ תקנ״א סי״ד.
110. קיצור הלכות ביהמ״צ להגר״ש איידער זצ״ל, ושו״ת רבבות אפרים שם בשם הגרמ״פ זצ״ל.
111. אמת ליעקב הערה 513, ודעת הגריש״א זצ״ל הובא בתורת המועדים עמוד קכ״ט.
112. דעת הגרח״ק שליט״א הובא שם.

18. **Washing Additional Garments:** When it is permissible to launder children's clothing, one may wash the quantity that is needed.[113]

    One may not add other garments that are not permissible to wash, to the load in the washing machine.[114]

19. **Exception to Laundering Garments for after Tishah B'Av:** If a person plans to embark on a trip during the Nine Days and knows that he will need laundered clothes to wear after Tishah b'Av, he may ask a non-Jew to launder his undergarments.[115]

20. **Doing Laundry for Health Reasons:** It is permissible to do laundry for health reasons[116] (e.g., washing a sick person's bedsheets and clothes).

21. **Leniencies for a Mourner:** If an *avel* reaches the end of *shloshim* (or of the first three months after the passing of a parent) during the Nine Days, it is permissible for him to trim his hair slightly (with a *shinui*, such as without using scissors) and launder his clothing without using detergent.[117] Some *poskim* permit a mourner in this situation to take an ordinary haircut and launder his garments in the normal fashion, unless his period of mourning ends during the week of Tishah b'Av.[118]

---

113. ואף שכתב המ"ב ס"ק פ"ג שלא יתכבסו הרבה יחד, מ"מ הסכמת הפוסקים דבזמננו שיש מכונת כביסה עדיף לכבס כל מה שצריך בב"א.
114. הסכמת הפוסקים.
115. מ"ב ס"ק ל"ט.
116. שו"ת שלמת חיים סי' של"ד-של"ה.
117. שו"ע שם סט"ו.
118. מ"ב ס"ק פ"ז ושעה"צ ס"ק צ"ג.

Laundering Garments ~ 175

4. Wearing New or Freshly Laundered Clothing

1. **Wearing Freshly Laundered Garments:** It is prohibited to wear freshly laundered clothes during the Nine Days even if they were washed long before. The Ashkenazic practice is to observe this restriction beginning on Rosh Chodesh Av; for Sephardim, this prohibition comes into effect only during the week of Tishah b'Av.[119]

2. **Using Clean Bedsheets, Towels, and Tablecloths:** This prohibition is not limited to clothes that are actually worn. It is also prohibited to use freshly laundered bedsheets, towels, and tablecloths.[120]

3. **Undergarments and Socks:** The *poskim* debate whether the prohibition to wear clean garments includes socks and undergarments. Some authorities contend that the prohibition encompasses all articles of clothing[121] (however, see below regarding Shabbos clothing). Other *poskim* rule that a person who perspires heavily and is accustomed to changing his clothes frequently, or who must change his garments to avoid skin irritation or discomfort, is permitted to wear freshly laundered undergarments and socks.[122] One should consult a Rav for a conclusive ruling.

---

119. שו"ע ורמ"א שם ס"ג.
120. שו"ע שם.
121. כן מבואר מהשו"ע והרמ"א שם ומהמ"ב סק"ו ומכל הפוסקים שכתבו להתיר כלי פשתן או הכתונת והפוהמקאות לענין שבת, הרי דבחול יש איסור בבגדי זיעה. וראה כף החיים ס"ק צ"א בשם הבא"ח. ועי' שו"ת מנחת יצחק ח"י סי' מ"ד. וכן דעת הגרי"י קניבסקי זצ"ל הובא בארחות רבינו ח"ב עמוד ק"ל.
122. עי' שו"ת שלמת חיים סי' רי"ז וסי' ר"כ, הגרמ"פ זצ"ל הובא בקיצור הלכות ביה"מ להגר"ש אייידער זצ"ל, הליכות שלמה פי"ד סי"ב. (ועי' ערוה"ש יו"ד סי' שפ"ט ס"ו שכתב להתיר לאבל להחליף בגדי זיעה אף בלי שילבש אותם אדם אחר.) ועי' מועדים וזמנים ח"ה סי' של"ח.

It is unclear to what extent the prohibition to wear clean clothes extends to pajamas and the like. Some *poskim* consider all forms of sleepwear like ordinary clothing, which may be worn freshly laundered only on Shabbos. Others consider pajamas to be similar to bedsheets, which may not be used when they are freshly laundered even on Shabbos. Other *poskim*, on the other hand, maintain that the status of pajamas and sleepwear is even more lenient than that of ordinary clothes, and that they are akin to undergarments, which some *poskim* permit wearing even during the week when they are freshly laundered.

4. **Preparing Garments before the Nine Days:** In light of the prohibition to wear freshly laundered garments during the Nine Days, it is important to prepare clothes in advance of the Nine Days to be worn during this time. This is accomplished by wearing each garment at some point before the Nine Days begin, so that it will no longer be considered freshly laundered.[123] (Those who observe the Sephardic custom need to prepare clothes only before the Shabbos prior to Tishah b'Av.) The halachah does not specify a precise amount of time for a garment to be worn prior to the Nine Days;[124] one should simply wear it long enough that it does not feel freshly laundered.[125]

5. **Clean Clothes for Children:** Any children whose clothing may be laundered during the Nine Days (see section 3 above) may also wear freshly laundered clothing.[126]

6. **A Person Who Did Not Prepare Clothing before the Nine Days:** If a person forgets to prepare clothing before the Nine

---

123. עי' רמ"א יו"ד סי' שפ"ט ס"ז לענין אבל לאחר שבעה שנותן לאדם אחר ללבוש כשעה א'.
124. עי' בש"ך יו"ד שם שכתב על דברי הרמ"א הנ"ל שא"צ שעה אחת ממש אלא זמן מה.
125. הליכות שלמה פי"ד סי"ד כ' שיהא לבוש זמן ניכר עד שאינו נראה כמכובס, ושם בהערה 45 כ' שהשיעור אינו תלוי בזמן מסויים אלא שישהה עמו עד שתתבטל הנאת הכיבוס.
126. הגריש"א זצ"ל הובא בתורת המועדים עמוד ק"ל.

Days, a valid solution is to change his clothes multiple times over the course of Shabbos, when it is permissible to wear freshly laundered garments (see paragraph 9 below), provided that he does not verbally state that he is doing so for the purpose of having garments to wear after Shabbos (and the garments are not noticeably meant for weekday use).[127] Some *poskim* add that if a person changes his garments throughout the day, it will be obvious that his intent is to prepare for after Shabbos, and therefore he should don fresh clothing only when it is natural to do so, such as in the morning or after a Shabbos afternoon nap.[128]

Some *poskim* state that one may wear freshly laundered garments during the Nine Days after placing them on the floor if this causes the garments to lose their feeling of freshness.[129] Of course, this is effective only if the floor is not clean or by stepping on the garments after placing them on the floor.

7. If the garments that a person prepared for the Nine Days become soiled, and he will suffer anguish or financial loss (e.g., in a workplace where he must maintain a well-groomed appearance) if he continues wearing them, it is permissible to wear freshly laundered clothing.[130] The garments should be placed on the floor before they are worn.

8. **A Guest:** A person who is lodging in a hotel or staying as a guest in another person's house is permitted to sleep on fresh bedsheets and to use freshly laundered towels. It is preferable to place the sheets and towels on the floor before using them.

---

127. הגרי"י קנייבסקי זצ"ל הובא באורחות רבינו ח"ב עמוד ק"ל.
128. בן איש חי הובא בכף החיים ס"ק צ"א. הליכות שלמה פי"ד סק"כ.
129. עי' שו"ת מנחת יצחק ח"י סי' מ"ד. אמנם, עי' הליכות שלמה פי"ד הערה 40 שהגרשז"א זצ"ל לא הורה כן.
130. הגרמ"פ זצ"ל הוב"ד בקיצור הל' ביהמ"צ שהגר"ש איידער זצ"ל.

However, a guest should not allow his host or the hotel staff to change his linens during his stay.[131]

9. **Wearing Clean Garments for a Mitzvah:** It is permissible to wear fresh clothes for the purpose of a mitzvah. Therefore, a woman may wear clean white undergarments and use a clean white bedsheet during the *shivah nekiim*.[132] Similarly, a person may wear freshly laundered clothing on Shabbos[133] (see paragraph 12 below regarding wearing Shabbos suits and dresses). Freshly laundered tablecloths may be placed on a table in honor of Shabbos, but it is customary to refrain from placing clean sheets on a bed even on Shabbos.[134]

See above (section 3, paragraph 14) regarding laundering garments or other items for use on Shabbos.

10. **Wearing New Garments:** It is prohibited to wear new garments during this period even if there is no need to recite *shehecheyanu* (i.e., if the *brachah* was recited upon the garment's purchase prior to Shivah Asar b'Tammuz because it needed no alterations, or it is an article of clothing that does not warrant the recitation of *shehecheyanu* at all[135]). This prohibition is observed by Ashkenazim throughout the Nine Days; according to Sephardic custom, it takes effect only during the week of Tishah b'Av.[136]

11. **Pressed Garments:** Garments that have been pressed (even if they were not freshly laundered) are considered similar to new garments and may not be worn during this period.[137] Consequently, it is customary to refrain from wearing Shabbos

---

131. שו"ת מנח"י שם.
132. רמ"א או"ח שם.
133. שם.
134. מ"ב ס"ק ל"ג.
135. עי' מ"ב ס"ק מ"ה.
136. שו"ע ורמ"א שם ס"ו.
137. מ"ב ס"ק מ"ד.

clothes during the Nine Days even if the garments have not been laundered, since such garments generally appear to have been newly pressed.[138] Nevertheless, the restriction on wearing such garments begins only from Shabbos Chazon.[139]

12. **Wearing Shabbos Finery on Shabbos Chazon:** Some authorities rule that Shabbos garments (which have the halachic status of newly pressed garments, as explained in the previous paragraph) are prohibited even on Shabbos itself.[140] (This pertains to Shabbos Chazon, the Shabbos immediately prior to Tishah b'Av. If there is another Shabbos after Rosh Chodesh that is not immediately prior to Tishah b'Av, the restriction applies only to Shabbos garments that are indeed freshly pressed or new.) These *poskim* rule that the only type of garments that may be worn on Shabbos are freshly laundered shirts and undergarments[141] (which may be worn even if they are new[142]). Other *poskim*, however, maintain that the *minhag* is to wear Shabbos clothes on Shabbos Chazon, even if Tishah b'Av itself falls on Shabbos.[143] The widespread practice is to follow this leniency.[144] Every individual should observe his family's *minhag*. Nevertheless, this leniency does not permit wearing new garments on Shabbos (with the exception of undergarments), even those that do not require the recitation of *shehecheyanu*.[145]

---

138. שם.

139. עי' מ"ב שם ובשעה"צ ס"ק מ"ו.

140. רמ"א שם ס"א ומ"ב ס"ק מ"ד. ועי' שעה"צ ס"ק מ"ו שכשחל ת"ב ביום ראשון או בשבת מותר ללבוש בגדי שבת בשבת הקודמת.

141. רמ"א שם וס"ג ומ"ב סק"ו.

142. ביה"ל ס"י ד"ה כלים חדשים.

143. מ"ב שם עפ"י הגר"א, ויש משנים בגד אחד, בשם הגר"י עמדין בשם אביו. ועי' בערוך השלחן סי"א שביאר מטעם אבילות בפרהסיא בשבת, וסיים דלפי"ז בזמננו שאין כ"כ הבדל בין שבת לחול בתמונת הבגד רק ביוקר וזול יש לאסור. וראה כה"ח ס"ק י"ג שמנהג ספרדים ללבוש בגדי שבת.

144. עי' מועדים וזמנים ח"ה סי' שמ"ג וח"ז סי' רנ"ו.

145. שו"ת אגר"מ או"ח ח"ג סי' פ'.

13. **Removing One's Shabbos Clothes Immediately after Shabbos:** For those who have the *minhag* to wear Shabbos clothes on Shabbos Chazon, there are various *minhagim* concerning whether the garments may be worn after the conclusion of Shabbos as well. Some change into weekday clothes immediately after Havdalah, while others continue wearing their Shabbos garments on Motzaei Shabbos. A person should follow his family's *minhag*.[146]

14. **Wearing Fresh Clothes at a *Bris Milah*:** In honor of a *bris milah*, the father, mother, *mohel*, *sandak*, and *kvatter* may wear freshly laundered garments or even Shabbos garments. Other honorees at a *bris milah* are not permitted to wear fresh garments.[147] Some *poskim* permit the grandparents and siblings at a *bris* to wear freshly laundered garments as well.[148]

15. **A Bar Mitzvah:** A bar mitzvah has the same halachic status as a *bris* in this regard, and the bar mitzvah boy and his parents may wear Shabbos clothes for a celebration on the day of his birthday (*bo bayom*).[149]

16. **An *Aufruf*:** A chassan and his parents may wear Shabbos garments for an *aufruf* on Shabbos Chazon (even if their custom is to refrain from wearing Shabbos clothes at that time).[150] However, the prohibition to wear new clothing remains in effect (even if *shehecheyanu* is not recited on the garments).[151] When Tishah b'Av itself falls on Shabbos, a chassan may wear Shabbos clothing at his *aufruf*, but the parents of a chassan should not deviate from their usual practice (i.e., if their

---

146. ראה הליכות שלמה פי״ד סכ״ח וס״ק ל״ח והערה 88.
147. רמ״א שם ס״א ובמ״ב סק״ג-ד. ועי׳ בשע״ת סק״ג. ויש להסתפק אם צריכים לפשוט אח״כ.
148. עי׳ שע״ת סק״ג. הליכות שלמה פי״ד ס״ט.
149. שו״ת דברי יציב או״ח ח״ב סי׳ רל״ח, קובץ תשובות ח״ג סי׳ ל״ה.
150. רמ״א שם ובמ״ב סק״ח.
151. מ״ב סק״ט.

minhag is to refrain from wearing Shabbos clothes on this particular Shabbos, they should not make an exception).[152]

17. **Wearing Fresh Clothes for a Shidduch:** Some authorities permit wearing freshly laundered clothes, and even Shabbos clothing, for a date, if the shidduch might be negatively affected otherwise.[153]

5. Sewing, Purchasing, and Mending Garments

1. **Making New Garments:** It is prohibited to make new garments, even those upon which the *brachah* of *shehecheyanu* would not be recited. This prohibition applies even to simple items such as socks. Making new garments is prohibited throughout the Nine Days even according to Sephardic custom.[154] However, one may fashion new garments for a wedding that will take place shortly after Tishah b'Av, only if the bride and groom were not previously married, and if there will not be sufficient time after the Nine Days for the garments to be made.[155]

2. **Hiring a Non-Jew to Fashion Garments:** Many *poskim* rule that one may hire a non-Jew to sew clothing that will be worn after Tishah b'Av, although it is preferable to wait until after Tishah b'Av to have the garments made, even by a non-Jewish tailor or seamstress.[156] While it is definitely prohibited to instruct a non-Jew to launder garments even for use after

---

152. מ״ב סק״י.
153. הגרי״י קניבסקי זצ״ל בשם החזו״א הוב״ד בארחות רבינו שם (ושם התיר בפגישה ראשונה), שו״ת שבט הלוי ח״ט סי׳ קל״א אות ד׳. וע״י הליכות שלמה פי״ד ס״י וס״ק ט״ו ובהערות לשם.
154. שו״ע שם ס״ז ובמ״ב ס״ק מ״ו.
155. מ״ב שם.
156. רמ״א שם ס״ז.

Tishah b'Av, the same restriction does not apply to employing a non-Jew to sew new garments. This scenario is viewed differently, since the completed garment is not yet in the Jew's possession; therefore, it is considered akin to an ordinary business transaction.[157] Some *poskim*, however, rule more stringently and prohibit instructing a non-Jew to fashion a garment, similar to the prohibition of laundering.[158] A person who wishes to follow the stringent opinion is not required to refrain from this until the week of Tishah b'Av.[159]

3. **Making Garments for Others:** It is customary to permit producing a garment for a non-Jew. The *minhag* is even to permit producing a garment for another Jew who placed an order for a new garment before Rosh Chodesh.[160] Nevertheless, some *poskim* maintain that fashioning a garment is comparable to laundering, which a Jew is forbidden to do for another Jew.[161] Here, too, a person who wishes to follow the stringent opinion need not refrain from producing garments until the week of Tishah b'Av.[162]

4. **Mending a Garment:** The above discussion pertains to the production of new garments; however, mending an old garment (e.g., sewing a tear or replacing a button) is permitted during this period.[163] Some *poskim*, though, prohibit tailoring or altering even an old garment to change its size.[164]

It is permissible to sew a name tag onto a garment (a

---

157. מ"ב ס"ק נ"ג.
158. דעת הגר"א הובא בביה"ל ד"ה ונהגו להקל.
159. מסקנת הביה"ל שם.
160. רמ"א שם ובמ"ב ס"ק נ"א-נ"ב.
161. דעת הגר"א הובא בביה"ל שם.
162. ביה"ל שם.
163. כף החיים ס"ק ק"ז בשם הבא"ח. הליכות שלמה פי"ד סט"ז. וכן משמע משו"ת אגר"מ או"ח ח"ג סי' ע"ט.
164. ארחות רבינו ח"ב עמוד קכ"ט.

common practice at this time of year, when children often prepare for summer camp).[165]

5. **Arranging the Threads on a Loom:** It is customary to prohibit arranging the threads of "*shesi*" or "*erev*" (the warp or weft) on a loom even if the garment will not be sewn until after Tishah b'Av, because the word "*shesi*" reminds us of the *even shesiyah*, which was lost with the destruction of the *Beis Hamikdash*.[166] This is prohibited even when done for others and even if one is not paid for the work. However, spinning the threads is not included in this restriction.[167]

6. **Buying Clothing:** Purchasing new clothing is also prohibited during this period.[168] This applies to all articles of clothing, including shoes, and even to basic garments such as undergarments.[169] (Purchasing new undergarments is certainly prohibited even for those who are lenient to wear freshly laundered undergarments.) It is prohibited to purchase new garments even for use after Tishah b'Av.[170] Some *poskim* rule that it is prohibited to buy even secondhand clothing (since it is new for the buyer).[171]

One should consult with a Rav regarding a purchase prior to Rosh Chodesh which will be delivered during the Nine Days.

7. **Buying *Tzitzis*:** Both a *tallis* and a *tallis katan* are considered articles of clothing and thus they may not be purchased during this time.[172]

---

165. אמת ליעקב הערה 509 משום שלא נחשב כתיקון בגדים.
166. שו"ע שם ס"ח עפ"י הירושלמי פסחים.
167. מ"ב ס"ק נ"ד.
168. רמ"א שם ס"ז.
169. עפ"י המ"ב ס"ק מ"ו.
170. מ"ב ס"ק מ"ט.
171. עי' שע"ת על ס"ז.
172. שו"ת אגר"מ או"ח ח"ג סי' פ'.

8. **Footwear for Tishah B'Av:** Some *poskim* permit buying non-leather footwear for Tishah b'Av if it is needed.[173]

9. **Purchasing Clothing at a Discounted Price:** It is permissible to buy a garment if a rare opportunity arises to purchase it at a significantly reduced price, such as a one-off seasonal sale, or if the item will not be available at all after Tishah b'Av.[174]

10. **Purchasing or Sewing Non-Clothing Items:** The prohibition of sewing or purchasing garments applies specifically to clothing and does not include other items. (However, any items that create joy may not be purchased during the Nine Days, as explained in section 2 above, and the Ashkenazic custom is to refrain from purchasing an item on which one would recite *shehecheyanu* at any time during the Three Weeks.)[175]

11. **Eyeglasses:** New eyeglasses are included in the prohibition to buy clothing. However, a person who has a need for new eyeglasses may have new lenses placed in his eyeglass frames. If it is impossible to fit the new lenses into the frames, he may purchase new eyeglass frames as well. Eyeglass frames that have broken may be repaired; if they cannot be repaired, one may purchase new frames.[176]

12. **Returns and Exchanges:** One may return clothing purchased prior to Rosh Chodesh to a store in exchange for credit or a refund. However, exchanging a garment for another garment is considered a purchase and is not permitted.

---

173. כף החיים ס"ק צ"ז. שו"ת אגר"מ או"ח ח"ג סי' פ'. אבל עי' חוט שני יו"ט עמוד שמ"ז שמחמיר בזה.
174. כן יש ללמוד מדברי המ"ב ס"ק י"א ושעה"צ ס"ק י"ב.
175. עי' מ"ב סוף ס"ק נ"ד, ועי' שו"ת אגר"מ או"ח ח"ג סי' פ"ב, ועי' הליכות שלמה פי"ד סכ"ב.
176. הליכות שלמה פי"ד ס"ק כ"ב.

Sewing, Purchasing, and Mending Garments

6. Abstaining from Meat and Wine

1. **Meat and Wine during the Nine Days:** The Ashkenazic custom is to refrain from consuming meat or wine throughout the Nine Days. There are two reasons for this custom: Meat and wine bring out happiness, and it also commemorates the fact that the *korbanos* and wine libations were discontinued when the *Beis Hamikdash* was destroyed.[177]

2. **The Onset of the Prohibition:** The prohibition to consume meat or wine takes effect at sunset on Rosh Chodesh. If a person davens *Maariv* before this time, the prohibition begins at that time. Moreover, if the community davens *Maariv* prior and thus becomes subject to the prohibition, even an individual who has not davened with them must begin observing this restriction. In an area where there are many shuls, an individual will become subject to this prohibition when the shul he usually attends has davened *Maariv* (or at *shekiah*).[178]

3. **Shechitah:** Ashkenazic custom also calls for *shechitah* not to be performed during this period, except for the benefit of a person who is ill or for a *seudas mitzvah* (such as a *bris milah* or *pidyon haben*), at which one is permitted to eat meat.[179] *Shechitah* may be permitted if one will suffer financial loss if it is not performed, but a portion of every animal that is slaughtered should be given to a poor person.[180] Some *poskim* permit the performance of *shechitah* in large cities where one can assume that there are many people who are permitted

---

177. שו״ע סי׳ תקנ״א ובמ״ב ס״ק נ״ח. (ויש מעד״מ שג״כ נוהגים בזה מר״ח עפ״י הבא״ח דברים סט״ו.)
178. מ״ב ס״ק נ״ו ובשעה״צ ס״ק נ״ו.
179. רמ״א שם ס״ט.
180. מ״ב ס״ק ס״א.

to eat meat (e.g., people who are ill or will be partaking in a *seudas mitzvah*).[181]

4. **Selling Meat:** In any event, stores where meat and poultry are sold may be open for business as usual during this time, and one may purchase meat to be used after Tishah b'Av. Since there are certain scenarios in which the consumption of meat is permitted, there is no concern that this may create *maris ayin* (the perception that one is eating meat during the Nine Days in violation of the prohibition).[182]

5. **Poultry:** The prohibition of consuming meat includes poultry (chicken, turkey, and duck) as well.[183]

6. **Foods Cooked with Meat:** Ashkenazic custom is to refrain from eating foods that have been cooked with meat, since the flavor of the meat is absorbed in any foods cooked together with it. Therefore, a person may not eat vegetables that have been cooked in a pot with meat, even if he is certain that he is not consuming any of the meat itself.[184] Fat and gravy from meat are certainly prohibited for consumption.

7. **Parve Foods Cooked in *Fleishig* Utensils:** It is permissible to consume parve foods that have been cooked in *fleishig* utensils. In fact, it is even permitted *lechatchilah* to use *fleishig* pots and other utensils for the preparation of parve foods, even if the utensils were used with meat within 24 hours.[185]

8. **A Small Quantity of Meat in Parve Food:** If a small quantity of meat falls into a parve food, such as if a utensil with meat residue is inserted into a parve food, the food remains permitted if the meat constitutes no more than one sixtieth

---

181. ערוך השלחן סכ"ה.
182. שו"ת אגר"מ או"ח ח"ד סי' קי"ב אות ג'. ועי' תשובות והנהגות ח"ב סי' רנ"ז.
183. שו"ע שם ס"י.
184. מ"ב ס"ק ס"ג.
185. מ"ב שם.

the volume of the parve food, or if the meat flavor cannot be detected.[186]

9. **Grape Juice:** The prohibition to drink wine includes even sweet and non-alcoholic beverages derived from grapes, such as grape juice (even though grape juice cannot be used for a wine libation on the *mizbeiach*).[187] However, wine vinegar is permitted.[188]

10. **Beer and Whiskey:** Alcoholic beverages not derived from grapes, such as beer and whiskey, are permitted.[189]

11. **Diluted Wine:** Wine that has been diluted with a ratio of six parts water to one part wine is permitted. Wine that has been diluted with a smaller quantity of water but still has a significantly diluted taste may be permitted in a case of need, such as if one is suffering from a headache. *Lechatchilah*, one should not add wine to food, even if it will constitute less than one sixth of the dish.[190]

12. **Artificial Grape Flavor:** Artificially flavored grape drinks are permitted.[191]

13. **Meat and Wine on Shabbos:** The consumption of meat and wine is permitted on Shabbos, even if it is the ninth of Av itself.[192] It is forbidden even to choose to be stringent and abstain from meat and wine.[193]

14. ***Seudah Shelishis* and *Melaveh Malkah*:** One may eat meat and drink wine even during *seudah shelishis*, even if *tzeis*

---

186. מ״ב שם ובשעה״צ ס״ק ס״ח.
187. שו״ע שם ס״י ובמ״ב ס״ק ס״ו. וראה הליכות שלמה פי״ד ס״ק י״ג בעניין מיץ ענבים.
188. רמ״א שם ס״ט ובמ״ב ס״ק נ״ז.
189. רמ״א שם סי״א.
190. עי׳ באר היטב ס״ק כ״ט ועי׳ שערי תשובה על ס״ט. אבל ראה תשובות והנהגות ח״ב סי׳ רנ״ט שמיקל לערב יין לעוגות ועוגיות, וראה שו״ת שבט הלוי ח״ט סי׳ קל״ב שמתיר לצורך קטנים.
191. פשוט.
192. שו״ע סי׳ תקנ״ד סי״ט. ואפי׳ קבל שבת מוקדם, מותר.
193. מ״ב סי׳ תקנ״א ס״ק נ״ט.

hakochavim has passed (provided that one has not recited the formula of *baruch hamavdil*).[194] However, it is prohibited to eat meat or drink wine on Motzaei Shabbos, even for the *melaveh malkah* meal.[195] (Some *poskim* rule that for the *melaveh malkah* meal it is permissible to eat leftover food that was prepared with the intent that it would be consumed on Shabbos.[196])

15. **Sampling Shabbos Foods on Erev Shabbos:** In general, there is a mitzvah to sample the Shabbos food on Erev Shabbos, to ensure that it will be enjoyable on Shabbos.[197] During the Nine Days, many *poskim* rule that one is only allowed to taste the food prepared for Shabbos without swallowing it.[198] Other *poskim*, however, do permit swallowing a taste of the food.[199]

16. **Drinking Wine at Havdalah:** It is permissible to drink wine for the sake of a mitzvah; therefore, one should recite Havdalah on wine or grape juice as usual. However, since the wine of Havdalah may be consumed by anyone who has listened to Havdalah, even a child of *chinuch* age, the *minhag* for Ashkenazim is to preferably give the wine to a child, rather than for the person reciting Havdalah to drink it. The child must have reached the age of *chinuch* with respect to Havdalah (approximately six years old), but should be younger than the age of *chinuch* for mourning the destruction of the *Beis Hamikdash* (approximately nine years). If a child of that age is not present, the person who recited Havdalah should drink the wine.[200] Some *poskim* disagree with this custom and maintain that even if a child is present, an adult may drink the wine.[201]

---

194. מ״ב ס״ק נ״ו.
195. כדמשמע במ״ב שם, שו״ת אגר״מ או״ח ח״ד סי׳ כ״א אות ד׳.
196. ברכי יוסף הוב״ד בשערי תשובה ס״ט, עי״ש, כף החיים ס״ק קמ״ד.
197. מ״ב סי׳ ר״נ סק״ב.
198. חוט שני ח״ה עמוד תט״ו.
199. שו״ת אור לציון ח״ג פרק כ״ו ס״ד. קובץ מבית לוי חי״ג עמוד מ״ט. ועי׳ שש״כ פמ״ב הערה רס״ו.
200. שו״ע ורמ״א שם ס״י, מ״ב ס״ק ס״ח וסק״ע.
201. עי׳ א״א בוטשאטש סי׳ תקנ״א, שו״ת שלמת חיים סי׳ של״ז, וכן נהג החזו״א הובא בדינים והנהגות פי״ח ס״ח, וכן נהג הגרש״ז זצ״ל הובא בהליכות שלמה פי״ד סכ״ז, ועי״ש ס״ק ל״ז דמאחר

Some authorities cite a *minhag* to use beer for Havdalah (in a locale where it is considered *chamar medinah*).²⁰²

17. **Reciting *Birkas Hamazon* with Wine:** Even when *birkas hamazon* is recited on a weekday by a group of three men or more (a *mezuman*), the Ashkenazic custom is to refrain from using a cup of wine during the Nine Days, even if a child is present who can drink it, since it is not obligatory to recite *birkas hamazon* with *zimun* over wine (even in the presence of ten men).²⁰³ However, at a *seudas mitzvah* one may recite *birkas hamazon* on wine and an adult may drink it.²⁰⁴

18. **A *Seudas Mitzvah*:** Meat and wine are permitted for consumption at a *seudas mitzvah* – such as a *bris milah*, *pidyon haben*, or *siyum* – for those who would normally attend the *seudah* at any other time of the year, such as relatives and close friends. Other participants, however, are not permitted to partake of the meat and wine even if they have been invited to join the *seudah*. During the week of Tishah b'Av, participation in a *seudas mitzvah* must be kept to a minimum, and only the *baalei simchah*, their close relatives (i.e., any family member who is not permitted to testify on their behalf in a *beis din*), and ten friends may partake of the meat and wine. (If Tishah b'Av falls on Shabbos, the preceding week does not have the halachic status of the *shavua shechal bo* in this regard, and anyone who would ordinarily participate in the *seudah* may eat meat and drink wine.)²⁰⁵

19. **Wine at a *Bris Milah*:** The cup of wine at a *bris milah* itself should preferably be given to a child to drink.²⁰⁶

שקטן שאמרנו היינו שהגיע לחינוך אבל לא הגיע להתאבל על ירושלים וכיון שלא נתבאר להדיא שיעור זה וקשה לשער הדבר, יש נוהגין לשתות בעצמו.

202. ערוך השלחן סכ״ו.
203. מ״ב ס״ק ע״א.
204. מ״ב ס״ק ע״ב.
205. רמ״א שם, מ״ב ס״ק ע״ה-ע״ז.
206. הגרש״ז זצ״ל הוב״ד בס׳ אוצר הברית ח״א עמוד קפ״ד.

20. **A *Bris Milah* after the Eighth Day:** Meat and wine may be consumed at a *seudah* for a *bris milah* even if it takes place after the eighth day (i.e., the *bris* was delayed).[207]

21. **Celebrating a *Siyum*:** One may not deliberately increase or decrease the pace of one's learning in order to schedule a *siyum* with a *fleishig* meal during the Nine Days.[208] (However, one may begin a learning program with the intent of completing a particular *limud* during the Nine Days.[209]) Furthermore, if a person does not generally celebrate a *siyum* with a *seudah*, it is preferable not to change his habit during the Nine Days.[210]

22. **When a *Siyum* May Be Held:** A *siyum* may be celebrated upon completing a *masechta* of Gemara, a full *seder* of Mishnayos, or a sefer of Tanach with its commentaries.[211]

23. **Participating in the Celebration of a *Siyum*:** Some *poskim* maintain that meat and wine may be consumed at a *siyum* only by participants who completed the learning or who support the yeshivah or *kollel*, as well as members of the staff and those who helped prepare the *seudah*.[212] Some authorities rule that an entire yeshivah or camp may partake of the meat at a *siyum* (even during the week of Tishah b'Av) because they normally eat together, like a family.[213]

24. **Partaking of a *Seudah* without Attending the *Siyum*:** A person may not eat meat that was sent to his home from a *siyum* or other *seudas mitzvah*.[214] However, a person may

---

207. עי' שע"ת ס"ק ל"ג.
208. מ"ב ס"ק ע"ג. ועי' שו"ת מנחת יצחק ח"ב סי' צ"ג.
209. ערוך השלחן סכ"ח.
210. מ"ב שם.
211. עי' שו"ת אגר"מ או"ח ח"א סי' קנ"ז ואמת ליעקב הערה 511.
212. עי' ביה"ל ס"י ד"ה וסיום מסכת.
213. הגרמ"פ זצ"ל הובא בקיצור הל' ביהמ"ץ להגר"ש איידער זצ"ל. ועי' שו"ת שבט הלוי ח"ו סוסי' ע"ב לענין נשים וילדים.
214. מ"ב ס"ק ע"ה.

partake of the meat at a *siyum* even if he missed hearing the actual recitation of the *siyum*.[215]

25. **Singing at a *Seudas Mitzvah*:** It is permissible to sing *zemiros* or songs praising the Torah at a *seudas mitzvah*.[216]

26. **A Bar Mitzvah:** According to most *poskim*, meat and wine may be consumed at a *seudas bar mitzvah* held on the boy's 13th birthday itself (*bo bayom*), as is the case at other *seudos mitzvah* (as in paragraph 18 above).[217] Some *poskim* prohibit this.[218]

27. ***Chanukas Habayis*:** Meat and wine may not be served at a *seudah* celebrating a *chanukas habayis*, even in Eretz Yisrael.[219]

28. **Children:** Many *poskim* rule that children should not eat meat or poultry during this period even if they are below the age of *chinuch* for mourning the destruction of the *Beis Hamikdash* (nine years), unless they are weak and must eat meat for health reasons.[220] (A child may be served meat or poultry if he refuses to eat other foods that can provide necessary nutrients.) There is more room for leniency prior to the week of Tishah b'Av.[221] Some authorities, however, cite grounds for leniency to permit children younger than the age of *chinuch* for mourning to eat meat under all circumstances.[222] Other *poskim* permit children to be served poultry or foods that have been cooked with meat, but rule that children should not be given meat

---

215. שו"ת תשובות והנהגות ח"ב סי' ר"י בשם הגרי"י קניבסקי זצ"ל. אבל ע" בשו"ת מנחת יצחק ח"ט סי' מ"ה שנקט להתיר רק לאלו שמסייעים בעריכת הסעודה.
216. הליכות שלמה פי"ד הערה 38.
217. הליכות שלמה שם ס"ח. וכתוב שם הערה 28 דמז' אב ואילך לא יעשו כן.
218. הגרח"ק שליט"א הוב"ד בתורת המועדים ס"ק מ"ז.
219. הליכות שלמה שם סי"א.
220. מ"ב סק"ע ובשעה"צ ס"ק ע"ו. וכן משמע מהמחזו"א סי' נ"ט סק"ג. וראה הליכות שלמה שם הערה 28 שהגרשז"א זצ"ל לא התיר אפי' אפי' לקטנים ביותר בני ג' וד' אפי' בשר עוף בכל צורך מיוחד.
221. עי' מ"ב ס"ק פ"ב בשם החי"א, וכ"ש הכא שהוא רק מנהגא.
222. שו"ת דברי יציב או"ח ח"ב סי' רל"ו. ובקיצור הל' ביהמ"צ להגר"ש אייךער זצ"ל כתב להתיר בקטן פחות מבן ט' אם רגיל בכל יום לאכול בשר וקשה להאכילו מאכלי חלב.

itself.[223] An individual should follow his family's custom in this regard or consult with a Rav.

For those who follow the more stringent opinion, meat should not be served to children even on Erev Shabbos. However, if the children in a family are accustomed to having a *seudah* on Erev Shabbos and going to sleep before the actual Shabbos meal, they may be permitted to eat meat at that time.[224]

29. **Eating Meat during Illness or after Birth:** A person who is ill is permitted to eat meat and drink wine even if his illness is not severe. This is also permitted for a woman within 30 days after birth. (Some *poskim* rule that if a woman after birth is not weak, she should refrain from eating meat from the seventh of Av through Tishah b'Av.) A nursing woman is likewise permitted to eat meat and drink wine if it is necessary for her milk.[225] According to some authorities, in these scenarios it is preferable to eat poultry rather than meat if it will be sufficient.[226]

30. **A Person with a Dairy Allergy:** Poultry is permitted for a person who is not ill or weak but is unable to eat dairy foods due to an allergy.[227]

7. Bathing and Showering

1. **Bathing during the Nine Days:** The *minhag* is to refrain from bathing or showering during the Nine Days.[228] According to

---

223. הגרי"ש א זצ"ל הובא בתורת המועדים עמוד קכ"ה.
224. עי' שו"ת אגר"מ או"ח ח"ד סי' כ"א אות ד'.
225. מ"ב ס"ק ס"א וס"ק ס"ד.
226. עי' מ"ב שם ועי' ערוך השלחן סכ"ו.
227. מ"ב ס"ק ס"ד.
228. שו"ע סי' תקנ"א סט"ז.

Ashkenazic custom, this restriction takes effect on the night of Rosh Chodesh.[229] This applies to any type of washing, whether bathing, swimming, or showering, even without soap or shampoo.

2. **Bathing in Cold Water:** The Ashkenazic custom is to refrain from bathing or showering even in cold water.[230] However, washing the hands, face, and feet in cold water is permitted[231] (except on Tishah b'Av itself; see Chapter Eight below).

3. **Bathing for Medical Reasons:** One may shower or bathe with hot water for medical purposes,[232] such as for a woman shortly before or after birth. Similarly, if a person is frail and has been advised by a doctor to bathe in hot water or take medicinal baths, such as sulphur baths, it is permitted even during the week of Tishah b'Av, but not on Tishah b'Av itself.[233]

    Swimming required for medical reasons (e.g., in the case of a paralytic condition) is permitted.[234]

4. **Bathing for a Mitzvah:** It is permissible to bathe in hot water for the purpose of a mitzvah. For example, a woman who must immerse in a *mikveh* should perform the *chafifah* in the usual manner, using hot water, and may immerse in a hot *mikveh*. (If her scheduled immersion is on the night of the tenth of Av or fell on the ninth and thus postponed until the tenth,

---

229. רמ"א שם סט"ז.

230. שם.

231. מ"ב ס"ק צ"ד. ומשמע מסתימת דבריו שהיתר רגלים הוא גם בזמננו שאין הולכים יחף, וכן דעת הגריש"א זצ"ל הוב"ד בתורת המועדים עמוד קל"ז. וכ"כ בשו"ת שבט הלוי ח"ז סי' ע"ז אות ב'. אמנם דעת הגריי"ק זצ"ל הובא בארחות רבינו ח"ב עמוד קל"ד והגרח"ק שליט"א בשמו הובא בתורת המועדים שם, שאין להתיר. עוד הובא בתורת המועדים שם לענין פניו, שדעת הגריש"א זצ"ל שגם הזקן בכלל ומאידך דעת הגרח"ק שליט"א שאינו בכלל. ובעניין עד היכן מקום ידיו ורגליו, בהליכות שלמה פי"ד ס"ק ל"ד איתא עד המקום שדרכו להתלכלך. ועי' ששכ"ל פמ"ב הערה קפ"ב.

232. מ"ב ס"ק פ"ח.

233. שעה"צ ס"ק צ"ד.

234. ומש"כ בהליכות שלמה פי"ד הערה 61 בשם הגרשז"א זצ"ל להחמיר, לכאורה הוא דוקא לצורך בריאות וחיזוק הגוף כללי ולא שיש צורך רפואה ממש בדבר.

see Chapter Eight, section 2, regarding when the *chafifah* is performed.) Before performing the *hefsek taharah*, a woman should wash herself in the usual manner with hot water.[235]

5. ***Tevilah* for a Man on Erev Shabbos:** A man who immerses in the *mikveh* every Erev Shabbos may do so even during the Nine Days,[236] albeit not in hot water.[237] If he sometimes opts not to immerse on Erev Shabbos, such as when he is busy or the weather is unfavorable, he may not immerse himself during the Nine Days[238] (even in cold water).

6. ***Tevilah* before Davening:** A person who immerses in a *mikveh* every day before davening may continue to do so during the Nine Days[239] (in cold water).

7. **Immersion for a *Sandak* before a *Bris*:** Some *poskim* permit a *sandak* to immerse in a *mikveh* before the *bris*.[240]

8. **Showering before *Tevilah*:** If a *mikveh* has a policy that a person must shower before immersing, he may do so[241] (in cold water).

9. **Bathing to Remove Dirt or Perspiration:** It is permissible to cleanse oneself of dirt.[242] Even warm water may be used if it is needed to remove the dirt.[243] Likewise, many *poskim* permit

---

235. רמ"א שם.
236. מ"ב ס"ק צ"ה.
237. שעה"צ ס"ק צ"ח.
238. מ"ב שם.
239. ערוך השלחן סל"ה, וראה כף החיים ס"ק ק"צ בשם הבא"ח לענין טבילת עזרא (וכתב שם שאם א"א לו לטבול בצונן או שאין שם כ"א חמין, מותר, כיון שיש תועלת גדולה בטבילה זו ועוד דאינו מכוין לתענוג רק להעביר הטומאה), וע" שו"ת שבט הלוי ח"ז סי' ע"ז. אמנם, דעת הגרח"ק שליט"א הוב"ד בתורת המועדים עמוד קל"ט שאין להתיר אלא טבילת עזרא. וכן בחוט שני יו"ט עמוד שמ"ז החמיר בדבר.
240. כה"ח שם בשם הבא"ח. אבל ע" תורת המועדים שם שהגרח"ק שליט"א פסק שאסור, וע"ש בדברי הגריש"א זצ"ל.
241. הגריש"א זצ"ל הוב"ד בתורת המועדים עמוד קל"ח. וע" הליכות שלמה פי"ד ס"ק כ"ט.
242. ערוך השלחן סל"ז, וכמו באבל יו"ד סי' שפ"א ס"א-ב.
243. שם.

washing in cold water to rid oneself of perspiration.[244] If soap is necessary to remove the sweat or dirt, it is permitted.[245] A person who must clean many parts of his body from dirt or perspiration is not required to wash each spot individually; he may cleanse his entire body at once instead.[246] Some *poskim* disagree with the above ruling and maintain that a person who has merely perspired and is not actually soiled may not wash his body even in cold water.[247] However, even according to these authorities, if specific body parts have a foul odor (such as the feet), one is permitted to wash those parts of the body and even to use soap if necessary.[248]

10. **Bathing in Lukewarm Water:** When bathing is permitted in cold water only (as opposed to bathing for medical reasons or a mitzvah purpose, in which case hot water may be used), some *poskim* permit the use of water that is lukewarm, if one does not derive pleasure from the warmth.[249]

11. **Using Soap or Shampoo:** If soap or shampoo is needed to remove dirt or perspiration (which is often the case when a person hasn't showered for a few days), it is permitted. (This is true even during the week of Tishah b'Av.)[250]

12. **Using a Wet Washcloth:** Some authorities maintain that it is permissible to clean the entire body with a slightly wet washcloth, since this is not considered bathing or showering.[251]

---

244. עי' שו"ת אגר"מ אבהע"ז ח"ד סי' פ"ד אות ד'. ועי' שו"ת שבט הלוי ח"ז סי' ע"ז, אבל כתב שיעשה דרך אבר אבר ולא בב"א והוסיף שהדבר מסור ליראי ה'. מתי להקל בזה. וראה עוד שם ח"ח סי' קכ"ז.

245. עי' שו"ת שלמת חיים סי' רי"ט, שו"ת שבט הלוי שם וששש"כ פמ"ב סנ"ב.

246. עי' מ"ב סי' תרי"ג סק"א. אמנם בשו"ת שבט הלוי ח"ח סי' ע"ז כתב שיעשה כן דרך אבר אבר.

247. ארחות רבינו ח"א עמוד שע"ו בשם החזו"א. וראה הליכות שלמה שם סי"ח וס"ק כ"ז והערה 62 שדעת הגרשז"א זצ"ל שאין להקל גם אם גורמת לו צער או שהוא איסטניס אא"כ מצטער ביותר וסבלו רב, אך בלי סבון. ומ"מ בס"ק כ"ו שם התיר רחיצה לצורך זיעה במוצאי ת"ב.

248. הליכות שלמה שם ס"ק כ"ד.

249. קיצור הלכות ביהמ"צ להגר"ש איידער זצ"ל.

250. שו"ת שבט הלוי ח"ח סי' קכ"ז.

251. הגריש"א זצ"ל הוב"ד בתורת המועדים עמוד ק"מ.

13. **Bathing Children:** Some authorities permit bathing young children (until approximately the age of five years).[252] One should consult with a Rav regarding whether older children may bathe regularly.

14. **Erev Shabbos on Rosh Chodesh Av:** When Rosh Chodesh Av falls on Friday, it is permissible to shower or bathe the entire body in hot water in the normal fashion, if one generally does so for Shabbos.[253] Soap and shampoo may be used as well.[254]

15. **Bathing on Erev Shabbos Chazon:** Many *poskim* rule that a person who generally bathes or showers with hot water on Erev Shabbos is permitted to wash his hair, hands, face, and feet in hot water for the sake of *kavod* Shabbos on Erev Shabbos Chazon (even if he has not perspired heavily or become soiled).[255] However, it is forbidden to bathe the entire body[256] or to use soap or shampoo.[257] (As mentioned above, many *poskim* permit washing the body to remove perspiration; therefore, a person who has perspired heavily may wash his hair, face, hands, and feet with hot water, and then wash the rest of his body with cold water to remove the sweat.[258]) Some *poskim* disagree with the above ruling and maintain that nowadays, when the standard practice is always to bathe the entire body daily in hot water, it is permitted to wash one's entire body with hot water for *kavod* Shabbos, as well as to use soap and shampoo.[259]

---

252. הגרי"ש א זצ"ל הוב"ל שם עמוד קל"ט.
253. מ"ב ס"ק פ"ט. וראה בט"ז ס"ק ט"ז בביאור הדבר.
254. הליכות שלמה שם סי"ט.
255. רמ"א שם סט"ז שיש מקילים, מ"ב ס"ק צ"ג. וכן המנהג עפ"י רוב בחו"ל, אמנם, בא"י יש נוהגין כדיעה ראשונה ברמ"א שדוקא בצונן מותר, וכ"ה בלוח א"י וכ"ה בהליכות שלמה שם סכ"ה.
256. כמבואר שם. ועי' בערוך השלחן סל"ו.
257. מ"ב ס"ק צ"ו.
258. שו"ת שבט הלוי ח"ח סי' קכ"ז.
259. הגרמ"פ זצ"ל והגרי"א העניקין זצ"ל הוב"ל בקיצור הלכות ביהמ"צ להגר"ש אייידער זצ"ל.

16. **When Tishah B'Av Falls on Shabbos:** When the eighth of Av falls on Erev Shabbos, one should wash for Shabbos before *chatzos*. A person who did not manage to do so is still permitted to wash (in keeping with the guidelines in paragraph 15 above) after *chatzos*.[260]

17. **Cutting Nails:** There is a difference of opinion among the *poskim* as to whether it is permissible to cut nails during the Nine Days (as mentioned above in section 2, paragraph 17). Nevertheless, it is certainly permissible to cut one's nails on Erev Shabbos, even if Tishah b'Av falls on Shabbos.[261]

18. **Applying Creams and Fragrances:** There is no prohibition to apply creams, perfumes, and certainly deodorant during this period. Regarding the use of these products on Tishah b'Av itself, see below, Chapter Eight, section 2.

---

260. ביה"ל סט"ז ד"ה בחפיפת הראש בחמין.
261. מ"ב סק"כ.

CHAPTER SEVEN
Erev Tishah B'Av

※

1. The Halachos of Erev Tishah B'Av
2. *Seudah Hamafsekes*
3. After the *Seudah Hamafsekes*
4. When Erev Tishah B'Av Falls on Shabbos

CHAPTER SEVEN

Erev Tishah B'Av

1. The Halachos of Erev Tishah B'Av

1. **Omitting *Tachanun* at *Minchah*:** Tishah b'Av has a unique status that sets it apart from other fast days. Although it is a day of mourning, it is also considered a *moed*, since it is destined to be observed as a Yom Tov after the *Beis Hamikdash* is rebuilt. Consequently, *Tachanun* is omitted at *Minchah* on the day before Tishah b'Av, as on any Erev Yom Tov.[1] When Erev Tishah b'Av coincides with Shabbos, *Tzidkascha* is omitted at *Minchah*;[2] however, *Av Harachamim* is recited before *Mussaf* as usual. (This is true even when the ninth of Av itself falls on Shabbos.)

2. ***Seudas Mitzvah* on Erev Tishah B'Av:** A *seudas mitzvah* such as a *bris* or *pidyon haben* that is held on Erev Tishah b'Av should be served before *chatzos*. As explained above (Chapter Six, section 6, paragraph 18), meat and wine may be served at a *seudas mitzvah* during the week of Tishah b'Av, but the *seudah* should be limited to no more than ten participants in addition to the *baalei simchah* and their close relatives.[3] If the

---

1. שו"ע סי' תקנ"ב סי"ב.
2. רמ"א שם.
3. רמ"א סי' תקנ"א ס"י ומ"ב ס"ק ע"ח.

seudah extends past *chatzos*, the participants may continue eating.[4]

3. **Pleasure Strolls:** After *chatzos* on Erev Tishah b'Av, one should not take a pleasure stroll[5] (and one certainly should not engage in other leisure activities[6]). This restriction applies even when Erev Tishah b'Av falls on Shabbos. When Tishah b'Av itself falls on Shabbos (and the fast is postponed until Sunday), one should not take a pleasure stroll at any time over the course of Shabbos.[7]

4. **Learning Torah after *Chatzos*:** Torah study is considered an activity that generates happiness and is therefore prohibited on Tishah b'Av (see Chapter Eight, section 4). The Rema cites a *minhag* to begin observing this restriction on Erev Tishah b'Av after *chatzos*.[8] According to this custom, when Erev Tishah b'Av falls on Shabbos, *Pirkei Avos* is not recited.[9] Torah learning is permitted on Shabbos prior to *chatzos* even when the ninth of Av itself falls on Shabbos.[10]

Some *poskim* dispute the Rema's ruling that one should not engage in Torah learning on Shabbos after *chatzos*. These *poskim* maintain that there can be no prohibition to engage in Torah study on Shabbos, even on the ninth of Av itself.[11] Many other authorities also dispute the notion that Torah learning is forbidden on Erev Tishah b'Av at any time, even on a weekday.[12] In light of these differences of opinion, there is no

---

4. שעה"צ סי' תקנ"א ס"ק פ"ט.
5. רמ"א סי' תקנ"ג ס"ב, ואף שכתב לא יטייל ערב ת"ב, כוונתו על לאחר חצות וכמש"כ למעלה מיניה לענין לימוד, וראה שערי תשובה סק"ה.
6. כן נראה פשוט שהכל נכלל ב"טיול".
7. עי' שע"ת שם בשם הברכ"י. (ומש"כ בשם הדגו"מ היינו על לימוד תורה.)
8. רמ"א שם.
9. שם.
10. מ"ב סק"ט. וראה שו"ת שבט הלוי ח"ו סי' ע' אות ו'.
11. מ"ב שם סק"י בשם הט"ז. ועי' ביה"ל ד"ה ולכן.
12. עי' מ"ב שם סק"ח בשם המהרש"ל, הגר"א, המאמר מרדכי והחיי אדם. ועי' ביה"ל שם.

objection if a person chooses to rely on the lenient view and engage in Torah study on a weekday Erev Tishah b'Av even after *chatzos*.[13] Furthermore, on Shabbos one may certainly rely on the lenient views and learn Torah at any time during the day.[14] According to all, *shenayim mikra v'echad targum* is permitted the entire day.[15]

Some authorities rule that although one may rely on the view that permits engaging in Torah study, public learning should be avoided. According to these *poskim*, a *shiur* should not be scheduled after *chatzos* on Erev Tishah b'Av when it falls on Shabbos, or the *shiur* should deal with topics related to Tishah b'Av. Nevertheless, if the attendees would not otherwise engage in Torah study, these authorities agree that there is no need to cancel the *shiur* or change its topic.[16] According to this view, *Avos U'banim* programs may be held as usual on Shabbos afternoon, as is common in many communities; these programs are not considered public learning sessions, since they are designated for fathers to learn independently with their sons.[17]

Other authorities, however, maintain that any *shiur* that regularly takes place on Shabbos should not be canceled on Erev Tishah b'Av, since the cancellation would constitute a public display of mourning, which is prohibited on Shabbos.[18]

Tehillim may be recited on Erev Tishah b'Av throughout the day.[19]

---

13. מ"ב שם.
14. מ"ב סק"י.
15. קיצור שו"ע סי' קכ"ה ס"ד כה"ח סי' תקנ"ח סקי"ט.
16. הגריש"א זצ"ל הובא בתורת המועדים עמוד קמ"ט.
17. שם עמוד ק"נ.
18. ראה שש"כ פס"ה הערה מ"ה.
19. הליכות שלמה פט"ז סק"ו סק"ח.

5. **Learning Topics of Sorrow in Depth:** There are certain topics that are permitted to be studied both on Tishah b'Av and on Erev Tishah b'Av (see Chapter 8, section 4). Although it is prohibited to study these subjects in depth (*b'iyun*) on Tishah b'Av itself, it is permissible to learn these topics *b'iyun* on Erev Tishah b'Av (even on a weekday).[20]

6. **Fasting on Erev Tishah B'Av:** A person should not commit to a fast on Erev Tishah b'Av, since it is too difficult for the average person to fast for two consecutive days. If a person has an existing commitment that obligates him to fast on Erev Tishah b'Av (e.g., he fasts every month on this specific date, or every Monday and Thursday), he may observe the fast and interrupt it to eat the *seudah hamafsekes* just before *shekiah*. Nevertheless, it is preferable to annul the vow that obligates him to fast. If a person has a *yahrtzeit* on Erev Tishah b'Av, he should stipulate on the first occurrence of the *yahrtzeit* that he will fast only until *chatzos*.[21]

2. *Seudah Hamafsekes*

1. **The Final Meal before the Fast:** The *seudah hamafsekes* is the final meal eaten before Tishah b'Av and incorporates various practices that intensify our mourning for the *Beis Hamikdash*. A meal must satisfy two conditions to be halachically defined as the *seudah hamafsekes* and therefore subject to these special halachos: It must take place after *chatzos*, and it must be the final meal before the fast. A meal held in the late afternoon will not be considered the *seudah hamafsekes* if it is to be followed by another meal that will include bread.[22] If a person plans to eat again without including bread in the

---

20. שם ס"א.
21. שו"ע סי' תקנ"ב סי"א ובמ"ב שם בכל הסעי'.
22. שו"ע סי' תקנ"ב ס"ט.

second meal, the first meal will be subject to the halachos of the *seudah hamafsekes*.[23]

2. **Meat and Wine Are Prohibited:** The consumption of meat or wine is prohibited at the *seudah hamafsekes*.[24] Although there is a general prohibition to consume meat or wine during the Nine Days, that restriction has the status of a *minhag*, whereas the prohibition at the *seudah hamafsekes* is an actual halachah that appears in the Gemara.[25] It is also customary to refrain from consuming poultry, fish, or unfermented wine at this meal.[26]

3. **Beverages:** Non-alcoholic beverages may be consumed at the *seudah hamafsekes*; however, a person should limit his consumption of these beverages. For example, a person who generally drinks three cups at a meal should drink only two at this time.[27] It is commendable to drink only water at the *seudah hamafsekes*; see paragraph 12 below. There is no limit on the quantity of water that may be consumed.[28]

It is prohibited to drink beer or any other alcoholic beverage at this meal, unless it is necessary for health reasons.[29] Some authorities add that sugary drinks such as soda should also not be consumed (unless there is a health reason for which one must have such a beverage), but tea and coffee are permitted.[30]

4. **The Limit of One Cooked Dish:** Only one cooked dish may be consumed at the *seudah hamafsekes*.[31] With regard to this halachah, the definition of a cooked dish is any food that has

---

23. שם ומ״ב סק״כ.
24. שו״ע שם ס״א.
25. מ״ב סק״ג.
26. שו״ע שם ס״ב.
27. רמ״א שם ס״א ומ״ב סק״ד.
28. מ״ב ס״ק ט״ו.
29. מ״ב סק״ד ושעה״צ סק״א.
30. עי׳ שערי תשובה ריש סי׳ תקנ״ב.
31. שו״ע שם ס״א.

Seudah Hamafsekes ~ 205

been cooked, fried, grilled, or prepared in any similar fashion.[32] The consumption of cooked dishes is limited in order to prevent the meal from bringing honor or physical enjoyment to the participants.[33] (Tea and coffee are not considered cooked dishes with respect to this halachah.)

5. **Two Versions of a Dish or Two Foods Cooked in a Single Pot:** If two different forms of a particular food item are prepared, each dish is considered a distinct cooked item, and one may not partake of both.[34] (If a large quantity of a food is prepared identically in two separate pots, it is considered a single cooked item.[35]) Two foods prepared together in the same pot are also considered different dishes, even if they share the same taste.[36] It is permissible, however, for each of the foods to be consumed by a different person.[37]

6. **Foods Generally Cooked Together:** Two food items that are usually cooked together, such as a vegetable and onions, are considered a single dish when they are prepared together.[38] However, foods that are prepared together often but not in the majority of instances, such as blintzes or pasta prepared with cheese, are viewed as two separate cooked dishes and may not be consumed at this meal. The cheese is considered a distinct food item because it is often eaten alone or with other types of food; it is not invariably prepared together with either of these items.[39]

7. **A Cooked Dish Generally Consumed with Other Foods:** A

---

32. רמ"א שם ס"ג.
33. מ"ב ס"ק י"א.
34. שו"ע שם ס"ג.
35. מ"ב סק"ח.
36. שו"ע שם. ועי' ביה"ל ד"ה וכן.
37. מ"ב סק"ט.
38. שו"ע שם. ועי' ביה"ל ד"ה שנותנים, דאפקא דוקא כשאחד בא להטעים השני.
39. מ"ב סק"י.

cooked food that is used to enhance another food item, such as a spread placed on bread, might nevertheless be considered a separate cooked dish. Thus, it would be prohibited to partake of an additional cooked dish along with this spread.[40]

8. **Pasteurized Foods:** Some authorities rule that pasteurized foods are considered cooked with respect to this halachah. Therefore, it would not be permissible to eat a pasteurized dairy food along with another cooked dish (such as an egg) at the *seudah hamafsekes*.[41]

9. **Foods That Are Edible when Uncooked:** Even foods that are edible when they are raw, such as vegetables, are viewed as cooked dishes with regard to the *seudah hamafsekes* if they have been prepared as such. (This stands in contrast to the laws of *bishul akum*, in which a distinction is drawn between foods that are edible in their uncooked state and those that cannot be consumed unless they are cooked.)[42]

10. **Uncooked Fruits and Vegetables:** Raw fruits and vegetables may be consumed at the *seudah hamafsekes* without restriction.[43] (See paragraph 12 below.) However, pickled vegetables should not be eaten.[44]

11. **Hard-Boiled Eggs:** Although any cooked food (other than meat, poultry, or fish) may be used at the *seudah hamafsekes*, the common custom is to eat a cold[45] hard-boiled egg, which is the food typically consumed by mourners.[46] (The round shape of an egg symbolizes the cycle of life and death, and the fact that it has no opening symbolizes the fact that the mourner

---

40. עי' שעה"צ ס"ק י"ח. והגרח"ק שליט"א הוב"ד בתורת המועדים עמוד קמ"ב הסתפק בדבר.
41. שו"ת אור לציון ח"ג פכ"ח ס"ב. אבל עי' כף החיים ס"ק י"ג.
42. שו"ע שם ומ"ב ס"ק י"א.
43. שו"ע שם ס"ד.
44. שע"ת ריש הסי' בשם שכנה"ג.
45. לשון הגהו"מ הובא בב"י, וכן העתיק המ"א ובאר היטב אבל המ"ב השמיטו.
46. רמ"א שם ס"ה, מ"ב ס"ק י"ג.

cannot open his mouth to question Hashem's decrees.) Aside from the egg, no other cooked food may be eaten. (The practice of eating other foods before sitting on the floor to eat the egg is in error, since all the foods consumed in the course of the meal are considered part of the *seudah hamafsekes*.)[47]

12. **The Preferable Practice:** It is commendable to eat a *seudah hamafsekes* consisting of only plain bread with salt and an egg, and to drink water rather than other beverages, if that will be sufficient.[48] On the other hand, a person should not minimize the quantity of food and drink that he consumes; he should make sure to eat and drink his fill so that the fast will not harm him.[49]

13. **Dipping the Bread in Ashes:** One should dip a small portion of the bread at the *seudah hamafsekes* in ashes.[50] This should be accompanied by the declaration, "This is the *seudah* of Tishah b'Av."[51]

14. **The Final Meal for a Person Exempt from the Fast:** A person who will not be fasting on Tishah b'Av (see Chapter Eight, section 1, for a discussion of possible exempting from the fast) should nonetheless eat the *seudah hamafsekes*, following all of the relevant halachos.[52]

15. **Sitting on the Floor:** It is customary to eat the *seudah hamafsekes* while seated on the floor,[53] in order to create an atmosphere of mournfulness and degradation.[54] If a person feels weak or will experience pain from sitting on the floor,

---

47. מ"ב ס"ק י"ד.
48. שו"ע שם ס"ו.
49. מ"ב ס"ק ט"ו.
50. רמ"א שם ס"ו עפ"י הירושלמי.
51. מ"ב ס"ק ט"ז עפ"י הירושלמי.
52. הליכות שלמה פט"ו ס"ב, שו"ת שבט הלוי ח"י סי' פ"ג.
53. שו"ע שם ס"ז.
54. מ"ב ס"ק י"ז, ולשונו "סעודה שפלה".

he may place a pillow beneath him.[55] Some *poskim* add that according to Kabbalah one should always sit on a mat or similar flat object rather than sitting directly on the floor. However, other *poskim* do not view this as a problem.[56]

Some authorities state that the custom to sit on the floor at the *seudah hamafsekes* does not apply to women.[57] However, it is a common practice for women to sit on the floor as well.

One may sit on a regular chair after the *seudah hamafsekes*, since the halachos of Tishah b'Av come into effect only at *shekiah*.[58]

16. **Wearing Leather Shoes:** It is not necessary to remove one's leather shoes at the *seudah hamafsekes*.[59]

17. **Avoiding the Formation of a *Zimun*:** Adult males should refrain from sitting together in groups of three or more during the *seudah hamafsekes*, so that they will not be required to recite *birkas hamazon* with a *zimun*. If three men are present, they should sit in separate rooms or in separate corners of the same room, where they cannot see each other.[60] If a group of men erroneously ate this meal together, they should nonetheless *bench* individually rather than reciting the *zimun*.[61]

---

55. מ"ב שם.
56. עי' שע"ת סק"ח שהביא מח' מהרי"ש ומהרי"ל ומסיק דמאחר דאיש יש תקנה ע"י דבר חוצץ יש לחוש לדברי קבלה שכתב מהר"ש. אמנם המ"ב לא הביאו וגם לא ציינו בשעה"צ לעי"ש. ועי' כף החיים ס"ק ל"ט שציידד לומר שליכא מח' וכל הענין עפ"י קבלה הוא לישב ע"ג אדמה ולא על קרקע מרוצף ומ"מ סיים שם שעדיף להחמיר גם על קרקע מרוצף.
57. הליכות שלמה פט"ו הערה 5.
58. מ"ב ס"ק י"ח.
59. רמ"א שם ס"ז.
60. שו"ע שם ס"ח.
61. מ"ב ס"ק י"ט.

18. **A Meal Prior to the *Seudah Hamafsekes*:** Because of the limitations on the foods that may be consumed at the *seudah hamafsekes*, the common practice is to have a proper meal with a variety of foods prior to the actual *seudah hamafsekes*, so that one will be sufficiently satiated before the fast.[62] However, since it is problematic to have two meals in close succession due to the halachic objection to reciting a *brachah she'einah tzrichah* (unnecessary *brachah* – in this case, *birkas hamazon* after the first meal and the *brachah rishonah* before the second), it is customary for the first meal to be served before *Minchah* and for the *seudah hamafsekes* to take place after *Minchah*.[63] A person should take care not to become satiated at the first meal to the point that he will not have an appetite at all for the *seudah hamafsekes*.[64]

It should be noted that if a person drinks water when he is not thirsty, he should not recite the *brachah* of *shehakol*.

19. ***Seudah Hamafsekes* on Shabbos:** For the halachos of *seudah hamafsekes* on Shabbos (when Erev Tishah b'Av falls on Shabbos or when Tishah b'Av itself falls on Shabbos and the fast is postponed until Sunday), see section 4 below.

3. After the *Seudah Hamafsekes*

1. **Eating and Drinking after the Meal:** After the *seudah hamafsekes* has concluded, the halachah does not presume that one has automatically accepted the fast. Therefore, it is permissible to eat and drink again at any time until *shekiah*.[65]

---

62. רמ"א שם ס"ט, ועי' מ"ב ס"ק כ"ב.
63. רמ"א שם ומ"ב ס"ק כ"א ושעה"צ ס"ק ט"ז.
64. מ"ב ס"ק כ"ב.
65. שו"ע סי' תקנ"ג ס"א.

2. **Declaring the Intent to Continue Eating:** Notwithstanding the above, it is preferable for a person to make a verbal stipulation at the conclusion of the meal that he does not intend to begin the fast until *shekiah*.[66]

3. **Accepting the Fast Verbally:** If a person explicitly declares that he does not intend to eat or drink more, or he verbally declares his acceptance of the fast, his commitment is binding and he is prohibited to eat or drink.[67] There is a dispute among the *poskim* as to whether a mental resolution to begin the fast is likewise binding.[68] If a person merely decides that he is full and will not need to continue eating or drinking, but he does not intend to begin formally fasting, this does not constitute acceptance of the fast, and he remains permitted to eat and drink.[69]

4. **The Onset of the Fast:** The fast of Tishah b'Av with all of its restrictions (washing, wearing leather shoes, and so forth, as will be discussed in the next chapter) begins at *shekiah*.[70] Unlike on Shabbos, Yom Tov, and Yom Kippur, there is no halachic requirement to add extra time (*tosefes*) to the fast.[71] If a person davens *Maariv* prior to *shekiah*, all the halachos of Tishah b'Av take effect at that time.[72] Leather shoes should be removed prior to *Barchu*.[73]

5. **When the Other Restrictions Take Effect:** Just as one may eat or drink until *shekiah*, the prohibitions of wearing leather shoes, washing, anointing, and sitting on a chair likewise

---

66. מ"ב סק"ב.
67. שו"ע שם ומ"ב סק"א.
68. רמ"א שם ס"א כתב שאינו קבלה, ובמ"ב סק"ב הביא בשם הב"ח והגר"א דהוי קבלה.
69. מ"ב שם.
70. שו"ע שם ס"ב.
71. מ"ב סק"ג.
72. שעה"צ סק"ט.
73. רמ"א שם ס"ב ומ"ב סק"ה.

do not take effect until *shekiah*.[74] If a person accepts the fast verbally prior to *shekiah* (see paragraph 2 above), this automatically renders him prohibited to wash or anoint himself as well.[75] (This is true only after *plag haminchah*; at any earlier time during the day, a person will become subject only to the prohibitions that he accepts explicitly.[76]) On the other hand, if a person verbally accepts the fast while wearing leather shoes, it is considered as if he has made an explicit stipulation that the prohibition to wear leather shoes should not be included, and therefore he is permitted to continue wearing his shoes until *shekiah*.[77]

4. When Erev Tishah B'Av Falls on Shabbos

1. **The Final Meal before the Fast:** When Tishah b'Av falls on Sunday, or the ninth of Av falls on Shabbos and the fast is postponed until Sunday, the usual halachos of the *seudah hamafsekes* are not applicable, and an ordinary meal should be served for *seudah shelishis*. One may even eat meat, wine, or any other delicacies at this meal.[78] However, one must cease eating prior to *shekiah*, since the fast begins at *shekiah*. It is important to be mindful of this, since it is quite common to continue the *seudah shelishis* meal past *shekiah* on an ordinary Shabbos.[79]

2. **Eating Meat:** There is no basis for refraining from eating

---

74. רמ"א שם.
75. מ"ב סק"ד.
76. שם.
77. מ"ב סק"ב ושעה"צ סק"ג.
78. שו"ע סי' תקנ"ב ס"י.
79. רמ"א שם ס"י, ומ"ב ס"ק כ"ד.

meat at this *seudah shelishis* as a measure of stringency. On the contrary, a person who deliberately abstains from eating meat due to the *aveilus* of Tishah b'Av would be viewed as transgressing the prohibition of mourning on Shabbos.[80] Even a person who generally does not eat meat at *seudah shelishis* may do so on this Shabbos.[81]

3. **Eating at the Table and *Bentching* with a *Zimun*:** As noted above, the laws of the *seudah hamafsekes* are not applicable to this meal; therefore, one should sit at the table rather than on the floor, and the entire family may have the meal together. It is even permissible for three adult males to eat together and to conduct a *zimun* at *birkas hamazon*.[82] The *poskim* debate whether it is permissible to share this meal with friends. Some rule that it is prohibited to have company at this particular *seudah*, while others maintain that a person who generally invites friends to join him for *seudah shelishis* may do so even on this Shabbos, since it would be akin to a public display of mourning if he refrained from inviting guests.[83]

4. **Singing *Zemiros*:** *Zemiros* may be sung as usual at the *seudah*.[84]

5. **A *Seudah* for a *Bris Milah*:** If a *bris milah* takes place on Erev Tishah b'Av when it falls on Shabbos, the *seudah* should be held before *Minchah*.[85] One need not limit the number of attendees.

6. **An *Aufruf*:** A chassan whose wedding will take place later in the week should certainly receive an *aliyah* on this Shabbos.

---

80. מ"ב ס"ק כ"ג.
81. שו"ת אגר"מ או"ח ח"ד סי' קי"ב אות א'.
82. מ"ב שם.
83. עי' מ"ב שם.
84. שו"ת אגר"מ שם, הליכות שלמה פט"ו הערה 33 בשם הגרשז"א זצ"ל, ושם כתוב שהורה רק לשיר הזמירות שרגילים לזמרן בשבתות הקבועים בסידור ולא להוסיף שירים אחרים.
85. מ"ב שם.

However, some *poskim* maintain that the Kiddush customarily held at an *aufruf* should be scheduled for the previous Shabbos instead.[86] Nevertheless, other *poskim* contend that refraining from holding a Kiddush and from throwing candies for a chassan would be a public display of mourning, which is prohibited on Shabbos. These authorities rule that the Kiddush of an *aufruf* should be held even on Erev Tishah b'Av, albeit on a modest scale.[87]

7. **A Stipulation at the End of *Seudah Shelishis*:** On Shabbos, it is not necessary to make a verbal stipulation at the conclusion of *seudah shelishis* that one does not intend to accept the fast until *shekiah* (see section 3, paragraph 3).[88]

8. **Observing the Laws of Tishah B'Av after *Shekiah*:** As mentioned at the beginning of this section, when the fast of Tishah b'Av is observed on Sunday, one must cease all eating and drinking at *shekiah* on Shabbos afternoon. (One may recite *birkas hamazon* after *shekiah*, including the passage of *retzei*.) However, it remains prohibited after *shekiah* to engage in explicit displays of mourning; therefore, one should continue sitting on a regular chair, and leather shoes and Shabbos clothes should not be removed. (Some *poskim* rule that a person who is at home should remove his shoes after *shekiah*, since people often take off their shoes at home, and it is therefore not considered an overt display of mourning.[89]) However, washing and anointing are prohibited after *shekiah*.

9. **Removing Leather Shoes after Reciting *Barchu*:** All the participants in a *minyan* should remove their leather shoes after *Barchu* at *Maariv* on Motzaei Shabbos (taking care not

---

86. הגרי"י קניבסקי זצ"ל הובא בארחות רבינו ח"ב עמוד קמ"ד.
87. הליכות שלמה שם סי"א ובהערות לשם.
88. שעה"צ סי' תקנ"ג סק"ז.
89. הגרש"א זצ"ל הוב"ד בתורת המועדים עמוד קמ"ח.

to touch their shoes or feet with their hands).[90] The *shaliach tzibbur*, however, should recite *baruch hamavdil* and remove his shoes prior to *Barchu*.[91]

10. **The Prohibition of *Hachanah*:** Bringing Tishah b'Av footwear to shul before reciting *baruch hamavdil* is forbidden due to the prohibition of *hachanah* (preparing on Shabbos for a weekday) even in an area that is surrounded by an *eruv*. Consequently, a person should bring his Tishah b'Av shoes to shul before Shabbos and store them in a safe place.[92] Likewise, one should not change into weekday clothing before reciting *baruch hamavdil* after *tzeis hakochavim*.[93]

11. ***Maariv* after *Tzeis Hakochavim*:** According to some authorities, the ruling in the previous paragraphs (9-10) is applicable only if one will begin davening *Maariv* before *tzeis hakochavim*. According to this view, if *Maariv* is scheduled to begin some time after *tzeis hakochavim*, the congregants should recite *baruch hamavdil* at home and change their shoes and clothes before going to shul.[94] (A person who generally waits until the *tzeis hakochavim* of Rabbeinu Tam before performing *melachah* is not required to wait until that time in order to change, provided that he generally relates to this practice as a stringency and abstains only from *melachos d'oraisa*.[95]) Indeed, when Tishah b'Av begins on Motzaei Shabbos, many congregations schedule *Maariv* at a slightly later time than on an ordinary Motzaei Shabbos, in order to

---

90. עי' מ"ב סי' תקנ"ג סק"ו שכתב שאם נגע ינקה ידיו בכל מידי דמנקי, ועי"ש בשעה"צ ס"ק ט"ו, רצ"ע שהרי לצורך תפילה מותר ליטול ידיו עי' סי' תרי"ג ס"ג, ובמ"ב סקי"ד.
91. רמ"א סי' תקנ"ג ס"ב, והטעם משום דאסור שום סימן אבילות בשבת, מ"ב סק"ו.
92. שש"כ פכ"ח ספ"ה (מהדו"ח) ופס"ב סמ"א.
93. שם.
94. שם ס"ק קפ"ט בשם הגרשז"א זצ"ל. ועי' שו"ת שבט הלוי ח"ז סי' ע"ז. ועי' מועדים וזמנים ח"ז סי' רנ"ו.
95. הליכות שלמה פט"ו ס"ק ט"ו.

give the congregants time to change their shoes and clothing after *tzeis hakochavim* before coming to shul.

Nevertheless, other *poskim* disagree with this ruling and maintain that even when *Maariv* begins after *tzeis hakochavim* and there is time to recite *baruch hamavdil* and perform *melachos* before davening, it is forbidden to make an overt display of mourning before reciting *Barchu*, such as removing one's leather shoes or sitting on the floor.[96]

One should follow the practice of the *minyan* he is davening with.

12. **Zemiros** before **Maariv**: Those who usually recite the *zemiros* of *Lamnatzeiach* and *L'Dovid* before *Maariv* should omit those passages on Tishah b'Av.[97]

Additional halachos regarding *Maariv* on the night of Tishah b'Av, as well as the halachos pertaining to Havdalah in this scenario, will be discussed below (Chapter Ten, section 2).

---

96. עי' שו"ת שלמת חיים סי' רכ"ז. וכן דעת הגרמ"פ זצ"ל הובא בקיצור הלכות ביהמ"צ להגר"ש איידער זצ"ל, אך דעתו שאם יהא הפסק רב לאחר אמירת ברכו לצורך כך כגון במחנה קיץ שיש הרבה אנשים, יש לחלצם קודם ברכו לאחר אמירת ברוך המבדיל. ועי' שו"ת שבט הלוי ח"ז סי' ע"ז דגם לפי זה את בגדי שבת מותר להחליף בביתו קודם הליכה לביהכנ"ס ואומר תחילה ברוך המבדיל, ורק הנעליים חולצים לאחר אמירת ברכו.

97. רמ"א סי' תקנ"ט ס"ב.

CHAPTER EIGHT

The Laws of Tishah B'Av

1. Fasting
2. Washing and Anointing
3. Wearing Shoes
4. Learning Torah
5. General Conduct on Tishah B'Av
6. Work and Business Dealings

CHAPTER EIGHT

The Laws of Tishah B'Av

Introduction: The ninth of Av has been established as a day of mourning for Klal Yisrael. The day primarily commemorates five tragedies: the sin of the *meraglim*, which prevented the Jewish people from entering Eretz Yisrael; the destructions of both the first and the second *Batei Mikdash*; the destruction of the great city of Beitar, which resulted in a multitude of fatalities; and the plowing of Yerushalayim and the site of the *Beis Hamikdash*.[1]

Aside from the fact that it is a fast day and a time for *teshuvah*, Tishah b'Av is unique among all other fast days in that its halachos include certain practices of mourning. Thus, in addition to the requirement to abstain from food and drink, several other activities are forbidden on Tishah b'Av as well: washing, applying oils or creams to the body, wearing leather shoes, engaging in marital relations, and learning Torah.[2]

The fast and other laws of Tishah b'Av come into effect at sunset. In this sense, Tishah b'Av is unlike the fast days of Tzom Gedaliah, Asarah b'Teves, and Shivah Asar b'Tammuz, on which the fast begins at daybreak. The prohibitions of Tishah b'Av extend until *tzeis hakochavim* of the following night. Unlike on Yom Kippur, though, there is no requirement to observe the prohibitions of Tishah b'Av for

---

1. מתני׳ תענית דף כו.
2. שם דף ל.

any extra time at the beginning and end of the day (i.e., there is no halachah of *tosefes hayom*).³

The details of the activities prohibited on Tishah b'Av will be discussed in this chapter. It should be noted that *Chazal* state that a person who mourns the destruction of Yerushalayim will be privileged to witness its rebuilding.⁴

1. Fasting

1. **The Obligation to Fast:** All adult males and females are obligated to fast on Tishah b'Av in memory of the terrible calamities that occurred on this day. The ultimate purpose of the fast is to inspire a person to engage in *teshuvah*⁵ (see introduction to Chapter Five).

2. **The Duration of the Fast:** The fast begins at *shekiah* on the eve of the ninth of Av (unlike the other three fast days, when the obligation to fast begins in the morning at *alos hashachar*) and concludes at *tzeis hakochavim*.⁶ There is no requirement to observe the prohibitions of Tishah b'Av for additional time either before or after the fast itself (unlike on Yom Kippur⁷).

3. **Pregnant and Nursing Women:** The obligation to fast on Tishah b'Av includes pregnant and nursing women, unlike on the other three public fasts⁸ (see Chapter Five, section 2). Nevertheless, some authorities rule that since most people today have weaker constitutions than in previous generations, and fasting is more difficult particularly in the hotter

---

3. עי׳ פסחים דף נד:, רמב״ם פ״ה הל׳ תעניות ה״ז.
4. תענית דף ל:, טור ושו״ע סי׳ תקנ״ד סכ״ה.
5. שו״ע סי׳ תקמ״ט ס״א.
6. שו״ע סי׳ תקנ״ג ס״ב.
7. מ״ב סי׳ תקנ״ג סק״ג.
8. שו״ע סי׳ תקנ״ד ס״ה.

climates, it is acceptable for pregnant and nursing women to refrain from fasting if they will become weak.[9] A Rav must be consulted for a conclusive ruling.[10] If a woman is experiencing difficulty with her pregnancy, or if she feels unwell during the first few months of a pregnancy, she is certainly accorded the status of an ill person, who is exempt from fasting[11] (see the following paragraph). A nursing woman is exempt from fasting if her baby may suffer harm if her milk supply is diminished or its quality is reduced.[12]

When Tishah b'Av falls on Shabbos and the fast is postponed until Sunday (*nidcheh*), a pregnant or nursing woman is certainly exempt from fasting even if she is only slightly unwell (a degree of illness categorized in halachah as a *michush*).[13]

4. **Fasting while Ill:** A person who is bedridden with illness and is therefore classified as *choleh kol haguf* (for instance, someone who is suffering from a fever), and who feels that he is too weak to fast, is permitted to eat and drink on Tishah b'Av even if he will not suffer actual harm from fasting. In such a situation, there is no need to consult a doctor to determine if the individual is able to fast.[14] (The same applies on the other three public fasts, but the laws of Yom Kippur are more stringent; see *Kitzur Halachos: Rosh Hashanah and Yom Kippur*, Chapter Eight.) On the other hand, if a person is not suffering from a serious ailment and is merely experiencing weakness, aches or pains, or some other form of physical

---

9. עי' הליכות שלמה פט"ז הערה 2 לענין מעוברת והערה 7 לענין מינקת (וכ' עד ט' חדשים לאחר הלידה). ועי' שו"ת אבן ישראל ח"ט סי' ס"ב אות י'.
10. עי' הליכות שלמה שם סוף הערה 2 מש"כ שהגרשז"א זצ"ל תמיד היה מדגיש שמעיקר הדין חייבת לצום וחקר כ"א את מצבה.
11. הליכות שלמה שם ס"א ו ב' ובהערות לשם, ועי' ס' תורת היולדת פמ"ח סק"ו.
12. עי' שערי תשובה סי' תקנ"ד סק"ו. ועי' הליכות שלמה שם סק"ז.
13. ביה"ל סי' תקנ"ט ס"ט ד"ה ואינו.
14. שו"ע סי' תקנ"ד ס"ו. ועי' חיי אדם כלל קל"ד ס"ב וערוה"ש סי' תקנ"ד ס"ז.

discomfort, such as a headache, backache, cough, or cold, he is still obligated to fast.[15]

When the fast of Tishah b'Av has been postponed from Shabbos to Sunday (*nidcheh*), even a person suffering from a minor ailment may be exempted from fasting.[16]

In any case of illness, a Rav should be consulted for a specific ruling.

5. **Resuming the Fast after an Interruption:** There is a dispute among the *poskim* regarding the case of a person who breaks his fast due to illness and then feels that he has strengthened himself sufficiently to fast for the remainder of Tishah b'Av. Some authorities maintain that he is required to resume the fast,[17] while others rule that he may eat without restriction for the remainder of the day.[18]

6. **A Woman after Childbirth:** Within the first 30 days after childbirth, when a woman is naturally in a weakened state, she is accorded the halachic status of a person who is ill and is therefore exempt from fasting.[19] (On Yom Kippur, the halachah is different; see *Kitzur Halachos: Rosh Hashanah and Yom Kippur*, Chapter Eight.) However, if a woman asserts that she is absolutely capable of fasting, then she is obligated to observe the fast.[20] Although the Rema notes that there is a *minhag* for a woman to fast on Tishah b'Av as long as seven days have elapsed since the birth (unless fasting could endanger her, or the ninth of Av falls on Shabbos and the fast is postponed until Sunday),[21] some *poskim* state that women are considered

---

15. שו"ע שם ובמ"ב ס"ק נ"א.
16. ביה"ל שם.
17. עי' שו"ת שבט הלוי ח"ט סי' קל"א אות ב'.
18. עי' מועדים וזמנים ח"ה סי' של"ה מה שאמר הגרי"ז בשם אביו הגר"ח.
19. שו"ע שם. ועי' מ"ב סק"ט.
20. מ"ב ס"ק י"ב.
21. רמ"א שם ס"ו, ועי' מ"ב ס"ק י"ג-ט"ז.

weaker today than in previous generations and this stringency should not be observed.[22] (See paragraph 3 above, where it is noted that many contemporary authorities exempt all nursing mothers from fasting. One should consult with a Rav on this matter.)

7. **Eating Ordinary Quantities of Food:** A person who is ill and is exempt from fasting is not required to eat "*shiurim*" (i.e., to eat in increments of less than a *kezayis* of food, separated by delays of *k'dei achilas pras*). Rather, it is permissible for him to eat in a normal fashion.[23] Likewise, there is no requirement to fast until *chatzos* in such a situation.[24]

8. **Breaking the Fast to Avoid Becoming Ill:** If a person is not actually ill yet, but feels he will likely become unwell if he observes the fast – e.g., a person who is prone to dehydration or who feels that he may faint if he abstains from eating – he is permitted only to eat or drink *shiurim*.[25] A Rav should be consulted regarding the precise quantity of food that constitutes a *shiur* and the amount of time that must be allowed to pass between increments of food.

9. **Swallowing Pills:** If a person is not halachically defined as suffering from illness but is experiencing a headache or some other form of pain, he is permitted to ingest pills to alleviate his symptoms; however, the pills should be taken without water. If he must ingest some liquid in order to swallow the pill, he may use a liquid with a bitter taste.[26] Some *poskim*

---

22. ערוך השלחן שם ס״ח. וע" שו״ת שבט הלוי ח״ו סי׳ ע׳.
23. עי׳ שו״ת שבט הלוי ח״ד סי׳ נ״ו שביאר שמש״כ הבה״ל ד״ה דבמקום חולי, מדובר על מי שעדיין לא נחלה אלא שצריך לאכול כדי שלא ידבק מהמחלה. וראה תשובות והנהגות ח״ב סי׳ רס״א בשם הגרי״ז. ועי״ש סי׳ רס״ד שלא יאכלו ב׳ תבשילים דעדיין צריכים להתאבל ולא עדיף מסעודת המפסקת. וראה מועדים וזמנים ח״ז סי׳ רנ״ב.
24. הליכות שלמה שם ס״ד.
25. עפ״י הבה״ל הנ״ל.
26. כף החיים ס״ק ל״ד.

permit drinking a small quantity of regular water in order to swallow a pill.[27]

10. **Involvement in Communal Affairs:** If a person is involved in communal affairs and he feels that engaging in those activities will likely weaken him to the extent that he will need to break his fast, some *poskim* maintain that he should nevertheless continue pursuing his communal activities on Tishah b'Av and when he becomes unwell he will break his fast.[28] Others disagree and rule that one must refrain from these activities if they will lead to breaking his fast.[29]

11. **The Elderly:** An elderly person who is weak is exempt from fasting, even if he or she is not ill and does not suffer from a specific medical condition.[30]

12. **Reciting Havdalah before Breaking the Fast:** When the fast of Tishah b'Av begins immediately after Shabbos, a person who is permitted to eat during the fast should recite Havdalah first. Havdalah should be recited over *chamar medinah* or grape juice, and the *pesukim* that precede Havdalah, as well as the *brachah* on *besamim*, should be omitted.[31] Even a woman must recite Havdalah before eating; however, some *poskim* rule that she should recite the *brachah* of *borei meorei ha'eish* only after drinking the beverage used for Havdalah.[32] See also Chapter Ten, section 2, paragraph 8, where it is noted that some *poskim* maintain that a woman should not recite the *brachah* of *borei meorei ha'eish*.

---

27. הליכות שלמה שם ס״ג וסק״ח. ועי״ש הערה 13 דאם הגלולה טעמה ערב יעטפנה בנייר דק.
28. עי' שו״ת אגר״מ או״ח ח״ד סי' קי״ד.
29. דעת הגריש״א זצ״ל הובא בתורת המועדים סי' תק״נ סק״ז.
30. עי' שו״ת אגר״מ שם. ועי' שו״ת אור לציון ח״ג פכ״ט ס״ה.
31. קיצור הלכות ביהמ״צ להגר״ש איידער זצ״ל בשם הגרמ״פ זצ״ל, הליכות שלמה שם ס״ז.
32. עי' הליכות שלמה שם ס״ח ובדבר הלכה לשם וארחות הלכה לשם.

Children are not required to recite Havdalah before eating on Tishah b'Av, even if they have reached the age of *chinuch*.[33]

13. **Rinsing the Mouth:** It is prohibited to rinse one's mouth on Tishah b'Av, unless one will suffer great distress as a result. (This halachah is more stringent on Tishah b'Av than on the other three public fast days; on any other fast, rinsing the mouth is permissible even to avoid minor distress, whereas on Tishah b'Av the discomfort must be significant. On Yom Kippur, rinsing the mouth is categorically forbidden, even if one will suffer severe discomfort as a result.) A person who is permitted to rinse his mouth on Tishah b'Av must bend forward while doing so, in order to ensure that he does not unintentionally swallow any of the water.[34]

It is also prohibited to use mouthwash or to brush one's teeth with toothpaste, even without water.[35]

14. **Children on Tishah B'Av:** Children are not required to fast on Tishah b'Av even for part of the fast (such as the night), nor is one obligated to have a child observe a *taanis shaos* (i.e., to delay his regular meals) as on Yom Kippur, even if the child has reached the age of *chinuch* for mourning the destruction of the *Beis Hamikdash*.[36]

15. **A Child Who Reaches Adulthood on a Postponed Fast:** When the ninth of Av falls on Shabbos and the fast is postponed, and a boy or girl turns bar or bas mitzvah on the day when the fast is observed, see above (Chapter Five, section 1, paragraph 8) as to whether they are obligated to observe the fast.

---

33. הליכות שלמה שם ס"ק י"ג. ועי' שו"ת שבט הלוי ח"ז סי' ע"ז אות ו'. ועי"ש ח"י סוסי' קע"ז.
34. מ"ב סי' תקס"ז ס"ק י"א.
35. הגרמ"פ זצ"ל הוב"ל בקיצור הלכות ביהמ"צ להגר"ש איידער זצ"ל ומטעם איסור רחיצה. אבל ע"י שו"ת מנח"י ח"ד סי' ק"ט.
36. ראה לשון המ"ב סי' תק"נ סק"ה. וכן מפורש בחיי אדם כלל קל"ג ס"ו וערוך השלחן סי' תקנ"ד ס"ז.

16. **Washing for Bread:** An ill person or a child who eats bread on Tishah b'Av should perform the procedure of *al netilas yadayim* in the normal fashion.[37]

17. **Donning Tefillin before Eating:** Regarding whether a person who is ill should put on his tefillin before eating on Tishah b'Av, see Chapter Nine, section 3, paragraph 7.

18. **If the Fast Is Broken in Error:** If a person erroneously eats or drinks on Tishah b'Av, he should nonetheless observe the remainder of the fast, as discussed above (Chapter Five, section 1, paragraph 9).

19. One should keep in mind that *Chazal* teach us that a person who transgresses the laws of Tishah b'Av by eating or drinking during the fast will not merit to see the *Beis Hamikdash* in its glory when it is rebuilt.[38]

2. Washing and Anointing

1. **The Prohibition to Wash:** Washing any part of the body, whether in hot or cold water, is prohibited on Tishah b'Av. It is prohibited even to place a single finger in water.[39]

2. **Washing to Remove Dirt:** Washing is prohibited only for the sake of deriving pleasure. Therefore, one may wash any part of the body that is dirty, but one must make sure to only wash that body part. For example, if a person's fingers are soiled, he may wash only his fingers and not the remainder of his hand.[40]

---

37. כף החיים סי׳ תקנ״ד ס״ק נ״ג. הליכות שלמה שם ס״ה.
38. תענית דף ל:, טור ושו״ע סי׳ תקנ״ד סכ״ה.
39. שו״ע סי׳ תקנ״ד ס״ז.
40. שו״ע שם ס״ט.

3. **Washing an Object:** It is permissible to rinse food or any other object even if one's hands will become wet in the process.[41]

4. ***Netilas Yadayim*:** Upon rising in the morning, one should wash *netilas yadayim* in order to remove the *ruach raah* that descends upon the hands during the night; however, the water should be poured only on the fingers until the knuckles.[42] Likewise, a person should wash only his fingers, rather than the entirety of each hand, before each of the three *tefillos* of the day (*Maariv*, *Shacharis*, and *Minchah*). The fingers should be washed prior to davening even if a person is not certain that his hands have become unclean.[43]

5. **Washing after Relieving Oneself:** After using the bathroom, a person who has touched a part of the body that is normally covered or has soiled his hands is permitted to wash only his fingers. If a person did not touch a covered part of the body and his hands are not soiled, the *poskim* disagree as to whether he may wash before reciting the *brachah* of *asher yatzar*. Consequently, it is advisable to make sure to touch a covered part of the body or to soil the hands so that it will certainly be permissible to wash one's fingers.[44]

6. A person who usually washes his hands three times after using the bathroom may wash his fingers three times, even though the basic halachic requirement would be satisfied by washing each hand once.[45]

7. **Washing All the Fingers:** A person who scratches his head or touches a part of the body that is usually covered should wash

---

41. מ"ב ס"ק י"ט.
42. שו"ע שם סי'.
43. מ"ב ס"ק כ"א.
44. רמ"א שם ס"ט ושו"ע סי' תרי"ג ס"ג ובמ"ב שם סק"ד. וראה שע"ת סי' תקנ"ד ס"ט.
45. מנחת שלמה ח"ב סי' נ"ח אות כ"ח. שו"ת מנחת יצחק ח"י סי' מ"ה.

Washing and Anointing ~ 227

all the fingers of that hand before learning Torah or reciting a *brachah*, even if only one finger was used.[46]

8. **Washing Only until the Knuckles:** In general, when washing the fingers (for *netilas yadayim* in the morning, after using the bathroom, and so forth), one is not required to be meticulous to make sure that absolutely no drops of water pass the knuckles.[47]

9. ***Birkas Kohanim* and Washing for Bread:** In Eretz Yisrael, where *birkas kohanim* is recited during davening, a *kohen* should wash his hands in their entirety, until the wrists.[48] Similarly, a person who is exempt from fasting and wishes to eat bread should wash his hands entirely until the wrists for *netilas yadayim*.[49]

10. **Immersing in a *Mikveh*:** A woman whose *leil tevilah* falls on the night of Tishah b'Av must postpone her immersion until the night following Tishah b'Av. This is because the immersion itself is not a mitzvah and therefore does not warrant violating the prohibition of washing on Tishah b'Av. (According to the laws of the Torah, a *niddah* is supposed to immerse in a *mikveh* seven days after she begins menstruating; however, a *takanah* was instituted that requires a *niddah* to wait until seven clean days have passed before immersing, just as a *zavah* would do. Consequently, the immersion is no longer in the prescribed time and thus does not have the status of a mitzvah.) Instead, immersing in a *mikveh* merely makes it possible to fulfill the mitzvah of marital relations, which is prohibited on Tishah b'Av in any event.[50]

---

46. מ״ב סי׳ תרי״ג סק״ו.
47. הגרח״ק שליט״א בשם החזו״א הובא בתורת המועדים עמוד קנ״ד.
48. רמ״א סי׳ תרי״ג ס״ג ובמ״ב סק״ז.
49. שש״כ פרק ל״ט סל״ג.
50. שו״ע סי׳ תקנ״ד ס״ח, ובמ״ב ס״ק י״ז.

A woman whose *leil tevilah* has been postponed until after Tishah b'Av, or if *leil tevilah* falls out on Motzaei Tishah b'Av, may perform the complete *chafifah* process on Erev Tishah b'Av (which is permitted in spite of the restrictions of the Nine Days) and then perform a brief, second *chafifah* after the conclusion of the fast (which involves showering, combing her hair, and inspecting her body),[51] or she may perform the complete *chafifah* after the conclusion of Tishah b'Av,[52] spending a minimum of one hour on her preparations. Some *poskim* express a preference for the latter option.[53]

11. **Performing the *Hefsek Taharah*:** A woman who performs a *hefsek taharah* on Tishah b'Av should wash the area of the *hefsek*, in keeping with the customary practice.[54] She should don a clean white garment immediately after performing the *hefsek taharah*, even prior to *tzeis hakochavim*.

12. ***Tevilah* before Davening:** A man may not immerse in a *mikveh* before davening. If he became *tamei* during the night, it is possible that it may be permitted. A Rav should be consulted for a conclusive ruling.

13. **Washing the Face:** Upon awakening in the morning, a person should not place his wet fingers on his face or eyes after *netilas yadayim*. However, it is permissible to wash crust off one's eyes, just as it is permissible to wash dirt off any part of the body.[55] If a person's fingers are only slightly damp after *netilas yadayim*, he may touch his face or eyes with his fingers if the moisture will not be transferred to the place that is touched.[56] An *istenis* (a particularly sensitive and finicky person) who will

---

51. מ"ב ס"ק י"ח. וע' ביה"ל סי' תקנ"א סט"ז ד"ה אם אי אפשר.
52. שעה"צ סי' תקנ"ד ס"ק כ"ד.
53. שיעורי שבה"ל סי' קצ"ט ס"ד.
54. רמ"א סי' תקנ"א סט"ז, שעה"צ ס"ק ל"ה.
55. שו"ע סי' תקנ"ד סי"א.
56. שו"ע שם ובמ"ב ס"ק כ"ב.

Washing and Anointing ~ 229

have no peace of mind throughout the day unless he washes his face is permitted to do so.[57]

14. **Using a Wet Towel:** Wiping the face or hands with a wet towel is permitted if the towel is not wet enough to moisten the areas it touches.[58]

15. **Entering a Body of Water:** As mentioned above, it is permitted to wash or otherwise come in contact with water for purposes other than pleasure. Consequently, a person who must pass through water in order to perform a mitzvah (e.g., going to see his rebbi) or to prevent a loss (e.g., in order to stand guard over a field) is permitted to do so. However, returning home through water is permitted only in the former case, in which the initial trip was for the sake of a mitzvah (since a person is liable to refrain from traveling for a mitzvah if he will not be able to return). A person who passed through water in order to avoid a financial loss is not permitted to traverse the body of water on his way back.[59]

16. **Soaking One's Feet and Cleaning a Wound:** It is permissible to wash or immerse part of the body in water to relieve pain; for example, if a person has walked a great distance, he may soak his feet in order to relieve the resultant ache.[60] Similarly, it is permissible to wash a wound.

17. **The Prohibition of *Sichah*:** Due to the prohibition of *sichah* (anointing), it is forbidden to apply any kind of cream, oil, makeup, perfume, or soap to the body on Tishah b'Av.[61] This

---

57. מ"ב שם.
58. רמ"א שם סי"ד, ומ"ב ס"ק כ"ז. ועי' שו"ת אור לציון ח"ג פכ"ט סי"ג שהתיר מגבות לחות.
59. שו"ע שם סי"ב וי"ג ובמ"ב ס"ק כ"ג-כ"ה.
60. שו"ע שם סי"ד.
61. שו"ע שם סט"ו, ובמ"ב ס"ק כ"ח.

prohibition applies to any part of the body, even a single finger.[62]

18. **Anointing for a Purpose Other than Pleasure:** The prohibition of anointing pertains only to the application of a substance for the sake of pleasure or enjoyment. Therefore, a person who suffers from skin irritation such as a rash, or who has sore or dry skin, is permitted to apply cream or oil to relieve those symptoms.[63] Similarly, soap may be used if it is necessary to remove dirt from the body; however, if one could achieve the same result with water alone, the soap may not be used. Applying a substance to the body to remove odor is also permitted;[64] therefore, one may use deodorant (either spray or stick) on Tishah b'Av.[65]

19. **Insect Repellent or Sunscreen:** Insect repellent and sunscreen may be applied to the skin on Tishah b'Av, since these substances serve only for protection.[66]

20. **Exception for a Kallah:** A recently married kallah within 30 days of her wedding is permitted to wash and to apply oils, makeup, or creams to her skin if it is necessary to prevent her from becoming unattractive to her husband.[67]

21. **Children:** Children who have reached the age of *chinuch* with respect to this halachah – i.e., they are old enough to understand the concept of mourning for the *Beis Hamikdash* and are capable of adhering to the halachos – are also

---

62. מ״ב ס״ק כ״ט.
63. שו״ע שם.
64. ביה״ל סט״ו ד״ה סיכה.
65. הליכות שלמה פי״ד הערה 56. קיצור הלכות ביהמ״צ להגר״ש איידער זצ״ל.
66. כן נראה פשוט.
67. מ״ב ס״ק כ״ט.

required to abide by the prohibitions of washing and applying cream or oil to the skin.[68]

3. Wearing Shoes

1. **The Prohibition to Wear Shoes:** The afflictions of Tishah b'Av include the prohibition to wear shoes, like the halachos of a mourner. This prohibition applies to leather footwear; shoes made of other materials may be worn.[69]

2. **Non-Leather Shoes:** Some *poskim* maintain that one should refrain from wearing non-leather shoes with proper soles that provide the same degree of comfort and protection as leather shoes, and only slippers with thin soles should be worn on Tishah b'Av.[70] In practice, the halachah does not follow this view, and all types of non-leather footwear may be worn on Tishah b'Av.[71] On Yom Kippur, however, it is commendable to be stringent in this respect.[72] (Some *poskim* were known to adopt the stringency of wearing only socks, without wearing shoes at all, on Tishah b'Av.[73])

3. **Shoes with Leather Components:** Shoes with any leather component, whether it is on the top or sole of the shoe, may not be worn on Tishah b'Av.[74] A shoe with a decorative piece of leather may be worn if the leather does not contribute to the

---

68. כשאר דיני חינוך. וראה אמת ליעקב הערה 514 שהתיר בתשעת הימים לילדים בקיטנה ליכנס לsprinkler רק עד שהגיעו לגיל הראוי להתאבל.
69. שו״ע סי׳ תקנ״ד סט״ז.
70. עי׳ שע״ת ס״ק י״א בשם שו״ת פמ״א.
71. סתימת המ״ב סק״ל, וכנראה שבא לאפוקי מהנ״ל דרך בס״ק ל״א בענין עור בשוליים ציין להשע״ת.
72. עי׳ מ״ב סי׳ תרי״ד סק״ה, ושעה״צ סק״ה, וצ״ל דרך התם משום חומרא דיוה״כ הביא דיעה זו.
73. הגרח״ק שליט״א הובא בתורת המועדים עמוד קנ״ו שכן נהג הגרהחזו״א והגריי״ק זצ״ל. וראה ארחות רבינו ח״ב עמוד קלח שהגרשהגריי״ק זצ״ל התיר נעלי גומי ולכן הנ״ל הוא רק שהחמיר על עצמו.
74. שו״ע שם ובמ״ב ס״ק ל״א.

form of the shoe and does not touch the foot; otherwise, even a small piece of leather will render the shoe prohibited to wear.[75]

4. **Shoes Made of Synthetic Leather:** Some *poskim* prohibit wearing shoes manufactured from a synthetic material that resembles genuine leather, due to the prohibition of *maris ayin*.[76] Other *poskim*, however, maintain that since synthetic leather is very common, it is not likely that the shoes will be mistaken by an observer for actual leather shoes.

5. **Wearing Leather Shoes for a Long Walk:** Technically, a person who must walk a long distance is permitted to wear leather shoes.[77] In the modern era, however, when comfortable and supportive footwear made of other materials is available, it is questionable whether this dispensation still applies.[78]

6. **Wearing Leather Shoes in the Company of Non-Jews:** Some *poskim* permit a person who must interact with non-Jews to wear leather shoes in order to avoid appearing undignified.[79] Nowadays, however, since wearing non-leather footwear in public is acceptable, this leniency likely does not apply.

7. **Standing on Leather:** One may stand on a leather mat or pillow.[80] It is certainly permissible to lie on a leather couch.

8. **Leather Orthotics:** Leather orthopedic insoles that are permanently attached to one's shoes may not be used on Tishah b'Av. If the orthopedic insoles are removable and are meant to be transferred between shoes, it is possible that they may be used (just as it is permissible to stand on a leather

---

75. עי' שו"ת אור לציון ח"ג פכ"ט סט"ו.
76. שו"ת מנחת שלמה סי' נ"ג אות ג'.
77. שו"ע שם סי"ז.
78. עי' שו"ת מנחת שלמה ח"א סי' צ"א אות כ"ה סק"ח.
79. רמ"א שם סי"ז ועי' מ"ב ס"ק ל"ה, שעה"צ ס"ק מ"ב, ובמ"ב ס"ק ל"ו בשם הח"א.
80. רמ"א סי' תרי"ד ס"ב.

pillow). A person who has difficulty walking without the inserts may be lenient in this regard.[81]

9. **Reciting the *Brachah* of *She'asah Li Kol Tzorki*:** Although leather footwear may not be worn on Tishah b'Av, many *poskim* maintain that one should nonetheless recite the *brachah* of *she'asah li kol tzorki* in *birchos hashachar*, which expresses our gratitude to Hashem for providing us with shoes.[82] Some have the practice, based on the teachings of the Arizal, to delay reciting this *brachah* until after nightfall at the conclusion of Tishah b'Av, when they don leather shoes.[83]

10. **Children:** Children at the age of *chinuch* (when they are old enough to understand the concept of mourning for the *Beis Hamikdash*) should preferably not wear leather shoes on Tishah b'Av.[84] Furthermore, since suitable alternative types of footwear are available nowadays, many refrain from allowing even younger children to wear leather shoes.

4. Learning Torah

1. **The Prohibition to Learn Torah:** It is prohibited to learn Torah on Tishah b'Av, just as a mourner is prohibited to learn, because Torah study gladdens the heart. (See Chapter Seven, section 1, regarding Torah study on Erev Tishah b'Av after *chatzos*.) One should refrain from learning any part of the Torah, including Chumash, Neviim, and Kesuvim, as well as Mishnayos, Midrash, Gemara, halachah, and aggadah. It

---

81. עי׳ שו״ת חלקת יעקב ח״ב סי׳ פ״ג.
82. מ״ב ס״ק ל״א, ובשעה״צ ס״ק ל״ט בשם הפמ״ג שכן נוהגין.
83. באר היטב ס״ק י״א, ועי׳ מעשה רב ס״ט שכן נהג הגר״א, ועי׳ בשערי תשובה סי׳ מ״ו ס״ח. ועי׳ בכף החיים סי׳ מ״ו ס״ק י״ז. וכן נהג החזו״א הובא בארחות רבינו ח״ב סי׳ קל״ט. וכן נהג הגרשז״א זצ״ל הובא בהליכות שלמה פט״ו הערה 19 ותפילה פ״כ הערה 88.
84. שו״ת אגר״מ יו״ד ח״א סוסי׳ רכ״ד, ועי׳ מועדים וזמנים ח״ז סי׳ רנ״א שנשאר בצ״ע על החכמ״א.

makes no difference if one studies the material superficially or in depth; any form of study is prohibited.[85]

2. **Topics That Evoke Sorrow:** It is permissible to study topics that evoke sorrow, such as *Sefer Iyov, Sefer Yirmiyah* (although the *pesukim* with messages of consolation must be skipped), *Midrash Eichah*, *perek V'Eilu Megalchin* (the third *perek* of *Maseches Moed Katan*, which deals with the halachos pertaining to a mourner), and the passages in the Gemara that discuss the destruction of the *Beis Hamikdash*, which can be found in *Perek Hanizakin* (the fifth *perek* of *Maseches Gittin*) and *Perek Chelek* (the eleventh *perek* of *Maseches Sanhedrin*).[86] It is also permissible to study the description of the *churban* at the end of *Maseches Taanis* in the Talmud Yerushalmi.[87] Similarly, one may read historical accounts and literature about suffering and destruction in the history of Klal Yisrael.[88]

3. **Learning Relevant Halachos:** One may also learn the halachos of Tishah b'Av and of mourning.[89]

4. **Learning *Mussar*:** Some authorities permit learning works of *mussar*, which inspire a person to repent. Other *poskim* rule that *mussar* works that include *pesukim* and *maamarei Chazal* should not be studied.[90]

5. **Learning *Al Derech Pshat*:** The permissible texts and topics may be studied only on a superficial level. In-depth learning and analytical discussions are prohibited.[91]

---

85. שו"ע סי' תקנ"ד ס"א.
86. שו"ע שם ס"א וס"ב ובמ"ב שם.
87. קיצור שו"ע כלל קכ"ד ס"ה.
88. הליכות שלמה פט"ז הערה 36.
89. הליכות שלמה שם שכן נהג הגרשז"א זצ"ל.
90. עי' שו"ת רבבות אפרים ח"א סי' שפו מה שהביא בשם הפוסקים בזה.
91. מ"ב סק"ד בשם הט"ז ומ"א, ובמ"ב סק"ה. אמנם החזו"א התיר ללמוד בעיון ועם חברותא, ועי' ארחות רבינו ח"ב עמ' קמ"ב.

Learning Torah ~ 235

6. **Thinking About Torah:** Although thinking about Torah is not considered equivalent to discussing it verbally (and therefore one is permitted to think about learning prior to reciting *birchos haTorah* in the morning), it is prohibited to think about one's learning on Tishah b'Av, since such thoughts tend to create joy.[92] Consequently, one may not even contemplate topics that may not be studied on Tishah b'Av, nor should one spend time trying to come up with questions and answers on such topics.[93]

7. **Recording Torah Thoughts in Writing:** It is prohibited to write down a *chiddush* or any Torah thought on Tishah b'Av. This is in contrast to the halachah concerning Chol Hamoed, when it is permitted to write.[94] However, it is permissible to jot down a reference or brief hint that will help one remember an idea after Tishah b'Av has ended.[95]

8. **Giving Halachic Rulings:** A Rav may not give a halachic ruling on a topic unrelated to Tishah b'Av, nor may he rule on monetary matters, unless the situation is urgent and the questioner cannot wait until after Tishah b'Av.[96]

9. **Teaching Torah to Children:** It is forbidden to teach Torah to children on Tishah b'Av.[97] The rationale for this prohibition is debated by the *poskim*: Some suggest that there is a prohibition for children to engage in Torah study, while others maintain that it is only because the teacher himself is prohibited to learn Torah. According to the latter view, since a child does not generally derive joy from his learning, the prohibition is only for an adult to teach children, but a child may learn any

---

92. שו"ע שם ס"ג ובמ"ב סק"ה.
93. מ"ב סק"ד וסק"ה.
94. שערי תשובה סק"כ. ערוה"ש סכ"ב.
95. כה"ח סי' תקנ"ד ס"ק ק"י.
96. מ"ב סק"ה.
97. שו"ע שם ס"א. ועי' מ"ב סק"ב דנחלקו הט"ז ומ"א אם מותר ללמוד עם התינוק דברים הרעים.

part of the Torah by himself. This is true only of children under the age of approximately 12 years; once a child has reached the age of 12, he is presumed to be old enough to understand and appreciate Torah learning and is therefore subject to the same prohibition as an adult. According to the *poskim* who maintain that the restriction pertains to the children themselves, Torah study is considered capable of bringing happiness to a child even if he does not fully understand what he learns, and children of any age are therefore forbidden to engage in Torah learning on Tishah b'Av.[98]

10. **Reciting Torah Passages in Davening:** Passages from the Torah that are included in the daily *tefillos* may be recited, such as the *parshiyos* of *Krias Shema*, the *parshah* of the *korban tamid*, the *mishnayos* of *Perek Eizehu Mekoman*, and the *braisa* of Rabbi Yishmael,[99] provided that one usually recites these passages on an ordinary day.[100] A *baal korei* may practice reading the Torah portion for *Minchah*. (The Torah reading of *Shacharis* may be studied by anyone, due to its sorrowful content.)[101] However, a person may not prepare the *leining* for the weekly *parshah* or perform *shenayim mikra v'echad targum*, even if he is accustomed to reciting a portion of the *parshah* every day.[102] There are divergent *minhagim* regarding whether *Pitum Haketores* should be recited on Tishah b'Av. Some omit this passage, since it is not universally recited on a daily basis (i.e., in some communities that follow *nusach* Ashkenaz, it is not part of the weekday davening) and therefore cannot be considered a part of the set *tefillos*.[103] Others, however, recite it

---

98. עי' ביה"ל ס"א ד"ה בטלים בו. וראה מש"כ בערוה"ש ס"ג שאף אם נוקטים שאין להם שמחה בפועל כלל מ"מ לנפש הישראלי יש שמחה.
99. שו"ע שם ס"ד.
100. הגרח"ק שליט"א הובא בתורת המועדים עמוד קנ"ט.
101. רמ"א שם ס"ד ומ"ב סק"ח.
102. מ"ב שם ושעה"צ ס"ק י"א.
103. רמ"א סי' תקנ"ט ס"ד ומ"ב סי' תקנ"ד סק"ז.

Learning Torah

on Tishah b'Av as well (in communities where it is recited on an ordinary weekday).[104] Many recite it at *Minchah* instead of *Shacharis*.

The bedtime *Krias Shema* may be recited along with all its accompanying *pesukim*.[105]

If a person has committed to recite *Perek Shirah* for forty consecutive days, he should recite it only on the night after Tishah b'Av and not during the fast.[106]

11. **Reciting *Krias Shema* after the *Zman*:** A person who missed the *zman* for *Krias Shema* should still recite the *Shema*, even though it is considered an act of Torah learning rather than a fulfillment of the mitzvah of reading the *Shema*.[107]

12. **Reciting *Tehillim*:** Some *poskim* permit reciting *Tehillim* beginning at the time of *Minchah*, since it is considered a form of davening rather than learning. However, other *poskim* maintain that this is prohibited.[108] Reciting *Tehillim* for a person who is ill is permitted even before *chatzos*.[109]

13. **Reading Other Material:** In addition to the prohibition of Torah study, it is also prohibited to divert one's attention from the mourning of Tishah b'Av, just as a mourner during the week of *shivah* may not engage in activities that will distract him from his loss. Therefore, a person should not read about topics of general knowledge (such as science, mathematics, and the like), nor may one read news articles, stories, history

---

104. כף החיים סי׳ תקנ״ט ס״ק מ״ח.
105. הגרח״ק שליט״א הובא בתורת המועדים עמוד קנ״ט (והוא עצמו רק נהג לומר פרשת שמע, בידך, והמפיל). וראה ס׳ אשי ישראל פל״ב ס״ק ל״ד.
106. שם בשם הגריש״א זצ״ל והגרח״ק שליט״א.
107. הליכות שלמה פט״ו ס״ז.
108. מ״ב סק״ז ובשעה״צ סק״ח.
109. ארחות רבינו ח״ב עמוד קמ״ב בשם החזו״א.

books, or any other form of literature that is not related to Tishah b'Av.[110]

5. General Conduct on Tishah B'Av

1. **Greeting Others:** One may not greet another person with the word "shalom" or any other form of greeting, such as "good morning," on Tishah b'Av.[111] One should also refrain from saying "goodbye" or any other type of parting words, such as "see you later."[112] One must be especially mindful of this when beginning and ending a telephone call.

2. **Responding to a Greeting:** If a person is greeted by someone who is not aware of the halachah, he should return the greeting in a quiet, somber manner.[113] If the other person might become offended by that response, it should be explained to him that the halachah does not permit extending greetings on Tishah b'Av, since it is a time of mourning.[114]

3. **Giving a Gift:** One may not send a gift or package to another person on Tishah b'Av.[115] This prohibition does not include sending money or a package to a person in need, as it is permissible to give *tzedakah*.[116]

4. **Walking in Public Places:** In order to avoid socializing or engaging in frivolous behavior, a person should refrain from

---

110. ראה ערוך השלחן יו"ד סי' שפ"ד ס"ט לענין אבל.
111. שו"ע סי' תקנ"ד ס"כ ובמ"ב ס"ק מ"א. וראה הליכות שלמה שם הערה 30 שה"ה שאילת מה שלומך או איך אתה מרגיש ששואל משום דרך ארץ, אסור (אם לא ששואל כן לחולה או סיבה אחרת).
112. הליכות שלמה שם.
113. שו"ע שם.
114. מ"ב ס"ק מ"ב.
115. מ"ב ס"ק מ"א.
116. כה"ח ס"ק צ"א.

walking around in public areas on Tishah b'Av.[117] (A person who has a need to walk outdoors for his health should do so alone and in areas where he will not encounter others.) In general, conversations should also be kept to a minimum.[118]

5. **The Prohibition of Marital Relations:** Marital relations are prohibited on Tishah b'Av. A husband and wife should not even sleep in the same bed.[119] The *poskim* debate whether the same laws pertaining to the *niddah* period (such as the requirement for a couple to refrain from touching or passing to each other), which are applicable on Yom Kippur, should be observed on Tishah b'Av as well. In practice, one should be stringent on this matter, even during the daytime.[120]

6. **Marital Relations when the Ninth of Av Falls on Shabbos:** Although the halachos of mourning do not apply on Shabbos even on the ninth of Av, some *poskim* maintain that the prohibition of marital relations, which is a private matter, is applicable nonetheless when the ninth of Av falls on Shabbos (as is the halachah regarding a person who becomes a mourner on Yom Tov). The Ashkenazic custom is to be stringent in this regard.[121] However, when a *leil tevilah* falls on Friday night, the woman should go to the *mikveh* as usual, and marital relations are permitted.[122] Similarly, if a man returns home from a trip on Erev Shabbos, marital relations are permitted on that Friday night.[123]

---

117. שו״ע שם סכ״א.
118. חיי אדם כלל קל״ה סי״ז.
119. שו״ע שם סי״ח.
120. עי׳ מ״ב ס״ק ל״ז ושעה״צ ס״ק מ״ד. והיום אין דרך לילך בבגדים מנוולים. ועי׳ בכה״ח ס״ק פ״ה שכתב להחמיר גם בשאר הרחקות. ובס׳ תורת המועדים עמוד קנ״ז הביא מהגרח״ק שליט״א שדעת הגריש״א זצ״ל שאפשר להקל בשאר הרחקות אפי׳ בלילה.
121. רמ״א שם סי״ט ומ״ב ס״ק ל״ט-מ׳.
122. מ״ב סק״מ.
123. שעה״צ ס״ק מ״ו.

7. **Altering One's Sleeping Arrangements:** It is commendable for a person to sleep in a fashion that affords him less comfort than on a typical night, such as by using fewer pillows than usual. Some people have the custom to sleep on the floor, and some place stones beneath their heads as an allusion to Yaakov Avinu, who experienced a vision of the *churban* when he lay down on *Har Hamoriah* to sleep with stones surrounding his head, as the Torah indicates in *Bereishis* 28:11.[124] A pregnant woman or any other person in a state of weakness is not required to sleep in an uncomfortable fashion.[125]

8. **Minimizing Pleasurable Activities:** In general, a person should avoid engaging in activities that generate honor or pleasure.[126] Consequently, some *poskim* prohibit smoking on Tishah b'Av. A person who is highly addicted to smoking may exercise leniency after *chatzos*, in the privacy of his own residence.[127] According to some *poskim*, one must refrain from smelling *besamim* or any other pleasant fragrances on Tishah b'Av.[128]

9. **Sitting on the Floor:** On Tishah b'Av, it is customary to sit on the floor rather than on a regular chair, as is the practice of an *avel* during *shivah*.[129] Unlike the other restrictions of Tishah b'Av, this halachah applies only until *chatzos*. After midday, one may sit on a regular chair.[130] Nevertheless, it is permissible to sit on the floor after *chatzos*, even though Tishah b'Av is

---

124. שו״ע ורמ״א סי׳ תקנ״א ס״ב. (ועי׳ מועדים וזמנים ח״ה סי׳ שמ״ב סי׳ שלדעת הגר״א סי׳ תקנ״ט צריך מעיקר הדין לישון על הארץ כדין אונן.)
125. רמ״א שם ומ״ב סק״ז.
126. רמ״א שם.
127. מ״ב סק״ח.
128. עי׳ שעה״צ סי׳ תקנ״ו סק״א דנחלקו הט״ז ומ״א אם בכלל אסור להריח בשמים משום תענוג או רק במוצ״ש אסור דהוי תענוג להשיב הנפש יתירה, ושדעת הגר״א משמע כהט״ז שתמיד אסור.
129. שו״ע סי׳ תקנ״ט ס״ג.
130. רמ״א ס״ג, מ״ב סק״י.

described as a *moed*.[131] (Some have the custom, based on the view of the Vilna Gaon, to sit on the floor throughout the day.)

There is no actual requirement to sit on the floor; the halachah merely prohibits sitting on an ordinary chair. Thus, one may stand as much as one wishes.[132]

10. **Sitting on a Low Chair:** If a person finds it difficult to sit directly on the floor, he may sit on a towel or pillow or on a low chair.[133] According to some *poskim*, the seat should not be higher than three *tefachim* above the ground;[134] however, other *poskim* require only that it be lower than a regular chair.[135] See Chapter Seven, section 2, paragraph 15, where it is noted that according to some authorities, there is a Kabbalistic prohibition to sit directly on the ground, and an intervening object should always be placed on the floor. Nevertheless, other authorities disagree and maintain that sitting directly on the floor is permissible even according to Kabbalah.[136]

11. **When a Regular Chair May Be Used:** A pregnant woman or a woman after birth may sit on a regular chair.[137] The same is true of an elderly or sick person. The person who holds the *sefer Torah* after *hagbaah* should also sit on a regular chair. Someone who must travel in a car or bus may sit in the seat as usual.[138] Some authorities are stringent that a person who travels by bus should stand whenever possible.[139]

---

131. מ״ב ס״ק י״ז.
132. ט״ז סק״ד. ועי׳ במועדים וזמנים ח״ה סי׳ שמ״א שבשעת אמירת קינות יש ענין דוקא לשבת על הארץ דרך אבילות ולא לעמוד.
133. מ״ב ס״ק י״א ועי׳ שעה״צ סק״ט.
134. כ״ה לענין אבל, ראה דע״ת סי׳ שפ״ז ס״ב, וכן עמא דבר.
135. ארחות רבינו ח״ב עמוד קל״ח בשם החזו״א, והליכות שלמה פט״ו הערה 25 בשם הגרשז״א זצ״ל.
136. עי׳ שע״ת סק״ג. ועי׳ מש״כ בפרק ז׳ בהערות שי״א שאין מחלוקת וכל הענין עפ״י קבלה הוא ע״ג אדמה.
137. כ״ה בערוה״ש יו״ד סי׳ שפ״ז ס״ג לענין אבל. וכ״כ בתורת היולדת פמ״ח סי״ב.
138. שם ס״ק י״ז בשם הגרי״ש זצ״ל.
139. הגרשז״א זצ״ל בהליכות שלמה שם ס״ו, אבל א״צ להימנע מנסיעה כאשר אין אפשרות לעמוד, שם סק״ז.

12. **Standing for a Rav or Elderly Person:** There is a difference of opinion among the *poskim* as to whether there is an obligation to stand up on Tishah b'Av when a Rav or elderly person passes by. It is customary to stand up as on any other day of the year, but it is questionable whether this is a full-fledged obligation.[140]

13. **Holding a Child:** It is prohibited for an *avel* during *shivah* to hold a child, since this might lead to playfulness.[141] Similarly, the *poskim* state that on Tishah b'Av a person should not hold a child for the purpose of playing with the child.[142] If a child needs to be held, it is certainly permitted to do so.

6. Work and Business Dealings

1. **Working on Tishah B'Av:** Working on Tishah b'Av was not formally prohibited by *Chazal*; however, a custom developed in some communities to refrain from working.[143] This practice has become the widespread *minhag*[144] and is therefore universally binding.

   The purpose of this restriction is to prevent one's attention from being diverted from the mourning of Tishah b'Av.[145]

2. **Until *Chatzos*:** The prohibition to work on Tishah b'Av remains in effect only until *chatzos*.[146] See paragraph 9 below regarding engaging in business after *chatzos*.

3. **Writing:** There is a dispute among the *poskim* as to whether writing is permitted on Tishah b'Av. Some authorities permit

---

140. עי' שערי תשובה סי' תקנ"ד סי"ב.
141. שו"ע יו"ד סי' שצ"א ס"א.
142. שו"ת תשובות והנהגות ח"ב סי' רנ"א.
143. מתני' פסחים דף נד:, שו"ע סי' תקנ"ד סכ"ב.
144. ביה"ל סכ"ב ד"ה במקום, מ"ב ס"ק מ"ה.
145. מ"ב ס"ק מ"ג.
146. רמ"א שם.

writing under any circumstances, while others permit it only in the select instances in which it is permitted on Chol Hamoed.[147]

4. **Food Preparation:** One may not engage in preparations for the meal following the fast until after *chatzos* (unless one is preparing for a *seudas mitzvah*).[148] However, one may cook or perform other forms of work in order to provide food for children or those who are ill.

5. **Conducting Business:** Conducting any form of business is prohibited before *chatzos*, even if no actual *melachah* is involved.[149] Even after *chatzos*, involvement in business is subject to the restrictions of the Nine Days.[150] (See Chapter Six, section 2, for details.)

6. **Forms of Prohibited Work:** The restriction on the performance of *melachah* includes activities that are only slightly time-consuming, as well as those that are defined as *maaseh hedyot* (of a non-professional nature). However, quick and simple activities such as lighting a candle, switching a light on or off, or tying a knot are permitted.[151] A person should, however, refrain from making his bed or tidying the house before *chatzos*.[152]

7. **Instructing a Non-Jew to Perform *Melachah*:** It is permissible to instruct a non-Jew to perform work on Tishah b'Av even in one's home.[153] However, one may not instruct a non-Jew to engage in activities that will attract the attention

---

147. עי׳ ביה״ל סוד״ה על ידי, וכוונתו שם ע״י עצמו.
148. שו״ע סי׳ תקנ״ט ס״י ומ״ב סק״מ. והיינו אף בדבר שלית ביה שיהוי, פשוט.
149. שו״ע סי׳ תקנ״ד שם.
150. שם.
151. רמ״א שם, מ״ב ס״ק מ״ג, ביה״ל ד״ה במקום.
152. ערוך השלחן סי׳ תקנ״ד סכ״א.
153. שו״ע שם סכ״ב. ועי׳ ביה״ל ד״ה על ידי, שדעת המט״י שאינו מותר אלא אם נותן לו המלאכה קודם ת״ב וכתב עליו הביה״ל דצ״ע כיון שיסוד ההיתר באמירה לעכו״ם הוא דליכא היסח הדעת ע״י.

of others, such as construction work.[154] (If a non-Jew was contracted before Tishah b'Av for a project, one may allow him to work on Tishah b'Av if he chooses to do so on his own accord.[155]) Similarly, a business that is open to the public may not be allowed to operate on Tishah b'Av prior to *chatzos*, even if it is to be managed by a non-Jew during that time, since people are generally aware when a business is owned by a Jew.[156]

8. **Preventing a Loss:** Work of any kind may be performed in order to prevent a loss (a scenario known as *davar ha'avud*) just as on Chol Hamoed.[157] One may take advantage of a rare opportunity to buy or sell an item at a good price, but the actual transaction must be carried out by a non-Jew.[158]

9. **Business Dealings after *Chatzos*:** Even after midday, when it is permissible to engage in *melachah* and business dealings, *Chazal* teach us that a person will not receive any blessing or profit from such activities.[159] This is true only if he becomes involved in the pursuit to the point that his attention is diverted from the mourning of Tishah b'Av.[160] Consequently, those who organize activities on Tishah b'Av for young children should not charge a fee; rather, the payment should be made in the form of a gift.[161]

10. **Working on Tishah B'Av when the Fast Is Postponed:** The halachos governing *melachah* and business dealings are the same when the fast of Tishah b'Av is a *nidcheh* (i.e., when the

---

154. מ"ב ס"ק מ"ו.
155. מ"ב סי' תקנ"א ס"ק י"ב.
156. שעה"צ סי' תקנ"ד סק"נ.
157. שו"ע שם סכ"ג.
158. מ"ב ס"ק מ"ח ועי' ביה"ל ד"ה דבר האבד.
159. שו"ע שם סכ"ד.
160. מ"ב ס"ק מ"ט.
161. דעת הגרי"ש א זצ"ל הוב"ד בתורת המועדים עמוד קס"א. ובס' אמת ליעקב הערה 524 כתב שמותר ליקח תשלום בת"ב בדרך הבלעה בצירוף שהוא מלאכה דלית ביה שיהוי והיסח הדעת.

ninth of Av falls on Shabbos and the fast is postponed until Sunday). In general, the laws of a postponed fast are identical to those of Tishah b'Av when it is observed on the ninth of Av itself; the sole exception is the added dispensation for a person who is slightly ailing to eat and drink.

CHAPTER NINE

Tefillos and *Minhagim* of Tishah B'Av

❦

1. The Night of Tishah B'Av
2. The Day of Tishah B'Av
3. *Tzitzis* and Tefillin
4. A *Bris* on Tishah B'Av

CHAPTER NINE
Tefillos and *Minhagim* of Tishah B'Av

1. The Night of Tishah B'Av

1. **The Order of Davening:** On the night of Tishah b'Av, *Maariv* is followed by the Full Kaddish, the reading of *Megillas Eichah*, and the recitation of *Kinnos*. An individual who is davening alone should recite *Eichah* and *Kinnos* on his own.[1]

2. **Removing the *Paroches*:** The *paroches* that covers the *aron kodesh* should be removed (or pulled to the side), as an allusion to the *pasuk* (*Eichah* 2:17) that states, "*Bitza emraso* – He carried out His word," which the Midrash expounds as indicating that the *paroches* at the entrance to the *Kodesh Hakodashim* was torn (*biza*) when the *Beis Hamikdash* was destroyed.[2]

3. **Dimming the Lights:** The lights in the shul should be dimmed, leaving only enough illumination for the congregants to read *Eichah* and *Kinnos*. This practice alludes to the *pasuk* (*Eichah* 3:6), "*B'machashakim hoshivani* – He caused me to sit

---

1. רמ"א סי' תקנ"ט ס"ב ובמ"ב סק"ד-ה.
2. רמ"א שם ס"ב, והוא עפ"י המדרש בוע פרפורין שלו, שמרמז לקריעת הפרוכת לפני הק"ק.

in darkness."³ The lights or candles at the *amud* should not be lit at *Maariv* or *Shacharis*, only at *Minchah*.⁴ The lights in one's home should also be dimmed.⁵

4. **Sitting on the Floor:** The congregants should sit on the floor during davening. The halachos regarding sitting on the floor are discussed in section 5 of the previous chapter.

5. **A Mournful Melody:** *Maariv* and *Eichah* should be recited in a slow, sorrowful tune reminiscent of a mourner's voice. The *baal korei* should begin reciting the *megillah* in a low tone and then raise his voice for each successive *perek*,⁶ pausing briefly between each *pasuk* and slightly longer between *perakim*. The final *pasuk* of each *perek* should be read in a louder tone than the rest of the *perek*.⁷

6. **Reciting a *Brachah* on *Megillas Eichah*:** There is a dispute among the *poskim* as to whether the *brachah* of *al mikra megillah* should be recited before the reading of *Megillas Eichah*.⁸ Every congregation should follow its custom.

7. **Reading Along in an Undertone:** The congregation should read *Megillas Eichah* quietly along with the *baal korei*.⁹ (According to some authorities, when the *megillah* is read from a kosher *klaf* one should not read along, as is the halachah with regard to an ordinary *haftarah*.)

8. **A Woman's Obligation:** Women are not obligated to hear

---

3. שו״ע שם ס״ג.
4. מ״ב ס״ק ט״ו.
5. הליכות שלמה פט״ו הערה 21, הגרח״ק שליט״א הוב״ד בתורת המועדים עמוד קס״ט.
6. רמ״א שם ס״א.
7. מ״ב סק״ב.
8. עי׳ מ״ב סי׳ ת״צ ס״ק י״ט.
9. מ״ב סי׳ תקנ״ט ס״ק ט״ו.

Megillas Eichah.[10] Nevertheless, a woman should try to recite the *megillah* if possible.[11]

9. **Reciting the *Pasuk* of "*Hashiveinu*" Aloud:** When the *baal korei* reaches the penultimate *pasuk* of the *megillah*, "*Hashiveinu Hashem eilecha*," the congregation should recite it aloud. After the conclusion of the *megillah*, the congregation should recite this *pasuk* aloud again and the *baal korei* should then repeat it. The recitation of *Kinnos* begins immediately thereafter.[12] (Some communities recite the *pasuk* of "*Hashiveinu*" aloud only once, after the *baal korei* has concluded the *megillah*.)

10. **Reciting *Uva Letzion* and *Kaddish*:** After *Kinnos*, the congregation recites *Seder Kedushah*, beginning with the words "*v'Atah kadosh*," before *Aleinu*. The *pasuk* beginning with the words "*uva letzion*" is omitted because it refers to redemption, which does not take place at night. The *pasuk* beginning "*va'ani zos brisi*" is likewise omitted, both because it is not appropriate to recite that *pasuk* in conjunction with *Kinnos* and because Torah study (to which the *pasuk* alludes) is prohibited.[13] The Full Kaddish without *tiskabel* is then recited, followed by *Aleinu*.

11. ***V'yehi Noam* and *Vayiten Lecha*:** When Tishah b'Av falls on Motzaei Shabbos, the passage of *V'yehi Noam* is not recited, since it refers to the construction of the Mishkan. Similarly, the passages beginning with *vayiten lecha* are not recited, since we do not work on Tishah b'Av.[14]

---

10. הגרח״ק שליט״א הוב״ד בתורת המועדים עמוד ק״ע.
11. ראה תשובות והנהגות ח״ב סי׳ ר״נ.
12. רמ״א שם ס״א.
13. שו״ע שם ס״ב ומ״ב סק״ו.
14. שו״ע ורמ״א שם, מ״ב סק״ז ט׳.

The Night of Tishah B'Av ∽ 251

2. The Day of Tishah B'Av

1. **Kinnos:** During the day, the recitation of *Kinnos* should preferably extend until close to *chatzos*, so that people will not come to perform *melachah* during this time.[15]

2. **Davening at *Neitz Hachamah*:** Although it is preferable to rise early for davening, if one will complete *Kinnos* long before *chatzos* as a result, it is better to begin davening later in order to finish closer to *chatzos*.[16] However, those who usually daven at *neitz*, in keeping with the *minhag* of *vasikin*, may do so on Tishah b'Av even if they will finish reciting *Kinnos* far in advance of *chatzos*.[17]

3. **Sitting in One's Regular Place:** Although many mourning practices are observed on Tishah b'Av, it is not necessary to change one's seat in shul; sitting on the floor is a sufficient display of *aveilus*.[18]

4. **Shacharis on Tishah B'Av:** Regarding the *brachah* of *she'asah li kol tzorki* in *birchos hashachar*, see Chapter Eight, section 3. For the halachos concerning the recitation of *korbanos*, the *mishnayos* of *Perek Eizehu Mekoman*, and the *braisa* of Rabbi Yishmael, see Chapter Eight, section 4. The halachos of donning the *tallis* and tefillin are discussed in the next section.

5. **Tachanun, Selichos, and Avinu Malkeinu:** *Tachanun* and *Selichos* are not recited on Tishah b'Av because of its unique status as a *moed*[19] (which derives from the fact that the *Beis Hamikdash* will eventually be rebuilt on this day). For the same reason, *Avinu Malkeinu*, which is typically recited at *Shacharis*

---

15. רמ"א שם ס"ג ובמ"ב ס"ק י"ג.
16. מ"ב ס"ק ט"ז.
17. ארחות רבינו ח"ב עמוד קמ"א שכן נהג החזו"א והגרי"י קניבסקי זצ"ל.
18. רמ"א שם ס"ד ומ"ב ס"ק כ"א.
19. שו"ע ורמ"א שם ס"ד.

and *Minchah* on a fast day, is not recited on Tishah b'Av. At the same time, a mourner may serve as *shaliach tzibbur* on Tishah b'Av, and a person who visits the Kosel should perform *kriah* as usual.[20]

6. **Krias HaTorah:** The passage of *Kel Erech Apayim* before *Krias HaTorah* is omitted, because of Tishah b'Av's status as a *moed*.[21] The Torah reading on the morning of Tishah b'Av is the passage in *Parshas Vaeschanan* beginning with the words "*ki solid banim*" (4:25-40). The *haftarah* is the passage in *Sefer Yirmiyah* beginning with the words "*asof asifeim*" (8:13, 9:1-23) and is read with the same cantillation as *Megillas Eichah*, aside from the final two *pesukim*, which are read in the ordinary tune of a *haftarah*.[22]

7. **Reciting *Kinnos* without Distraction:** During the recitation of *Kinnos*, one should not leave the shul to engage in unnecessary conversation. One should certainly refrain from any idle chatter or frivolity in shul, and from engaging in conversation with a non-Jew, which will surely divert one's attention from mourning.[23]

8. **The Conclusion of *Shacharis*:** The recitation of *Kinnos* is followed by *Ashrei*. *Lamnatzeiach* is omitted due to the status of the day as a *moed*[24] and the *pasuk* beginning with the words "*va'ani zos brisi*" is omitted in *Uva Letzion*. The Full Kaddish without *tiskabel* is recited. *Shacharis* concludes with *Aleinu*. Some congregations omit *Pitum Haketores*[25] and the *Shir Shel Yom*.[26]

---

20. הליכות שלמה פט״ו הערה 45.
21. רמ״א שם ס״ד.
22. רמ״א שם ובמ״ב ס״ק י״ח.
23. שו״ע שם ס״ה ובמ״ב ס״ק כ״ב-כ״ג.
24. רמ״א שם.
25. שם.
26. קיצור שו״ע כלל קכ״ד ס״ג.

9. **Reading *Eichah* after *Kinnos***: It is commendable for every individual to read *Eichah* during the day of Tishah b'Av as well.[27] Some congregations have the custom to conduct a second public reading of the *megillah* after *Kinnos*.[28] (The *brachah* of *al mikra megillah* is not recited.) This custom is observed in many communities in Eretz Yisrael.

10. **A Mourner during the First Three Days of *Shivah***: A mourner is not permitted to go to shul on the evening of Tishah b'Av during the first three days of the *shivah*; however, he is permitted to go to shul during the day.[29]

11. **Visiting a Cemetery**: After *Shacharis* on Tishah b'Av, it is customary to visit a cemetery.[30] If there is no Jewish cemetery in the vicinity, one should visit even a non-Jewish cemetery. The purpose of this practice is to internalize the sense that we are no better off than the deceased.[31] One should not venture within four *amos* of any *kever*, even that of a Jew. In light of the fact that Tishah b'Av is not a time for outings and that idle chatter is discouraged, visits to the cemetery should be conducted with no more than one other person for company, to prevent one from being distracted from mourning over the *churban*.[32] If one will need to wear leather shoes in order to visit a cemetery, it is preferable not to go.[33]

12. ***Tziduk Hadin* at a *Levayah***: If there is a *levayah* on Tishah b'Av, *tziduk hadin* is not recited, since Tishah b'Av is a *moed*.[34]

13. **Preparing Food after *Chatzos***: It is customary to refrain

---

27. מ"ב סק"ב.
28. ערוך השלחן סי' תקנ"ט ס"ב.
29. שו"ע שם ס"ו ובמ"ב ס"ק כ"ד.
30. רמ"א שם ס"י.
31. מ"ב ס"ק מ"א. אבל בערוה"ש ס"ז כתב שאין ללכת רק על קברי ישראל.
32. מ"ב שם.
33. שם.
34. רמ"א שם ומ"ב ס"ק מ"ב.

from beginning food preparations for the conclusion of the fast until after *chatzos*,³⁵ so that during the morning one will be occupied solely with contemplating the destruction of Yerushalayim and with reciting *Kinnos*.³⁶ Nevertheless, one may prepare food for children who need to be fed prior to *chatzos*. (When Tishah b'Av falls on Thursday and it will be difficult to prepare for Shabbos, one may begin the preparations for Shabbos after *chatzos* as well.³⁷)

14. **Returning the *Paroches* to Its Place:** It is customary to return the *paroches* to its place before *Minchah*.³⁸

15. ***Shir Shel Yom*:** In many congregations, the *shir shel yom* is recited before *Minchah*.³⁹ Some recite it after *Minchah*.

16. **Washing Hands before *Minchah*:** A person should wash his hands before davening *Minchah*, albeit only until the knuckles.⁴⁰

17. **Torah Reading and *Haftarah*:** As on any other *taanis tzibbur*, a Torah reading and *haftarah* are included in *Minchah*. (In Sephardic communities, there is no *haftarah* on a fast day.)

18. ***Bentching Gomel* and Receiving an *Aliyah* for a Bar Mitzvah:** A person who must recite the *brachah* of *hagomel* should recite it at the Torah reading of *Minchah*, rather than at *Shacharis*.⁴¹ Similarly, a boy who becomes bar mitzvah on Tishah b'Av should receive an *aliyah* at *Minchah* rather than at *Shacharis*.⁴²

---

35. שו״ע שם ס״י.
36. ביה״ל ס״י ד״ה עד לאחר חצות.
37. הגרש״א זצ״ל הוב״ד בתורת המועדים עמוד קע״ג.
38. כף החיים סי׳ תקנ״ט ס״ק י״ט וכמו בטלית.
39. קיצור שו״ע כלל סי׳ קכ״ד סי״ט.
40. מ״ב סי׳ תקנ״ד ס״ק כ״א. ויל״ע דלכאורה ׳צריך׳ ליטול ולא רק דמותר.
41. כף החיים שם ס״ק ל״ח.
42. הליכות שלמה פט״ו ס״ח.

19. ***Nacheim***: In *Shemoneh Esrei* of *Minchah*, we insert a passage beginning with the words "*nacheim Hashem Elokeinu es aveilei Tzion*" in the *brachah* of *bonei Yerushalayim*. This passage is inserted specifically in the *Shemoneh Esrei* of *Minchah* because the *Beis Hamikdash* was set on fire in the afternoon. (This is the *minhag* of Ashkenazim; however, the Sephardic custom is to recite this passage in all three *tefillos* of the day.)[43] If a person forgets to recite the passage of *Nacheim* in the proper place, he should recite it after the *brachah* of *retzei*, before the words "*v'sechezenah eineinu*"; in this case, the *brachah* of *menachem Tzion* at the conclusion of the passage should be omitted.[44] If he neglects to include the passage in the *brachah* of *retzei*, he should recite it at the end of *Shemoneh Esrei*, before the words "*yiheyu leratzon*."[45] If he realizes his error only after that point, he should not repeat *Shemoneh Esrei*.[46]

20. **Reciting *Nacheim* when One Is Not Fasting:** A person who is not fasting should omit the passage of *Aneinu* (see below) but nevertheless should recite *Nacheim*.

21. ***Nacheim* in *Birkas Hamazon*:** A person who eats bread on Tishah b'Av should recite the passage of *Nacheim* in the third *brachah* of *birkas hamazon*. Most *poskim* rule that this should be done at any point during the day, even in the morning.[47] Some *poskim*, however, maintain that *Nacheim* should not be recited.[48] If a person forgets to recite *Nacheim* in *birkas*

---

43. שו"ע ורמ"א סי' תקנ"ז ס"א.
44. מ"ב סי' תקנ"ז סק"ב, ועי' ביה"ל ד"ה בונה ירושלים.
45. כף החיים סי' תקנ"ז סק"ב.
46. שו"ע שם.
47. רמ"א שם, ובמ"ב סק"ה.
48. עי' מ"ב שם שיש חולקים. ועי' כף החיים ס"ק י"א שאין לאומרו מאחר שיש מפקפקים שב ואל תעשה עדיף שיש חשש הפסק.

hamazon, he should not return to the place of his error, nor should he repeat *birkas hamazon*.[49]

22. **Inserting *Aneinu* in the *Shemoneh Esrei*:** The passage of *Aneinu* is recited during the *brachah* of *shomea tefillah* at *Minchah*, as on other fast days.[50] A person who forgets to recite this passage should not return to that *brachah*,[51] but he should insert it before the words "*yiheyu leratzon*."[52] If he forgets to insert it then, he does not repeat *Shemoneh Esrei*.

23. ***Aneinu* for the *Shaliach Tzibbur*:** As on other fast days, *Aneinu* is recited by the *shaliach tzibbur* as a separate *brachah*, after the *brachah* of *goel Yisrael*, both at *Shacharis* and at *Minchah*.[53] If the *shaliach tzibbur* forgets to recite *Aneinu* and realizes his mistake before concluding the *brachah* of *refaeinu*, even if he has already recited the words "*baruch Atah*," he should immediately recite *Aneinu* and then repeat the *brachah*.[54] If he realizes his mistake only after reciting Hashem's Name, he does not go back; rather, he should recite *Aneinu* in the *brachah* of *shomea tefillah*, before the words "*ki Atah shomea*," and should omit its concluding *brachah*.[55] If he neglects to include it in this *brachah* as well, he should recite it after the *brachah* of *sim shalom*.[56]

24. **The Conclusion of *Minchah*:** After the chazzan's repetition of the *Shemoneh Esrei*, the Full Kaddish with *tiskabel* is recited,

---

49. מ"ב שם.
50. שו"ע שם.
51. שו"ע שם.
52. שו"ע סי' תקס"ה ס"ב, מ"ב שם סק"ו, ועי' שעה"צ שם סק"ו שבדיעבד יכול לאמרו גם לאחר יהיו לרצון כל שלא עקר את רגליו.
53. מ"ב סי' תקנ"ז סק"ג.
54. שו"ע סי' קי"ט ס"ד ובמ"ב ס"ק ט"ז.
55. רמ"א סי' קי"ט ס"ד ובמ"ב ס"ק י"ט.
56. מ"ב שם.

followed by *Aleinu*. *Tachanun* and *Avinu Malkeinu* are not recited at *Minchah* on Tishah b'Av.

3. *Tzitzis* and Tefillin

1. **Wearing *Tzitzis* on Tishah B'Av:** It is customary to refrain from wearing a *tallis* at *Shacharis* on the morning of Tishah b'Av and to wear only a *tallis katan* beneath one's shirt. There is an allusion to this practice in the comment of the Midrash on the *pasuk* (*Eichah* 2:17), "*bitza emraso*," which translates literally as "He carried out His word." The Midrash explains that the word *bitza* is related to the Aramaic word *biza* ("tore"), and the word *emraso* can be understood as a reference to the Aramaic word *imra* ("garment"). The Midrash thus explains the *pasuk* to mean that Hashem tore His royal garments, so to speak; therefore, we do not wear a *tallis*, which contains *techeiles* and therefore resembles a royal garment.[57] The *poskim* debate whether a person who removes his *tallis katan* at night should recite the *brachah* of *al mitzvas tzitzis* when donning the garment in the morning.[58] Consequently, some *poskim* had the practice of wearing their *tzitzis* to sleep on the night of Tishah b'Av, in order to avoid this halachic dilemma.[59]

2. **Grasping the *Tzitzis* during *Shacharis*:** In most communities, it is customary to refrain from taking hold of the *tzitzis* of the *tallis katan* during *Baruch She'amar* and *Krias Shema* on the morning of Tishah b'Av.[60]

3. **Tefillin:** It is also customary to refrain from wearing tefillin on the morning of Tishah b'Av, since the *pasuk* states (*Eichah*

---

57. שו״ע סי׳ תקנ״ה ס״א. מ״ב שם סק״א.
58. עי׳ מ״ב סק״ב.
59. הגרשז״א זצ״ל הובא בהליכות שלמה פט״ו הערה 32.
60. תורת המועדים עמוד קס״ב בשם הרבה פוסקים.

2:1), "*Hishlich mishamayim eretz tiferes Yisrael* – He cast the glory of Yisrael from the heavens to the earth," and the term *tiferes Yisrael* may be interpreted as referring to tefillin.[61]

4. **The Sephardic Custom:** There are divergent customs among Sephardim regarding wearing a *tallis* and tefillin on Tishah b'Av.[62] A person should daven with a congregation that follows his family's customs.

5. **Wearing a *Tallis* and Tefillin at *Minchah*:** Both the *tallis* and tefillin should be worn at *Minchah* on Tishah b'Av. The appropriate *brachos* should be recited.[63] A person who usually wears Rabbeinu Tam's tefillin should do so on Tishah b'Av as well.[64] Due to the prohibition of Torah study on Tishah b'Av, many authorities maintain that the passages of *Shema*, *Vehayah*, and *Kadesh* should not be recited, even if one generally recites these passages upon putting on tefillin.[65] Nevertheless, some *poskim* consider the passages to be part of the order of davening and therefore rule that they should be recited.[66]

6. The reason we wear *tallis* and tefillin at *Minchah* is that the *Beis Hamikdash* was set on fire at that time, commencing the atonement for our *aveiros.* Alternatively, the *tallis* and tefillin provide us with some comfort during our mourning. At the same time, it should be noted that the reason the prohibition to wear a *tallis* and tefillin is lifted in the afternoon is that it is only a *minhag.* The other prohibitions of Tishah b'Av,

---

61. שו"ע שם ס"א. מ"ב שם סק"א.
62. עי' כף החיים סי' תקנ"ה סק"ד. ועי' שו"ת אור לציון ח"ג פכ"ט סכ"ב.
63. שו"ע שם.
64. מ"ב סק"ד.
65. מ"ב סק"ה.
66. עי' באר היטב סק"א (אבל רק כתב פרשת ק"ש) וכה"ח סי' תקנ"ד ס"ק י"ט (אבל רק כתב שם על פרשת קדש והיה כי יביאך ולא פרשת שמע). שו"ת שבט הלוי ח"י סי' פ"א.

Tzitzis and Tefillin

which were instituted by *Chazal*, remain in effect until *tzeis hakochavim*.[67]

7. **Designating a *Shomer*:** There is a dispute among the *poskim* as to whether a person must designate a *shomer* before engaging in *melachah*, sleeping in a manner that constitutes *sheinas keva*, or having a meal (in the case of someone who is allowed to eat on Tishah b'Av) if he has not yet fulfilled the mitzvah of wearing tefillin. Some rule that a *shomer* is not required, since some authorities maintain that the mitzvah of tefillin is not actually in effect on Tishah b'Av at all, just as a mourner is exempt from wearing tefillin on the first day of mourning.[68] (Those who adopt this position acknowledge that the halachah does not follow this opinion; nevertheless, they consider it sufficient grounds to exempt a person from designating a *shomer*.) Other *poskim*, however, maintain that a *shomer* is indeed required.[69]

4. A *Bris* on Tishah B'Av

1. **The Timing of a *Bris*:** According to Ashkenazic custom, a *bris milah* on Tishah b'Av should be performed immediately after the recitation of *Kinnos*; there is no need to delay it until after *chatzos*.[70] On the other hand, although a *bris* should generally be performed as early as possible in the day, on Tishah b'Av a

---

67. מ"ב סק"ג.
68. הגריש"א זצ"ל הוב"ד בתורת המועדים עמוד קס"ב.
69. דעת הגרח"ק שליט"א הוב"ד שם. וראה שש"כ פס"ב ס"ק ק"ח שדעת הגרשז"א זצ"ל שמותר לחולה לאכול בבוקר אחר תפילה וא"צ להניח תפילין אבל אחר חצות אין לאכול קודם שיניח תפילין. אמנם, עי' שו"ת שבט הלוי ח"ט סי' קל"ג שנקט שגם בבוקר יניח החולה תפילין בביתו לפני שיאכל.
70. רמ"א סי' תקנ"ט ס"ז.

bris milah should not be conducted before *Kinnos*, since a *bris milah* is a mitzvah that is associated with happiness.[71]

2. **Lighting Candles:** Although it is customary to dim the lights on Tishah b'Av, candles should be lit in honor of the *bris* (if that is one's custom) as on any other day.[72]

3. ***Besamim*:** Even those who usually bring *besamim* to a *bris milah*[73] do not do so on Tishah b'Av.[74]

4. **Drinking the Wine:** The *brachos* should be recited over a cup of wine. If the mother is not fasting (see Chapter Eight, section 1, regarding when a woman is exempt from fasting after birth) she should drink from the *kos*, provided that she heard the *brachah* and has not engaged in an interruption. If she did not hear the *brachah* or she engaged in some kind of interruption, the *kos* should be given to a child instead.[75] (Drinking *malei lugmov* – a cheekful of wine – is not essential; it is sufficient for a small quantity of the wine to be consumed.[76]) It is preferable for the child who receives the wine to have reached the age of *chinuch* with respect to reciting *brachos* but to be younger than the age of *chinuch* for mourning the *churban* (in general, this refers to a child between the ages of six and nine).[77] Some authorities maintain that the wine should always be given to a child and not to the mother, since wine is not a standard beverage today and is therefore prohibited even for a person who is exempt from fasting.[78]

---

71. מ"ב ס"ק כ"ה.
72. מ"ב ס"ק ט"ו.
73. עי' שו"ע יו"ד סי' רס"ה ס"א.
74. שו"ע סי' תקנ"ט ס"ז ובמ"ב ס"ק כ"ז.
75. שו"ע שם. אמנם ביוה"כ אין נותנים לתינוק לשתות דלמא אתי למסרך אלא נותנים מעט לרך הנימול, רמ"א סי' תרכ"א ס"ג.
76. ט"ז יו"ד סי' רס"ה סק"י.
77. שעה"צ סי' תקנ"ט ס"ק כ"ו.
78. תורת היולדת פמ"ח סק"כ בשם הגריש"א זצ"ל.

5. **Reciting *Shehecheyanu*:** In Eretz Yisrael, where the *brachah* of *shehecheyanu* is customarily recited at a *bris*, it is recited even on Tishah b'Av.[79]

6. **Wearing Shabbos Clothes:** After the recitation of *Kinnos*, the parents of the baby, the *mohel*, and the *sandak* may change their clothes and even don Shabbos clothes in honor of the *bris*; however, they should not wear new or freshly laundered clothing. (It is questionable whether freshly pressed Shabbos clothes may be worn.)[80] Leather shoes are not permitted.[81] After the *bris*, the celebrants must change back to their regular attire.[82]

7. **Wearing a *Tallis*:** If the *sandak* wishes to don a *tallis* as is customary at a *bris*, we do not object, but it is preferable not to.[83]

8. **A *Bris* when the Fast Has Been Postponed:** If a *bris* is performed on Sunday, the tenth of Av (i.e., the ninth of Av has fallen on Shabbos and the fast has been postponed until Sunday), the parents of the baby, the *mohel*, and the *sandak* (but not the *kvatter* or any of the other honorees at the *bris*) are permitted to break their fasts after davening *Minchah*. They are also permitted to bathe, since the day has the status of a Yom Tov for them,[84] as well as to don leather shoes.[85] Although they may put on fresh clothes and leather shoes even before the *bris* takes place, they may eat or drink only after

---

79. שו"ת שבט הלוי ח"י סי' פ"ד אות ג'.
80. שו"ע ורמ"א שם ס"ח, ובמ"ב ס"ק ל"א-ל"ג. (וצ"ל ש"לבנים" היינו מכובסים דלא מצאנו נ"מ בין לבנים וצבעונים.)
81. ביה"ל ס"ח ד"ה ומותר ללבוש.
82. מ"ב ס"ק ל"ד.
83. שע"ת סי' תקנ"ה סק"ב. ועי' שע"ת סי' י"ח סק"ב. וראה הליכות שלמה פט"ו ס"ט.
84. שו"ע שם ס"ט. (וראה ערוה"ש ס"ט שכתב על רחיצה - רק פניו, ידיו ורגליו.)
85. שו"ת שבט הלוי ח"ז סי' ע"ז.

the *bris* has been performed.[86] The other prohibitions of Tishah b'Av (learning Torah, laundering garments, and so forth) still apply.[87] Some authorities, however, are stringent with the above ruling and a Rav should be consulted.

9. **Davening *Minchah* at the Earliest Possible Time:** In the case discussed in the previous paragraph, Ashkenazic custom permits the participants in the *bris* to daven *Minchah* at the *zman* of *Minchah Gedolah* and break the fast immediately thereafter; they are not required to wait until the *zman* of *Minchah Ketanah*.[88] In Sephardic communities, however, there are divergent customs in this regard.[89]

10. **A *Bris* That Has Been Delayed:** When Tishah b'Av is *nidcheh*, as above, Ashkenazic custom permits the participants to engage in the aforementioned activities even if the *bris* took place after the eighth day of the baby's life.[90] Among Sephardim, there are divergent customs in this regard as well.[91]

11. **Reciting Havdalah:** The participants in a *bris* in the aforementioned scenario must recite Havdalah on a *kos* before breaking their fasts.[92]

12. **Delaying the *Seudah* until Nightfall:** Although it is permitted for the participants in the *bris* to eat, they should not engage in a large *seudah*. The actual celebratory *seudah* should be delayed until the night.[93]

---

86. עי' שע"ת סי' תקנ"ט ס"ק ט"ו.
87. עי' שו"ת נודע ביהודה תנינא יו"ד סי' רי"ג. ועי"ש בסו"ד שצריך להחליף הבגדים אח"כ משום מ"ע והגם שמותרים להמשיך לאכול ולשתות במשך כל היום אבל יעשו כן בביתו.
88. מ"ב ס"ק ל"ז ובשעה"צ ס"ק ל"ט. ועי' הליכות שלמה פט"ז סק"ז.
89. עי' כף החיים סי' תקנ"ט ס"ק ע"ד.
90. כן משמע מדברי המ"ב ס"ק ל"ח, וכ"פ הגרשז"א זצ"ל הוב"ד בשש"כ פס"ב ס"ק קט"ז.
91. עי' שע"ת שם סוס"ק ט"ו, ועי' כף החיים ס"ק ס"ט.
92. מ"ב ס"ק ל"ז.
93. מ"ב ס"ק ל"ו. ובשו"ת שבט הלוי ח"י סי' פ"ד כתב שאין לאכול ביחד רק מותר לכ"א לאכול לבד.

A Bris on Tishah B'Av 263

13. **A *Pidyon Haben*:** When Tishah b'Av is *nidcheh*, some authorities permit a *pidyon haben* to be performed and the father and *kohen* to break their fasts after *Minchah*, provided that Sunday (rather than Shabbos) is the actual 31st day after the child's birth.[94] Nevertheless, it is customary to delay a *pidyon haben* until after the conclusion of the fast[95] or, according to some authorities, to perform the actual *pidyon haben* on Tishah b'Av itself but to delay the *seudah* until the night.[96] A Rav should be consulted for a practical ruling.

---

94. מ"ב ס"ק ל"ח. ויש לעיין מה דין אם הבן.
95. הליכות שלמה פט"ו סט"ו, ועיי"ש בהערות.
96. שו"ת שבט הלוי ח"ו סי' ע' אות י"א.

CHAPTER TEN

Tishah B'Av on Sunday

1. Halachos Pertaining to Shabbos
2. Halachos Pertaining to Motzaei Shabbos
3. Halachos Pertaining to Sunday Night

CHAPTER TEN

Tishah B'Av on Sunday

Introduction: Tishah b'Av is observed on Sunday in two scenarios: when the ninth of Av falls on Sunday, and when the ninth of Av falls on Shabbos and the fast is postponed until the following day. In both scenarios, there are unique halachos pertaining both to Erev Tishah b'Av and to Havdalah either during or after the fast. When the ninth of Av falls on Shabbos and the fast is postponed, there are also variations in the halachos concerning the night and day after Tishah b'Av. The relevant halachos that were discussed in previous chapters will be reviewed briefly below.

1. Halachos Pertaining to Shabbos

1. **Torah Study:** In general, it is customary to refrain from regular Torah study on Erev Tishah b'Av after *chatzos* and to learn only those topics that are permitted to be studied on Tishah b'Av. In accordance with this custom, many refrain from reciting *Pirkei Avos* in shul after *Minchah* when Erev Tishah b'Av falls on Shabbos. On the other hand, Torah study is permitted on Shabbos before *chatzos*, even if Shabbos is the ninth of Av itself. Some *poskim* disagree with the practice of refraining from Torah study on Shabbos after *chatzos*, and some maintain that Torah study should continue as usual even when Erev Tishah b'Av falls on a weekday. In light of this difference of opinion, a person who wishes to learn Torah as usual on Shabbos is permitted to do so. Nevertheless, the

permissibility of teaching Torah in public, such as conducting *shiurim* after *chatzos* (on topics not related to Tishah b'Av) is a matter of dispute among the *poskim*. See Chapter Seven, section 1, for more details.

2. **Leisure Activities:** One must refrain from engaging in leisure activities after *chatzos* on Erev Tishah b'Av, even on Shabbos. When the ninth of Av falls on Shabbos, this restriction is in effect throughout the day. See Chapter Seven, section 1, for more details.

3. **Marital Relations:** When the ninth of Av falls on Shabbos, Ashkenazic custom prohibits marital relations unless it is a *leil tevilah*. There is no requirement, though, to observe the *harchakos* practiced when the wife is a *niddah*. When the eighth of Av falls on Shabbos, marital relations are permitted.

4. ***Av Harachamim* and *Tzidkascha*:** *Av Harachamim* is recited before *Mussaf* even when the ninth of Av itself falls on Shabbos (in spite of the fact that Tishah b'Av has the status of a *moed*). *Tzidkascha* is not recited at *Minchah* even when the ninth of Av falls on Sunday.

5. ***Seudah Hamafsekes*:** The usual halachos of the *seudah hamafsekes* do not apply on Shabbos, regardless of whether it is the eighth or the ninth of Av. An ordinary *seudah shelishis* should be conducted, and even meat and wine may be consumed, but the meal must conclude prior to *shekiah*. (If three adult males eat together, a *zimun* should be conducted.) One may still eat or drink after reciting *birkas hamazon* (even without making a verbal stipulation) until sunset. See Chapter Seven, section 4, for more details.

6. **Singing at *Seudah Shelishis*:** Regular Shabbos *zemiros* may be sung even at *seudah shelishis* (until *shekiah*), but one should refrain from singing other joyous songs.

7. **Other Practices of Mourning:** Although one must stop

eating and drinking at *shekiah*, one may not engage in any practice of *aveilus* until after Shabbos, i.e., at *tzeis hakochavim*. Thus, a person should not sit on the floor or remove his leather shoes or Shabbos clothes before nightfall. (Nevertheless, after *shekiah* it is prohibited to wash any part of the body for pleasure, even in cold water, or to perform an act of *sichah*, such as applying perfume.)

There are various opinions among the *poskim*, and consequently various customs, regarding the appropriate time to remove leather shoes and Shabbos clothes when Tishah b'Av begins immediately after Shabbos. Some congregations begin *Maariv* slightly after the conclusion of Shabbos so that the congregants can change their shoes and clothes at home after *tzeis hakochavim* before coming to shul. In other communities, the congregants bring their Tishah b'Av footwear to shul before Shabbos and change their shoes after *Barchu*, while they change out of their Shabbos clothes after davening. See Chapter Seven, section 4, for a detailed discussion of this subject. (Note: According to Sephardic custom, the halachos of *shavua shechal bo* are not observed before Tishah b'Av when the ninth of Av falls either on Shabbos or on Sunday; consequently, Sephardim must remember not to don freshly laundered clothing after Shabbos.)

8. **Taking a Pill on Shabbos to Prepare for the Fast:** Some *poskim* rule that one may take a pill on Shabbos to make the fast easier if the pill is mixed with food. It is preferable for the pill to be mixed with the food before Shabbos.[1] A Rav should be consulted for a practical ruling.

---

1. קובץ מבית לוי עמוד מ"ג. ולענין רפואה ממש למי שיש לו מיחוש לקחת התרופה ע"י תערובות מאכל מע"ש, עי' שו"ת אגר"מ או"ח ח"ב סי' פ"י שאין היתר אלא במין תרופה שהדרך לקחתו בתוך מאכל ומשקה ובד"כ מערבבו סמוך לאכילתו ועכשיו שינה לעשותו מע"ש. ומאידך, עי' שש"כ פל"ד ס"ה וס"ק כ"ז שכתב להיפוך שדוקא כשאין הדרך לקחתו במאכל ומשקה מותר בכה"ג. ועי' שו"ת שבט הלוי ח"ג סי' ל"ו, וח"י סי' פ"ד סק"ו. וראה ארחות שבת פכ"ב ס"ק רפ"ד בשם הגרי"ש א.

2. Halachos Pertaining to Motzaei Shabbos

1. **Reciting *Baruch Hamavdil*:** After *tzeis hakochavim* one must recite the words *"baruch hamavdil bein kodesh l'chol"* before beginning any preparations for Tishah b'Av. Therefore, a *gabbai* should recite this formula before arranging the tables and benches in the shul for the night's *tefillos*, and an individual must recite *baruch hamavdil* before changing his clothes or shoes. Similarly, after *seudah shelishis* it is prohibited to clear the table or tidy the kitchen before reciting *baruch hamavdil*, unless one is disturbed by the mess or the food will spoil. (One should not clean up, i.e., wash dishes etc. until after *chatzos* on Tishah b'Av day.)

2. **The Passages of *L'Dovid* and *Lamnatzeiach*:** In congregations where the *mizmorim* of *L'Dovid* and *Lamnatzeiach* are generally recited before *Maariv* on Motzaei Shabbos, these prayers should be omitted when Shabbos is followed by Tishah b'Av.[2]

3. ***Atah Chonantanu*:** The passage of *Atah chonantanu* is inserted in the *Shemoneh Esrei* as on a regular Motzaei Shabbos. If a person forgets to recite *Atah chonantanu*, he should not return to that point in the *Shemoneh Esrei* to correct his error; however, he must be careful to recite the formula of *"baruch hamavdil bein kodesh l'chol"* before performing any *melachah*. Women who do not daven *Maariv* must be especially mindful of this.[3]

4. **The Passages of *V'yehi Noam* and *Vayiten Lecha*:** The

---

2. רמ״א סי׳ תקנ״ט ס״ב. מ״ב סי׳ רצ״ג סק״א.

3. מ״ב סי׳ תקנ״ו סק״ב. וראה הליכות שלמה תפילה פי״ד ס״ז שיש לדון אם לכתחילה יש לנשים להתפלל ערבית מאחר שאין הבדלה על הכוס, וראה שם הלכות ת״ב פט״ו הערה 52 שא״א לחייבם.

passages beginning with the words "*v'yehi noam*," which are generally recited after *Shemoneh Esrei* on Motzaei Shabbos, should be omitted. The passages beginning with "*vayiten lecha*" are omitted as well.[4]

5. **Havdalah:** The Havdalah recited over wine is postponed until the conclusion of Tishah b'Av on Sunday night.

6. **The *Brachah* of *Borei Meorei Ha'eish*:** After *Maariv*, before the reading of *Megillas Eichah*, the *brachah* of *borei meorei ha'eish* is recited over a flame. A person who did not recite or hear the *brachah* at that time should recite it whenever he remembers during the night.[5] If he does not remember until the following day, he should not recite the *brachah* at a later time, even at Havdalah at the conclusion of Tishah b'Av. This is because the *brachah* of *borei meorei ha'eish* relates specifically to Motzaei Shabbos, the time when fire was created.[6]

7. **Deriving Benefit from the Flame:** It is important to note that in order to be *yotzei* the *brachah* of *borei meorei ha'eish* by hearing it from someone else, one must be sufficiently close to the flame that some benefit can be derived. A person who is too far from the flame to derive benefit will not be *yotzei*, even if he holds up his hands and gazes at his fingernails. If a person recites the *brachah* for others, it is preferable for everyone to be seated; however, *b'dieved* the listeners will be *yotzei* even if they stand.[7]

8. **The *Brachah* of *Borei Meorei Ha'eish* for Women:** It is questionable if a woman may recite the *brachah* of *borei meorei ha'eish*.[8] Consequently, there is a dispute among the *poskim* as to what a woman should do when Tishah b'Av begins

---

4. שו"ע ורמ"א סי' תקנ"ט ס"ב.
5. שו"ע סי' תקנ"ו ס"א ומ"ב סק"א.
6. מ"ב סק"ד.
7. עי' שש"כ פס"א ס"ק מ"ד.
8. עי' ביה"ל סי' רצ"ו ס"ח.

after Shabbos. Some authorities maintain that a man should preferably refrain from reciting the *brachah* in shul, or should have the intention not to be *yotzei* when it is recited in shul, so that he will be able to recite it for his wife or daughters at home. *B'dieved*, if the males in the family have fulfilled their obligation with the *brachah* recited in shul, the women and girls should recite the *brachah* themselves.[9] Other authorities rule that this is actually the preferable procedure: Men should fulfill their obligations by hearing the *brachah* in shul before the reading of *Eichah*, and women should recite the *brachah* on their own.[10] All *poskim* agree that a man who was already *yotzei* cannot be *motzi* a woman. When *Maariv* is delayed for some time after *tzeis hakochavim* (i.e., to remove clothes and shoes before going to shul), the recommended practice is to recite the *brachah* at home to be *motzi* the women.

9. **The *Brachah* on *Besamim*:** The *brachah* on *besamim* is not recited when Tishah b'Av begins on Motzaei Shabbos, since inhaling the fragrance of *besamim* is a form of pleasure that is prohibited on Tishah b'Av.[11] The *brachah* is also not recited at the conclusion of Tishah b'Av, since it is relevant only on Motzaei Shabbos, when the *neshamah yeseirah* departs.[12]

10. **Havdalah before Eating on Tishah B'Av:** According to many *poskim*, a person who will not be fasting on Tishah b'Av should recite Havdalah over a *kos* on Motzaei Shabbos before eating. He should recite the *brachah* of *borei meorei ha'eish* on a lit candle, but the *brachah* of *borei minei besamim* and the *pesukim* at the beginning of Havdalah should be omitted.[13] If a person eats only during the day, he should recite Havdalah

---

9. דעת הגרש"ז א זצ"ל הובא בשש"כ פס"ב ס"ק צ"ח.
10. שו"ת שבט הלוי ח"ז סי' ע"ז.
11. שו"ע שם ובמ"ב שם, ועי"ש שעה"צ סק"א.
12. שו"ע שם ובמ"ב סק"ה.
13. עי' שע"ת סי' תקנ"ו סק"א בשם ברכ"י בשם כנה"ג.

prior to eating and not at night.[14] *Lechatchilah*, Havdalah should be recited over a *chamar medinah* (such as beer in *chutz la'Aretz*), but if a person cannot use such a beverage, he may recite Havdalah over wine or grape juice. Havdalah may be recited over wine or grape juice *lechatchilah* if a child (between the ages of six and nine) will drink the wine.[15]

11. **Listening to Havdalah on Tishah B'Av:** When a man recites Havdalah on Tishah b'Av, he can recite it even for others who are fasting. The listeners are then not required to repeat Havdalah at the conclusion of the fast.[16]

12. **Havdalah for a Woman on Tishah B'Av:** A woman who is not fasting should preferably not recite Havdalah herself; instead, her husband (or any adult male) should recite it on her behalf even if he is fasting. The man should recite Havdalah with the intent to be *yotzei* and for the members of his household to fulfill their obligations, and it should be given to a child (between the ages of six and nine) to drink. If no adult male is available to recite Havdalah for a woman who must break her fast, she should recite Havdalah herself and give it to a child to drink. If no child is available, she should drink it herself.[17] However, it is preferable for her to recite Havdalah over a *chamar medinah*, such as beer in *chutz la'Aretz*.

13. **Havdalah for a Child:** According to many *poskim*, a child does not need to recite or hear Havdalah before eating on Tishah b'Av, even if he has reached the age of *chinuch*. A child

---

14. כף החיים סי׳ תקנ״ו סק״ט, שו״ת מנחת יצחק ח״ח סי׳ ל׳, תשובות והנהגות ח״ה סי׳ קס״ט סק״ט.
15. כה״ח שם, שש״כ פס״ב סמ״ו, ועי׳ שו״ת שבט הלוי ח״ז סי׳ ע״ז. ומ״מ דעת הגרח״ק שליט״א שחולה אינו מבדיל ואינו דומה למש״כ המ״ב סי׳ תקנ״ט לענין בעל ברית בת״ב נדחה שמבדיל קודם שאוכל.
16. שע״ת שם בשם הברכ״י שכן דעתו נוטה קצת, ובשש״כ שם נפסק כן למעשה.
17. שש״כ שם סמ״ח.

should fulfill his obligation to hear Havdalah at the conclusion of Tishah b'Av.[18]

14. **Leniencies when the Fast Is Postponed:** Although a person must generally be bedridden with illness in order to be exempt from fasting on Tishah b'Av, there is greater room for leniency when the ninth of Av falls on Shabbos and the fast is postponed until Sunday. In that case, a person may be exempt from fasting even if he is merely experiencing pain; see Chapter Eight, section 1.

3. Halachos Pertaining to Sunday Night

1. **The Passage of *Atah Chonantanu*:** If a person forgets to recite the passage of *Atah chonantanu* during the *Shemoneh Esrei* on Motzaei Shabbos, he should not include it in the *Shemoneh Esrei* on Motzaei Tishah b'Av.[19] If he erroneously eats on Motzaei Tishah b'Av before Havdalah, it is questionable if he must repeat the *Shemoneh Esrei* of *Maariv*.[20] (On a regular Motzaei Shabbos, a person who omits *Atah chonantanu* and makes the mistake of eating before Havdalah must repeat the *Shemoneh Esrei*.[21]) In practice, the *Shemoneh Esrei* should not be repeated in this situation.

2. **Havdalah:** As noted above, Havdalah on a *kos* should be recited on Sunday night rather than on Motzaei Shabbos. This Havdalah consists only of the *brachos* of *borei pri hagafen* and *hamavdil*; the *brachos* of *borei minei besamim* and *borei meorei*

.18 ארחות רבינו ח"ב עמוד קמ"ה בשם הגריי"ק שליט"א, שש"כ שם סמ"ה, ועי' שו"ת שבט הלוי ח"י סי' קע"ז. ועי' מועדים וזמנים ח"ז סי' רנ"ה. אמנם, בתורת המועדים עמוד קס"ד הביא שדעת הגריש"א זצ"ל שיבדילו לעצמם קודם שיאכלו.

.19 מ"ב סי' תקנ"ו סק"ג.

.20 שש"כ שם ס"ק צ"ה.

.21 שו"ע סי' רצ"ד ס"א ובמ"ב סק"ד.

ha'eish are omitted.[22] The *pesukim* beginning with the words "*hinei Keil yeshuasi*" are likewise omitted.[23] Wine or grape juice should be used for Havdalah; *chamar medinah* is not necessary. The wine should be consumed by the person who recites Havdalah; there is no need to give it to a child. This is true even if the ninth of Av falls on Sunday and Havdalah is therefore recited on the night of the tenth of Av, when some of the prohibitions of the Nine Days are still in effect.[24] Nevertheless, it is prohibited to drink wine for any other purpose until the following morning.

3. **Drinking Water before Havdalah:** A woman who is waiting for her husband to return from shul to recite Havdalah may drink water after *tzeis hakochavim* even before Havdalah.[25] Some authorities rule that if a woman feels that she must eat, she may recite Havdalah herself.[26]

4. ***Kiddush Levanah***: Regarding the mitzvah of *Kiddush Levanah*, see Chapter Eleven, section 1, paragraph 4.

5. **Activities Prohibited after Tishah B'Av:** When the ninth of Av falls on a weekday, certain prohibitions remain in effect until *chatzos* of the following day; see Chapter Eleven, section 2. However, when the ninth of Av falls on Shabbos and the fast is observed on the following day, only the prohibition to eat meat and drink wine remains in effect on Sunday night (for Ashkenazim). This prohibition is lifted on the following morning, and it is also waived in the event of a *seudas mitzvah*. When the ninth of Av itself falls on Sunday, the usual halachos of Motzaei Tishah b'Av are in effect, and the prohibitions extend until *chatzos* on Monday.

---

22. שו"ע סי' תקנ"ו ס"א.
23. שש"כ שם סמ"ד.
24. מ"ב סק"ג.
25. שו"ע סי' רצ"ו ס"א.
26. הגריש"א זצ"ל הובא בתורת המועדים עמוד קס"ה. ועי' שו"ת שבט הלוי ח"ד סי' נ"ד סק"ז וח"ח סי' קכ"ט.

CHAPTER ELEVEN

Motzaei Tishah B'Av

1. The Conclusion of the Fast
2. Prohibitions on Motzaei Tishah B'Av
3. Exceptions to the Prohibitions
4. Conduct after a Postponed Fast

CHAPTER ELEVEN

Motzaei Tishah B'Av

1. The Conclusion of the Fast

1. **Breaking the Fast:** The fast of Tishah b'Av concludes at *tzeis hakochavim*. (The exact time can be found on a calendar.) Unlike on Yom Kippur, one need not extend the fast after *tzeis hakochavim* (i.e., the halachah of *tosefes hayom* does not apply).[1]

2. **Eating and Drinking before *Maariv*:** After *tzeis hakochavim*, a man may drink but should preferably refrain from eating until after he has davened *Maariv*. If he feels the need to eat, he may do so, but he should refrain from consuming a *kebeitzah* of baked mezonos or bread. Women are permitted to eat without restriction immediately after *tzeis hakochavim*.

3. **Havdalah on Sunday Night:** When Tishah b'Av is observed on a Sunday, Havdalah must be recited before one may eat. See Chapter Ten, section 3, for details of the halachos of Havdalah.

4. **When to Recite *Kiddush Levanah*:** There are different *minhagim* regarding when the mitzvah of *Kiddush Levanah* should be performed during the month of Av. According to one *minhag*, *Kiddush Levanah* is not recited at the conclusion of Tishah b'Av (or any fast day) because it should be recited

---

1. מ"ב סי' תקנ"ג סק"ג.

with joy.[2] According to this custom, *Kiddush Levanah* should likewise not be recited during the Nine Days[3] and should be postponed instead until after Tishah b'Av.[4] Many *poskim*, however, maintain that *Kiddush Levanah* should indeed be recited on Motzaei Tishah b'Av, after one has broken the fast and put on leather shoes.[5] According to Kabbalah, *Kiddush Levanah* should be recited on Motzaei Tishah b'Av.[6] It is customary in Chassidic, Sephardic, and Yerushalmi communities, as well as in congregations that follow *nusach* Sephard, to recite *Kiddush Levanah* after *Maariv* on Motzaei Tishah b'Av.

If a person davens with a congregation whose custom is to recite *Kiddush Levanah* immediately after *Maariv*, he should recite it along with the congregation even though he will not have a chance to break his fast or change his shoes.[7]

A third *minhag* is not to postpone *Kiddush Levanah* at all but to recite it at the earliest opportunity during the month of Av.[8] (This is the practice in congregations that follow the *minhagim* of the Vilna Gaon.)

When Tishah b'Av falls on Thursday, *Kiddush Levanah* should be delayed until Motzaei Shabbos.[9]

---

2. רמ"א סי' תכ"ו ס"ב.
3. רמ"א סי' תקנ"א ס"ח.
4. מ"ב סי' תכ"ו סק"י.
5. מ"ב ס"ק י"א.
6. באר היטב סי' תכ"ו סק"ד בשם האריז"ל.
7. שעה"צ שם סק"ט. אא"כ יכול לקדש בציבור למחר.
8. מעשה רב סי' קנ"ט, ערוך השלחן סי' תכ"ו ס"ח.
9. מ"ב סק"י.

2. Restrictions on Motzaei Tishah B'Av

Introduction: The *Beis Hamikdash* was set on fire toward the end of the day on the ninth of Av, and it continued to burn throughout the tenth of Av. Although the destruction took place primarily on the tenth of Av, we mourn its destruction on the day when it began, the ninth of Av.[10] Nevertheless, it is customary to continue observing some practices of mourning on the tenth of Av as well. Ashkenazic custom, in keeping with the ruling of the Rema, calls for these halachos to be observed until *chatzos* of the tenth of Av. In general, the prohibitions are the same as those observed during the Nine Days; however, there are certain leniencies stemming from the fact that these restrictions were instituted as a *minhag* and not as a *gezeirah* of *Chazal*, as will be explained below.

1. **Meat and Wine:** The *minhag* is to abstain from the consumption of meat and wine until after midday on the tenth of Av.[11] (The *minhag* of Sephardim is to refrain from consuming meat or wine until the conclusion of the day.[12]) A person who wishes to practice a higher level of stringency should preferably abstain from meat and wine throughout the day.[13] Parve foods that were cooked together with meat may be consumed, as long as one makes sure not to consume any of the meat itself.[14] (During the Nine Days, however, even parve foods cooked with meat are prohibited for consumption.)

2. **Bathing, Haircuts, Laundering Garments, and Wearing Freshly Laundered Clothing:** The prohibition of showering and bathing, which begins during the Nine Days, remains

---

10. תענית דף כט.
11. רמ"א סי' תקנ"ח ס"א.
12. שו"ע שם. שו"ת אור לציון ח"ג פכ"ט סכ"ו.
13. עי' שע"ת שם סק"א.
14. ביה"ל ד"ה שלא לאכול בשר.

in effect until after *chatzos* on the tenth of Av. Likewise, the prohibitions to take a haircut, launder garments, and wear freshly laundered clothing remain in effect until that time.[15] (Some Sephardim do not observe these prohibitions and refrain only from consuming meat or wine.[16])

3. **Marital Relations:** Marital relations should be avoided on the night following Tishah b'Av, unless it is a *leil tevilah* or the husband has returned from a journey or will be traveling on the following day.[17]

4. **Reciting *Shehecheyanu*:** The *minhag* to refrain from reciting *shehecheyanu* after Shivah Asar b'Tammuz remains in effect until *chatzos* on the tenth of Av.[18]

5. **Music:** Playing musical instruments and listening to music is also prohibited until *chatzos*.[19]

3. Exceptions to the Prohibitions

1. **A *Seudas Mitzvah*:** It is permitted for all the guests at a *seudas mitzvah* on Motzaei Tishah b'Av to partake of meat and wine. Since this prohibition has the status of a *minhag* and was not actually instituted by *Chazal*, it is waived in the case of a *seudas mitzvah*. This is unlike the halachah pertaining to the Nine Days, when only relatives and friends are permitted

---

15. מ"ב סק"ג. ועי' בביה"ל ד"ה עד חצות היום, שאף שיש מקילים בדבר מ"מ קשה להקל. ולענין רחיצה, ראה הליכות שלמה פי"ד ס"ק כ"ו שיש להקל מחמת צער, ועי' תשובות והנהגות ח"ב סי' ר"ס שרק צריך למנוע ממים חמים.
16. שו"ע סי' תקנ"א ס"ד. שו"ת אור לציון שם.
17. מ"ב סי' תקנ"ח סק"ב.
18. שע"ת שם סק"ב.
19. עי' מ"ב שם.

to eat meat and drink wine at a *seudas mitzvah*.[20] Music is also permitted at such an occasion.[21]

2. **A Woman after Birth:** A woman within 30 days of birth who fasted on Tishah b'Av (see Chapter Eight, section 1) is permitted to eat meat (and drink wine if necessary) in order to regain her full strength.[22]

3. **Reciting *Birkas Hamazon* with a *Kos*:** If a person generally recites *birkas hamazon* over a *kos* (containing wine or grape juice) when there is a *zimun*, he may do so on Motzaei Tishah b'Av as well.[23]

4. **Extenuating Circumstances:** Under extenuating circumstances, some authorities permit bathing and laundering garments.[24] Therefore, a person who has perspired heavily and has an unpleasant odor may shower (and wear freshly laundered clothes).[25] Similarly, a person who is about to leave for a trip and requires clean clothing may launder his clothes.[26]

5. ***Kavod* Shabbos:** When Tishah b'Av falls on Thursday and the tenth of Av is Friday, these prohibitions are waived for the sake of *kavod* Shabbos. Therefore, it is permissible to take a haircut, shave, and launder garments for Shabbos.[27] Garments that are not needed for Shabbos may not be laundered at this time. Similarly, one may put on clean garments and bathe before

---

20. מ"ב שם.
21. משמעות המ"ב שם.
22. שע"ת שם.
23. ביה"ל ד"ה שלא לאכול בשר.
24. מאחר שיש מקילים לגמרי ונוקטים שהמנהג בעשירי הוא רק מבשר ויין כדאיתא בביה"ל ד"ה עד חצות.
25. תשובות והנהגות ח"ב סי' רס"ס.
26. קובץ מבית לוי עמוד ל"ח.
27. מ"ב סק"ג.

Exceptions to the Prohibitions ~ 283

chatzos only if the purpose is for Shabbos.²⁸ The consumption of meat and wine, however, remains prohibited until *chatzos*.²⁹

6. **Preparing for Shabbos on Thursday Night:** Some *poskim* maintain that the dispensation to bathe and to launder garments in honor of Shabbos comes into effect only on Friday morning,³⁰ while others permit these activities on Thursday night.³¹ There is another opinion that maintains that it is preferable to launder garments on Thursday night due to the *takanah* instituted by Ezra to always refrain from laundering on Erev Shabbos, but one should bathe only on Friday.³²

4. Conduct after a Postponed Fast

1. **Meat and Wine:** When the fast of Tishah b'Av is observed on Sunday, the tenth of Av, the prohibitions that typically apply on the day following the fast are relaxed. Nevertheless, the consumption of meat and wine remains prohibited until the following morning.³³ (This is the Ashkenazic custom; the halachah is different for Sephardim.³⁴)

2. **The Other Prohibitions:** Taking haircuts, shaving,³⁵ bathing

---

28. שש"כ פמ"ב ס"ה וס"ק ט"ז. (אבל עי' שו"ת מחזה אליהו סי' פ"ו). ודעת הגריש"א זצ"ל הוב"ד בתורת המועדים עמוד קס"ז שאם מכבסים לכבוד שבת (ומותר גם בלילה כשיש צורך) מותר להוסיף באותה מכונה גם בגדים שאינם לצורך שבת. ובשש"כ שם בתיקו"מ ובהליכות שלמה פט"ו ס"ק כ"ז כ' כאשר אין רגילים לכבס בגדים מועטים במכונה מותר להוסיף.
29. ערוך השלחן ס"ב.
30. עי' שע"ת שם וערוך השלחן שם. וכן דעת הגרמ"פ זצ"ל הוב"ל בקיצור הל' בין המצרים להגר"ש איידער זצ"ל.
31. שש"כ שם, הגריש"א זצ"ל הוב"ד תורת המועדים שם. והיינו דוקא אם הוא לכבוד שבת שלא יתרחץ עו"פ לפני שבת.
32. חוט שני.
33. רמ"א סי' תקנ"ח ס"א.
34. עי' ברכ"י סק"ב ושו"ת אור לציון ח"ג פכ"ט סכ"ו.
35. מ"ב סק"ד.

in hot water, laundering garments, and wearing freshly laundered clothes[36] are permitted immediately after the conclusion of the fast. Some *poskim*, however, prohibit playing or listening to music until the morning.[37]

3. **Havdalah on Sunday Night:** Havdalah is recited over wine or grape juice. The person reciting Havdalah may drink the wine; it is not necessary to give it to a child, even if the ninth of Av itself fell on Sunday.[38] The *brachah* of *borei meorei ha'eish* is not recited (even if one neglected or was unable to recite the *brachah* on Motzaei Shabbos), since it commemorates the creation of fire, which took place on Motzaei Shabbos. Similarly, the *brachah* on the *besamim* is omitted because it is relevant only on Motzaei Shabbos, when the *neshamah yeseirah* departs.[39] The *pesukim* typically recited before Havdalah should also be omitted.[40]

---

36. ששכ"ב פס"ב סמ"ט.
37. קיצור הלכות בין המצרים להגר"ש איידער זצ"ל. וכ"ה בלוח א"י. וכן דעת הגריש"א זצ"ל הובא בהלכות חג בחג פ"י הערה ט'.
38. שו"ע סי' תקנ"ו ס"א ובמ"ב סק"ג, אע"פ שבמוצאש"ק חזון איתא שאם יש תינוק יתן לתינוק, לילה זו קלא, שעה"צ סק"ז.
39. שו"ע שם ובמ"ב סק"ד-ה'.
40. ששכ"ב פס"ב סמ"ד.

CHAPTER TWELVE

Zecher L'churban in a Home

※

1. The Basic Obligation
2. Parameters of a *Zecher L'churban*
3. Places Requiring a *Zecher L'churban*

CHAPTER TWELVE

Zecher L'churban in a Home

Introduction: After the destruction of the *Beis Hamikdash*, *Chazal* instituted various *takanos* requiring us to limit our joy in certain ways, to serve as a constant reminder of the *churban*.[1] This is referenced in the *pasuk*, "*im lo aaleh es Yerushalayim al rosh simchasi* – if I do not remember Yerushalayim at the beginning of all my rejoicing" (*Tehillim* 137).

This chapter discusses the halachah of *zecher l'churban* – the requirement to leave a portion of a wall unfinished in a new or refurbished home in order to serve as a reminder of the destruction of the *Beis Hamikdash*. Building or renovating a home is considered an activity that generates joy, and *Chazal* required us to leave one square *amah* of a wall in a new or renovated home unfinished in order to diminish that joy. The *zecher l'churban* should be located near the entrance to the home, where it is noticeable.

Other *takanos* intended to commemorate the *churban* will be discussed in Chapter Thirteen.

1. The Basic Obligation

1. **An Unfinished Patch on a Wall:** When a home is built or renovated, an area of one square *amah* must be left unfinished

---

1. ב"ב דף ס:

on one of its walls, to commemorate the *churban* of the *Beis Hamikdash*.[2]

2. **Eretz Yisrael and the Diaspora:** This halachah is equally applicable in Eretz Yisrael and in *chutz la'Aretz*.[3]

3. **One *Zecher L'churban* for a Home:** There is no need to have a *zecher l'churban* in every room of a house. It is sufficient to leave a single area of the wall unfinished near the entrance to the house (see section 2, paragraph 5).[4]

4. **The Measurement of an *Amah*:** As noted above, the *zecher l'churban* must measure one square *amah*. Some *poskim* rule that an *amah* is equal to 48 centimeters,[5] while other halachic authorities evaluate an *amah* as a measurement of 54 centimeters[6] or 57.6 centimeters.[7] One may rely on the smaller, more lenient measurement if necessary, since this halachah is *d'rabbanan*.

5. **The Shape of the Unfinished Patch:** It is preferable for the unfinished area of the wall to be in the shape of a square, with both a length and a width of one *amah* each, rather than a rectangle with the same area.[8]

2. Parameters of a *Zecher L'churban*

1. **An Unplastered Area:** It is not sufficient to leave an area

---

2. שו"ע סי' תק"ס ס"א. והנה המחבר נקט כלשון הרמב"ם שאין בונים לעולם בנין מסויד ומכוייר כבנין המלכים וכו' כלומר דלא מהני שיור אמה לזה (עי' ב"י תחילת סי' תק"ס), ומ"מ כתב המ"ב סק"א שהמנהג כהטור דמהני שיור על אמה בכ"ג. ובלא"ה בזמננו דרך הבנייה הוי כמו טחין וסדין ולא מסיידין הכל כמלכים.

3. פשוט, דלא מצאנו פוסקים שיחלקו. וכ"ה בלוח א"י סי' כ"ג שנוהג בישוב.

4. שע"ת סק"א.

5. הגרא"ח נאה בשיעורי תורה ש"ו אות ז'.

6. שו"ת אגר"מ או"ח ח"א סי' קל"ו והוא 53.9 ס"מ, וכתב שאולי יש להחמיר 58.4 ס"מ.

7. חזו"א בשיעורין של תורה.

8. פמ"ג מ"ז סק"א וא"א סק"א, שע"ת שם. אמנם לא הובא במ"ב.

on the wall unpainted; the *zecher l'churban* must also be unplastered.[9] (It is also not sufficient to paint the walls a color that is different from the plastered square *amah*.[10])

2. **Wallpaper:** When a wall is covered with wallpaper or some other type of material rather than being plastered or painted, one must also leave an area of one square *amah* uncovered.[11]

3. **A Cement Wall:** A cement or brick wall that will not be plastered, painted, or finished in any other way does not require a *zecher l'churban*.[12]

4. **Painting the Square Black or Hanging a Sign:** Some have the custom to paint the square *amah* black and to write the words "*zecher l'churban*" in that space.[13] Although the technical requirement is to leave an area of the wall without any paint or plaster at all, there are some grounds for this custom.[14] Nevertheless, there is no halachic basis for painting this area of the wall any color other than black (the color that indicates mourning), even if the words "*zecher l'churban*" are written in the square. It is certainly not sufficient to place a sign bearing the words "*zecher l'churban*" on the wall.[15]

5. **The Placement of the *Zecher L'churban*:** The *zecher l'churban* must be on the wall opposite the doorway, so that it will be visible to someone entering the house.[16] It may also be placed above the doorway if the members of the household spend time in that area of the house and the empty square will be

---

9. עי' מ"ב סק"ב. ומש"כ שם ללמד זכות על הנוהגים היתר היינו על סיד שאינו לבן ביותר (וגם ע"ז כתב שהוא דוחק), אמנם בזמננו שהוא לבן ביותר בודאי אסור לכו"ע.
10. דלא מצינו בפוסקים שיחלקו בדבר.
11. מ"ב סק"ג.
12. מ"ב סק"ב.
13. מ"ב סק"ג ושעה"צ סק"ח.
14. שם.
15. פשוט, דהרי אפילו המקילין הוא דוקא בשחור. ועי' שו"ת אגר"מ ח"ח סי' פ"ו.
16. שו"ע שם ומ"ב סק"ג.

constantly seen.[17] However, if the family members do not spend time in that portion of the house, the *zecher l'churban* must be positioned opposite the doorway so that it will be visible to a person entering the house.[18]

6. **A House with Two Entrances:** A house with two entrances requires only one *zecher l'churban*. The *zecher l'churban* should be positioned opposite a door that is in regular use, or at least above the doorway, if the area is frequented by the occupants of the home.

3. Places Requiring a *Zecher L'churban*

1. **Residential Homes:** The obligation to leave an area of the wall unfinished applies only to a residence. A *zecher l'churban* is not required in a shul, beis midrash, yeshivah, or school.[19]

2. **Public Buildings:** There is no obligation to leave an area of the wall unfinished in a building or facility that is open to the public.[20]

3. **A Home Purchased from a Non-Jew:** If a person purchases a home without a *zecher l'churban* from a non-Jew, he is not obligated to scrape away a portion of the paint or plaster to create a *zecher l'churban*.[21] However, if he refurbishes the walls in the vicinity of the entrance to the home, he must leave

---

17. מ"ב שם.
18. כמבואר שם.
19. ביה"ל סי' תק"ס ס"א ד"ה שאין בונין. (אמנם עי' שו"ת מהר"ם בר ברוך סי' של"ג שכ' דצריך להניח אמה בביהכנ"ס.)
20. כמבואר במ"א סק"ב שהוא המקור לדברי הביה"ל הנ"ל דדוקא "ביתו", ועי' פמ"ג סק"ב. הגרח"ק שליט"א הוב"ד בתורת המועדים סי' תק"ס סק"ב. וכן עמא דבר. מיהו, עי' בשו"ת מנחת אלעזר ח"ג סי' ס"ו אות ג'. (ויש לעיין לענין סוכה שצובע אם יש חיוב לשייר אמה, דאם הטעם בבהכנ"ס משום מצוה הרי בסוכה פטור, אבל אם הטעם דלאו ביתו יש להסתפק בביתו שהוא דירת עראי. וראה לשון השע"ת.)
21. שו"ע שם.

an area unfinished.[22] Hiring non-Jewish workers to build or renovate a home does not exempt a Jewish owner from the obligation to create a *zecher l'churban*.

4. **A Home Purchased from a Jew:** If a person buys a home from another Jew and finds that a *zecher l'churban* has not been made, he is obligated to scrape away one square *amah* of the paint and plaster. If it is possible that the seller himself bought the home in its current state from a non-Jew, rather than building or refurbishing it himself, the buyer may assume that the Jewish seller had previously purchased the home from a non-Jew and therefore was not obligated to leave an unfinished area as a *zecher l'churban*. Hence, he is likewise not required to create a *zecher l'churban*.[23]

5. **A Home Intended for Sale or a Rental:** When a home is built or renovated for the purpose of being sold or rented to a tenant, the owner is not required to create a *zecher l'churban*.[24] Consequently, if a person buys a home from a Jew who built or renovated it (whether the owner is a private individual or a Jewish-owned company), he is likewise not required to fashion a *zecher l'churban*, since the seller did not have such an obligation.[25]

6. **A Rented Home:** A tenant who rents a home from a non-Jew has no obligation to create a *zecher l'churban*. If the home is rented from a Jew, the tenant is obligated to request permission to scrape away a *zecher l'churban* (unless the home was originally built or renovated to serve as a rental or was

---

22. מ"ב סק"ד.
23. שו"ע ומ"ב שם.
24. עי' שו"ת אגר"מ או"ח ח"ג סי' פ"ו. אמנם, לענין בנה להשכיר, ראה דעת הגריש"א זצ"ל והגרח"ק שליט"א הובאו בתורת המועדים עמוד קע"ו שלדעת הגריש"א זצ"ל יש חיוב על השוכר (אא"כ יצטרך לריב עם המשכיר) ולהגרח"ק שליט"א יש חיוב על המשכיר (אא"כ בנה להשכיר לגוי).
25. אגר"מ שם. ויש לעיין כשנקונה דירה בדמי קידמה pre-construction, אולי צריך לבקש שישיירו אמה על אמה בשבילו.

Places Requiring a Zecher L'churban 293

originally purchased from a non-Jew). If the owner refuses to permit this, the tenant is exempt from the obligation. If a tenant will renovate his rental apartment, he should leave a patch of wall unfinished as a *zecher l'churban*.[26]

---

26. עי׳ פמ״ג סי׳ תק״ס א״א סק״ד. וראה ארחות רבינו ח״ב עמוד קמ״ח. ובשו״ת אגר״מ שם מסיק שפטור בכ״ג.

CHAPTER THIRTEEN

Other Halachos Commemorating the *Churban*

※

1. Limitations at a *Seudah*
2. Music
3. Halachos Pertaining to a Wedding
4. Other Forms of Mourning

CHAPTER THIRTEEN

Other Halachos Commemorating the *Churban*

1. Limitations at a *Seudah*

1. **Omitting a Dish:** Another *takanah* instituted by *Chazal* to show mourning for the *churban* is the requirement to omit a food item when hosting a meal at which guests are present.[1]

2. **A Meal with Guests:** The *poskim* state that the requirement to omit a food item applies only at a festive meal attended by guests, not at an ordinary family meal.[2]

3. **Shabbos and Yom Tov Meals:** This halachah does not apply to the meals served on Shabbos and Yom Tov, for we do not engage in displays of mourning on Shabbos and Yom Tov. It does apply, however, to a *seudas mitzvah*, including a *bris*

---

1. ב״ב שם. שו״ע סי׳ תק״ס ס״ב.
2. עי׳ שו״ת שבט הלוי ח״י סי׳ פ״ה. ושם כתב ״ודבר פשוט דבנים הסמוכים על שולחן אביהם אינם בכלל זה״, ויש לעי׳ אם כוונתו דכשיש סעודה גדולה עם בנים שאינם סמוכים על שולחן אביהם שחייב לשייר.

Limitations at a Seudah ✑ 297

or wedding.³ The Purim *seudah* is not included in this obligation.⁴

4. **Omitting an Insignificant Dish:** It is not necessary to omit a main dish from the meal; one may satisfy this requirement even by omitting a dish of relatively little importance.⁵

5. **Leaving an Empty Space on the Table:** If the absence of a particular food item will not be noticeable, the place on the table that it would typically occupy should remain empty. If the omitted food is one that is generally served at meals, and its absence is therefore noticeable even without an empty space, it is not necessary to leave an empty space on the table.⁶

6. **The Contemporary Practice:** This halachah is generally not observed today. Some *poskim* justify this by explaining that the practice would not be noticeable at a meal nowadays. Since our meals do not consist of specific predetermined food items, it would not draw attention if a particular dish was omitted. Likewise, we do not have the practice of placing every food item in a consistent spot on the table; therefore, leaving an empty space on the table would likewise not draw attention.⁷

7. **Fancy Dishes:** In general, one should not place a complete array of fancy dishes on a table for display; some component of the array should be left out, as a sign of mourning over the *churban*. This halachah does not apply at the Pesach Seder.⁸

---

3. מ"ב סק"ה.
4. ראה שערי תשובה ריש סי' תרצ"ה.
5. מ"ב סק"ו.
6. עי' שו"ע שם ומ"ב סק"ז ושעה"צ ס"ק ט"ו-ט"ז.
7. עי' ביה"ל ד"ה וכן, בשם החי"א. ועי' ערוך השלחן סי' תק"ס ס"ו, וכן בכף החיים סי' תק"ס ס"ק י"ח, אבל סיים שעכ"פ יניח מקום פנוי על השולחן שיהא ניכר שהוא בבוונה. רצ"ל, שלגבי סוגי תבשילים ג"כ בזמננו אין דברים קבועים ויש כ"כ הרבה סוגים ומינים שונים שמתחלפים כל יום וכל סעודה שלא תהא ניכר החיסרון. וכמו"כ אין מקום קבוע בשלחן להנחת המאכלים אלא מונחים הכל בערבוביא ומקומות סוגי המאכלים מתחלפים.
8. ראה מ"ב סי' תע"ב סק"ו.

8. **Al Naharos Bavel:** On an ordinary weekday, one should recite the passage of *Al Naharos Bavel* before *birkas hamazon*. This passage is not recited on Shabbos, Yom Tov, or any other day when *Tachanun* is omitted, when we recite *Shir Hamaalos* instead.[9]

2. Music

1. **Playing or Listening to Music:** Another *takanah* instituted by *Chazal* to commemorate the *churban* is the prohibition to play or listen to music, which generates joy.[10] According to some *poskim*, the prohibition applies only to playing or listening to music on a regular basis or while drinking wine.[11] Other *poskim* take a more stringent view and prohibit playing or listening to music for enjoyment at any time, even if one does not drink wine. According to these *poskim*, music and singing are permitted only for work purposes (e.g., to keep a production line moving in sync, etc.).[12] One may rely on the lenient opinion.[13]

2. **While Drinking Wine:** All authorities agree that it is prohibited to listen to music or to sing while drinking wine, even if one does not do so on a regular basis. Therefore, one should not drink wine in a restaurant where music (either live or recorded) is played.[14] Nevertheless, one need not protest if others drink wine in such a setting, since some authorities

---

9. מ"ב סי' א' ס"ק י"א. והרבה נוהגים באמירת על נהרות בבל רק בימי בין המצרים או מר"ח אב עד ת"ב, וצ"ע.
10. גיטין דף ז.
11. רמ"א סי' תק"ס ס"ג. ולדעת השו"ע שם יש ב' דינים, בכלי - בין לנגן בין לשמוע - אסור בכ"ג, ושירה בפה אסור דוקא על היין.
12. מ"ב ס"ק י"ג בשם הב"ח.
13. עי' שו"ת שבט הלוי ח"ו סי' ס"ט. אמנם, מהמ"ב שם משמע שדעתו שיש לנהוג כהב"ח. ועי' שו"ת אגר"מ או"ח ח"א סי' קס"ו שבע"נ יחמיר על עצמו.
14. מ"ב ס"ק י"ב.

permit listening to music or singing while drinking wine during a meal; according to those *poskim*, the prohibition of music or singing applies only when one drinks wine outside the context of a meal.[15] At the same time, some authorities adopt an even more stringent stance and prohibit listening to music while eating in any public venue, even when one is not drinking wine at all.[16]

3. **Listening to Music at a Set Time:** Another practice that is unanimously prohibited by the *poskim* is listening to music at a consistent set time, even if it is not accompanied by the consumption of wine (as explained above in paragraph 1). Therefore, it is prohibited to listen to music every day after work, or at dinner, or every morning when one wakes up. This prohibition applies to recorded music as well.[17] Some *poskim* permit singing without musical accompaniment (even on a regular basis) when one is not drinking wine; thus, some authorities permit listening to recorded *chazzanus* even at a meal, provided that wine is not served.[18]

4. **Playing Music for Income:** It is permissible to learn to play an instrument for the purpose of earning a livelihood. Likewise, one may play an instrument as a source of income.[19] However, according to some authorities, a parent should not offer music lessons to his children solely for the sake of teaching them a skill, providing them with enjoyment, or keeping them occupied.[20]

---

15. עי' שעה"צ ס"ק כ"ג.
16. עי' שו"ת אגר"מ יו"ד ח"ב סי' קל"ז.
17. שו"ת אגר"מ שם סי' קמ"ב.
18. עי' שו"ת אגר"מ או"ח ח"א סי' קס"ו. אמנם עי' שו"ת שבט הלוי ח"ח סי' קכ"ז אות ב' שנקט שההקלטה הוי ככלי שיר.
19. שו"ת תשובות והנהגות ח"א סי' של"ג.
20. עי' שו"ת שבט הלוי ח"ו סי' ס"ט, ועי' שו"ת אגר"מ ח"ג סי' פ"ז.

5. **Singing to Praise or Thank Hashem:** Singing is permitted, even while drinking wine, if one is praising or thanking Hashem.[21] (Using *pesukim* from Tanach as lyrics in a song is always prohibited.[22] The details of this halachah are beyond the scope of this work.[23])

6. **Music at a Wedding or *Seudas Mitzvah*:** Music may be played for a mitzvah, such as at a wedding, when we rejoice with the chassan and kallah.[24] However, even at a wedding the music should not be overly joyous.[25] It is also customary to permit music at any *seudas mitzvah*.[26] The custom in Yerushalayim (which was established in later years and was not instituted by *Chazal*) is to limit music at weddings.[27]

7. **Using Music to Lift One's Spirits:** The *poskim* rule that a person who feels depressed or angry is permitted to play or listen to music in order to improve his mood, as this is considered a form of *refuah* and not merely enjoyment. Similarly, playing or listening to music to inspire oneself to greater devotion to Hashem and passion in one's *avodas Hashem* is viewed as a mitzvah and is therefore permitted.[28]

8. **Exercise and Driving:** One may listen to music while exercising.[29] One may also listen to music in order to stay awake while driving.[30]

---

21. שו"ע שם.
22. עי' מ"ב ס"ק י"ד.
23. עי' שו"ת אגר"מ יו"ד ח"ב סי' קמ"ב.
24. רמ"א שם.
25. מ"ב ס"ק ט"ז.
26. כף החיים ס"ק ל"ד, שו"ת אגר"מ או"ח ח"א סי' קס"ו. ועי' שו"ת אגר"מ שם דצ"ע אם מותר בסעודה לאסיפת צדקה.
27. עי' שו"ת שלמת חיים סי' תתפ"ט ותר"צ.
28. עי' שו"ת שבט הלוי ח"ו סי' ס"ט וח"ח סי' קס"ז.
29. נכלל במש"כ בסוטה שם והובא במ"ב שם.
30. פשוט.

Music ~ 301

9. **Singing to Put Children to Sleep:** A mother may sing to put her children to sleep.[31]

10. **A Musical Ring Tone or Door Chime:** Music may be used as a ring tone on a telephone or as a door chime. Some *poskim* prohibit using an alarm clock that wakes one up with music, since the daily use of such a clock constitutes an act of listening to music at a set time every day.[32] If one turns off the alarm clock immediately upon awakening, however, it is permitted.[33]

3. Halachos Pertaining to a Wedding

1. **Placing Ashes on a Chassan's Head:** Another *takanah* instituted by *Chazal* to commemorate the *churban* is the practice of placing ashes on a chassan's head before the *chuppah*.[34]

2. **The Placement of the Ashes:** The ashes should be placed on the spot where the chassan wears his tefillin.[35] The person placing the ashes there and the chassan recite, "*Im eshkachech Yerushalayim tishkach yemini*" (*Tehillim* 137:5).[36]

3. **Removing the Ashes before the *Chuppah*:** The standard practice is to remove the ashes before the *chuppah* takes

---

31. שעה"צ ס"ק כ"ה.
32. הליכות שלמה תפילה פי"ג סי"ח.
33. כן נראה פשוט שגם הגרשז"א זצ"ל יתיר אם אינו אלא להקיצו ע"י הקול פתאומי.
34. ב"ב דף ס:, שו"ע תק"ע ס"ב. ולשון השו"ע באבה"ע סי' ס"ה ס"ג 'צריך לתת אפר בראש החתן' משמע שאחר מניח לו (בשונה מלשונו באו"ח שם 'לוקח אפר מקלה ונותן בראשו') וכן נוהגים שהמסדר קידושין נותן האפר בראש החתן.
35. שם.
36. ט"ז סי' תק"ס סק"ד.

place.[37] Some have the custom to leave the ashes in place during the *chuppah*.

4. **Breaking a Cup:** It is customary to break a cup during the *chuppah* to commemorate the *churban*.[38] The chassan typically breaks the cup[39] while reciting the *pasuk* "*im eshkachech Yerushalayim*."[40]

5. **Using an Intact Glass:** A cup that is whole should be used for this purpose. Breaking the glass does not constitute *bal tashchis*, since it is broken for a purpose: to remind the celebrants of the *churban*.[41]

6. **Using a Glass:** It is customary to use specifically a cup made of glass for this purpose.[42]

7. **Breaking a Dish at the *Tenaim*:** Another *minhag* is to break a dish at the writing of the *tenaim*.[43] It is customary to use a dish made of porcelain or china.[44] In this case, it is preferable to use a dish that is already broken or chipped.[45]

8. **Head Adornments for a Chassan and Kallah:** Another *takanah* commemorating the *churban* is for a chassan to refrain from wearing any adornments on his head, and for a kallah to refrain from wearing adornments on her head that are made of genuine silver, gold, or precious stones.[46] If the

---

37. ערוך השלחן אבה"ע סי' ס"ה ס"ה. אמנם ראה ערוך השלחן או"ח סי' תק"ס ס"ו שכ' שבמקומו לא נהגו בהנחת אפר.
38. עי' ברכות דף לא., תוס' שם ד"ה אייתי, רמ"א תק"ס ס"ב ואבה"ע סי' ס"ה ס"ג.
39. דרכ"מ סי' תק"ס סק"ב ולשון הרמ"א באבה"ע שם.
40. ט"ז שם.
41. מ"ב סק"ט. ועי' פמ"ג מ"ז סק"ד.
42. שע"ת ס"ב. ועי' פמ"ג שם. והוא להראות שכמו שזכוכית שנשברה יש תקנה ה"ה בני ישראל בגלות.
43. מ"ב שם.
44. שע"ת שם. ועי' פמ"ג שם.
45. שעה"צ סק"כ בשם הפמ"ג שם, עי"ש.
46. משנה סוטה דף ס"ט ובגמ' שם, שו"ע סי' תק"ס ס"ד. ועי' מ"ב ס"ק י"ז-י"ח.

body of an adornment is made of a different material, some authorities permit using it even if it contains diamonds or a component made of genuine silver or gold.[47]

4. Other Forms of Mourning

1. **Omitting a Piece of Jewelry:** In order to commemorate the *churban*, *Chazal* also instituted a *takanah* requiring a woman who adorns herself with all her jewelry to leave out one piece.[48]

2. **Omitting Jewelry on Shabbos and Yom Tov:** This requirement applies even on Shabbos and Yom Tov. Even though it is not permissible to display *aveilus* on these days, the absence of a single piece of jewelry is not considered a visible display of mourning.[49]

3. **Jewelry Worn on a Daily Basis:** This halachah does not require a woman to refrain from wearing a piece of jewelry that is part of her standard attire (such as a necklace, bracelet, earrings, or rings). Rather, it simply prohibits a woman to wear all of her jewelry at once.[50] For example, a woman who owns several rings should not wear them all at once.

4. **Dressing Ostentatiously in Public:** In general, a woman should not dress in an ostentatious manner in public, since it has the potential to evoke jealousy from non-Jews and to bring about negative consequences.[51]

5. **Enjoyment without Happiness:** In general, it is permissible

---

47. מ"ב ס"ק י"ח.
48. ב"ב שם, שו"ע שם ס"ב. ותמה הח"א, הוב"ד בביה"ל ד"ה וכן, למה לא נהגו כהיום.
49. שעה"צ ס"ק י"ג.
50. כדמוכח משעה"צ הנ"ל. וראה לשון המ"ב סק"ח.
51. מ"ב סק"ח ושעה"צ ס"ק י"ח.

to relax and enjoy oneself, as long as it is not a *taanug sheyesh simchah* (a form of pleasure that generates joy).[52]

6. **Filling One's Mouth with Laughter:** In general, it is prohibited to fill one's mouth with laughter, since this can cause a person to forget the mitzvos and to commit *aveiros*.[53] This prohibition relates to involving oneself in frivolities for an extended period of time; it does not prohibit occasional laughter or humor.[54] Even when observing mitzvos involving joy, such as on the holidays of Chanukah and Purim, a person should not fill his mouth with laughter.[55]

---

52. מ"ב סק"י בשם המ"א עפ"י הגמ' בשבת דף סב.
53. שו"ע שם ס"ה ובמ"ב סק"כ. ועי' כף החיים סק"מ בשם תנא דבי אליהו שמביא חרון אף לעולם והפירות מתמעטין ע"י ורעות רבות באות ע"י.
54. ערוך השלחן סי' תק"ס ס"ח.
55. מ"ב שם בשם הט"ז.

Other Forms of Mourning ∾ 305

CHAPTER FOURTEEN

The Halachos of *Kriah*

❦

1. Rending One's Garments for Yerushalayim and the *Makom Hamikdash*
2. The Procedure for *Kriah*
3. Exemptions from Performing *Kriah*

CHAPTER FOURTEEN

The Halachos of *Kriah*

1. Rending One's Garments for Yerushalayim and the *Makom Hamikdash*

1. **The Obligation to Perform *Kriah*:** A person who sees the Old City of Yerushalayim in ruins should recite the words *"Tzion midbar hayasah Yerushalayim shemamah"* and should perform *kriah*.[1] (The exact procedure for *kriah* will be discussed in the following section.)

2. **Tearing *Kriah* upon Seeing the Old City Today:** Although the Old City of Yerushalayim no longer lies in ruins and is not under the jurisdiction of non-Jews, many *poskim* rule that one must still perform *kriah* upon seeing it, either since a non-Jewish presence remains in Yerushalayim (i.e., the churches and mosques),[2] or because the city is controlled by non-religious authorities.[3] Nevertheless, other *poskim* argue that there is no obligation to perform *kriah* nowadays,

---

1. שו"ע סי' תקס"א ס"ב. ובענין הרואה ערי יהודה, שו"ע שם ס"א, עי' ספר ארץ ישראל סי' כ"ב שאין נוהגים לקרוע היום שאין יודעים בדיוק גבולותיהן של ערי יהודה ועוד שהרי כשבאים לירושלים מצד מערב פוגעין תחילה בירושלים לפני שאר ערי יהודה. ועי' שע"ת סי' תקס"א בענין העיר חברון.
2. שו"ת מנחת שלמה ח"א סוף סי' ע"ג. והחזו"א זצ"ל נהג לקרוע בשער יפו, הובא באראחות רבינו ח"ב עמוד קמ"ח.
3. שו"ת שבט הלוי ח"ז סי' ע"ח. ועי' מועדים וזמנים ח"ה סי' שמ"ח.

Rending One's Garments for Yerushalayim and the Makom Hamikdash ∽ 309

since Yerushalayim has been rebuilt and is under Jewish jurisdiction.[4]

3. **Tearing *Kriah* at the Site of the *Beis Hamikdash*:** Upon seeing the location of the *Beis Hamikdash* (see below regarding the exact parameters), one should bow and recite the words, "*Beis kodsheinu v'sifarteinu asher hilelucha avoseinu hayah l'sreifas eish, v'chol machamadeinu hayah lecharbah*" (*Yeshayah* 64:10), followed by the performance of *kriah*,[5] while reciting the words "*baruch dayan emes.*"[6] One then declares, "*ki chol derachav mishpat, Keil emunah v'ein avel tzaddik v'yashar hu, v'Atah tzaddik al kol haba aleinu ki emes asisa va'anachnu hirshanu.*" Finally, one should recite *perek* 79 of *Tehillim* while mourning the *churban*.[7]

4. **Performing *Kriah* from Afar:** The obligation to perform *kriah* upon seeing the site of the *Beis Hamikdash* or the city of Yerushalayim is limited to when one sees these locations clearly and up close. Viewing the sites from a distance does not trigger the requirement to perform *kriah*.[8]

5. **The *Kosel Hamaaravi*:** There is a dispute among the *poskim* as to whether a person must tear *kriah* upon seeing the Kosel Hamaaravi, since the Kosel is one of the walls of *Har Habayis*, rather than a wall of the *azarah*. Some *poskim* rule that one should perform *kriah* only upon seeing the floor of the *azarah*[9] (which is visible from *Har Hazeisim* to the east or from some elevated areas in the Old City to the west) or upon seeing

---

4. שו"ת אגר"מ או"ח ח"ד סי' ע' אות י"א וח"ה סי' ל"ז. ובשו"ת שבט הלוי הביא שם מסיק שהמנהג לא לקרוע.
5. שו"ע שם ובמ"ב סק"ו.
6. מ"ב שם. ובשו"ת אגר"מ יו"ד ח"ג סי' קכ"ט אות ה' כתב שיכול להזכיר מלכות ויאמר ברוך אתה ה' מלך העולם דיין האמת.
7. מ"ב שם.
8. מ"ב סק"ג ו'. וכדעת המ"א עפ"י תוס' פסחים דף מט. ד"ה אם, שא"צ מקום על שם צופים דוקא.
9. ראה ס' עיר הקודש והמקדש ח"ג פ"ב. ועי' תשובות והנהגות ח"א סי' של"א.

310 ~ Chapter Fourteen: *The Halachos of Kriah*

the Dome of the Rock[10] (which is visible from the descent to the Kosel). However, other *poskim* rule that *kriah* should be performed even upon seeing the Kosel itself.[11] (This is the common practice, although generally a visitor to the Kosel will also see the Dome of the Rock anyway.)

6. **Seeing Both the Old City and the *Makom Hamikdash*:** When a person first sees the Old City of Yerushalayim before arriving at the site of the *Beis Hamikdash*, he should make a tear in his garment, the length of a *tefach*, to commemorate the destruction of Yerushalayim. Then, upon seeing the *makom hamikdash*, he should tear an additional *tefach*, at a distance of the breadth of three fingers from the first tear. If he arrives in Yerushalayim from the opposite direction and sees the *makom hamikdash* before seeing the Old City of Yerushalayim (e.g., if he visits *Har Hazeisim* first), he should merely make a small tear upon seeing Yerushalayim.[12] (A person may postpone tearing until he reaches the *makom hamikdash* and only tear once, but he should preferably close his eyes when entering the Old City.[13]) However, as noted in paragraph 2 above, some *poskim* rule that the requirement today is to perform *kriah* only upon seeing the *makom hamikdash* and not for the Old City of Yerushalayim.

7. ***Kriah* for Women:** Women are also obligated to perform *kriah*.[14] She should wear two garments and tear the outer one.

---

10. כן איתא בב"ח סי' תקס"א, וס' ארץ ישראל סי' כ"ב. וע" מועדים וזמנים ח"ז סי' רנ"ז.
11. כן איתא בב"ח שם, ארחות רבינו ח"ב עמוד קמ"ח-קמ"ט בשם החזו"א והגרייי"ק זצ"ל, שו"ת אגר"מ או"ח ח"ד סי' ע' אות י"א.
12. שו"ע שם ס"ב ובמ"ב סק"ח-ט'.
13. ארחות רבינו ח"ב עמוד קמ"ח בשם הגרייי"ק זצ"ל.
14. עיי"ש עמוד קמ"ט.

8. **Kriah for Children:** There is no requirement for a child to perform *kriah*, even for the purpose of *chinuch*.[15] Children who have reached the age of bar or bas mitzvah are required to perform *kriah* even though their garments are technically owned by their fathers.[16]

9. **Performing *Kriah* Once in 30 Days:** The obligation to perform *kriah* is limited to once in 30 days.[17] See section 3 for further details.

2. The Procedure for *Kriah*

1. **How to Tear the Garment:** *Kriah* must be performed while one is standing and without the use of a tool such as a knife or scissors.[18] (However, one may begin an incision with a knife or scissors and then tear the required *tefach* with one's hands.)

2. **Tearing a Garment Next to the Heart:** *Kriah* should be performed on the front of the garment, next to the heart. Therefore, the tear should be made on the left side of the chest.[19]

3. **Tearing the Outermost Garment:** Technically, the halachah requires a person to tear all his layers of clothing until he reveals his heart.[20] However, *kriah* is not required on an

---

15. שם עמוד קנ״ד בשם הגריי״ק זצ״ל.
16. תשובות והנהגות ח״ה סי׳ קס״ה. ועי׳ בתורת המועדים עמוד קפ״ו שהסתפק הגרח״ק שליט״א באופן שלא ידוע להאב שבנו הולך להכותל.
17. שו״ע שם ס״ה.
18. שו״ע שם ס״ד, מ״ב ס״ק י״ב. אמנם ראה שו״ת אבן ישראל ח״ח סי׳ מ״ג שיש להקל לקרוע בכלי. וראה ספר א״י סי׳ כ״ב.
19. שו״ע שם ומ״ב ס״ק י״ג.
20. שו״ע שם. וכל הנ״ל הוא כדין קריעה על אביו ואמו.

undershirt[21] or *tzitzis*.[22] Furthermore, the *minhag* is to tear only the outermost layer of clothing, i.e., a jacket or shirt.[23] A person may remove his jacket first and tear only his shirt.[24] It is not necessary to remove a coat, since many *poskim* maintain that a coat does not require *kriah*.[25]

4. **Wearing an Old Garment:** One may intentionally wear an old jacket or shirt while visiting these locations in order to avoid tearing a more valuable article of clothing.[26] In keeping with the aforementioned custom of tearing only the outermost layer of clothing, one may wear the old shirt on top of one's regular shirt and tear only the old shirt.

5. **Tearing the Same Garment Twice:** A garment that was already torn when one visited the Old City or the *makom hamikdash* may be used for *kriah* on subsequent visits. In this case, it is necessary only to slightly enlarge the existing tear. A garment that was torn after the passing of a relative may also be worn for this purpose, but a complete *kriah* of one *tefach* should be performed.[27]

6. **Repairing the Tear:** After performing *kriah*, one may never completely repair the tear. However, beginning on the day after the *kriah*, one may sew the tear in a non-professional manner, with uneven stitches, so that the damage remains noticeable.[28] (A woman may sew the tear on the same day in a non-professional manner.)

---

21. רמ"א יו"ד סי' ש"מ ס"י.
22. תשובות והנהגות ח"א סי' של"א.
23. ספר ארץ ישראל סי' כ"ב ס"ד, מנחת שלמה סי' ע"ג אות א', שו"ת אבן ישראל ח"ח סי' מ"ג, תשובות והנהגות ח"א סי' של"א.
24. תשובות והנהגות ח"א סי' של"א. ובכך יוצא העיקר הדין שהרי קרע כל בגדיו ובבגדי זיעה וציצית א"צ קריעה.
25. ט"ז יו"ד סי' ש"מ סק"ה, ואפי' לפי הש"ך שם סק"כ ונקוה"כ שם י"ל שא"צ לקרוע.
26. גליון מהרש"א יו"ד סי' ש"מ ס"ט.
27. תורת המועדים עמוד קפ"ג בשם הגרח"ק שליט"א בשם חמיו הגריש"א זצ"ל.
28. שו"ע סי' תקס"א ובמ"ב ס"ק י"ד-ט"ו. וביו"ד סי' ש"מ סל"ט, ובדין קורע על אביו ואמו.

3. Exemptions from Performing *Kriah*

1. **Shabbos and Yom Tov:** On Shabbos and Yom Tov, one does not perform *kriah*.

2. **Erev Shabbos and Erev Yom Tov:** *Poskim* discuss whether one is required to perform *kriah* after midday on Erev Shabbos or Erev Yom Tov. Some rule that there is no obligation. Others, however, disagree.[29]

3. **Chol Hamoed:** On Chol Hamoed, one is not obligated to perform *kriah*.[30]

4. **Days When *Tachanun* Is Omitted:** The common custom is to refrain from performing *kriah* on a day when *Tachanun* is omitted.[31] However, some *poskim* maintain that there is an obligation to perform *kriah* even on such a day.[32]

5. **A Person Who Has Seen the Locations within the Past 30 Days:** As mentioned in section 1, paragraph 9, a person who has seen the Old City of Yerushalayim or the *makom hamikdash* within 30 days is exempt from performing *kriah*. If he was exempt from performing *kriah* on his previous visit (e.g., he visited these locations on Shabbos or Yom Tov), many *poskim* rule that he is nonetheless exempt from performing *kriah* if he visits the location again within 30 days.[33] Some

---

29. ראה סי׳ ארץ ישראל סי׳ כ״ב סי״א, ספר עמק ברכה עמוד קנ״ג, שו״ת אגר״מ או״ח ח״ה סי׳ ל״ז אות ב׳, ועי״ש יו״ד ח״ג סי׳ נ״ב אות ד׳ אם לבוש בגדי שבת. אמנם, בתשובות והנהגות ח״א סי׳ של״ד הביא שהחזו״א צווח על הנוהגים להקל. וכן הובא בארחות רבינו סוף עמוד קמ״ט שהורה החזו״א שמחוייבים לקרוע בע״ש אחר חצות.
30. ס׳ ארץ ישראל שם, ארחות רבינו שם בשם הגריי״ק זצ״ל.
31. הליכות שלמה תפילה פט״ז הערה 17 (אבל כתב שאין לזה מקור בדברי הפוסקים).
32. דעת החזו״א הובא בארחות רבינו ח״ב עמוד קמ״ט שבר״ח ובשאר ימים שא״א תחנון חייב לקרוע.
33. כן משמע מהמ״ב ס״ק י״ז, מנחת שלמה סי׳ ע״ג אות ח׳, וכן נהגין כמוש״כ ס׳ הערות מו״ק דף כ: בשם הגריש״א זצ״ל.

authorities disagree and obligate a person to perform *kriah* in such a case, since he did not do so on his previous visit.[34]

6. **A Child who Turns Bar or Bas Mitzvah:** A child who becomes bar or bas mitzvah within 30 days after seeing the Old City or the *makom hamikdash* is still exempt from performing *kriah* for the duration of the 30 days, even though the obligation of *kriah* takes effect only when a child reaches adulthood.[35]

7. **A Person Who Forgot to Perform *Kriah*:** A person who forgets to perform *kriah* and realizes his mistake only after leaving the area is not required to perform *kriah* even if he remembers later on the same day.[36] Furthermore, if he returns to the area within 30 days, many *poskim* rule that he is exempt from performing *kriah*, even though he did not perform the procedure on his previous visit.[37] According to the authorities cited in paragraph 5 above, who obligate a person to perform *kriah* upon seeing the Old City or the *makom hamikdash* within 30 days if he was exempt from *kriah* on his previous visit, the obligation to perform *kriah* would certainly apply in this case as well.

8. **A Resident of Yerushalayim:** Technically, a person who lives in Yerushalayim but did not see the *makom hamikdash* within 30 days is obligated to perform *kriah*. However, some *poskim* maintain that a person who lives in the Old City of Yerushalayim may be lenient in this regard and need not perform *kriah* when he visits the *makom hamikdash*.[38] Some

---

34. שו"ת אגר"מ יו"ד ח"ג סי' נ"ב אות ד'.
35. מ"ב ס"ק י"ז.
36. כן מצדד מנחת שלמה שם (מיהו ראה הליכות שלמה שם סכ"ו שכל עוד שיש לו שעת חימום חייב לקרוע), וכן מסיק בשו"ת אגר"מ או"ח ח"ה סי' ל"ז, ועי' הערות מהגריש"א זצ"ל מו"ק דף כו. ועי' תשובות והנהגות ח"ד סי' קל"א בשם החזו"א.
37. מנחת שלמה שם.
38. עי' שע"ת סי' תקס"א בשם הרדב"ז והברכ"י. וראה ס' ארץ ישראל סי' כ"ב ס"ט.

Exemptions from Performing Kriah ∽ 315

poskim rule further that anyone who lives anywhere in Yerushalayim, even outside the Old City, is exempt from *kriah*.[39]

9. **Transferring Ownership of One's Clothing:** Some *poskim* discuss whether a person can exempt himself from *kriah* by transferring ownership of his clothing to someone else (using a "*kinyan chalifin*" or "*kinyan sudar*," after which he "borrows" the garments back) so that his clothes no longer belong to him and he is therefore not entitled to tear his garments. However, it is not proper to exempt oneself from this obligation.[40]

Many *poskim* maintain that a person does not become exempt from the obligation of *kriah* by transferring ownership of his clothing to someone else.[41]

---

39. הליכות שלמה תפילה פכ״ג ס״ק מ״ד והערה 116 בשם הגרשז״א זצ״ל. וראה מש״כ במעדני שלמה עמוד נ״ח בשם הגרשז״א זצ״ל. ועי׳ תשובות והנהגות ח״ה סי׳ קס״ה. אמנם דעת הגריש״א זצ״ל הוב״ד בתורת המועדים עמוד קפ״ז שבודאי לא נאמר על השכונות הרחוקות.

40. עי׳ שו״ת שבט הלוי ח״ז סי׳ ע״ח. ועי׳ שו״ת אבן ישראל ח״ח סי׳ מ״ג שדן לענין להפקיר בגדיו בפני שלשה שהרי יהא מחוייב לזכות בה כדי לקיים המצוה ומסיק שאינו מועיל.

41. דעת הגריש״א זצ״ל בהערות שם דף כו:, שו״ת אור לציון ח״ג פ״ל ס״ה, ועי׳ מועדים וזמנים ח״ז סי׳ רנ״ז, וכן דעת הגרח״ק שליט״א הוב״ד בתורת המועדים עמוד קפ״ז שאינו מועיל להפקיר שהרי אין דין קריעה דוקא על בגד שלו ובגד זה מותר לקורעו מפני שהוא הפקר. וראה מש״כ במעדני שלמה עמוד ס׳ בשם הגרשז״א זצ״ל.

INDEX

Usage note: This comprehensive index is not intended to indicate the halachah in any particular case, but to allow the reader to find the place in this sefer that discusses that halachah. Please make sure to look up the referenced citations to see a full discussion of each topic.

A

a capella
   see music

ahavah rabbah/ahavas olam
   birchos haTorah, fulfilling obligation of by reciting, 120

ahavas olam
   birchos haTorah, fulfilling obligation of after daytime sleep by reciting, 121

Akdamus Milin
   Shavuos morning, recited, 104

alarm clock
   waking up with to music, 302

alcoholic beverages
   sefiras haomer, imbibing before counting, 39

Aleinu
   sefiras haomer, reciting before, 17

aliyah l'regel
   commemorating by visiting Kosel, 108

allergy
   Nine Days, eating poultry during because of, 193

al mitzvas tzitzis
   Tishah b'Av, reciting on, 258

alos hashachar
   birchos hashachar, reciting beforehand, 123
   hanosein lasechvi vinah, reciting beforehand, 123-124
   kiyor passage of *Korbanos*, reciting before, 124
   korban tamid passage of *Korbanos*, reciting before, 124
   netilas yadayim beforehand, if needs to be repeated, 115-116
   sefiras haomer, counting until, 24
   Shavuos night, eating or drinking after, 113
   Shivah Asar b'Tammuz, eating or drinking before, 141
   studying Torah after, before *birchos haTorah*, 120

Index ⟿ 317

studying Torah after, before washing hands, 116

terumas hadeshen passage of *Korbanos*, reciting before, 124

amah
   measurement of, 290

Aneinu
   ate by mistake, reciting, 143, 152
   Behab, reciting on, 82
   child reciting, 152
   fast days, reciting on, 149-150, 151-152
   not fasting, if recited, 143, 152, 256
   omitted by *shaliach tzibbur* erroneously, 150, 257
   omitted erroneously, 151, 257
   shaliach tzibbur and congregation fasting in order to recite, 150
   Tishah b'Av, reciting on, 257

anger
   music, using to calm, 301

anointing
   Tishah b'Av, children required in avoiding, 231-232
   Tishah b'Av, cream, using on, 230-231
   Tishah b'Av, deodorant, using on, 231
   Tishah b'Av, Erev Tishah b'Av coinciding with Shabbos, 214
   Tishah b'Av, insect repellent, using on, 231
   Tishah b'Av, irritated skin, putting cream on, 231
   Tishah b'Av, kallah, exception for, 231
   Tishah b'Av, makeup, using on, 230, 231
   Tishah b'Av, oil, using on, 230-231
   Tishah b'Av, perfume, using on, 230
   Tishah b'Av, prohibition of, 230-231
   Tishah b'Av, prohibition of begins at, 211, 214
   Tishah b'Av, soap, using on, 230-231
   Tishah b'Av, sunscreen, using on, 231

antibiotics
   fasting while still taking, 145

Asarah b'Teves
   bathing on, 147
   Friday, when falls out on, 149
   neviim instituted, 139
   nursing women fasting on, 143
   objective of, 139
   pregnant women fasting on, 143
   showering on, 147
   see fast day

Aseres Hadibros
   Shavuos morning, reading on, 104
   standing for reading of, 104

asher yatzar
   reciting after sleepless night, 115

ashes
   seudah hamafsekes, dipping bread in at, 208
   wedding, placing on chassan's head at, 302

Ashkenazim
   cutting hair of Sephardic person during Three Weeks period, 158
   Nine Days period, observed as mourning, 163-164
   reciting *brachah* on *mitzvas aseh shehazman grama*, 6
   sefirah period, when observed, 62-63
   sefiras haomer, inserting "*laomer*" or "*baomer*", 13
Atah chonantanu
   Tishah b'Av that is also Motzaei Shabbos, if forgotten, 274
aufruf
   Erev Tishah b'Av on Shabbos, celebrating on, 213-214
   Nine Days period, wearing freshly laundered clothing in honor of, 181
   sefirah period, chassan cutting hair or shaving before, 58
Australia
   mashiv haruach, when recited in, 74-75
aveilus
   Lag Baomer, being *shaliach tzibbur* on, 68
   Nine Days period, when *shloshim* ended during, 175
   sefirah period, haircut after *shloshim* during, 59
   Shabbos, when Tishah b'Av follows, 269
   Tishah b'Av, being *shaliach tzibbur* on, 253
   Tishah b'Av, *shivah* coinciding with, going to shul, 254
   see kriah, onen, zecher l'churban
avel
   see aveilus
Av Harachamim
   Erev Tishah b'Av, reciting on, 201, 268
   Rosh Chodesh, reciting on, 78
   sefirah period, recited during, 78
   Shabbos Mevarchim, reciting on, 78
   Shavuos, reciting on, 107
Avinu Malkeinu
   Behab, omitting on when coincides with Pesach Sheni, 83
   fast days, reciting on, 150-151
   Tishah b'Av, omitted on, 252, 258
Avos U'banim
   Erev Tishah b'Av on Shabbos, holding program on, 203

B
bal tashchis
   uprooting fruit tree prohibited because of, 134
bal tosif
   omitting words in *sefirah's Leshem Yichud* because of, 16
baomer
   concluding *sefirah* recitation with, 12-13
barber
   Three Weeks period, servicing non-Jewish customer, 159

Index ༳ 319

barley

   chadash considerations for, 94

bar mitzvah

   18th of Tammuz on Sunday, fasting when on, 142

   kriah after, when saw Yerushalayim or *makom hamikdash* within 30 days, 315

   Nine Days period, meat and wine at *seudah* for, 192

   Nine Days period, wearing fresh clothes in honor of, 181

   sefirah period, haircut for, 58

   sefirah period, music and dancing at, 49

   sefirah period, occurring during regarding counting with *brachah*, 7

   sefirah period, *seudah* for during, 56

   Tishah b'Av, receiving *aliyah* on in honor of, 255

baruch hamavdil bein kodesh l'chol

   Tishah b'Av after Shabbos, reciting, 270

Baruch She'amar

   Tishah b'Av, *tzitzis*, holding during recitation of, 258

bas mitzvah

   kriah after, when saw Yerushalayim or *makom hamikdash* within 30 days, 315

   sefirah period, haircut for, 58

bathing

   Asarah b'Teves, on, 147

   Motzaei Tishah b'Av, on, 281-282, 284-285

   Nine Days period, *chafifah* during, 194-195

   Nine Days period, children, 197

   Nine Days period, cold water for, 194

   Nine Days period, dirt, cleansing from, 195-196

   Nine Days period, during, 193-198

   Nine Days period, eighth of Av on Erev Shabbos, 198

   Nine Days period, Erev Shabbos Chazon, 197

   Nine Days period, Erev Shabbos on Rosh Chodesh, 197

   Nine Days period, lukewarm water, using, 196

   Nine Days period, medical reasons requiring, 194

   Nine Days period, *mikveh* during, 194-195

   Nine Days period, mitzvah purpose for, 194-195

   Nine Days period, perspiration, cleansing from, 195-196

   Nine Days period, shampoo, using for, 196

   Nine Days period, soap, using for, 196

   Nine Days period, sponge or washcloth, using for, 196

   sefirah period, during, 60

   Shivah Asar b'Tammuz, on, 147

   see mikveh, showering, washing

bedding
  Nine Days period, laundering during, 170
  Nine Days period, using freshly laundered during, 176, 179
beer
  chadash considerations for, 94
  Havdalah before eating on Tishah b'Av, making with, 273
  Nine Days period, drinking during, 189
  Nine Days period, Havdalah, using for, 190
  seudah hamafsekes, drinking at, 205
Behab
  accepting on oneself to fast on, 81
  Aneinu, reciting on, 82
  custom of fasting on after Pesach, 80-81
  feeling unwell during, 82-83
  Krias HaTorah portion for, 82
  mi shebeirach, recited in shul for those participating in, 81
  Selichos, reciting on, 82
  seudas mitzvah, breaking fast to participate in, 82-83
bein hametzarim
  see Three Weeks
bein hashemashos
  sefiras haomer, counting during, 18, 21
  sefiras haomer, counting on Erev Shabbos during, 21

sefiras haomer, remembered yesterday's count during, 28
beis hakevaros
  see cemetery
Beis Hamikdash
  Al Naharos Bavel, reciting before *birkas hamazon* to commemorate, 299
  dish, omitting at *seudah* to show mourning for loss of, 297-298
  jewelry, not wearing all at once to commemorate destruction of, 304
  kriah, performing in remembrance of, 309-316
  music, limiting in commemoration of *churban* of, 299-302
  Nine Days period, abstaining from meat and wine to commemorate destruction of, 186
  sefiras haomer, praying for rebuilding of after, 16
  singing, limiting in commemoration of *churban* of, 299-302
  Three Weeks period, mourning destruction of during, 163
  Tishah b'Av commemorates destruction of and plowing of site of, 219
  weddings, minimizing joy at in commemoration of destruction of, 302-304
  zecher l'churban, obligation of, 289-293
  see kriah, music, singing, weddings, *zecher l'churban*

Index ∽ 321

beis midrash
   zecher l'churban, if required, 292
Beitar
   Tishah b'Av commemorates destruction of, 219
besamim
   Havdalah after Tishah b'Av, at, 272
   Tishah b'Av, smelling on, 241, 261, 272
birchas hamitzvos
   standing during recitation of, 9
birchos hashachar
   after sleeping in the morning, 124
   after staying awake all night, 123
   before *alos hashachar*, 123
   before midnight, reciting, 124
   see Korbanos
birchos haTorah
   after daytime nap, 120-121, 122
   after staying awake all night, 119-120
   after waking up during night, 122
   reciting mentally, 121
   repeating after recited at night, 122
   sheinas keva necessitating recitation of, 120
   Torah study before hearing, after *alos hashachar*, 120
   see birchos hashachar
birkas hamazon
   Al Naharos Bavel, reciting before on weekdays, 299
   Erev Tishah b'Av, after *shekiah*, 214

   Motzaei Tishah b'Av, with *kos*, 283
   Nine Days period, using wine for, 190
   retzei recited in following *sefiras haomer* at *seudah shelishis*, 23
   Tishah b'Av, *Nacheim* added on, 256-257
   see retzei, zimun
birkas kohanim
   Tishah b'Av, washing hands before, 228
b'iyun
   Erev Tishah b'Av, studying Torah, 204
blood drawing
   Erev Shavuos, refraining from on, 99
bonfire
   see fire
borei atzei besamim
   made on fragrant plants, 134
borei isvei besamim
   made on fragrant plants, 134
borei meorei ha'eish
   benefiting from flame when recited, 271
   sitting when recited, 271
   Tishah b'Av after Shabbos, when recited, 271, 272
   Tishah b'Av after Shabbos, women reciting, 272
   women reciting, 271-272
   see Havdalah

brachah

brachah acharonah, when snacking intermittently, 110-111

brachah rishonah, when snacking intermittently, 110

cheesecake, *rishonah* and *acharonah* on, 131-132

Eichah, reciting on, 250

flowers, made on inhaling scent of, 134

hagomel, on Tishah b'Av, 255

hesech hadaas, necessitates new recitation of, 110-111

location changing, necessitates new recitation of, 110, 112

netilas yadayim, reciting on after sleepless night, 113-116

Megillas Rus, reciting on, 106

shiur ikul, new *brachah acharonah* required after it passes, 110-111

snacking intermittently, when water, when not thirsty for, 210

see al mitzvas tzitzis, birchas hamitzvos, birchos hashachar, birchas haTorah, birkas hamazon, borei meorei ha'eish, brachah levatalah, Elokai neshamah, hamaavir sheinah, hanosein lasechvi vinah, hatov vehameitiv, hefsek, hesech hadaas, sefiras haomer: brachah, she'asah li kol tzorki, shehecheyanu

brachah levatalah

when teaching child, 7

brachah she'einah tzrichah

seudah hamafsekes, avoiding when planning, 210

bread

using for both milk and meat meals, 126-127, 130

bride

see kallah

bris milah

Behab, eating at during, 82-83

Erev Tishah b'Av, on, 201, 213

Nine Days period, *seudah* for, 190-191, 201-202

Nine Days period, wearing fresh garments in honor of, 181

Nine Days period, wine for, child drinking, 190

sefirah period, haircuts for participants in, 58

sefirah period, music and dancing at, 49

sefirah period, *seudah* for, 56

sefirah period, *shehecheyanu* recited at, 55

Shivah Asar b'Tammuz, celebrants of fasting on, 143

tenth of Av on Sunday, procedure for, 262-263

Tishah b'Av, procedure for, 260-263

Tishah b'Av, *seudah* for at night, 263

Tishah b'Av, wearing fresh garments in honor of, 262

bus

Tishah b'Av, sitting in during, 242

business
> Nine Days period, conducting during, 165-166
> Tishah b'Av, conducting on, 244
> *see* work

C

candles
> Lag Baomer, lighting on, 71
> Shavuos night, when lit, 100-101

car
> Tishah b'Av, sitting in during, 242
> *see* driving

cemetery
> Tishah b'Av, visiting on, 254

chadash
> barley, 94
> beer, 94
> *chutz la'Aretz*, if prohibited in, 90-92
> definition of, 88, 89
> Eretz Yisrael, no leniency applies, 92-93
> grains, times when commonly prohibited, 94
> guide to common situations of, 93-95
> malt, 94
> oats, 94
> prohibition of, 87
> rye, 94
> spelt, 94
> uncertain, determining status of, 89, 95
> vessels used for baking, status of, 89-90
> wheat, 94
> *see yashan*

chafifah
> Nine Days period, performing during, 194-195
> Shivah Asar b'Tammuz, performing on, 147
> Tishah b'Av, when performed when using *mikveh* after, 229

chair
> Tishah b'Av, bus, sitting or standing while on, 242
> Tishah b'Av, car, sitting on regular one while traveling, 242
> Tishah b'Av, elderly person sitting in regular one, 242
> Tishah b'Av, *hagbaah* performer sits in regular one, 242
> Tishah b'Av, pregnant woman sitting in regular one, 242
> Tishah b'Av, prohibition of sitting in begins at, 211
> Tishah b'Av, sitting on low one during, 241-243
> Tishah b'Av, woman after childbirth, sitting in regular one, 242

challah
> *see* bread

chanukas habayis
> Nine Days period, meat and wine at, 192

chassan
- ashes, placing on head before *chuppah*, 302-303
- head adornments for, limiting, 303-304
- Isru Chag, fasting on, 108
- Lag Baomer, fasting on, 69
- *sefirah* period, haircut and shave before *aufruf*, 58
- Shivah Asar b'Tammuz, fasting on, 143

chassidim
- *sefiras haomer*, counting after Seder, 17

chatzos
- *birchos hashachar*, reciting before during night, 124
- tenth of Av, restrictions of extending to, 281-282
- waking up before, if *birchos haTorah* required, 122

chazzanus
- listening to at a meal, 300

cheese
- cheddar, eating meat after, 128
- hard, eating meat after, 128
- Parmesan, eating meat after, 128
- Swiss, eating meat after, 128
- see cheesecake

cheesecake
- *brachah acharonah* on, 131-132
- *brachah rishonah* on, 131

chicken
- napping after meal of, eating dairy earlier, 130
- same as meat regarding eating dairy after, 129
- *see* poultry

children
- *Aneinu*, reciting on fast day, 152
- Bar mitzvah during *sefirah* period, 7
- fasting on final three of childhood, 142
- haircut for, first on Lag Baomer, 71
- Havdalah, waiting for before eating on Tishah b'Av, 225, 273
- *kriah*, performing, 312
- music lessons for, 300
- Nine Days period, bathing during, 197
- Nine Days period, crafts, buying for, 165
- Nine Days period, laundering clothing for, 174-175
- Nine Days period, meat and wine for during, 192-193
- Nine Days period, toys, buying for, 165
- *sefirah* period, cutting hair during, 57
- *sefirah* period, music during for, 50, 51-52
- *sefiras haomer* and, 6-7
- *sefiras haomer*, if fulfilled when helping child with, 34
- Shivah Asar b'Tammuz, fasting on, 141-142
- singing to sleep, 302
- Tishah b'Av, anointing on, 231-232

Index ∽ 325

Tishah b'Av, eating before Havdalah, 225
Tishah b'Av, fasting on, 225
Tishah b'Av, food, preparing for on, 255
Tishah b'Av, holding on, 243
Tishah b'Av, playing with on, 243
Tishah b'Av, shoes on for, 234
Tishah b'Av, Torah study on, 236-237
Tishah b'Av, washing for bread on, 226, 228
Tishah b'Av, washing on, 231-232

chinuch
children's obligation in fasting on Shivah Asar b'Tammuz, 141-142
children's obligation in *sefiras haomer*, 6-7
sefirah period, children's obligation regarding cutting hair, 57
Three Weeks period, children's obligation regarding cutting hair, 159

choleh
see illness

Chol Hamoed
kriah not performed on, 314
sefirah period, music and dancing during on, 52

chukos hagoyim
trees in home or shul question of, 134-135

chuppah
see wedding

churban
see Beis Hamikdash, kriah, zecher l'churban

cleaners
see laundering: Nine Days period

clothing
Nine Days period, buying during, 165, 168, 184, 185
Nine Days period, delivered during but bought before, 184
Nine Days period, exchanging at store during, 185
Nine Days period, eyeglasses buying or repairing during, 185
Nine Days period, laundering during, 170-175
Nine Days period, laundering for Shabbos during, 173
Nine Days period, making, 182
Nine Days period, mending, 183
Nine Days period, non-Jew sewing, 182-183
Nine Days period, preparing for use during, 177-178
Nine Days period, returning to store during, 185
Nine Days period, sewing during, 182-183
Nine Days period, using freshly laundered during, 176-182
Nine Days period, using new during, 176
sefirah period, for bride and groom, 55
sefirah period, *shehecheyanu* on during, 54, 55

Three Weeks period,
purchasing during, 162

Three Weeks period,
wearing new during, 162

see *kriah*, laundered clothing:
Nine Days period, laundering:
Nine Days period, sheitel, shoes

coffee
  seudah hamafsekes,
  drinking at, 205, 206

combing
  sefirah period, during, 60

convert
  see *ger*

counting the *omer*
  see *sefiras haomer*

crafts
  Nine Days period, buying for
  children during, 165

creams
  Nine Days period,
  using during, 198
  Tishah b'Av, using on, 230-231

Crusades
  Av Harachamim composed
  in response to, 78

D

dairy
  Shavuos, custom of eating
  on, 125-126, 128

dancing
  sefirah period, during, 48, 49, 52
  sefirah period, during Chol
  Hamoed, 52

sefirah period, lessons
for during, 50

sefirah period, when haircuts
permitted, 52-53

Shabbos, on, 135

Three Weeks period, during, 157

Yom Tov, on, 135

see music, singing

date
  Nine Days period, wearing freshly
  laundered clothes for, 182
  sefirah period, haircut
  or shave for, 59
  Three Weeks period, haircut
  or shaving during for, 160

day
  sefiras haomer, counting
  during, 25

daybreak
  see *alos hashachar*

deodorant
  Nine Days period,
  applying during, 198
  Shivah Asar b'Tammuz,
  applying on, 149
  Tishah b'Av, using on, 231

depression
  music, lifting with, 301
  sefirah period, listening to
  music during because of, 52
  Three Weeks period, listening to
  music during because of, 158

diapers
  cloth, laundering during
  Nine Days period, 174

Index ∽ 327

dish
   omitting at *seudah* to show mourning for loss of *Beis Hamikdash*, 297-298

doctors
   fasting when work will be affected, 146

Dome of the Rock
   kriah, performing upon seeing, 311

doorbell
   musical, 302

drinking glasses
   washing before using from meat or dairy meal, 131

driving
   music, listening to while, 301
   see car

dry cleaning
   see laundering: Nine Days period

dryer
   Nine Days period, putting wet clothes into during, 171

E

eggs
   seudah hamafsekes, eaten at, 207-208

Eichah
   see Megillas Eichah

Eizehu Mekoman
   passage of, reciting on Tishah b'Av, 237

elderly
   supporting oneself during *sefiras haomer*, 10
   Tishah b'Av, standing up for, 243

engagement
   Nine Days period, finalizing and celebrating during, 169
   sefirah period, celebrating during, 48
   sefirah period, haircut or shave before, 59
   sefirah period, *seudah* for during, 56
   Three Weeks, finalizing and celebrating during, 156

Elokai neshamah
   reciting after sleeping only in morning, 124
   reciting after staying awake all night, 123

Erev Shabbos
   Asarah b'Teves falling out on, 149
   kriah, if performed on, 314
   Nine Days period, children eating meat on during, 193
   Nine Days period, *mikveh* use on during, 195
   Nine Days period, sampling Shabbos food on during, 189
   sefirah period, haircut on during, 62, 66-67
   sefirah period, music during, 52
   sefiras haomer, counting early on, 21, 22
   see Shabbos

Erev Shavuos
  blood drawing on, 99
  medical procedures on, 99
  mikveh, immersing in on, 101
  see Shavuos
Erev Tishah b'Av
  aufruf on, when on Shabbos, 213-214
  Av Harachamim, recited on, when on Shabbos, 201, 268
  Avos U'banim program on, when on Shabbos, 203
  birkas hamazon, reciting after *shekiah* of, 214
  bris on, 201-202, 213
  fasting on, 204
  leisure activities on, 202, 268
  Maariv after, when on Shabbos, 215-216, 269
  pidyon haben on, 201-202
  Pirkei Avos, reciting when on Shabbos, 202, 267
  seudah hamafsekes, 204-210, 212-213
  seudas mitzvah on, 201-202
  Shabbos, *seudah hamafsekes* on, 212-213, 214
  Shabbos, showing mourning after *shekiah*, 214
  Shenayim mikra v'echad targum, reciting on, 203
  shiur on when on Shabbos, 203, 268
  stroll, taking on, 202
  Tachanun omitted on, 201
  Tehillim, reciting on, 203
  Torah study on, 202-204, 267-268
  Tzidkascha omitted on, when on Shabbos, 201, 268
  yahrtzeit on, fasting, 204
  zemiros, when on Shabbos, 213
  see *seudah hamafsekes*
Erev Yom Tov
  kriah, if performed on, 314
  eulogies
    see *hespedim*
  exchanges
    Nine Days period, clothing during, 185
  excrement
    sefiras haomer in presence of, 8
  exercising
    music, listening to while, 301
  eyeglasses
    Nine Days period, buying new during, 185
    Nine Days period, repairing during, 185

F

fast day
  Aneinu recited on, 149-150, 151-152
  antibiotics, fasting while still taking, 145
  ate by mistake on, 142-143, 226
  Avinu Malkeinu, recited on, 150-151
  childbirth, women observing after, 144

Index ~ 329

children fasting on, 141-142

doctors observing when work affected, 146

elderly people fasting on, 224

exempt from, observing anyway, 145

haftarah at *Minchah* on, 151

illness, fasting while experiencing, 144-145, 221-223, 274

Krias HaTorah, on, 151

medicine, taking on, 145-146

neviim instituted, 139

nurses observing when work affected, 146

nursing women fasting on, 143

objective of, 139

pills, swallowing on, 145-146, 223-224

pregnant women fasting on, 143

Selichos, recited on, 150

working during, when observance will be prevented, 146

see Aneinu, Asarah b'Teves, Behab, fasting, Shivah Asar B'Tammuz, Tishah b'Av, Tzom Gedaliah

fasting

Erev Tishah b'Av, 203

Isru Chag, on, 108

Lag Baomer, on, 68-69

Shavuos, on, 103

Sivan, prohibited during until Shavuos, 84

yahrtzeit, on Erev Tishah b'Av, 204

see Asarah b'Teves, Behab, fast day, Shivah Asar B'Tammuz, Tishah b'Av, Tzom Gedaliah

fingernails

Nine Days period, trimming during, 169, 198

sefirah period, trimming during, 60

Three Weeks period, trimming during, 160

fire

Lag Baomer, lighting on, 71

fish

seudah hamafsekes, eating at, 205

fleishig

see dairy, meat and milk

floor

Nine Days period, washing and polishing during, 172

seudah hamafsekes, sitting on during, 208-209

Tishah b'Av, sitting on during, 241-242, 250, 252

flowers

brachah made on inhaling scent of, 134

muktzeh status of on Yom Tov, 132

placing in water on Yom Tov, 133

removing from water on Yom Tov, 133

scent of, inhaling during davening, 134

Shavuos, adorning shuls and homes with on, 132

theft, avoiding while picking, 135

vase of, adding water to on Shabbos or Yom Tov, 133

vase of, moving on Yom Tov, 133

see trees

Friday

see Erev Shabbos

fruit

sefirah period, *shehecheyanu* on new, 53-54

funeral

see levayah

furniture

Nine Days period, buying during, 164

G

gardening

Nine Days period, during, 168

garments

see clothing

ger

converted during *sefirah* period, 8

gifts

Nine Days period, giving or receiving during, 165

Tishah b'Av, giving on, 239

glasses

see drinking glasses, eyeglasses

gomel bentching

see hagomel

grape juice

Nine Days period, prohibited, 188

see wine

greetings

Tishah b'Av, giving and receiving on, 239

groom

see chassan

guest

Nine Days period, using fresh linen, 178-179

H

habit

mashiv haruach, creating, 76

mashiv haruach, of saying, 75

hachanah

bringing footwear to shul when Erev Tishah b'Av on Shabbos, 215, 269

decorating house when Shavuos is Motzaei Shabbos, 132-133

hachnassas sefer Torah

sefirah period, celebrating, 49-50

Shavuos appropriate time for, 107

haftarah

Shavuos morning, custom to stand, 105

Shavuos morning, of, 105, 107

hagbaah

Tishah b'Av, sitting on regular chair after, 242

hagomel

Tishah b'Av, reciting on, 255

haircutting

barber, non-Jewish customer during Three Weeks period, 159

Motzaei Tishah b'Av, on, 281-282, 283, 284-285

Nine Days period, *avel* concluding *shloshim* during, 175

sefirah period, Arizal's stringency regarding, 60

sefirah period, *avel* at conclusion of *shloshim*, 59

sefirah period, bar mitzvah boy engaging in, 58

sefirah period, bas mitzvah girl engaging in, 58

sefirah period, *bris milah* participants engaging in, 58

sefirah period, chassan before *aufruf*, 58

sefirah period, children engaging in, 57

sefirah period, combing hair during, 60

sefirah period, date, 59

sefirah period, engagement party, 59

sefirah period, engaging in during, 56-60

sefirah period, Friday in honor of Shabbos, 62, 66-67

sefirah period, Lag Baomer, 62-64, 66, 67, 70, 71

sefirah period, medical needs requiring, 59

sefirah period, mustache, 56

sefirah period, *pidyon haben* participants engaging in, 58

sefirah period, Rosh Chodesh, 67

sefirah period, shaving during, 56

sefirah period, someone else's hair, 60

sefirah period, wedding, 59

sefirah period, women engaging in, 56-57

Shivah Asar b'Tammuz, taking on, 148

Three Weeks period, barber and non-Jewish customer, 159

Three Weeks period, bar mitzvah boy engaging in, 160

Three Weeks period, *bris milah* participants engaging in, 159

Three Weeks period, children receiving, 159

Three Weeks period, engaging in during, 158-161

Three Weeks period, *pidyon haben* participants engaging in, 160

Three Weeks period, tefillin have *chatzitzah* without, 160

Three Weeks period, women engaging in, 158, 160

see shaving

hakamas matzeivah

Lag Baomer, holding on, 69

Hallel

Shavuos, recited on, 103

hamaavir sheinah

reciting after sleeping only in morning, 124

reciting after staying awake all night, 123

hanosein lasechvi vinah

reciting before *alos hashachar*, 123-124

Har Sinai
    covered with flora at time of Torah giving, 132
Hashem sefasai tiftach
    reciting when repeating Shemoneh Esrei, 74
hatov vehameitiv
    Nine Days period, reciting during, 165
    Three Weeks period, reciting during, 162-163
Havdalah
    Nine Days period, beer, using for, 190
    Nine Days period, wine, using for, 189-190
    sefiras haomer, counting before/after, 22-23
    Shavuos, when first night of is Motzaei Shabbos, 102
    Tishah b'Av, children before eating, 273
    Tishah b'Av, drinking water before hearing, 275
    Tishah b'Av, listening to when made on, for one still fasting, 273
    Tishah b'Av night, ate before, 274
    Tishah b'Av on Sunday, not eating until after, 224-225
    Tishah b'Av on Sunday, postponed until Sunday night, 271
    Tishah b'Av on Sunday, procedure of, 274-275, 285
    Tishah b'Av, reciting when eating on, 272-273
    Tishah b'Av, women making themselves, 273, 275
    Tishah b'Av, women who are not fasting, 273
    see *Atah chonantanu*, *borei meorei ha'eish*
hazkaras neshamos
    see *Kel Malei Rachamim*
hefsek
    between *brachah* and *sefirah*, 10
    see *hesech hadaas*
hefsek taharah
    Nine Days period, performing during, 195
    Tishah b'Av, performing on, 229
heker
    after meat meal, while eating parve at dairy meal, 130-131
    between meat and dairy eaters at same table, 130
hesech hadaas
    necessitates new *brachah* recitation, 110-111
    Torah study, from, 119
    see *hefsek*
hespedim
    Lag Baomer, delivering on, 69
    Pesach Sheni, delivering on, 84
home
    sefirah period, moving to, 55
    sefirah period, renovating, 55
    sefirah period, *shehecheyanu* recited on purchasing, 55
    see *zecher l'churban*

Index ↝ 333

hotel
   Nine Days period, guest in using fresh linen, 178-179

house
   see home

I

illness
   fasting in situation of, 144-145, 221-223, 274
   Nine Days period, laundering for someone suffering from, 175
   Nine Days period, meat or wine during because of, 193
   sefirah period, cutting hair because of, 59
   sefirah period, listening to music during because of, 52
   sefiras haomer, leaning during because of, 10
   Three Weeks period, listening to music during because of, 158
   Three Weeks period, reciting *shehecheyanu* on fruit eaten during because of, 162
   Tishah b'Av, chair, using regular one because of, 242
   Tishah b'Av, resuming fast after broken in case of, 222
   Tishah b'Av, washing for bread on in case of, 226
   see fast day

insect repellent
   Tishah b'Av, using on, 231

instruments
   learning to play, 300

   see music

intent
   sefiras haomer, not to fulfill mitzvah of, 19, 31
   see sefiras haomer: intent during

interruption
   see hefsek

ironing
   Nine Days period, during, 170

Isru Chag
   eating/drinking more than usual on, 108
   fasting on, 108
   sefirah period: music and dancing on, 52
   Tachanun on, 107

J

jewelry
   Nine Days period, purchasing during, 164
   not wearing all at once to commemorate destruction of *Beis Hamikdash*, 304

joy
   happiness, without, 304-305
   Nine Days period, minimizing during, 164

K

Kabbalas haTorah
   source of custom to study Torah night of Shavuos, 109

Kabbalas Shabbos

sefiras haomer, counting yesterday's after, 29

Kah E-li

Shavuos, reciting on, 107

kallah

head adornments for, limiting, 303-304

Isru Chag, fasting on, 108

Lag Baomer, fasting on, 69

Shivah Asar b'Tammuz, fasting on, 143

Tishah b'Av, makeup, using on, 231

Tishah b'Av, washing and anointing on, 231

kavanah

see intent, *sefiras haomer*: intent during

Kel Erech Apayim

Lag Baomer, if said on, 68

Pesach Sheni, if said on, 83

Sivan, if said during, 84

Tishah b'Av, if said on, 253

Kel Malei Rachamim

sefirah period, reciting during, 79

Kiddush

fulfilling via hearing recitation of, 4

sefiras haomer, before/after, 22-23

Shavuos eve, delaying until night, 100

Shavuos, following with dairy foods before meat meal, 131

Kiddush b'makom seudah

eating enough *mezonos* after Kiddush to satisfy requirement of, 131

Kiddush Levanah

Av, delaying until after Tishah b'Av, 280

Av, reciting at earliest opportunity, 280

Motzaei Tishah b'Av, reciting on, 279-280

Tishah b'Av on Thursday, delaying until after Shabbos, 280

Kinnos

distractions, avoiding during recitation of, 253

extending recitation of, 252

Tishah b'Av, recited on, 249, 251-252, 253

kiyor

passage of, reciting before *alos hashachar*, 124

korban omer

offered on Pesach, 3

see chadash

Korbanos

kiyor passage, reciting before *alos hashachar*, 124

korban tamid passage, reciting before *alos hashachar*, 124

terumas hadeshen passage, reciting before *alos hashachar*, 124

korban shtei halechem

dairy meal followed by meat meal commemorates, 125, 126

Index ∾ 335

offered on Shavuos, 3

korban tamid

   passage of, reciting before *alos hashachar*, 124

   passage of, reciting on Tishah b'Av, 237

Kosel

   kriah, performing upon seeing, 310-311

   Shavuos, visiting on day of and days after, 108

   Tishah b'Av, performing *kriah* when visiting on, 253

   see Beis Hamikdash, *kriah*

kriah

   bar or bas mitzvah within 30 days of seeing, if obligated, 315

   Beis Hamikdash, performing upon seeing site of, 310-311

   children performing, 312, 315

   Chol Hamoed, not performed on, 314

   clothing, transferring ownership of, if obligated, 316

   coat, if required on, 313

   Erev Shabbos or Yom Tov, if performed on, 314

   forgot to perform, 315

   Kosel, if performed upon seeing, 310-311

   obligation to perform, 309, 312

   old garment, using for, 313

   procedure for, 309, 310

   repairing garment after performed, 313

   Shabbos, not performed on, 314

   Tachanun omitted, if performed, 314

   tearing, how performed, 312-313

   thirty days, obligation of limited to once every, 312, 314, 315

   Tishah b'Av, performing on, 253

   torn garment, using for, 313

   transferring ownership of garment, if obligated, 316

   tzitzis, if required on, 313

   undershirt, if required on, 313

   women performing, 311

   Yerushalayim, performing upon seeing, 309-310, 311

   Yerushalayim resident, if obligated, 315-316

   Yom Tov, not performed on, 314

   see Beis Hamikdash

Krias HaTorah

   baal korei preparing for, on Tishah b'Av, 237

   Behab, portion read on, 82

   discrepancy in when traveling to or from Eretz Yisrael, 79-80

   fast days, *aliyah* for non-faster, 151

   fast days, on, 151

   Shavuos, readings for, 103, 106-107

   Tishah b'Av, order of, 253, 255

Krias Shema

   passing around fragrant flowers during *brachos* of, 134

   precedence of before *sefiras haomer*, 17, 23-24

Tishah b'Av, reciting
at bedtime, 238

Tishah b'Av, reciting on, 237-238

Tishah b'Av, *tzitzis*, holding
during recitation of, 258

ksivah

  see writing

kvatter

  Nine Days period, wearing fresh
clothing in honor of *bris milah*, 181

  sefirah period, cutting hair
or shaving during, 58

L

Lag Baomer

  avel as *shaliach tzibbur* on, 68

  candles, lighting on, 71

  cutting hair on, 62-64, 66, 67, 69

  fasting on, 68-69

  festivity on, 70

  fire, lighting on, 71

  hakamas matzeivah on, 69

  hespedim on, 69

  Kel Erech Apayim on, 68

  Lamnatzeiach on, 68

  Meron, visiting on, 70-71

  music and dancing on, 53

  night of, music and dancing on, 53

  sefiras haomer, if fulfilled
when said that tonight is, 35

  Tachanun on, 67, 68

  Tzidkascha omitted at
Minchah beforehand, 68

  tziduk hadin on, 69

  upsheren on, 71

  wedding on, 66, 67, 69-70

Lamnatzeiach

  Lag Baomer, if said on, 68

  Pesach Sheni, if said on, 83

  Sivan, if said during, 84

  Tishah b'Av, if said on, 253

landscaping

  Nine Days period, during, 167, 168

language

  sefiras haomer, when one
doesn't understand, 11

laomer

  concluding *sefirah*
recitation with, 12-13

laughter

  "filling one's mouth with", 305

laundered clothing: Nine Days period

  aufruf, wearing in honor
of during, 181

  bar mitzvah, wearing in
honor of during, 181

  bedding, using during, 176, 179

  bris milah, in honor of, 181

  children's, wearing during, 177

  date, wearing during
because of, 182

  guests using during, 178-179

  mitzvah purpose, 179

  Motzaei Tishah b'Av, wearing
on, 281-282, 284-285

  pajamas, wearing during, 177

  preparing before Nine
Days for, 177-178

pressed garments,
wearing, 179-180
prohibition of wearing during, 176
Shabbos, on, 179, 180
Shabbos, wearing after, 181
sheets, using during, 176, 179
shidduch date, wearing
during because of, 182
shivah nekiim, during, 179
sleepwear, wearing during, 177
socks, wearing during, 176
tablecloths, using during, 176, 179
towels, using during, 176
undergarments, wearing
during, 176

laundering: Nine Days period
adding clothes to permissible washing machine load, 175
after Tishah b'Av, for, 170, 175
avel concluding *shloshim* during, 175
bedding during, 170
children's clothes during, 174-175
clean clothing unavailable, 172
cleaners, giving clothing to, 173
cleaners, remaining open during, 174
diapers, cloth, during, 174
dirty clothing only available, 172
dryer, putting wet clothes into during, 171
floors, washing and polishing during, 172
illness, for someone suffering from, 175
ironing during, 170
mitzvah purpose, for, 172-173
Motzaei Tishah b'Av, on, 281-282, 283, 284-285
non-Jew, instructing to engage in, 170-171, 175
non-Jew, laundering for, 173-174
prohibition of, 170
Shabbos, for, 173
sheets during, 170
shivah nekiim, for, 172-173
soaking stained garment, 171
spot cleaning during, 171
tablecloths during, 170
towels during, 170
washing machine, turning on immediately before Nine Days begin, 171
see clothing, laundered clothing: Nine Days period, Shabbos Chazon, sheitel, shoes

laundromat
Nine Days period, remaining open during, 174

leaning
sefiras haomer, during, 9-10

learning
see Torah study

leather
orthotics, using on Tishah b'Av, 233-234
using or standing on on Tishah b'Av, 233
see shoes

338 ∽ *Index*

Leshem Yichud
   sefiras haomer, omitting words in, 16
   sefiras haomer, reciting before, 16

levayah
   Tishah b'Av, *tziduk hadin* not recited, 254

loom
   Nine Days period, arranging threads on during, 184

lo plug
   reason for requirement of *netilas yadayim* after sleepless night, 114-115
   see *netilas yadayim*

M

maakeh
   Nine Days period, constructing during, 168

Maariv
   Erev Shabbos, counting *sefiras haomer* after when still day, 29
   Erev Shabbos, davening before *shekiah*, 21, 29
   sefiras haomer, counting before, 21-22
   sefiras haomer, intent assumed if after, 31
   sefiras haomer, reciting after, 17, 18, 19-22
   sefiras haomer, when after *plag haminchah*, 20
   sefiras haomer, when before sunset, 19-20
   sefiras haomer, when immediately after *shekiah*, 19
   sefiras haomer, when to count when late to, 23-24
   Shavuos eve, delaying until night, 100
   Tishah b'Av, customs of, 249-251
   Tishah b'Av, Erev Tishah b'Av on Shabbos, procedure for, 215-216, 269
   Tishah b'Av, restrictions of begin at when davening before *shekiah*, 211

makeup
   Tishah b'Av, kallah using on, 231
   Tishah b'Av, using on, 230, 231

malt
   chadash considerations for, 94

marital relations
   Erev Tishah b'Av on Shabbos, 268
   Motzaei Tishah b'Av, on, 281-282
   Shavuos, on eve of, 102-103
   Shivah Asar b'Tammuz, on eve of, 147, 149
   Tishah b'Av on Shabbos, 240, 268
   Tishah b'Av, prohibited on, 219, 228, 240

marriage
   see wedding

mashiv haruach u'morid hageshem
   Australia, when recited in, 74-75
   corrected *toch k'dei dibbur*, 75
   erroneously omitted, 71
   erroneously recited, 73-75

Index ～ 339

habit of saying correctly, creating, 76

one who davened alone on first day of Pesach, 73

public announcement that recitation stopped, 72

recitation of stopped on first day of Pesach, 71-73

southern hemisphere, when recited in, 74-75

uncertain if said, 75-76

see morid hatal

matzah

Pesach Sheni, eating on, 83

meal

see seudah

meat

Motzaei Tishah b'Av, food cooked with, 281

Motzaei Tishah b'Av, restrictions on, 275, 281, 284

Nine Days period, abstaining during, 186-193

Nine Days period, bar mitzvah, eating at, 192

Nine Days period, *bris milah*, eating at, 190-191, 201-202

Nine Days period, *chanukas habayis*, eating at, 192

Nine Days period, childbirth, eating after, 193

Nine Days period, children abstaining from, 192-193

Nine Days period, food cooked in meat utensils, 187

Nine Days period, food cooked with, 187-188

Nine Days period, illness requiring, 193

Nine Days period, *melaveh malkah*, eating at, 188-189

Nine Days period, nursing requiring, 193

Nine Days period, onset of prohibition of consuming, 186

Nine Days period, *pidyon haben*, eating at, 190, 201-202

Nine Days period, poultry included in prohibition of consuming, 187

Nine Days period, sampling Shabbos food, 189

Nine Days period, *seudah shelishis*, eating during, 188-189

Nine Days period, *seudas mitzvah* permitted in, 190, 201-202

Nine Days period, Shabbos, eating on, 188-189

Nine Days period, *siyum*, eating at, 190, 191-192

Nine Days period, storeowner selling during, 187

seudah hamafsekes, eating at, 205, 212-213, 268

Shivah Asar b'Tammuz, eating on night after, 149

Yom Tov *seudah* including, 129

see dairy, meat and milk, poultry, *shechitah*

meat and milk

bread at meals of, switching, 126, 130

chicken, same as meat regarding eating dairy after, 129

dairy after meat, procedure to follow, 129

dairy meal after meat before sufficient time has passed, 129-130

dairy meal after meat, but only eating parve, 130-131

glasses, requirement to be washed between meals of, 131

meat after dairy, procedure to follow, 127-128

meat after hard cheese, 128

napping after meat/chicken meal, beginning dairy meal sooner, 130

parve food cooked in meat pot, eating dairy after, 129

parve food cooked with meat, eating dairy after, 129

parve food cut with meat knife, eating dairy after, 129

preparing dairy meal after eating meat, 130-131

removing bread and dairy products before meat meal, 126-127

tablecloth, using different for meals at same time, 130

tablecloth, using for both meat and milk meals, 127, 130

table, using same one for at the same time, 130

see cheese, dairy, parve

medical procedures

Erev Shavuos, refraining from on, 99

Three Weeks period, refraining from during, 163

medicine

fast days, taking on, 145-146

see pills

Megillas Eichah

brachah, reciting on reading of, 250

Hashiveinu recited out loud at public reading, 251

mournful tone, read in, 250

Tishah b'Av, recited on, 249, 254

women listening to, 250-251

Megillas Rus

brachah on reading of, 106

Shavuos morning, reading on, 105

melachah

sefiras haomer, abstaining from before counting, 38, 41-43

melaveh malkah

Nine Days period, meat and wine at, 188-189

meraglim

sin of commemorated by Tishah b'Av, 219

Meron

Lag Baomer, visiting on, 70-71

midnight

see chatzos

miktzas hayom kekulo

sefirah period reflects, 62, 63

mikveh

Nine Days period, constructing during, 168

Index ∾ 341

Nine Days period, using during, 194-195

Tishah b'Av, using on, 228-229

see tevilah

milchig

see dairy, meat and milk

milk and meat

see meat and milk

Minchah

plag haminchah, davening before/after, 20

minyan

sefiras haomer, starting meal before counting when regular at, 39-40

Selichos, preferably recited with, 150

mi shebeirach

Behab, recited for observers of, 81

mitzvas aseh shehazman grama

sefiras haomer's status as, 5-6

woman reciting *brachah* on, 6

mitzvos tzrichos kavanah

sefiras haomer, if required for, 30-31

moed

Tishah b'Av considered, 201, 252-253, 268

mohel

Nine Days period, wearing fresh clothing in honor of *bris milah*, 181

sefirah period, cutting hair or shaving during, 58

Three Weeks period, cutting hair or shaving during, 159

Tishah b'Av, wearing fresh clothing in honor of *bris milah*, 181, 262

morid hatal

announcing recitation of on first day of Pesach, 72

erroneously omitted, 73

reciting during summer months, 73

see mashiv haruach u'morid hageshem, vesein tal u'matar livrachah

morning

sefiras haomer, repeating count in, 24

Motzaei Shabbos

sefirah period: music during on, 52

Tishah b'Av on, 270-273

see Atah chonantanu, Havdalah

Motzaei Tishah b'Av

bathing on, 281-282, 283, 284-285

birkas hamazon with *kos* on, 283

chatzos of tenth of Av, restrictions extending to, 281

fast ends at *tzeis hakochavim*, 279

haircuts on, 281-282, 284-285

Havdalah after, when on Sunday night, 274-275, 279, 285

Kiddush Levanah, reciting on, 279-280

laundered clothes, wearing on, 281-282, 284-285

laundering clothes on, 281-282, 283, 284-285

Maariv, eating or drinking before on, 279
marital relations on, 282
meat, eating on, 275, 281, 284
music, listening to or playing on, 282, 284-285
postponed fast, after, 284-285
restrictions on, 281-282
seudas mitzvah on, 282-283
shehecheyanu, reciting on, 282
Thursday night, restrictions abated in honor of Shabbos, 283-284
water, drinking before Havdalah, 275
wine, drinking on, 274-275, 281, 283, 284
women after childbirth, eating meat on, 283
women waiting for Havdalah, 275

mourner
see *aveilus*, *onen*

mourning
during Nine Days period, 163
during *sefirah* period, 47
during Three Weeks period, 155
Tishah b'Av observance, part of, 219
see *aveilus*, *onen*

mouthwash
Tishah b'Av, using on, 225

moving
Nine Days period, during, 166
Three Weeks period, during, 166

muktzeh
flowers, status of on Yom Tov, 132

music
alarm clock, 302
anger, calming with, 301
children, learning to play, 300
churban, commemorating by limiting, 299-302
depression, lifting with, 301
door chimes, 302
driving, staying awake while with, 301
exercising with, 301
inspirational purposes, using for, 301
learning to play for livelihood purposes, 300
lessons, children receiving, 300
playing for livelihood purposes, 300
restaurant, drinking wine in while playing, 299-300
mitzvah purpose, for, 301
mood, improving via, 301
Motzaei Tishah b'Av, on, 281-282, 285
recorded, listening to, 300
ring tones, 302
sefirah period, a capella music during, 50-51
sefirah period, Chol Hamoed, 52
sefirah period, exercising with during, 51
sefirah period, "hold" music during, 51

sefirah period, involuntary listening, 51

sefirah period, keeping awake with, 51

sefirah period, lessons for during, 51

sefirah period, listening to during, 49-53

sefirah period, listening to for someone who is ill, 52

sefirah period, practicing during, 51

sefirah period, recorded music during, 50

sefirah period, singing during, 52

sefirah period, stories with background music during, 51-52

sefirah period, when haircuts permitted, 52-53

set times, listening to at, 300, 302

seudas mitzvah, playing at, 301

Shivah Asar b'Tammuz, listening to on, 148

Three Weeks period, children listening to during, 158

Three Weeks period, listening to, 157, 158

Three Weeks period, playing instruments during, 157

Three Weeks period, *seudas mitzvah* celebration with, 158

wedding, playing at, 301

wine, listening to while drinking, 299-300

work purposes, listening to for, 299, 300

see Lag Baomer, singing

mussar

Tishah b'Av, studying on, 235

mustache

sefirah period, trimming during, 56

Three Weeks period, trimming during, 158

N

Nacheim

Tishah b'Av, recited on, 256

nails

see fingernails

name tag

Nine Days period, sewing onto clothing during, 182-183

napping

dairy meal after, beginning sooner, 130

Shabbos afternoon for Shavuos that night, 102

neitz hachamah

Tishah b'Av, davening at, 252

neshamah

returning to person reason for *netilas yadayim* in morning, 113

see netilas yadayim

netilas yadayim

alos hashachar, repeating when washed before, 115-116

brachah on, 114-116

daytime sleep, requirement of after, 116-117

neshamah returning in morning reason for, 113

requirement of in morning, reasons for, 113-115

ruach raah and, 113-117

sheinas arai, not required after, 116

sheinas keva, requirement of after, 116-117

sleeping part of night, requirement of after, 116

sleepless night, requirement of after, 114-115

studying Torah beforehand, when *alos hashachar* already passed, 116

Tishah b'Av, on, 227

see sleep, Torah study

night

counting *omer* at, 4, 17, 18

Nine Days

air travel during, 169

bathing during, 193-198

beer, drinking during, 188, 190

business, conducting during, 165-166

class photos during, 169

clothing, buying during, 165, 168, 184, 185

clothing, laundering during, 170-175

clothing, making during, 182

clothing, preparing beforehand for use during, 177-178

clothing, pressed, wearing during, 179-180

clothing, wearing freshly laundered during, 176-182

clothing, wearing new during, 176, 179

construction during, 167

court case during, 169

cream, applying during, 198

deodorant, using during, 198

engagement, finalizing and celebrating during, 169

fingernails, trimming during, 169, 198

floors, washing and polishing during, 172

fragrances, using during, 198

gifts, giving or receiving during, 165

graduation pictures during, 169

grape drinks, drinking during, 188

grape juice, drinking during, 188

hatov vehameitiv during, 165

landscaping during, 167

laundering clothing during, 170-175

leasing new home during, 166

litigation during, 169

loom, arranging threads on during, 184

meat, abstaining from during, 186-193

mending during, 183

mikveh use during, 194-195

mitzvah purpose, purchasing or construction for during, 168

Index ∾ 345

mourning intensified during, 163, 164

moving into new home during, 166

nails, cutting during, 169

painting home during, 167

perfume, using during, 198

purchasing items which engender joy during, 164-165, 168

purchasing new home during, 166-167

renovations during, 166, 167

repairs to home during, 167

Rosh Chodesh, beginning from *shekiah* of, 164

sefarim, purchasing during, 165

selling home during, 166

selling items which engender joy during, 164

sewing during, 182-183

Shabbos clothes during, 179, 180

shechitah, abstaining from during, 186-187

sheitel, washing and setting during, 172

shoes, polishing during, 171-172

showering during, 193-198

siyum during, 190, 191-192

spinning thread during, 184

swimming during, 169, 194

tefillin, purchasing during, 168

tevilah during, 194-195

tzitzis, purchasing during, 168

wallpapering home during, 167

whiskey, drinking during, 188

wine, abstaining from during, 186, 188-193

see Erev Tishah b'Av, laundered clothing: Nine Days period, laundering: Nine Days period, meat, *shavua shechal bo*, Three Weeks, Tishah b'Av, wine

numbers

sefiras haomer, cardinal vs. ordinal for, 12

sefiras haomer, unusual formulation for, 11

nurses

fasting when work will be affected, 146

nusach Ashkenaz

baomer, using for *sefirah* formula, 13

tefillos, reciting at *sefiras haomer*, 16

nusach Sephard

laomer, using for *sefirah* formula, 13

tefillos, reciting at *sefiras haomer*, 16

O

oats

chadash considerations for, 94

odor

sefiras haomer in presence of, 8

oil

Tishah b'Av, using on, 230-231

omer

see korban omer

onen
    sefiras haomer, performing, 7-8

oness
    sefiras haomer, missed count because of, 26

orthotics
    Tishah b'Av, using on, 233-234

P

painting
    Nine Days period, during, 167
    Nine Days period, shul during, 168

pajamas
    Nine Days period, using freshly laundered during, 177

paroches
    Tishah b'Av, removed on, 249
    Tishah b'Av, replaced for *Minchah*, 255

Parshas Hashavua
    compensating for missing when traveling between Eretz Yisrael and outside it, 80
    discrepancy between reading of in Eretz Yisrael and outside it, 79-80

parties
    sefirah period, during, 55-56

parve
    cooked in meat pot, eating dairy after, 129
    cooked with meat, eating dairy after, 129
    cut with meat knife, eating dairy after, 129
    eating at dairy meal, after eating meat, 130-131
    see meat and milk

Perek Eizehu Mekoman
    see Eizehu Mekoman

Perek Shirah
    Tishah b'Av, reciting on, 238

perfumes
    Nine Days period, applying during, 198
    Tishah b'Av, using on, 230

Pesach
    mashiv haruach u'morid hageshem, recitation stopped on, 71
    morid hatal, beginning on, 72
    sefiras haomer begins on, 3
    Tefillas Tal, reciting on first day of, 72
    vesein brachah, recitation of begins on, 77

Pesach Sheni
    Avinu Malkeinu, omitting on, 83
    hespedim on, 84
    Lamnatzeiach, reciting on, 83
    matzah, custom of eating on, 83
    Selichos, omitting on, 83
    Tachanun, omitting on, 83

Pesukei D'zimrah
    passing around fragrant flowers during, 134

phone
    musical ring tones for, 302

pidyon haben
    Behab, eating at during, 82-83

Index 347

Erev Tishah b'Av, on, 201

Nine Days period, *seudah* for, 190, 201-202

sefirah period, haircut or shaving for, 58

sefirah period, *seudah* for during, 56

Three Weeks period, haircut or shaving for, 160

Tishah b'Av, procedure for when on, 264

pills

 fast days, taking on, 145-146, 223-224

 Shabbos, taking on to prepare for Tishah b'Av, 269

Pirkei Avos

 Erev Tishah b'Av, reciting when on Shabbos, 202, 267

 sefirah period, beginning reciting during, 79

Pitum Haketores

 Tishah b'Av, reciting on, 237-238, 253

placemats

 used to separate between meat and dairy eaters at same table, 130

plag haminchah

 Maariv after, 20

 sefiras haomer, not saying day after, 33

poultry

 Nine Days period, allergic to dairy, eating when, 193

 Nine Days period, children eating, 192-193

 Nine Days period, preferred over meat, 193

 Nine Days period, prohibited from eating, 187

 seudah hamafsekes, eating at, 205

 see meat

prayers

 see *tefillos*

R

Rabi Akiva

 students of dying during *sefirah* period, 47, 61, 67

Rabi Shimon bar Yochai

 candles in honor of *yahrtzeit* of, 71

 fire in honor of *yahrtzeit* of, 71

 Lag Baomer, *yahrtzeit* of, 67

 Meron, visiting on Lag Baomer, 70-71

 music and dancing in honor of *yahrtzeit* of, 53

Rabi Yehuda HaChasid

 sefirah period, *tzavaah* of regarding haircut on Rosh Chodesh, 67

railing

 see *maakeh*

Rav

 sefiras haomer, embarrassed because missed day, 27

 Tishah b'Av, giving halachic ruling on, 236

 Tishah b'Av, standing up for during, 243

Rav Yosef Karo
  Divine revelation, merited through Shavuos night study, 109
restaurant
  wine, drinking at while music playing, 299-300
returns
  Nine Days period, clothing during, 185
retzei
  Erev Tishah b'Av, reciting after *shekiah*, 214
  seudah shelishis, reciting at after *sefiras haomer*, 23
Rosh Chodesh
  sefirah period, haircut on, 67
  sefirah period, listening to music on, 52
ruach raah
  netilas yadayim in morning and, 113-117
  see *netilas yadayim*
Rus
  see Megillas Rus
rye
  chadash considerations for, 94

S

safek brachos lehakel
  reciting *brachah* when unsure if counted *sefiras haomer*, 5
sandak
  Nine Days period, immersing in *mikveh* before acting as, 195
  Nine Days period, wearing fresh clothing in honor of *bris milah*, 181
  sefirah period, cutting hair or shaving during, 58
  Three Weeks period, cutting hair or shaving during, 159
  Tishah b'Av, wearing *tallis*, 262
  Tishah b'Av, wearing fresh clothing in honor of *bris milah*, 262
school
  zecher l'churban, if required, 292
seamstress
  Nine Days period, non-Jewish making clothing during, 182-183
Seder
  sefiras haomer, reciting afterward, 17-18
sefarim
  Nine Days period, purchasing during, 165
sefer
  sefiras haomer, if said while reading from, 35
sefer Torah
  see *hachnassas sefer Torah*
sefirah period
  a capella music during, 50-51
  bar mitzvah, music and dancing at during, 49
  bar mitzvah, *seudah* for during, 56
  bathing during, 60
  bris milah, music and dancing at during, 49
  bris milah, *seudah* for during, 56
  clothing, buying new during, 54

Index 349

combing hair during, 60
cutting hair during, 56-60
dance lessons during, 50
dancing during, 48, 49
dinners during, 49, 55-56
engagement, celebrating during, 48
fingernails, trimming during, 60
hachnassas sefer Torah, celebrating during, 49-50
home, moving to during, 55
home, renovating during, 55
mourning during, 47
music during, 49-53
music lessons during, 51
nails, trimming during, 60
parties during, 55-56
penalty for not observing mourning during, 48
pidyon haben, *seudah* for during, 56
Pirkei Avos, reciting during, 79
Sephardic custom of, 61-62
seudas mitzvah during, music and dancing at, 49
shaving during, 56, 57
shehecheyanu during, 53-55
sheva brachos, celebrating during, 48-49
showering during, 60
siyum, music and dancing at during, 49
siyum, *seudah* for during, 56
social gatherings during, 55-56
swimming during, 55
tenaim, celebrating during, 48
trips during, 55
vort, celebrating during, 48
vort, *seudah* at during, 56
waxing during, 57
wedding, attending during, 59, 65-66
wedding during, 48
when observed, 61-65
when observed, changing from year to year, 64
see haircutting, Lag Baomer, music, shaving, *shehecheyanu*, Shloshes Yemei Hagbalah
sefiras haomer
activity before, abstaining from, 37-39, 42-43
alos hashachar, counting until, 24
"*baomer*" – concluding with, 12-13
bein hashemashos, counting during, 18
bein hashemashos, counting for previous day during, 28
cardinal numbers for, 12
children's obligation of, 6-7
congregation, counting with, 23
day, counting during, 25
days, counting in formula, 13-15
Erev Shabbos, counting early on, 21
grammar of formula of, 15
Havdalah, counting before/after, 22-23
hefsek during, 10

incorrect count, 27, 36

individual's obligation, 4

informing other of night's count, 31-33

intent not to fulfill mitzvah of, 19, 32

interruption after *brachah* for, 10

Kabbalas Shabbos, counting yesterday's after when still day, 29

Kiddush, counting before/after, 22-23

language recited in, 11, 33

"*laomer*" – concluding with, 12-13

leaning during, 9-10

Leshem Yichud, reciting before, 16

Maariv, counting before when davening later, 21-22, 23-24

meal, beginning before counted, 37-39, 40-41

mid'oraisa or *mid'rabbanan*, 3

missing a count, 25-27

mistake in count of, 15, 36-37

mitzvah of, 3

morning, counting again in, 24

night, counting at, 4, 17, 18

obligation to count, 4

onen's obligation, 7

ordinal numbers for, 12

prayers afterward, 16

procedure for counting, 9-16

sleeping before counting, 38

standing during, 9-10

time of counting, 17-19, 24

time zones, counting when switching between, 29-30

thought, fulfilling via, 10

toch k'dei dibbur, correcting mistake during, 36-37

Torah study, engaging in before counting, 39, 40

tzeis hakochavim, counting after, 18-19

tzibbur, counting with, 23

uncertain if counted, 26

uncertain if counted correctly, 27-28

understanding the count, 11

unsure what day to count, 37

unusual counts, 11, 33

weeks, counting in formula, 13-15

women's obligation of, 5-6

writing, fulfilling via, 10-11

wrong day counted, 27

see Maariv, sefirah period, *sefiras haomer: brachah, tenai*

sefiras haomer: brachah

Bar mitzvah, reciting when falls during *sefirah* period, 7

child, teaching to recite, 6

convert reciting, 8

counting immediately after recitation of, 36

day, counting during without, 25

ger reciting, 8

hearing from someone else, 5

hefsek after, 10

intent assumed if after, 31

interruption after, 10

missed day anticipated,
counting with, 29

missed day, counting with, 25-27

omitting, to count again after
tzeis hakochavim with, 19

proper intent during, 35-36

Rav, reciting if embarrassed
because missed day, 27

reciting, 9

standing during, 9-10

unable to recite, 8

unsure if counted correctly,
reciting, 27-28

unsure if counted, reciting, 5

woman reciting, 6

see *sefiras haomer, sefiras
haomer*: intent during

sefiras haomer: intent during

answering affirmatively to
another, if assumed, 34

asking if correct day,
if assumed, 34

assumed absent if before
tzeis hakochavim, 33

assumed if after *brachah*, 31

assumed if after *Maariv*, 31

brachah of *shaliach tzibbur*, intent
to not to fulfill obligation with, 35

child, when assisting, 34

correcting someone
else, if assumed, 34

if assumed when weeks
not said, 33-34

if required, 30-31

incorrect count in mind, 36

incorrectly thought
mistake made, 37

informing other of
night's count, 31-33

Lag Baomer, when said
that tonight is, 35

language, if assumed
when different, 33

not to fulfill mitzvah, 19, 31, 32

number, when said alone, 33

proper, during *brachah*
recitation, 35-36

repeating *sefirah* if didn't have, 31

sefer, if said while reading from, 35

see *kavanah, mitzvos
tzrichos kavanah*

Selichos

Behab, omitting on when
concides with Pesach Sheni, 83

Behab, reciting on, 82

fast days, reciting on, 150

Tishah b'Av, omitted on, 252

Sephardic

bachur learning in Ashkenazic
yeshivah, cutting hair
during Three Weeks, 158

marrying into family
during *sefirah* period, 6

sefirah period, when
observed, 61-62

sefiras haomer, inserting
"*laomer*" or "*baomer*", 13

shavua shechal bo, observed
as mourning time before
Tishah b'Av, 163-164

seudah
  dairy, custom of holding on Shavuos, 125-126, 128
  dish, omitting at to show mourning for loss of *Beis Hamikdash*, 297-298
  engagement, celebrating during Three Weeks, 156
  halachic definition of, 39
  music, listening to during, 299-300, 301
  sefiras haomer, beginning before counted, 37-39, 40-41
  sefiras haomer, interrupting because of, 38, 40-41
  sefiras haomer, designating *shomer* to remind about, 39-41
  singing, listening to during, 299-300, 301
  see dairy, meat, meat and milk

seudah hamafsekes
  ashes, dipping bread in at, 208
  beer at, 205
  beverages at limited, 205
  bread dipped in ashes eaten at, 208
  chair, sitting on after, 209
  coffee at, 205
  cooked dishes at, 205-208
  definition of, 204
  drinking after over, 210-211
  eating after over, 210-211
  eggs eaten at, 207-208
  exempt from fast, eating, 208
  fish refrained from at, 205
  floor, sitting on during, 208-209
  food at limited, 205-206
  meal precedes, before *Minchah*, 210
  meat prohibited at, 205
  pasteurized food at, 207
  poultry refrained from at, 205
  Shabbos, when coincides with, 212-213, 268
  shoes, wearing at, 209
  soda at, 205
  tea at, 205
  uncooked food at, 207
  wine prohibited at, 205
  zimun at, 209, 213

seudah shelishis
  clearing after, 270
  Erev Tishah b'Av, when falls on, 212-213, 268, 270
  sefiras haomer during, 23
  Yom Tov after Shabbos, how fulfilled, 102

seudas mitzvah
  Behab, breaking fast for on, 81-82
  dish, omitting at to show mourning for loss of *Beis Hamikdash*, 297-298
  Erev Tishah b'Av, on, 201
  Motzaei Tishah b'Av, on, 282-283
  music, playing at, 301
  Nine Days period, food for sent home, 191
  Nine Days period, *birkas hamazon* with wine, 190
  Nine Days period, meat and wine permitted at, 190-192, 201-202

Nine Days period, singing at, 192

sefirah period, making, 56

sefirah period, music and dancing at during, 49

sewing

   Nine Days period, for someone else, 183

   Nine Days period, hiring non-Jew to, 182-183

   Nine Days period, mending clothing, 183

   see clothing

sfek sfeika

sefiras haomer, reciting *brachah* because of when unsure if counted correctly, 27-28

Shabbos

   Al Naharos Bavel, not recited on, 299

   clapping on, 135

   dancing on, 135

   kriah not performed on, 314

   mourning on, 269

   napping on even though may necessitate repeating *birchos haTorah*, 121

   napping on in preparation for Shavuos, 102

   Nine Days period, laundering clothing for, 173

   Nine Days period, meat and wine on, 188-189

   pills, taking on to prepare for Tishah b'Av, 269

   preparing for Yom Tov on, 102

   sefirah period, *shehecheyanu* recited on during, 55

   sefiras haomer, counting when still day but after *Kabbalas Shabbos*, 29

   Shir Hamaalos recited before *birkas hamazon* of, 299

   Tishah b'Av following, 267-275

   vase, adding water to on, 133

   see Erev Shabbos, Erev Tishah b'Av, Havdalah, Kabbalas Shabbos, *melaveh malkah, seudah shelishis*, Shabbos Chazon

Shabbos Chazon

   aufruf on, wearing freshly laundered items on, 181

   bathing before, 197

   freshly laundered items, using on, 179

   meat, eating on, 188-189

   Motzaei Shabbos, meat or wine on, 189

   Motzaei Shabbos, wearing Shabbos clothes, 181

   new clothing, wearing on, 180

   pressed clothing prohibited from, 180

   Shabbos clothing, wearing on, 180

   wine, drinking on, 188-189

Shabbos Mevarchim

   Av Harachamim, reciting on during *sefirah* period, 78

   Kel Malei Rachamim, reciting on during *sefirah* period, 79

Shacharis

   Shavuos, additions to, 103-107

Tishah b'Av, changes to, 252-253
shaliach tzibbur
   Lag Baomer, *avel* being on, 68
   sefiras haomer, intent not to fulfill obligation with *brachah* of, 35
   Tishah b'Av, *avel* being on, 253
shaving
   Lag Baomer, engaging in on, 70
   sefirah period, *bris milah* participants engaging in, 58
   sefirah period, chassan before *aufruf*, 58
   sefirah period, date, 59
   sefirah period, engagement party, 59
   sefirah period, engaging in, 56
   sefirah period, wedding, 59
   sefirah period, women engaging in, 56-57
   sefirah period, work requires, 57
   Three Weeks period, during, 158
   Three Weeks period, women engaging in, 160
   Three Weeks period, work requires, 159
   see haircutting
shavua shechal bo
   clothing, laundering during, 170
   clothing, wearing freshly laundered during, 176-182
   clothing, wearing new during, 179
   Sephardic custom of observing mourning before Tishah b'Av, 163-164

Tishah b'Av on Shabbos or Sunday, when observed, 163-164
   see Nine Days, Three Weeks
Shavuos
   Akdamus Milin recited on morning of, 104
   Aseres HaDibros, reading on morning of, 104
   Av Harachamim, reciting at *Shacharis* of, 107
   birchos hashachar, reciting after staying awake on night of, 123
   birchos haTorah, reciting after staying awake on night of, 119-120
   candle lighting for, when performed, 100-101
   clapping on, 135
   dairy, custom of eating on, 125-126, 128
   dancing on, 135
   fasting on, 103
   flowers, adorning shuls and homes with on, 132
   greenery, adorning shuls and homes with on, 132
   hachnassas sefer Torah, appropriate time for, 107
   haftarah on morning of, 105, 107
   Hallel, reciting on, 103
   Isru Chag of, customs of, 107-108
   Kah E-li, reciting on, 107
   Kiddush on eve of, 100, 102
   Kosel, visiting on and on days after, 108
   Krias HaTorah on, 103, 106-107

Maariv on eve of, additions to, 101-102

Maariv on eve of, delaying until night, 100

marital relations on eve of, 102-103

meals of, various customs of dairy and meat foods, 126, 128, 131

Megillas Rus, reading on morning of, 105-106

milchig, custom of eating on, 125-126

netilas yadayim after studying on night of, 113-117

Pirkei Avos, reciting when falls on Shabbos, 79

Shabbos, when falls out after, 102

Shacharis of, additions to, 103-107

Staying awake on night of, 108-113

Torah study on night of, 108-110

tosefes Yom Tov for, 100

trees, custom of placing in shuls and homes on, 134

tzitzis, brachah on after awake on night of, 117-118

when celebrated, 99

Yetziv Pisgam, reciting during *haftarah* of, 107

Yizkor, reciting on, 107

zman matan Toraseinu, known as, 99

see Erev Shavuos, flowers, meat and milk, *netilas yadayim, seudah, Tachanun*, Torah study

she'asah li kol tzorki

Tishah b'Av, reciting on, 234

shechitah

Nine Days period, prohibition of engaging in during, 186-187

see meat

sheets

Nine Days period, laundering during, 170

Nine Days period, using freshly laundered during, 176, 179

shehecheyanu

bris milah, reciting at when on Tishah b'Av, 262

sefirah period, clothing that is new, 54

sefirah period, home purchased, 55

sefirah period, making opportunity for, 54

sefirah period, reciting during, 53-55

sefirah period, reciting on Shabbos, 55

sefiras haomer, if recited on, 9

Shavuos, recited on eve of, 102

Three Weeks period, reciting during, 161-162

sheinas arai

definition of, 121

not necessitating *birchos haTorah*, 120, 122

not necessitating *netilas yadayim*, 116

sheinas keva

chicken meal, eating dairy sooner after, 130

daytime, if necessitates *birchos haTorah*, 120-121

definition of, 121

necessitates *birchos haTorah*, 120, 122

necessitates *netilas yadayim*, 116-117

waking up after, but before *chatzos*, if necessitates *birchos haTorah*, 122

sheitel

Nine Days period, combing on, 172

Nine Days period, washing and setting during, 172

shekiah

Erev Shabbos, davening *Maariv* before, 21

sefiras haomer, counting before if no consequence, 32-33

sefiras haomer, counting immediately after, 18, 19

sefiras haomer, counting on Erev Shabbos before, 21

sefiras haomer, remembered yesterday's count after, 27

Tishah b'Av, fast starts at, 210, 211, 214

Shema

see *Krias Shema*

shema koleinu

drought, reciting *vesein tal u'matar* in during, 77

Shemoneh Esrei

mashiv haruach, uncertain if said correctly, 75-76

precedence of before *sefiras haomer*, 17

repeating, reciting *Hashem sefasai tiftach* when, 74

see *mashiv haruach u'morid hageshem, morid hatal, vesein tal u'matar livrachah*

shenayim mikra v'echad targum

Erev Tishah b'Av, reciting on, 203

Tishah b'Av, reciting on, 237

when traveling to or from Eretz Yisrael, 80

sheva brachos

sefirah period, celebrating during, 48-49

Shivah Asar b'Tammuz, on night before or after, 148

shinui makom

necessitates new *brachah rishonah*, 110, 112

see *brachah*

Shir Shel Yom

Tishah b'Av, saying on, 253, 255

shiur

Erev Tishah b'Av, holding on, 203, 268

shiur ikul

definition of, 111

when passes, necessitates new *brachah acharonah*, 110-111

see *brachah*

shiurim

eating in increments of while fasting in case of illness, 223

Index ∽ 357

shivah
   Tishah b'Av, going to shul on during, 254

Shivah Asar b'Tammuz
   alos hashachar, begins at, 141
   alos hashachar, waking at to eat before, 141
   ate by mistake on, 142-143
   baalei simchah fasting on, 143
   bar mitzvah on 18th of Tammuz on Sunday, fasting on, 142
   bathing on, 147
   bris, celebrants still fast, 143
   brushing teeth on, 148-149
   chafifah on, 147
   childbirth, fasting on after, 144
   children fasting on, 141-142
   deodorant, applying on, 149
   drinking before *alos hashachar* of, 141
   duration of, 141
   eating before *alos hashachar* of, 141
   exempt from, making up the fast, 145
   haircut on, 148
   illness, fasting on in case of, 144-145
   leather shoes, wearing on, 148
   marital relations on, 147, 149
   meat, eating on night after, 149
   music, listening to on, 148
   neviim instituted fast of, 139
   nursing women fasting on, 143
   objective of, 139
   pregnant women fasting on, 143
   requirement to fast on, 140
   rinsing mouth on, 148-149
   Shabbos, postponing when falls on, 149
   sheva brachos, on night before or night of, 148
   showering on, 147
   Three Weeks, mourning period of begins on, 156
   Tishah b'Av prohibitions, observing on, 147-148
   toothbrushing on, 148-149
   tragedies commemorated by, 140-141
   tzeis hakochavim, ends at, 141
   washing on, 147
   wedding on night before, 148
   wine, drinking on night after, 149
   women fasting on, special considerations, 143-144
   see fast day

shivah nekiim
   Nine Days period, laundering garments for, 172-173
   Nine Days period, using laundered garments for, 179

Shloshes Yemei Hagbalah
   hachnassas sefer Torah, celebrating during, 49-50

shloshim
   sefirah period, haircut at end of, 59

shoes
  Nine Days period, buying during, 185
  Nine Days period, buying non-leather footwear for during, 185
  Nine Days period, polishing during, 171-172
  seudah hamafsekes, wearing at, 209
  Tishah b'Av, children wearing on, 234
  Tishah b'Av, Erev Tishah b'Av coinciding with Shabbos, 214-215, 269
  Tishah b'Av, leather footwear prohibited, 232-233
  Tishah b'Av, long walk, wearing on, 233
  Tishah b'Av, non-leather, if prohibited on, 232
  Tishah b'Av, non-Jews, wearing when in company of, 233
  Tishah b'Av, orthotics made of leather, 233-234
  Tishah b'Av, prohibited on, 219, 232-234
  Tishah b'Av, prohibition of wearing begins at, 211-212, 214
  Tishah b'Av, synthetic leather, if prohibited, 233
  see leather
shomea k'oneh
  fulfilling Kiddush obligation via, 4
  fulfilling *sefiras haomer* obligation via, 4-5, 26

shomer
  tefillin, designating one before fulfilling mitzvah of, 260
shopping
  Nine Days period, during, 164-165
showering
  Nine Days period, before *tevilah*, 195
  Nine Days period, during, 193-198
  Nine Days period, medical reasons requiring, 194
  sefirah period, during, 60
  see bathing
shtei halechem
  see korban shtei halechem
shul
  Nine Days period, renovating or painting during, 168
  Shavuos, custom of placing flowers and trees in on, 132, 134
  Tishah b'Av, lights of dimmed on, 249-250, 261
  zecher l'churban, if required, 292
sichah
  see anointing
singing
  chazzanus, listening to at a meal, 300
  churban, commemorating by limiting, 299-302
  Nine Days period, *seudas mitzvah* during, 192
  praising Hashem by, 301
  restaurant, drinking wine in while, 299-300

Index ∽ 359

sefirah period, engaging
in during, 52

thanking Hashem by, 301

Three Weeks period,
engaging in during, 157

Three Weeks period,
for children, 158

seudah shelishis, when
immediately preceding
Tishah b'Av, 268

sleep, putting children to with, 302

wine, listening to while
drinking, 299-300, 301

work purposes, listening
to for, 299, 300

see music, *zemiros*

siyum

Nine Days period, eating
at when missed, 192

Nine Days period, food
for sent home, 191

Nine Days period, held for, 191

Nine Days period, *seudah*
for, 190, 191-192

sefirah period, music
and dancing at, 49

sefirah period, *seudah*
for during, 56

sleep

necessitating *netilas
yadayim*, 116-117

sefiras haomer, before counted, 38

Tishah b'Av, in less comfortable
manner on, 241

see alarm clock, *alos hashachar*,
napping, *netilas yadayim*, *sheinas
arai*, *sheinas keva*, Torah study

smoking

Tishah b'Av, on, 241

soap

Nine Days period, using
for bathing, 196

Tishah b'Av, using on, 230-231

socks

Nine Days period,
making during, 182

Nine Days period, using freshly
laundered during, 176

soda

seudah hamafsekes,
drinking at, 205

song

see music, singing

southern hemisphere

mashiv haruach, when
recited in, 74-75

spelt

chadash considerations for, 94

spinning

Nine Days period, during, 184

standing

sefiras haomer, during, 9-10

stipulation

see tenai

Sunday

Tishah b'Av falling out on, 267-275

sunscreen

Tishah b'Av, using on, 231

sunset
  see shekiah
surgery
  sefiras haomer, counting with brachah when scheduled, 29
swimming
  Nine Days period, during, 169, 194
  Nine Days period, medical reasons requiring, 169, 194
  sefirah period, during, 55
  Three Weeks period, during, 160
  see bathing, showering

T

taanis
  see fasting
taanis chalom
  Shavuos, on, 103
table
  using same one for meat and dairy meals at same time, 130
tablecloth
  Nine Days period, laundering during, 170
  Nine Days period, laundering for Shabbos during, 173
  Nine Days period, using freshly laundered during, 176, 179
  switching between dairy and meat meals, 127, 130
  using different for meat and dairy meals at same time, 130
Tachanun
  Al Naharos Bavel not recited on days omitted, 299
  Erev Tishah b'Av, omitted, 201
  Isru Chag, reciting on, 107-108
  kriah, if performed on days omitted, 314
  Lag Baomer, 67, 68
  Pesach Sheni, reciting on, 83
  Shavuos, reciting on six days after, 108
  Sivan, reciting during, 84
  Tishah b'Av, omitted, 252
tadir
  sefiras haomer, determining placement of, 17, 21-22, 23-24, 41
tailor
  Nine Days period, non-Jewish making clothing during, 182-183
Tal
  see Tefillas Tal
tallis
  Tishah b'Av, sandak wearing, 262
  Tishah b'Av, wearing at Minchah, 259
  see tzitzis
tallis katan
  see tzitzis
tea
  seudah hamafsekes, drinking at, 205, 206
teeth
  see toothbrushing
Tefillas Tal
  reciting on first day of Pesach, 72

Index ⸺ 361

tefillin
    haircut to remove *chatzitzah* during Three Weeks period, 160
    Nine Days period, purchasing during, 168
    shomer, designating before fulfilling mitzvah of, 260
    Tishah b'Av, wearing on, 259
tefillos
    sefiras haomer, after recitation of, 16
Tehillim
    Erev Tishah b'Av, reciting on, 203
    Tishah b'Av, reciting on, 238
telephone
    see phone
temimos
    requirement that *sefiras haomer* be, 17, 25, 26
tenai
    sefiras haomer, counting before *tzeis hakochavim* with, 19, 20
tenaim
    dish, breaking at writing of, 303
    sefirah period, celebrating during, 48
terumas hadeshen
    passage of, reciting before *alos hashachar*, 124
teshuvah
    objective of fast days to spur to, 139, 220
tevilah
    Nine Days period, before davening, 195

Nine Days period, cutting nails for, 169
Nine Days period, performing, 194-195
Nine Days period, showering before, 195
sefirah period, cutting hair during for, 56
Three Weeks period, cutting hair during for, 158
Tishah b'Av, before davening, 229
see mikveh
theft
    flowers, avoiding while picking, 135
thought
    sefiras haomer, fulfilling via, 10
Three Weeks
    caution during, 163
    children, haircuts for during, 159
    children, music or singing for during, 158
    clothing, purchasing during, 162
    clothing, wearing new during, 162
    cutting hair during, 158-160
    cutting hair during, for women, 158, 160
    dancing during, 157, 158
    engagement, finalizing during, 156
    engagement *seudah* during, 156
    fingernails, cutting during, 160
    garments, purchasing during, 162
    hatov vehameitiv, reciting during, 162-163

362 ∽ *Index*

mourning *Beis Hamikdash* during, 163

mourning observed during, reason for, 155

mourning period of, when begins, 156

moving into new home during, 166

musical instruments, playing during, 157

music, listening to during, 157

nails, cutting during, 160

seudas mitzvah during, celebrating, 158

shaving during, 158, 160

shehecheyanu during, 161-162

singing during, 157

swimming during, 160

upsheren during, 160

wedding during, 156

see haircutting, Nine Days, music

tikkun leil Shavuos

Shavuos night, custom to study on, 110

time zone

sefiras haomer, counting when switching between, 29-30

tircha

prohibition of on Yom Tov, 133

Tishah b'Av

accepting the fast restrictions verbally or mentally, 211, 212

Aneinu, reciting on, 257

anointing on, 230-231

ate or drank erroneously, continuing fast after, 226

Avinu Malkeinu, omitted on, 252-253, 258

bar mitzvah on tenth of Av on Sunday, fasting on, 225

besamim, smelling on, 241, 261, 271

birkas hamazon on, 256

bris milah on, 260-263

brushing teeth on, 225

business, conducting on, 244, 245

cemetery, visiting on, 254

chafifah, when performed when using *mikveh* after, 229

chair, sitting in low one on, 211, 241-243

childbirth, fasting after, 222-223

children, eating before Havdalah on, 225

children, fasting on, 225

child, playing with on, 243

community affairs, engaging in will create difficulty in fasting on, 224

deodorant, using on, 231

duration of, 219, 220

Eichah recited on, 249-250, 254

elderly people fasting on, 224

elderly people sitting in low chair on, 242

elderly people, standing up for them on, 243

fasting on, obligation of, 220

floor, sitting on during, 241-242, 250, 252

food preparation on, 244, 254-255

gifts, giving on, 239

Index ~ 363

gomel bentching on, 255
greetings on, 239
Havdalah when eating on, 272-273
Havdalah when on Sunday, 224-225, 270-273, 274-275, 285
housecleaning on, 244
illness, fasting in situation of, 221-223, 274
illness, resuming fast after broken because of, 222
illness, washing for bread in case of, 226, 228
Kinnos recited on, 249, 251-252, 253
Krias HaTorah on, 253, 255
lights dimmed on, 249-250, 261
Maariv, customs of, 249-251
Maariv, Erev Tishah b'Av on Shabbos, procedure for, 215-216, 269
Maariv, restrictions begin at when before *shekiah*, 211
makeup, using on, 230, 231
marital relations on, 219, 228, 240, 268
mikveh use on, 228-229
Minchah, customs of, 255-256, 257-258, 259
moed, called, 201, 252-253, 268
Motzaei Tishah b'Av, 274-275, 279-285
mourning, diverting attention from during, 238-239
mourning part of observance of, 219
mouthwash, using on, 225

Nacheim, reciting on, 256
neitz hachamah, davening at on, 252
netilas yadayim on morning of, 227
neviim instituted, 139
nursing woman fasting on, 220-221
objective of, 139, 220
perfume, using on, 230
pidyon haben on, 264
pills, taking on, 223-224
pregnant woman fasting on, 220-221
Rav, standing up for on, 243
reading general knowledge material on, 238-239
rinsing mouth on, 225
seudah hamafsekes, 204-210, 212-213
Shabbos, taking stroll when falls out on, 202
Shacharis, customs of, 252-253, 258-259
she'asah li kol tzorki, reciting on, 234
shekiah, fast begins at, 210, 211, 214, 219
shoes, prohibited on, 219, 232-234
shoes, removed at *Barchu* of *Maariv*, 211, 214-215, 269
sleeping in less comfortable manner on, 241
smoking on, 241
soap, using on, 230-231
socializing, minimizing on, 239-240

stroll, taking on, 202, 239-240
Sunday, when falls out on, 267-275
Tachanun, omitted on, 252-253, 258
tefillin, wearing on, 258-259
tevilah on, 228-229
toothbrushing on, 225
Torah study on, 202, 204, 234-238, 267-278
tragedies commemorated by, 219
transgressing restrictions of, penalty for, 226
tzedakah, giving on, 239
tzitzis, wearing on, 258, 259
washing on, 211, 219, 226-230, 255
work on, 243, 244-245
work on, via non-Jew, 244-245
writing on, 243-244
see anointing, Erev Tishah b'Av, fast day, *Kinnos, Megillas Eichah*, Motzaei Tishah b'Av, *seudah hamafsekes*, shoes, Torah study, washing

toch k'dei dibbur
  interruption of after *brachah*, 10
  mashiv haruach, correction of mistake within, 75
  sefiras haomer, correction of mistake within, 36-37
  vesein tal u'matar, correcting erroneous recitation of within, 78

toothbrushing
  Shivah Asar b'Tammuz, on, 148-149
  Tishah b'Av, on, 225

Torah reading
  see Krias TaTorah

Torah study
  Erev Tishah b'Av, engaging in on, 202-204
  sefiras haomer, engaging in before, 39, 40
  Shavuos night, *birchos hashachar* after staying awake for, 123
  Shavuos night, *birchos haTorah* after staying awake for, 119-120
  Shavuos night, eating or drinking during, 110-113
  Shavuos night, exerting oneself to study throughout, 110
  Shavuos night, material studied on, 110
  Shavuos night, *netilas yadayim* after, 113-117
  Shavuos night, second night, studying on, 110
  Shavuos night, source of custom, 108-109
  Shavuos night, studying *tikkun leil Shavuos*, 110
  Shavuos night, *tzitzis* after staying awake for, 117-118
  snacking intermittently during, conduct regarding *brachos*, 111
  snacking intermittently during, repeating *brachos rishonah* and *acharonah*, 110-111
  Tishah b'Av, children engaging in on, 236-237
  Tishah b'Av, davening, Torah passages from, 237-238

Tishah b'Av, engaging in on, 202, 204

Tishah b'Av, halachic rulings, conveying, 236

Tishah b'Av, halachos of and of mourning, 235

Tishah b'Av, *mussar*, 235

Tishah b'Av, prohibited on, 219, 234-235

Tishah b'Av, sorrowful topics, 235

Tishah b'Av, *Tehillim*, 238

Tishah b'Av, thoughts of, 236

Tishah b'Av, writing notes about, 236

see netilas yadayim

tosefes Yom Tov

   Shavuos, on eve of, 100

towels

   Nine Days period, laundering during, 170

   Nine Days period, using freshly laundered during, 176

toys

   Nine Days period, buying for children during, 165

travel

   Nine Days period, by air during, 169

   Parshas Hashavua, discrepancy of Eretz Yisrael and outside, 79-80

   sefiras haomer when switching between time zones, 29-30

trees

   fruit trees, uprooting, 134

   Shavuos, placing in shuls and homes on, 134

trips

   sefirah period: during, 55

tzedakah

   Tishah b'Av, giving on, 239

tzeis hakochavim

   sefiras haomer, assumed no intent for if before, 33

   sefiras haomer, beginning activity from half hour before, 38

   sefiras haomer, counting after, 18-19

   sefiras haomer, remembered yesterday's count before, 28

   Tishah b'Av ends at, 279

tzibbur

   sefiras haomer, counting with, 23

Tzidkascha

   Erev Tishah b'Av, omitted on, 201, 268

   Lag Baomer, omitted on *Minchah* before, 68

tziduk hadin

   Lag Baomer, reciting on, 69

   Tishah b'Av, reciting on, 254

tzitzis

   brachah on after sleepless night, 117-118

   kriah not required on, 313

   Nine Days period, purchasing during, 168, 184

   Tishah b'Av, *Shacharis* of, holding, 258

   Tishah b'Av, wearing on, 258, 259

see tallis

Tzom Gedaliah
  neviim instituted, 139
  nursing women fasting on, 143
  objective of, 139
  pregnant women fasting on, 143
  see fast day

U

undergarments
  kriah of, 313
  Nine Days period, buying new during, 184
  Nine Days period, using freshly laundered during, 176, 180

upsheren
  Lag Baomer, custom of performing on, 71
  Three Weeks period, holding during, 160

urine
  sefiras haomer in presence of, 8

Uva Letzion
  Tishah b'Av, changes in recitation of, 251, 253

V

vase
  see flowers

Vayiten Lecha
  sefiras haomer counted before recitation of, 23
  Tishah b'Av on Motzaei Shabbos, not recited, 251, 270-271

vesein brachah
  announcing recitation of, 77
  Pesach, beginning recitation of on, 77

vesein tal u'matar livrachah
  drought, reciting during, 77
  Pesach, discontinuing recitation of on, 77
  recited erroneously, 77-78
  see vesein brachah

vinegar
  Nine Days period, from wine, 188

vort
  see engagement

V'yehi Noam
  Tishah b'Av on Motzaei Shabbos, not recited, 251, 270-271

W

wallpapering
  Nine Days period, during, 167
  zecher l'churban, leaving uncovered for, 291

washing
  Tishah b'Av, bathroom, after using, 227-228
  Tishah b'Av, before davening, 227, 255
  Tishah b'Av, before Torah study, 227-228
  Tishah b'Av, *birkas kohanim*, before, 228
  Tishah b'Av, *chafifah* when going to *mikveh* after, 229

Index ~ 367

Tishah b'Av, Erev Tishah b'Av coinciding with Shabbos, 214

Tishah b'Av, face, 229-230

Tishah b'Av, food or other objects, 227

Tishah b'Av, *hefsek taharah*, for, 229

Tishah b'Av, kallah, exception for, 231

Tishah b'Av, *netilas yadayim* in morning, 227

Tishah b'Av, pain, removing by, 230

Tishah b'Av, prohibited on, 219, 226

Tishah b'Av, prohibition of begins at, 211, 214

Tishah b'Av, removing dirt by, 226

Tishah b'Av, upon eating when exempt from fasting, 226, 228

Tishah b'Av, water, passing through on, 230

Tishah b'Av, wet towel, using for, 230

Tishah b'Av, wound, 230

washing machine

Nine Days period, turning on immediately before begins, 171

waxing

sefirah period, engaging in during, 57

wedding

ashes, placing on chassan's head at, 302-303

cup, breaking at, 303

dish, breaking at, 303

head adornments for chassan and kallah, limiting, 303-304

music, playing at, 301

Nine Days period, making clothing for during, 182

sefirah period, attending during, 59, 65-66

sefirah period, Lag Baomer, 66, 67, 69-70

sefirah period, marrying into Sephardic family during, 6

sefirah period, prohibition of, 48

Shivah Asar b'Tammuz, holding on night before, 148

Three Weeks period, holding during, 156

Western Wall

see Kosel

wheat

chadash considerations for, 94

whiskey

Nine Days period, drinking during, 188

wine

Havdalah with when eating on Tishah b'Av, 273

Motzaei Tishah b'Av, *birkas hamazon* with, 283

Motzaei Tishah b'Av, restrictions on, 274-275, 281, 284

Nine Days period, abstaining from during, 186, 188-193

Nine Days period, bar mitzvah, drinking at, 192

Nine Days period, *birkas hamazon* with, 190

Nine Days period, *bris milah*, drinking at, 190-191, 201-202

Nine Days period, *chanukas habayis*, drinking at, 192

Nine Days period, childbirth, drinking after, 193

Nine Days period, children abstaining from, 192-193

Nine Days period, diluted, 188

Nine Days period, food, adding to, 188

Nine Days period, grape juice included in prohibition, 188

Nine Days period, Havdalah with, 189-190

Nine Days period, illness requiring, 193

Nine Days period, *melaveh malkah*, drinking during, 188-189

Nine Days period, mitzvah purpose for drinking, 189

Nine Days period, nursing requiring, 193

Nine Days period, onset of prohibition of consuming, 186

Nine Days period, *pidyon haben*, drinking at, 190, 201-202

Nine Days period, *seudah shelishis*, drinking during, 188-189

Nine Days period, *seudas mitzvah* permitted in, 190, 201-202

Nine Days period, Shabbos, drinking on, 188-189

Nine Days period, *siyum*, drinking at, 190, 191-192

restaurant, drinking in when music playing, 299-300

seudah hamafsekes, drinking at, 205, 268

Shivah Asar b'Tammuz, drinking on night after, 149

Tishah b'Av, drinking on night after, 274-275, 281, 284

see beer, whiskey

women

borei meorei ha'eish, reciting, 271-272

brachah on *sefiras haomer*, reciting, 6

brachah on *sefiras haomer*, reciting in presence of, 8

craving fruit during pregnancy, reciting *shehecheyanu* during Three Weeks period, 161

Eichah, listening to, 250-251

fasting, after childbirth, 144, 222-223

fasting, when nursing, 143, 220-221

fasting, when pregnant, 143, 220-221

jewelry, not wearing all at once to commemorate destruction of *Beis Hamikdash*, 304

kriah, performing upon seeing Yerushalayim or site of *Beis Hamikdash*, 311

Motzaei Tishah b'Av, eating meat when after childbirth, 283

Nine Days period, *hefsek taharah* during, 195

Index ~ 369

Nine Days period, meat or wine after childbirth, 193

Nine Days period, meat or wine while nursing, 193

Nine Days period, *mikveh* use during, 194

Nine Days period, preparing for *tevilah* during, 169, 194-195

ostentatious dressing, avoiding to minimize jealousy, 304

sefirah period, cutting hair on, 56-57

sefirah period, observing same as husband, 65

sefirah period, waxing on, 57

sefiras haomer, obligation of, 5-6

seudah hamafsekes, sitting on floor at, 209

Shavuos, lighting candles for, 100-101

Three Weeks period, cutting hair on, 158

Tishah b'Av, Havdalah after, 272, 273, 275

Tishah b'Av, pregnant or after birth, sitting on a regular chair during, 242

see *chafifah, hefsek taharah, mikveh, tevilah*

work

fast day, when observance will be prevented by, 146

sefirah period, shaving during for, 57

Tishah b'Av, on, 243, 244-245

see business

wound

Tishah b'Av, washing on, 230

writing

sefiras haomer, fulfilling via, 10-11

Tishah b'Av, performing on, 242-243

Tishah b'Av, Torah thoughts on, 236

Y

yashan

definition of, 88

see *chadash*

Yerushalayim

kriah, performing on seeing ruins of, 309-310

resident of, obligation in *kriah*, 315-316

Tishah b'Av commemorates plowing of, 219

weddings, custom to limit music at in, 301

see *kriah*

yeshivah

zecher l'churban, if required, 292

Yetziv Pisgam

haftarah of Shavuos, reciting during, 107

Yizkor

Shavuos, reciting on, 107

Yom Tov

Al Naharos Bavel not recited on, 299

clapping on, 135

dancing on, 135
flowers, *muktzeh* status of on, 132
flowers, placing in or removing from water on, 133
kriah not performed on, 314
meals of should include meat, 129
napping on even though may necessitate repeating *birchos haTorah*, 121
Shir Hamaalos recited before *birkas hamazon* of, 299
tircha, prohibition of on, 133
vase, adding water to, 133
vase, moving on, 133

Z

zakein
  see elderly

zecher l'churban
  beis midrash, if required, 292
  black, painting area of, 291
  brick wall not requiring, 291
  cement wall not requiring, 291
  doorway, placing opposite, 291-292
  doorway, when there are more than one, 292
  Jew, purchased home without from, 293
  method of making, 289-290
  non-Jew, purchased home from, 292-293
  non-Jews working in home, still required, 293
  placement of, 291-292
  plastering area of, 290-291
  public buildings, if required, 292
  rented home, obligation of, 293-294
  rent, home intended for, 293
  requirement of, 289
  sale, home intended for, 293
  school, if required, 292
  shul, if required, 292
  sign replacing, 291
  wallpaper, leaving area for uncovered, 291
  yeshivah, if required, 292
  "*zecher l'churban*" written in square of, 291
  see Beis Hamikdash

zemiros
  seudah hamafsekes on Shabbos, singing at, 213, 268
  see singing

zimun
  seudah hamafsekes, avoiding requirement of at, 209
  seudah hamafsekes on Shabbos, conducting, 268
  see birkas hamazon

zman matan Toraseinu
  Shavuos known as, 99